The Bipolar Teen

The BIPOLAR TEEN

What You Can Do to Help Your Child and Your Family

DAVID J. MIKLOWITZ, PhD
ELIZABETH L. GEORGE, PhD

ROBINSON
London

Constable & Robinson Ltd
3 The Lanchesters
162 Fulham Palace Road
London W6 9ER
www.constablerobinson.com

First published in the United States in 2008 by The Guilford Press,
a division of Guilford Publications, Inc.,
72 Spring Street, New York, NY 10012

First published in the United Kingdom by Robinson,
an imprint of Constable & Robinson Ltd 2008

A copy of the British Library Cataloguing in
Publication Data is available from the British Library.

Important Note
This book is not intended as a substitute for medical advice or
treatment. Any person with a condition requiring medical attention
should consult a qualified medical practitioner or suitable therapist.

ISBN 978-1-84529-726-8

Printed and bound in the United States of America

1 3 5 7 9 10 8 6 4 2

This book is dedicated to the memory of three major figures in the field of family therapy and severe psychiatric illness: Michael J. Goldstein, Ian R. H. Falloon, and Lyman C. Wynne. It is also dedicated to those families with whom we have worked, with admiration for their courage in navigating the rough seas of bipolar disorder.

Contents

Contents

Preface

In 1987 I (D.J.M.) had a conversation with a parent that I'll never forget. I had just published my dissertation, whose key finding was considered novel, even doubtful, at the time. I had found that late adolescents and young adults who had been hospitalized for a manic bipolar episode were more likely to have a recurrence within 9 months if they were living in high-conflict families than in low-conflict families. My psychiatric colleagues thought we had failed to take into account some biological or genetic variable or that those who relapsed had just not taken their medications. Bipolar disorder was, after all, a genetic and biological illness, no different from diabetes or hypertension. Despite an exhaustive review, however, I never did find such a variable.

Then the mother of an 18-year-old with bipolar disorder asked me to explain my findings. When I did, she waited, looking at me blankly, and finally said, "That's it?" I explained the finding again, thinking she hadn't understood.

She had.

Her response? "Well, duh!"

It was certainly no surprise to her that family stress could be associated with relapse—she could give me innumerable examples of family conflicts that had precipitated mood swings in her son. As we continued to talk, I told her how compelled I felt to understand what families did wrong that made people like her son relapse and how we could keep them from doing it.

She continued to listen with interest and then said, pointedly, "Why don't you study what families do *right*? Maybe you'll find out why some people *don't* relapse."

Over the past 20 years, my colleagues and I have studied just that—what families do right—and how they could do more of it to keep their children well and out of the hospital. When I went to the University of Colorado as a faculty member in 1989, I started a study with, among others, a young graduate student named Liz George, who had an upbeat interpersonal manner and a way of getting even the most difficult patients and family members to open up. We conducted a large-scale study of our new psychoeducational intervention, called *family-focused treatment* (FFT), for adults with bipolar disorder and their parents or spouses. Our study showed that a 9-month course of FFT combined with medications was highly effective in staving off recurrences of the disorder and keeping patients from having ongoing symptoms of mania and depression. The treatment also helped keep people with the disorder on their medications and led to better family relationships. We learned a great deal during the 8-year study about what strategies families could use to keep their sons and daughters well. In 2002, I published a book for adult bipolar patients and their families—*The Bipolar Disorder Survival Guide* (Guilford Press)—which distilled what we'd learned into a set of recommendations for managing the illness.

In the late 1990s, after having received numerous phone calls from parents of teenagers who wanted FFT, we decided to redesign our treatment program for younger bipolar patients who had just been diagnosed. We were immediately struck with the different challenges faced by their parents: how could they get help for their teenager when they couldn't even get agreement from doctors that he or she was really bipolar? Their teens seemed to cycle in and out of mood phases with astonishing rapidity, which sometimes looked like true bipolar episodes and at other times looked more like "meltdowns." Were their kids really ill with bipolar disorder, or did they have some other diagnosable problem, like attention-deficit/hyperactivity disorder or conduct disorder? Were their teens overly hormonal, distressed, or just plain bratty? The level of functional impairment we observed in these kids convinced us that this was more than just teenage angst: it looked more like a younger version of what we were seeing in our adult bipolar patients.

Sadly, there was no support or treatment system available to the families of these teens to help them through the repeated crises they faced. The families who contacted us had sometimes broken up over their teen's illness. Parents blamed themselves for not having nurtured their children enough, for having worked when their children were young, or even for having passed on bad genes.

Over the past 10 years, we've developed a version of FFT for families with bipolar teens. We've learned a great deal about how the disorder should be diagnosed, how it differs from other disorders, and how it affects and is affected by families. We've learned how to explain to family members—including teens' siblings—what causes the disorder in language they can understand, how to point them in the direction of the right treatments, and how to make sure the teen is committed to an effective treatment regimen. In so doing, we've confirmed what we've believed for a long time: that the best treatment for bipolar disorder is a combination of medication and psychotherapy, rather than one without the other.

Most important for this book, we have learned a great deal about successful illness management tools the family can use—how to keep a teen well when she's stable, how to recognize the oncoming train of mania and intervene before it's too late, and how to help pull teens out of deep depressions. We've learned how parents can recognize their teen's suicidal impulses and what to do when they first see them. Last, we've learned how important it is for parents to communicate with teachers and guidance counselors to make sure their teen is not just labeled with a "behavior problem" and grouped with all the other children with this label, some of whom they resemble but most of whom they do not.

It's our intention in this book to provide you with these necessary illness management tools in an easy-to-digest format. We hope it will help you on the challenging journey through the ups and downs of bipolar disorder. We hope it will help you keep your family together, recognize and build on your teen's strengths, and make you optimistic about the future.

A Word of Thanks

Many people deserve our warmest and most sincere thanks for their help, not only with the writing of this book, but with the raw material from which we drew our conclusions. Our colleagues at the University of Colorado, who have worked with us for many years and helped us navigate some of the most difficult family situations we've ever encountered, deserve our special gratitude: Dawn Taylor, PhD, Chris Schneck, MD, W. Edward Craighead, PhD, Adrine Biuckians, MA, Kim Mullen, MA, Tina Goldstein, PhD, Eunice Kim, PhD, Carol Beresford, MD, Richard Suddath, MD, Alisha Brosse, PhD, Isabelle Guillemet, MD, Jeff Richards, MA, Teri

Simoneau, PhD, Charles Judd, PhD, Marianne Wamboldt, MD, Fred Wamboldt, MD, Vicky Cosgrove, MA, Joanne Friedman, MA, Cheryl Chessick, MD, Michael Allen, MD, Marshall Thomas, MD, and Emily Kean, PhD.

We'd also like to thank our wonderful colleagues at the University of Pittsburgh School of Medicine, who originally acquainted us with the wondrous world of childhood bipolar disorder and encouraged us throughout the years to pursue our muse: Ellen Frank, PhD, David Kupfer, MD, David Axelson, MD, Boris Birmaher, MD, David Brent, MD, Michael Thase, MD, Amy Schlonski, LCSW, Kim Poling, LCSW, Tim Winbush, LCSW, Sue Wassick, RN, and Mary Beth Hickey.

We wish to thank the two best editors in the universe, Chris Benton and Kitty Moore at The Guilford Press. Thanks for believing in us, for being so generous with your time and expertise, and for holding our hands through the long days and nights of writing and revising. Without your creativity, encouragement, and fabulous senses of humor, this book would never have come to pass.

Finally, we would like to thank our spouses, Mary Yaeger and Tony George; our kids, Ariana Miklowitz, Dylan George, and Christofer George; and our parents and siblings, Gloria Miklowitz (an accomplished author of over 60 books for children), Paul Miklowitz, PhD (a professor of philosophy), Peggy Carter, Joan and Julio George, and the Levergood–George clan. Thanks for sticking by us. The special memory of my father, Julius Miklowitz, PhD, who taught me the value of hard work and an academic life, came to me frequently as I worked on this book. Liz recognizes the dedication and perseverance of her father, Charlie Levergood, who, at the age of 76, is still writing books and short stories.

PART I

Understanding Bipolar Disorder in Teens

1 "What's Happening to My Teenager?"

Emilia, a 44-year-old single parent who worked as a waitress during the day and managed a health care supply business at night, was getting increasingly concerned about her son, Carlos, age 14. For the last 2 weeks Carlos had been "wired" and "snapping at everyone." He would explode into tirades when the Internet went down for even a few minutes, if his sister took too long in the bathroom in the morning, or if the dog wanted his attention when he was busy. Emilia suspected he had been staying up most nights well after she had gone to bed and on at least two occasions had not gone to sleep at all. She felt nervous and fearful about an odd stare he had developed and about his unusual ideas about religion, death, burial, and the afterlife. Carlos said he believed in reincarnation, which was not in itself unusual, but he also believed he could communicate with his former soul via email. He had become more irritable and disrespectful of her since he had turned 13 (for example, by swearing and occasionally shoving her out of his way), but this new behavior was a big change for him. She wondered whether she had been in denial about the milder odd behaviors that she had been seeing in her son for a long time.

Emilia decided she was not spending enough time with her son or her 12-year-old daughter, Yolanda. One Saturday, Carlos awoke at noon as usual after having been up until 4:00 A.M. the night before "doing experiments in instant messaging." Because Yolanda was at a birthday party, Emilia suggested that they see a movie with one of his friends. Although she was initially delighted that he wanted to go, she felt hurt and frustrated when an innocent conversation about which movie to see turned into a shouting match.

After the movie, Carlos said good-bye to his friend and they headed home. Carlos took his soft drink into the car and began sloshing the ice around loudly in his mouth. Suddenly, he angrily turned to her and said, "I want to go to Pizza Hut." She explained calmly that she had defrosted a steak and didn't want it to go to waste and that they had already spent $25 on the movie, popcorn, and other snacks. Carlos started yelling that he was hungry and that she'd better turn the car around and go back to Pizza Hut "or else." Emilia couldn't believe her son was demanding that she now take him out for dinner and said sharply, "You know I never give in to you when you get like this."

Carlos dumped his soft drink in her lap and then picked up a stray auto map binder that had fallen out of her glove compartment and hit his mother on the head with it. She stomped on the brakes and the car swerved. She pulled over, and they began a screaming match during which he scratched her. She felt angry, hurt, and at the same time feared for her physical safety. To escape a situation that had escalated beyond her control, she finally agreed, against her better judgment, to take Carlos to Pizza Hut.

He ordered his food and ate it quickly. They got back in the car. They were silent for the rest of the evening. When she got home, Emilia poured herself a stiff drink and drank it alone in her bedroom. She heard a knock on her door. "Mom, can I come in?," Carlos said in a plaintive voice. She let him in. He sat on the edge of her bed shaking, with the empty stare she had seen earlier that week that had made her shudder. He said, "Mom, what happens when you die? If you kill yourself, does that mean you'll go to hell?"

Emilia was devastated. What had made her son act this way? Was he just going through a strange teenage phase? Was she a bad parent, and should she have seen this coming years ago? Where could she get help? And what would happen to her and her daughter while they were trying to deal with this overwhelming problem? Would they be able to stay together as a family? Emilia desperately wanted answers, but scanning websites and reading brochures didn't give her nearly enough information.

Having a teenager who is developing or has developed bipolar disorder is extremely upsetting, frustrating, even heartbreaking. The ups and downs of adolescent bipolar disorder are difficult to manage, and its rippling effects on the family can exhaust your energies. Whether your teen is having mood problems but hasn't received a diagnosis, has already been diagnosed but is just starting treatment, or has been in treatment for some time, you'll benefit from knowing as much as possible about the adolescent form of this disorder. Knowing how to recognize episodes of the illness before they build, how to get your teenager the most up-to-date treatments, and how best to respond so that your teen's condition is more likely to stabilize will boost your confidence and energy.

This book is for you if:

- You think your teenager (ages 12–18) or preteen may have bipolar disorder but it has not been diagnosed yet, and you want to gather information to see if the diagnosis is applicable.
- Your teenager has recently been diagnosed and you want to know more about what kind of treatment he or she should be getting.
- You have been dealing with bipolar disorder in your child for several years and want to learn new skills for coping with it now that your child is entering the already challenging phase of adolescence.

Knowing the facts about adolescent bipolar disorder will help you accept and learn to cope with it, and, in turn, help your teen and other family members come to terms with the illness. Each of the following chapters describes the problems you and your teen and family are probably facing, and provides a set of solutions we've found effective in our work with families like yours. If your son or daughter was diagnosed with bipolar disorder as a child, you may already have a pretty firm grasp of the fundamentals and prefer to go straight to the chapters of current interest. But chances are that you'll find some new information on the fundamentals. Everything in this book is based on up-to-date research findings as well as clinical wisdom from our own practices and those of our colleagues.

"What Is Bipolar Disorder?"

If you're not yet familiar with the full list of bipolar symptoms and how the disorder is diagnosed, you'll find complete explanations in Chapters 2 and 3. But essentially bipolar disorder is an illness involving extreme fluctuations in mood, usually from the highest of highs to the lowest of lows, like what Carlos was experiencing. The highs are called *mania* and the lows *depression,* which is why the disorder once was and sometimes still is called *manic–depression.*

Although bipolar disorder is difficult to deal with at any age, in our experience it is particularly challenging for teenagers and their families. For example, the shifts from high to low or low to high can occur even more quickly in teens than in adults. As Emilia observed in her son, teens can quickly change from elated, happy, and highly energized to angry, irritable, or morose, with suicidal despair. Some teens even experience mania and depression simultaneously. When manic, teens, like children and adults, experience euphoria, intense irritability, an inflated sense of self (grandiosity), increased energy and activity, rapid speech and thinking, distractibility, impulsive and reckless behavior, and a decreased need for sleep. When depressed, they feel intensely sad, lose interest in life, feel fatigued, slowed down, guilty, hopeless, and suicidal; they cannot sleep or they sleep way too much. For kids who are already undergoing huge developmental changes, these symptoms create an enormous burden in their young lives.

It's hard to say how many teens actually have bipolar disorder at any one time because so much depends on accurate diagnosis. Many people are not diagnosed until years after the symptoms appear—or at all. We know that about one in 25 adults (4% of the population) has bipolar disorder and that about half of these develop bipolar disorder in their childhood or teen years. The average age at first onset of bipolar disorder is between 15 and 19. This means that there is a good chance your teen is not the only one in his high school class who is suffering the mood swings of bipolar disorder.

Whoever they may be, teens with bipolar disorder usually have significant difficulties in school, not just at home. People with the disorder—young and old—have trouble managing their work, relationships, and family life. They are often codiagnosed with disorders like attention-deficit/hyperactivity disorder (ADHD; as in Carlos's case). Others have anxiety disorders, substance (drug or alcohol) abuse, or learning disabilities, all of which can complicate the process of getting an accurate diagnosis and appropriate treatment.

Fortunately, though, we're learning more and more about how to help teens with bipolar disorder, both with medication and with coping methods that pick up where medicine leaves off. Sharing them with you is the goal of this book.

In Part I you'll find up-to-date information about the symptoms, causes, and course of bipolar disorder over time. What does the disorder look like, and how is it experienced by the bipolar teen (Chapter 2)? How is it diagnosed (Chapter 3)? How will you experience it as a parent, and how will it look to other members of your family, like siblings (Chapter 4)? How does the disorder look at different stages of development? What happens to bipolar teens as they enter adulthood?

"Why Is It So Hard for Anyone to Tell Me What's Wrong?"

> Emilia took Carlos back to see the psychiatrist who had evaluated him when he turned 13. That's when he was diagnosed with ADHD, a diagnosis that had also been suggested by an elementary-school teacher. The physician met with Emilia and listened sympathetically, but seemed uninterested in her recounting of the increasingly hostile interactions she had been having with Carlos. He met briefly with Carlos, who said little other than "I just get pissed off sometimes."
>
> Carlos's psychiatrist told Emilia that he still believed Carlos had ADHD. He renewed Carlos's prescription for Adderall, a stimulant medication, and recommended he start taking Zoloft, an antidepressant, for his morose mood.

The parents we work with have usually been told many different things about what is wrong with their teen. Most have been told at one point or another that their teen has ADHD. Often this is true, although not always. Many are told that the teen is just depressed, anxious, or going through the ups and downs of growing up. You may have gone through numerous lengthy evaluations where the same questions were asked again and again, only to be told that your teen was going through "growing pains" or "a phase." The truth is that the distinction between bipolar disorder in teens and other disorders—and even between bipolar disorder and normal teenage development—is very hard to make (see Chapter 4). Professionals are not always reliable in making this distinction.

Securing an accurate and reliable diagnosis is the first step toward obtaining proper treatment for your child. Fortunately, there are things you can do to maximize your chances of getting an accurate diagnosis, but this process is still fraught with the potential for trial and error. Some studies have found that the lag time between the onset of bipolar disorder and getting first treatment for it can average 8–9 years! This typically happens, as it did with Carlos, when the child is repeatedly treated for the wrong conditions because he has never had the benefit of a proper diagnostic evaluation.

If you've had this experience, you, like Emilia, may feel frustrated and angry at the mental health system. But you may be able to resolve your doubts and answer nagging questions by reading Chapter 3, where you'll learn how doctors diagnose bipolar disorder in teens and how they distinguish it from ADHD, oppositional defiant disorder, and a host of other mental health complications. You'll learn how to get a proper referral for a diagnostic evaluation, what questions you should ask of the mental health provider who performs it, and what you can do if you're not satisfied with the results.

You'll become familiar with the term *comorbidity*, which means the codiagnosis of two or more disorders in the same person (for example, bipolar disorder in conjunction with ADHD). Knowing about illness comorbidities will help you select among the various treatment alternatives for your teen because the medications recommended for comorbid illnesses are often quite different. Hopefully, you will feel less isolated by knowing that many other parents have gone through the long and often frustrating process of finding the right diagnosis for their teens.

Still, one of the greatest difficulties associated with bipolar disorder is its effects on family life. You, and most parents coping with the illness, probably feel considerable stress and have had to make great sacrifices financially, practically, or emotionally. Emilia stopped inviting friends over for fear that she would be embarrassed by one of Carlos's "meltdowns." Chapter 4 offers a frank discussion of how bipolar disorder will affect your family. What are the various stages families go through in learning to accept the realities of the disorder? How will it affect your teen's healthy siblings? How can your family work to recognize your teen's strengths despite the disruption caused by the illness? Although your situation may differ from those described, they will give you some ideas (which will be built on later) for dealing with the stress caused by the illness.

"Why Can't I Get a Handle on What This Illness Is and Is Not?"

Before I was diagnosed, I felt like my life was a 100-piece jigsaw puzzle. Now it seems like 1,000 pieces and the first 100 don't even seem to belong to the same puzzle.

—A 17-year-old teen with bipolar disorder

Kids with bipolar disorder do all the things normal teens do: they argue with their parents, take unnecessary risks, experiment with drugs or alcohol, and have mood swings. How do you know when your child is behaving like a normal teenager and when he or she is starting to become manic or depressed? What is the teen experiencing internally, and how might that be different from what healthy teens experience?

Emilia went back and forth between believing there was something wrong with Carlos and believing he was just an annoying teen. Carlos argued this point fervently: "I don't act any different than any of my friends. It's just you who freaks out, unlike their parents."

To make matters even more complicated, once you become acquainted with the disorder, you may find yourself overly concerned that every small change in your teen's behavior heralds a new episode of illness. This is an understandable confusion, and it's easy to err in one direction or another. Even professionals, including us, sometimes mistake a normal reaction to a stressful situation for the beginning of mania—or, worse, mistake a burgeoning manic episode for normal adolescent behavior. Chapter 4 offers the wisdom regarding this tough distinction that we've collected with the help of many bipolar adolescents and their families. When you see your teen start to act angry or defiant, it helps to have some guidelines to fall back on in determining whether it's the normal assertion of independence or the extreme, unfocused irritability that is a key symptom of bipolar disorder.

"Why Is This Happening to My Child?"

In the 2 weeks immediately after Carlos started taking Adderall and Zoloft, he started getting worse. For nearly a week, he stayed up most of the night without any need to catch up on sleep during the day. He said that sleep was a waste of his time. He seemed constantly angry and on the brink of hitting Emilia. He knocked over a lamp and slammed doors. After he verbally threatened Yolanda, Emilia began to fear for her daughter's safety. He talked incessantly about a book he had obtained on occult powers and witchcraft. He started collecting odd fragments of wood and trash and used them to build a prayer altar in his room.

Things came to a head one morning when Emilia insisted Carlos get out of bed in time to get to school. He groaned and cursed at her. Later that morning, after she assumed he had already left, she found him in the bathroom with a razor, scratching "I hate you" in his arm. She called the police, and Carlos was admitted to a hospital.

Once her son was admitted, Emilia met with the inpatient attending psychiatrist, Dr. Roswell, a woman who specialized in mood disorders among teens. Dr. Roswell took a thorough history of Carlos's development, symptoms, and family history and asked questions that Emilia had never been asked before. Dr. Roswell told her that Carlos's mood and behavioral problems were probably the end result of a family history of mood disorders, although no one in the family had been diagnosed with bipolar disorder. Carlos's father had been intermittently depressed and alcoholic. Emilia herself had had several episodes of depression, one immediately following Carlos's birth and another when her husband left. Carlos's paternal grandfather had been "a ramblin', gamblin' man" (her words) who had never had a fixed address for very long.

After a week-long hospitalization, Carlos was diagnosed with bipolar disorder and started on a regimen of Depakote (a mood stabilizer) and Seroquel (an atypical antipsychotic). Dr. Roswell agreed to see him on an outpatient basis in her practice. Carlos and Emilia began a family educational program along with other families of bipolar teens, which met weekly during the evening at the hospital's outpatient clinic.

The group meetings, while highly informative, left Emilia with a combination of frustration, worry, and intense sadness. For her, the issues surrounded grieving over the loss of who she thought Carlos would be: a bright, artistically talented, and creative young man. She began to think she would spend her life taking him in and out of hospitals. These events were equally hard on Carlos, who, despite his bravado, expressed the worry that he would always be mentally ill and that he would never have a career or his own family. Privately, both Carlos and his mother agonized over the question "Why him?" How could this have happened?

Part of coming to terms with bipolar disorder is accepting that it may have been inherited and that your child is biologically prone to future episodes. Knowing that what's wrong with your teen has a name and a biochemical basis may alleviate some of the guilt and nagging fears that you or your teen's other parent may harbor. You may believe that you somehow caused the symptoms because of your parenting style, a divorce, inadequate nurturing when your child was a baby, or other life circumstances. But it may also raise a series of questions for you: Will the illness last for the rest of his life? Will my other children get the illness? Do I have it and just not know it? Will my teen have to take medications forever, and what will these medications do to him?

These questions and others about treatment are answered in Part II. In Chapter 5 we lay out our biopsychosocial model for treating teens with the illness, which emphasizes the interaction of psychological, environmental, and biological factors in causing episodes of the disorder. For example, stress elicits symptoms in most bipolar children, but teens are also particularly likely to create their own stressful circumstances, especially within the family. This biopsychosocial model is important in understanding why we combine medications with psychotherapy in treating the illness.

The biological basis for the disorder will also help you understand your teen's medical treatment. For example, if you know that your teen is biologically predisposed to manic episodes, you will know to be cautious about the use of antidepressant medications, which can cause depressed teens to become manic if used without accompanying mood stabilizers. Carlos was already developing mania at the time his first doctor encouraged him to take the antidepressant Zoloft. This medication accelerated his mania and eventually led to the recognition of his bipolar disorder.

"What Can Be Done to Treat My Child?"

In our experience, the biggest concern of parents is getting their teen into treatment and making sure the teen stays in treatment. Emilia succeeded in getting Carlos to see a psychiatrist, but getting him to follow through on his medications was another matter entirely. You can feel particularly hurt if your child does not see the need for treatment despite the fact that her mood swings are having a clearly negative impact on you and other members of your family. You may also be frustrated and angry if you and your spouse don't share the same vision about what needs to be done.

Our first goal in Part II is to acquaint you with available treatments for bipolar teenagers. Having all of this in one place will consolidate a lot of the information that you'd ordinarily have to seek from websites, radio and television programs, and the things your doctor tells you. Chapter 6 explains what we know about the different medications used to treat bipolar disorder. Medications for bipolar teens, which usually fall into the mood stabilizer and atypical antipsychotic classes, are often used in combination. The array of available medications is changing constantly, but there are "old standbys" like lithium that still play an important role in stabilizing kids with the disorder.

Many teens with bipolar disorder benefit from individual, family, or group therapy (Chapter 7) in addition to medication. Many of these treatments have not been tested experimentally in bipolar teens, but we know a lot about them from studies of bipolar adults or teens with depression. Psychotherapy and support groups (as in Carlos's case) can also help you to learn to cope with the illness. They can provide a forum for teens to vent about and develop solutions to problems in their peer relationships. Psychotherapy is an essential adjunct to medication in managing the ups and downs of bipolar disorder, even though the positive results may not be obvious right away.

"How Can I Help My Child Stay in Treatment?"

When Carlos and Emilia began attending support groups, Emilia felt like her eyes were being opened. Other parents' descriptions of their kids' problems seemed to mirror her own, and for the first time she felt not quite as alone. Carlos, in contrast, hated going to the groups. He described the other kids in the group as "losers" and "whiners" and said he had no intention of going back. He also began to toy with his medications, sometimes leaving tablets around the house or forgetting where he left his pill bottles. He disliked Dr. Roswell and saw her as lacking in understanding, prone to using "big words that don't mean anything," and uninterested in his religious and spiritual beliefs.

As a parent, much of the responsibility for your teen's ongoing stability will fall on you. This means finding ways to keep your teen compliant with his medications. Toward this end, it's important to develop an alliance with your child's treatment providers, even when you find yourself frustrated by our imperfect mental health care system.

Teens are notorious for going off the medications intended to stabilize their moods. Getting Carlos to accept the necessity of Depakote or Seroquel was a long and arduous process that involved several more illness episodes before he finally agreed to take them consistently. Your teen may be going through something similar. Maybe your teen keeps changing her mind about medications. Or maybe she has finally begun to accept the need for them—but has agreed to take only one of two that have been prescribed. At one point Carlos was willing to take a stimulant medication for ADHD because it made him feel hyper and racy, but was not willing to take a mood stabilizer to prevent mania. Your teen may accept medications at first and then stop taking them (like Carlos) or never agree to take them in the first place.

Sometimes teens resist medications because of unpleasant side effects. No one likes to take medications every day, especially ones that can cause acne, weight gain, insomnia, headaches, shakiness, or fatigue—even though some side effects can be ameliorated by the physician. Other issues are more complicated to resolve, such as when medications make a teen feel like a "mental patient." But there are more and less effective ways to get a teenager to commit to a medication regimen. In Chapter 8, we offer some methods for discussing medications with your child, negotiating dosage levels with doctors to minimize side effects, and monitoring whether the medications are helping your teen's mood or causing more problems than they are worth. Getting your child—and sometimes your other family members as well—to buy into his treatments will make your life and your child's life much easier.

"How Can I Keep My Child from Getting Worse?"

Understanding the diagnosis and getting appropriate medication treatments are only two parts of the complex puzzle of keeping bipolar teens well. Bipolar disorder waxes and wanes. It follows a "relapse–remission" course in which teens have episodes followed by periods of better functioning followed by more episodes. Knowing the triggers for your child's symptomatic periods and what the early warning signs look like (and how they are experienced by your child) is essential to preventing illness recurrences. This book will help you recognize when your child is cycling into an episode of mania, depression, or mixed disorder. You'll learn how to develop a relapse prevention plan that involves identifying triggers for mood episodes or suicidality, identifying early symptoms, and introducing preventative or palliative measures (Chapters 10–13).

For most teens, there is a brief but recognizable period when they are becoming ill but are not there yet. Emilia noticed that Carlos began to snap at everybody and developed an odd stare when he was getting manic. Many of the parents we work with say things like "I know he's getting manic when he gets that look in his eyes" or "When she gets depressed, she starts looking like a rag doll, flopping around, like her arms and legs are useless sticks that she has to drag along."

You may have noticed some signs that your child is getting worse, and also felt the frustration of trying to distinguish a true sign of oncoming illness from an ordinary change in mood. If your teen has not yet been diagnosed, or perhaps was just recently diagnosed, his "cycling pattern" (that is, when the onsets and offsets of illness episodes occur and how they develop) may not be clear yet. In Chapter 11, you'll find useful information about how to identify the early warning signs of mania and what to do when you see them. Emilia learned to recognize Carlos's "odd stare" and religious preoccupations as signs that he needed an increase in his atypical antipsychotic medication (Seroquel). As a result, on at least one occasion she was able to keep him out of the hospital. You will feel empowered when you learn to apply similar principles to your unique situation.

A key tool is to know when to communicate with the psychiatrist. You and your family members need to have an agreed-on plan to call the psychiatrist for an emergency medication change. Sometimes these changes can be quick and easy, like increasing the dosage of a mood stabilizing medication. At other times, the interventions are more complicated and may require hospitalization to keep the teen safe and give new medications a chance to take effect.

A separate set of tools can be used when a teen is getting depressed (Chapter 12). Depression can have a sudden onset in adolescents and can be difficult to distinguish from mania (and sometimes even coexists with it). In many ways, we know more about how to manage depression than mania since there is a larger literature on the self-management of depression. In Chapter 12, we'll acquaint you with techniques such as behavioral activation (developing a plan for keeping your child physically active and engaged with her environment) and cognitive restructuring (helping her identify and challenge pessimistic thinking).

In Chapter 13, you'll become familiar with techniques that can be used should your teen express suicidal thoughts. Emilia was understandably worried that Carlos's intellectual preoccupation with death and the afterlife were suicidal thoughts in disguise. In fact, bipolar disorder in teens is associated with a high risk of suicidal behavior, but fortunately there are things you can do to prevent this behavior. Preventing suicide is more than just being sympathetic. It can involve, for example, removing from the house weapons that could cause harm or drugs that could cause overdose.

"How Can I Help My Child Stay Well over the Long Haul?"

After talking with other parents, Emilia began to understand the importance of keeping Carlos on a consistent sleep schedule. When he got home from the hospital, he started staying up most of the night instant-messaging his friends or talking on his cell phone. Later, Emilia discovered that Carlos had called someone in Venezuela and someone else in Newfoundland, but her son had little memory of these calls. Emilia insisted that Carlos go to bed at 11:00 and be up by 7:00 the next day for school, which he had begun to miss. The lack of predictable family routines, however, made enforcing these rules nearly impossible.

Dr. Roswell encouraged Carlos to take Seroquel in the evening to help him fall asleep. Reluctantly, Carlos began recording his bedtimes, wake times, and mood each day on an online sleep–wake chart Emilia had obtained in the group. Carlos called the chart "lame" and said it made him feel like a mental patient, but he used it, and over the next several weeks his mood began to stabilize.

Much of helping your teen stay well involves acquainting yourself and your teen with *self-management techniques*, such as keeping a regular sleep–wake cycle, avoiding overstimulation at night, keeping a mood and sleep chart, avoiding drugs or alcohol, and learning to keep family stress to a minimum (Chapters 9–10). These habits and skills that can help your son or daughter maintain a stable mood can be viewed as tools in a toolkit that will work with some problems and not others. Not all of them will fit every nail or screw that needs pounding or tightening, but their availability will make you feel empowered to cope with even the most stressful situations. As with medication, however, getting your teen to use these strategies can be a challenge, which is why in Part III we'll offer lots of examples of how to get a teen to follow through. We also provide worksheets for recording your mutual efforts, which you'll find well worth your time. As Emilia said, "Managing this illness really involves changing your whole routine. It's not something you can medicate away."

Even more important than the practicalities of managing the disorder is experiencing a sense of hope and communicating this to your teen. You may feel defeated by the wrong turns that treatment can take or angry at doctors for making promises that haven't been fulfilled. Emilia certainly felt this way. But knowing that you have hope for his future is extremely important to your teen, even if he doesn't know it yet. Throughout this book, we will give you many reasons to remain optimistic and offer many ways to communicate this optimism to your child.

"Can My Teenager Lead a Normal Life at School and with Friends?"

Carlos got out of the hospital on a Saturday afternoon and was back in school on Monday. At 11:00 Tuesday morning Emilia got a call from the guidance counselor that Carlos was waiting to be picked up. He had cursed at a teacher, overturned a desk, and angrily walked out of class. The counselor raised the possibility that Carlos wasn't ready for high school, that perhaps he was too immature. Emilia tried to explain what she knew about Carlos's bipolar disorder. The counselor did not acknowledge her use of the term *bipolar* but said that she had worked with many kids in the "SED [seriously emotionally disturbed] category." She mentioned something about special education classes or home schooling. Emilia protested that Carlos was not seriously emotionally disturbed, that he was taking medications, that he was ordinarily a fine student, and that he just needed time to stabilize. The counselor asked if there were "problems at home." Emilia eventually hung up, feeling she had no advocate in the school setting.

Around this time, Carlos began withdrawing from his friendships. He had never been a particularly social child, but the friends he had were good ones. Now, however, he seemed uninterested in going to their houses, although he continued to "binge on instant messaging," as Emilia put it. The phone calls he had with his friends sounded short and perfunctory, like "a series of grunts," unlike the lively and humorous conversations he used to enjoy.

Bipolar disorder takes a heavy toll on the functioning of a teenager. Unlike children with ADHD, teens with bipolar disorder can be functioning well and then suddenly "take a dive" in their school performance, from straight A's to F's or from being punctual and conscientious to cutting classes. Often, the deterioration coincides with a significant episode of mania or depression. Unfortunately, schools are often not set up to handle the myriad of mental health diagnoses that are brought to them, including bipolar disorder, Asperger syndrome, or ADHD. Like Emilia, you may have experienced significant conflict with teachers and school guidance counselors and may feel that the people who are supposed to help you are causing more problems than they solve.

Some schools deal with the complexities of psychiatric disturbance by lumping all children into one category, like "seriously emotionally disturbed" or "in need of special education." Yet this solution glosses over the important differences between children who have quite different psychiatric problems. A teen like Carlos, for example, needs a different school program from one with ADHD. Carlos needed classes that started at later times, more frequent breaks during the day, the availability of a school counselor when he had mood swings, and special help with arithmetic. A teen with ADHD may need behavioral plans that have been developed for this disorder, which may include training in how to maximize attention and minimize distraction, organizational skills, memory or recall strategies, and social skills.

Chapter 14 is devoted to helping your child succeed in school. In our experience, parents of bipolar teens can be quite effective in navigating the school system and are often quite helpful to each other in making this happen. What kinds of educational plans can be made for a bipolar teen, and how are these different from what would be proposed for a teen with ADHD or a learning disability? What are the pros and cons of disclosing your teen's bipolar disorder to teachers or fellow parents? How can you help your teen deal with the stigma of the disorder in the school system or with peers?

In our experience, school counselors and teachers are usually willing to help but are overwhelmed by the number of students in their charge. In all likelihood, your teen will need a "Section 504 plan" or an "individualized educational plan" (IEP). These are written, agreed-on educational protocols whose objective is to maximize your child's learning potential. To develop these plans—and, even more important, to make sure they are actually implemented—you will need to be assertive with your child's school authorities. You will need to walk a fine line between advocating for your child and not alienating teachers or counselors who can react defensively to these demands.

Finally, because of their difficulty regulating emotions, teens with bipolar disorder often have trouble negotiating healthy peer relationships within the school setting. Keeping your child involved with peers is essential to her mood stability. We will talk about treatment strategies for managing social relationships in Chapters 7 and 14.

"How Do I Keep This Illness from Destroying Me and My Family?"

Emilia had been having difficult interactions with Carlos since he had been a little boy, but they had gotten worse since puberty. The behaviors that counselors had told her reflected her son's "normal developmental quest for independence" seemed more like poisonous verbal brawls that made her feel ineffective and threatened. Carlos was no longer a little boy and towered over her physically. She was beginning to feel afraid of him. To make matters worse, Emilia had to deal with relatives and friends who said "He's just being a teenage boy" or "He's a brat. Don't let him get so much control over you" or "Take him over your knee" or "Send him to a military academy." Another friend who was schooled in mental health care asked, "Do you think maybe he's been sexually abused by someone and hasn't told you? Could he be taking drugs?" These responses made Emilia feel like her competence as a parent was more and more in question.

Emilia was simultaneously having problems of her own. Her job was very stressful, and the business was not going well. Financially, she was barely making ends meet. She got minimal child support from her ex-husband, who played a marginal role in Carlos's and Yolanda's lives. When he did make an appearance, he usually brought lavish gifts for the kids and took them out with his latest girlfriend. Whenever this happened, Carlos seemed to escalate his anger and hostility toward his mother.

Emilia began drinking to alleviate an increasing anxiety that seemed to pervade her consciousness from almost the moment she woke up. To make matters worse, Yolanda began having problems. In apparent imitation of Carlos, she was beginning to swear and kick household furniture when she didn't get her way.

One time, in a particularly vulnerable moment in her support group, Emilia began crying, saying, "I didn't think my life would turn out this way. I had all these dreams for me and my kids. Maybe I just wasn't meant to be a parent."

It would be an understatement to say that being the parent of a bipolar teenager is a rough road. It can turn your life upside down and have negative, rippling effects on your relationships, your work, and your other kids. Although bipolar disorder is often glibly compared to medical diseases like diabetes, such comparisons gloss over the stigma and shame experienced by parents of the psychiatrically ill. Like Emilia, you may have already experienced a great deal of practical burden from dealing with the illness, such as lost income from work, huge financial costs, and strained relationships. The emotional burden can be equally crippling. You may end up feeling like you need mental health services yourself, as parents of bipolar people often do. Moreover, because this illness is transmitted genetically, some parents are simultaneously dealing with their own mood disorder as well as their kid's, or with mood disorder in a spouse or other members of the family.

Our research has found that a person's family environment during and just after a manic episode has a significant influence over the possibility of a recurrence in the following year. This is not surprising; many psychiatric illnesses are strongly affected by the family environment. Fortunately, there are things you can do to take care of yourself, your spouse, and your other children while still staying on top of the care your teen with bipolar disorder needs.

A major purpose of this book is to give you some tools for managing your own emotional states and reactions to stressful circumstances in your family. Some of these tools are practical skills like learning how to respond when your teen is blowing up at you; how to solve problems collaboratively before they get out of hand; and when and when not to negotiate with your teen (Chapter 9). Other tools involve in-the-moment "mindfulness" techniques such as refocusing, breathing, or distancing yourself from disturbing thoughts. These emotional self-regulation skills will keep you from losing control yourself when you're being provoked.

You may find Chapters 4 and 9 to be the most useful of all. They look at questions such as: How is the family affected by bipolar disorder? How can the family create a positive, protective environment for the teen that also protects the parents' marriage and the well-being of the other children? What is the parent's role, the affected teen's role, and the sibling's role in maintaining this balance?

Throughout these chapters we'll refer frequently to our family therapy techniques. We have found in numerous studies that family education and skills training can prevent recurrences and stabilize mood in those taking medications for bipolar disorder. Other research groups have shown that support groups like the one Emilia took part in can stabilize a child's mood disorder. We'll acquaint you with many of the skills we train families to use, such as effective listening, negotiating strategies, and problem solving.

We offer a number of exercises for practicing illness management techniques with your family members. If you can master these techniques when things are calm, they will be much more effective when things get tense. Parents who get in the habit of using effective communication and problem-solving skills can help their teenager stabilize more completely and help their other children cope with stress caused by the illness.

Emilia and Carlos: Epilogue

Carlos is 18 now, and things have gotten better for him, Emilia, and Yolanda. He obtained a G.E.D. (a high school graduation equivalent certificate) and eventually enrolled in community college. Central to his stabilization was his eventual willingness to accept that he had bipolar disorder and needed to take medications for it. This came about gradually, not overnight, through a combination of meetings with his psychiatrist, a good individual therapist, and the education and support that Emilia got through her multifamily group. Carlos still has significant mood swings and often complains of an ongoing depression that he can't shake. His rage attacks are fewer and farther between, and he and Emilia have developed a civil, if not exactly close, relationship. Yolanda never developed bipolar disorder. She has had her own problems in high school, and received counseling, but is otherwise a normally functioning teenager.

Emilia has developed close relationships with parents in her support group, which still meets monthly, even years later. They have developed a system by which parents substitute for each other when feeling overly stressed. For example, on one recent Saturday night in which she was fighting with both kids, Emilia's friend Nancy agreed to come over to the house with her husband. Emilia left for a few hours. The kids seemed to welcome this change, and when their mother came back, they had both calmed down.

Emilia still struggles with her urge to drink. She goes to AA groups and obtains support from her sponsor. She is still employed but decided that trying to manage a business at night was too much. She is more philosophical these days about the cards she was dealt in life: "I wouldn't wish this illness on anyone or their family. But I guess it's made me a stronger person than I might have been otherwise." She gets considerable satisfaction from helping other parents whose children have just been diagnosed with bipolar disorder.

A key message of this book is to remain hopeful. Many parents are dealing with the same kinds of problems that you are. Our knowledge of this illness isn't complete, but there are things you can do to make life better for your teen and you.

Emilia and Carlos's story is only one of many we have heard. Many children have much better outcomes, and some have had worse. But we hear a common theme in these stories: when you, as the parent, come to accept the illness and are successful in getting your teen the best treatment available, your teen will eventually come to see the value of your efforts, even if hostile to them early on. Accepting bipolar illness is a lifelong process. We hope the information and strategies we offer here will make your journey more successful and hopeful.

2

A Close Look
at the Symptoms

Sixteen-year-old Justin was breaking rules at home, ditching classes at school, and had most recently run away from home to spend a few days with his friends. Though his friends slept after being out all night, Justin stayed up and wrote lyrics for a new song he'd been working on. He believed he would be a great rock star some day and that having to obey a curfew and go to school was interfering with his plans. When he returned home, he was angry and sullen and then exploded and started yelling when his mother tried to talk to him. His father stepped in and tried to restrain him, but Justin knocked his father down and ran out of the house, still yelling. Later his friends dropped him off at a party, where he got drunk. Because the party was full of high school kids, the police were called. They took Justin to juvenile detention for being drunk and belligerent. When his parents picked him up, he began angrily talking about being stifled by them. He then threatened to kill himself if they made him go home with them. His parents took him to the emergency room for a safety evaluation.

Each major player in this case study had a different explanation for Justin's behavior. Justin believed his parents were responsible for his erratic behavior, faulting them for not supporting his dreams of becoming a rock star and wanting him to toe the "corporate" line.

Justin's parents were initially confused and angry about his behavior. In their eyes, he appeared disrespectful and rebellious. As time went on, they became fearful. When Justin got belligerent and threatening, they knew his behavior was more than they could handle safely and decided to get help. After the latest blowup, they felt sad and guilty, knowing that Justin was in a lot of pain and they couldn't seem to alleviate it.

Justin's 14-year-old brother, Zach, thought Justin was being a jerk. He didn't understand why Justin was being so hostile to their parents when Mom and Dad were just trying to keep Justin safe. Zach silently vowed that he would never be like his brother and decided he would be the "good" kid to give Mom and Dad a break.

Justin's friends said he was just a typical teenager—trying to find himself and figure out where he was headed. They did admit, however, that he was "hyper" and hard to keep up with.

The hospital staff saw many of the signs of bipolar disorder in Justin and admitted him to the hospital for observation. The facts that he needed less sleep than his friends, that he had grandiose ideas of rock stardom, that he bounced between sullen irritability and rage, and that he had threatened suicide were all consistent with the diagnostic criteria for bipolar disorder. But first they had to rule out a substance abuse problem since Justin had been drinking—and possibly using drugs—when brought in.

Bipolar disorder is a challenge to diagnose because people with the illness, as well as some of those around them, often see the symptoms as making sense in the context of their life. Justin thought his goals and behavior were perfectly normal and felt terribly misunderstood by his family. This conviction was in part reinforced by his friends, who saw him as high-strung but otherwise fine. Even family members may confuse the low-grade symptoms of mania (the "up" side of bipolar mood swings) with the affected person's personality, especially when these symptoms have been evident for years. To complicate matters, teenagers are already angst-driven and moody due to developmental changes, so how can parents be sure that something is truly wrong rather than that their child is just going through a typical, if harrowing, teenage phase?

All these factors make diagnosing bipolar difficult. Therefore, it's critical to get the best evaluation available, a process covered separately in Chapter 3. In this chapter we'll help you pull together everyone's observations so that you can see whether, in fact, your teenager needs a professional evaluation for bipolar disorder. Knowing what the symptoms might look like from different vantage points will also help your family contribute their indispensable knowledge of your teen to his evaluation, and help you begin the process of coping with the disorder in daily life.

Bipolar disorder looks different from different family members' perspectives:

Teens' perspectives on why they behave in these erratic ways:
"I'm fine; everyone else is crazy."
"If I'm crazy, so are all my friends."
"I'm so screwed up, life is hopeless."

Parents' perspectives:
"It's the kid's fault—he's a bad kid; he's lazy."
"It's all my fault; I'm a bad parent."
"It's the environment—the teachers are too hard on her."
"His friends are bad for him."
"There's something wrong with her brain."

Siblings' perspectives:
"My brother is a jerk."
"She just does this stuff to get attention."
"All my parents care about is him and his bad behavior."
"I can't wait until I don't have to deal with her anymore."

What Symptoms Does Your Teenager Have?

How difficult it is to answer this question may depend in part on how long you've been noticing symptoms in your teen. Early symptoms often appear long before the full-blown symptoms of a diagnosable bipolar disorder, so concerns may have been lurking in the back of your mind for quite some time. In that case it may or may not be that hard to bring them to the surface now. Sometimes bipolar symptoms appear all at once without warning in teens, in which case you may be able to identify them quite easily. Either way, it can be helpful to take a more systematic look at the behaviors you're seeing.

A good start would be to fill out the Mood Disorder Questionnaire on pages 25–26, which is based on both the criteria doctors use to diagnose bipolar disorder in teens and insights from clinical experience with teen patients. Take a few minutes to fill out the questionnaire now, being sure to note whether your observations occurred during the same period of time and whether they caused any problems with your teen's normal functioning. Try thinking about your teen's behavior in the last week or during a time when his behavior was of greatest concern to you.

The questionnaire has three sections. For section 1, write down the numbers 1–13 on a piece of paper and answer each question with a yes or no (or you can just copy this page). Answer section 2 with a yes or no. Choose the answer in section 3 that best fits your situation and write it down.

If you found yourself unsure about how to answer the questions, read the rest of this chapter and then go back to the questionnaire. The rest of this chapter will give you a closer view of how the symptoms may appear to parents, teachers, professionals, and the teens themselves.

Once you've completed the questionnaire, take a look at your answers. If you answered yes to more than one of the items under (1), answered yes to item (2), and rated her problems under (3) as being at least mild, you should definitely read on. By itself, this questionnaire does not tell you if your child has bipolar disorder, but if your child meets these criteria, you should arrange a thorough psychiatric evaluation.

Chapter 3 will tell you more about the way mental health practitioners view bipolar disorder in teens. To be diagnosed, your teen will have to meet certain criteria, and the clinician will want to rule out other illnesses, a particular problem in the case of bipolar disorder. If your teen hasn't yet been diagnosed, you may also want to take your answers to the questionnaire to the first meeting. If your teen has already been diagnosed, do your answers to the questionnaire match what the diagnosing professional reported in his or her assessment of your teen? If not, you might want to bring up any inconsistencies between your and the doctor's viewpoints at your next office visit.

The Hallmark Symptoms of Mania and Hypomania

As you know from Chapter 1, bipolar disorder is defined by mood swings between mania or hypomania and depression. Each has certain hallmark symptoms that best distinguish bipolar disorder from other conditions. The Mood Disorders Questionnaire should have helped you get a preliminary idea of whether your teen is suffering any of these hallmark symptoms. The following descriptions will help you fill in the picture of your teen.

If you've been concerned about your child's behavior but are unsure whether bipolar disorder is a possibility, the teen years may clarify what's

THE MOOD DISORDER QUESTIONNAIRE

Instructions: Think about your adolescent and please answer each question as best you can.

1. Has there ever been a period of time when your child was not his/her self and . . .

. . . felt so good or so hyper that other people thought your child was not his/her normal self, or was so hyper that your child got into trouble?	**Yes**	**No**
. . . felt so irritable that he/she shouted at people or started fights or arguments?	**Yes**	**No**
. . . got much more self-confident than usual?	**Yes**	**No**
. . . got much less sleep than usual and found he/she didn't really miss it?	**Yes**	**No**
. . . was much more talkative or spoke much faster than usual?	**Yes**	**No**
. . . thoughts raced through his/her head or your child couldn't slow his/her mind down?	**Yes**	**No**
. . . was so easily distracted by things around him/her that he/she had trouble concentrating or staying on track?	**Yes**	**No**
. . . had much more energy than usual?	**Yes**	**No**

Source: Wagner K. D. et al. (2006). Validation of the Mood Disorder Questionnaire for bipolar disorder in adolescence. *Journal of Clinical Psychiatry, 67*(5), 827–830. Reprinted by permission.

... was much more active or did many more things than usual? **Yes** No

... was much more social or outgoing than usual, for example, telephoned friends in the middle of the night? **Yes** No

... was much more interested in sex than usual? **Yes** No

... did things that were unusual for him/her or that other people thought were excessive, foolish, or risky? **Yes** No

... spent money and got him/her or your family into trouble? **Yes** No

2. **If you checked YES to more than one of the above, have several of these ever happened during the same period of time?**

3. **How much of a problem did any of these cause your child—like being unable to go to school; having family, money or legal troubles; getting into arguments or fights? Please select one response.**

   No problem   Minor problem   Moderate problem   Serious problem going on. That's when some of the symptoms of mania may appear that are less likely to be in the behavioral repertoire of young children (or at least are harder to assess): spending, immodest attire, grandiose thinking, and increased sexual activity. Hypomania—low-grade mania—is a more difficult mood state for teens and parents to identify, particularly if your teen has experienced a lot of depression. You may interpret a more upbeat mood—acting unrealistic, goofy, silly, and happy for no apparent reason—as just a relief from depression. But if hypomania shows its other side—increased anger and irritability that may lead to snapping at others—you're likely to be more concerned.

Euphoria and Elation

When I am manic I feel like a cheetah. I'm strong, powerful, and fast. No one can tame me.

—Lewis, age 14

Mania and hypomania—the "up" moods of bipolar disorder—take one of two primary shapes: (1) euphoria or elation, or (2) irritability. The mania of bipolar disorder is usually depicted as involving a true "high" mood, yet not all teens experience mania as a pleasant state. In fact, some studies have not found elation in teenage patients at all, only irritability.

Teens who do get elated during mania or hypomania often feel a sense of well-being, confidence, and power. In other cases parents notice something is wrong when the teen's feelings don't match her life circumstances. This was the case with 13-year-old Marcy, who happily reported, "Everything is great in my life—I have lots of friends, school is great, and I'm going to have a great life," despite the fact that she had only one casual friend that lived in another state, was failing several classes in school, and wasn't getting along with anyone in her family.

When hypomanic or manic, elated teens display a distinct lack of ability to question their contentment. Your teen may interpret any "reality check" you try to offer as you being critical and trying to rain on her parade. When Justin's parents tried to point out that his health and grades were suffering as a consequence of his elated behavior, he showed no insight into the reality of his situation, got angry at the parents he saw as the real problem, and stormed off to get involved in more trouble.

Grandiosity

My friend and I are going to drive to California and become back-up dancers for Britney Spears.

—Danielle, age 15

As many as 86% of youth with bipolar disorder demonstrate *grandiosity*—an inflated sense of self or of one's abilities—although this symptom can be hard to distinguish from typical adolescent bravado. Again, it's the teen's lack of realism that usually reveals grandiosity as a symptom of mania. When asked if she had been taking dance lessons or had any connections that would get her this job, Danielle responded defensively, "No, but I'm sure it will all work out."

Milder forms of grandiosity are particularly difficult to recognize. After all, it is age-appropriate for kids to have dreams of doing great things—take the 14-year-old who claims he's going to become a professional basketball player, for example. Kids who are very bright and creative may have lofty ideas of what they are capable of accomplishing, and their grandiosity may be especially difficult to recognize. Sometimes it takes time for a parent to realize that it's no longer age-appropriate for an 18-year-old to be clinging to his 14-year-old dreams.

If you have questions about whether your teen has grandiose ideas or is behaving in a grandiose manner, you may get a clearer picture from her teacher or siblings. To them, your teen's grandiosity may show up as a persistent "know-it-all" attitude that is hard to miss because it is so annoying. Fourteen-year-old Kenneth's parents recalled with some regret that when their son was in kindergarten and first grade, they had been told numerous times that he was repeatedly challenging his teacher in the classroom—reports they took as a sign of his intelligence and great academic prospects. By the time he was a freshman in high school, they realized that acting like he was smarter than the teacher was probably an early sign of his illness.

Grandiosity is even more frustrating for siblings. Typically, the bipolar adolescent consistently makes brothers and sisters feel stupid or inadequate. While hypomanic, 13-year-old Roy spurned every advance his 11-year-old brother, Ben, made to connect with him by ridiculing anything Ben said as being incorrect or stupid. Even when Ben was sharing information that Roy didn't have, Roy would begin screaming at his younger brother, "You are so wrong and so stupid! Get away from me! I hate you!" Roy believed that no one paralleled his intellect, least of all his younger brother, and would go to extremes to keep him in his place. Roy was unlikely to behave in this way when his mood was stable.

Decreased Need for Sleep

> He's up in his room until 2:00 or 3:00 in the morning listening to music, playing video games, and making quite a lot of noise. Then he is up around 6:00 A.M. making food and slamming doors. He heads out for a bike ride and, once his friends are up, hangs out with them all day. He doesn't appear to be tired at all, even when they are. All of us, however, are exhausted.
>
> —Mother of 13-year-old Paul, diagnosed with a manic episode

The decreased need for sleep that comes with mania is not the same thing as *insomnia*, the inability to fall asleep or stay asleep, which leads to being tired the next day. Teens like Paul can go with little or no sleep and continue to function as if they've slept normally. About 40% of youth with bipolar disorder experience this symptom of mania. If your teen has long been having bipolar symptoms, you may be used to the late nights and early waking—he may have even shown this symptom during infancy. But if your teen is just starting to show signs of bipolar disorder, you'll find this symptom very disruptive; when it disturbs your own sleep, it can become hard to function, let alone handle a rebellious, labile teen. Your own physical health can begin to suffer, as can your teen's, who will be more vulnerable to illnesses due to lack of sleep. Although your teen may claim he can get along without sleep, becoming sleep-deprived often leads to an increase in irritability and attacks of rage, which take their toll on the health of your other family members. In Chapter 6, we discuss medications for sleep disturbance, and in Chapter 10, we discuss ways to help your teen regulate his sleep–wake cycle.

Racing Thoughts and Flight of Ideas

> When I have all these thoughts and ideas in my head I end up thinking all day. By the end of the day my brain is really tired. . . . I'm not able to concentrate because my mind is too busy and full of so many ideas.
>
> —Marcus, age 12

What Marcus described takes two different forms, both of which can make it very hard for bipolar teens to concentrate on schoolwork. Racing thoughts come one at a time but move so quickly that the teen can't focus on one thought before another one inserts itself. "Flight of ideas" doesn't necessarily mean that thoughts move quickly; instead multiple thoughts occur all at once, which makes it hard to focus on any single one. One study found that 71% of youth with bipolar disorder experienced racing thoughts and/or flight of ideas, but this is a symptom on which parents and teens often disagree. Parents may not be able to see this symptom, and teens may have a hard time describing it clearly. Unless asked, kids don't usually volunteer information about racing thoughts. To help them figure out what we mean, we often tell kids that racing thoughts could be described as the songs on an iPod playing on fast forward. In response many say their mind is constantly running and they can't shut it off.

Hypersexuality

> She has always been hypersexual. When she was 3 and 4 years old, she was constantly masturbating in public. We would go home and take her to her room, where she would masturbate for extended periods. This behavior has continued into adolescence. She will still spend hours in her room self-stimulating.
> —Mother of a 15-year-old with bipolar I disorder

Hypersexuality is a symptom of the manic or hypomanic phase of bipolar disorder. Once again, it can be tough to distinguish from the usual prepubertal hormones and adolescent sexual experimentation. Parents respond in different ways to this behavior in their child. You may view it as just a behavior for limit setting and boundaries, or you may be quite concerned, especially if other kids in the family are exposed to it. "When she gets hyper," said the mother of one 16-year-old, "she does the most disgusting things. She will lick my face and laugh. Then she will take her pants off, pull her panties up between her buttocks, and start jumping around the house. I have two younger girls in the house that should not be exposed to this type of sexual behavior."

Some parents worry, justifiably, that their teenager will be rejected by her peers over this behavior. "I was horrified when I discovered that my daughter was giving suggestive notes to the boys in her sixth-grade class," lamented the mother of a 12-year-old with bipolar disorder. "I'm really scared that other girls won't want to be friends with her."

When teens get older and hypersexual feelings turn to early experimentation, the risks become more palpable. Adolescent girls often later regret the consequences of this symptom. Even though their sexual behavior was driven by an illness, the symptom and its consequences can change the way a young girl views her sexuality, as it did for Marissa, who said this at age 16: "I always wanted to be a virgin when I got married, but I guess that won't happen now. I had sex when I was 13 with a guy who was much older. I wanted to do it at the time, but later I felt sick to my stomach, violated, guilty, and confused." Marissa was pregnant 1 year later.

Kids like Marissa struggle to make sense of sexual events they've been exposed to much too early in life. Sometimes, the fallout will include depression and anxiety. Fourteen-year-old Wendy said, "The anxiety started the day after I had sex with my boyfriend. My stomach started hurting, and I had intense anxiety because I knew that a stomachache happened if you were pregnant. Well, since then I've been anxious about being pregnant even though I know I'm not."

Hypersexuality occurs in less than half of youth with bipolar disorder, but because of its high potential to have serious consequences, it is especially important to keep it from escalating. Chapter 6 discusses medications to help control the symptoms of mania (including hypersexuality), and Chapter 11 gives you suggestions on how to help prevent your teen from acting on these impulses when she is in the earliest phases of mania.

Irritability

Several studies have reported that irritability is the most common symptom among kids and adolescents who develop bipolar disorder. We've certainly seen this in the teenagers we treat, who often say every little thing a parent or sibling does gets on their nerves. When asked what makes them irritable, many say, "Everything. It doesn't matter what it is, if I'm in a bad mood, no one can do anything without pissing me off." Sometimes, though, chronic irritability can be fixated on one family member, as it was with the 14-year-old who said about her mother, "I just hate her. She's always so stupid. Everything she does bugs me."

Irritability is often the symptom behind the intense aggressive outbursts that are so difficult for parents of bipolar teens to deal with. Although the more subtle forms of irritability may be hard to identify as behavior that needs mental health attention, the rage attacks leave little doubt. Adolescents with bipolar disorder can become very angry and rage at their parents for hours. They appear to have an unlimited amount of energy for these negative interactions. Typically after his rages Justin would sleep up to 4 hours due to complete mental and physical exhaustion.

Sometimes during these rage attacks, the teen may become threatening or physically abusive toward the parent or a sibling. For parents who have experienced this level of aggressiveness when their child was younger, having him move into adolescence may be particularly frightening. As a child grows larger and stronger, these aggressive outbursts may result in physical injury to any family members involved in trying to calm or subdue him. "Now that he's become so large, we have started walking on eggshells trying not to do or say anything that might upset him," said the mother of 16-year-old Evan. "He is stronger than we are, and my husband has a back condition. We don't want him to hurt either of us. We feel like hostages in our own home."

One of our clients took the bedpost off his mother's bed and threatened to kill her with it. Another teen, during a manic rage, aggressively jumped on his mother's back and would not let go. Often the teen does not remember these events and therefore doesn't understand the full scope of his behavior. Many don't see themselves as responsible for the outburst, ascribing the incident to the parent's stupidity or some other negative trait. It is especially frustrating to try to come up with solutions when your teen doesn't agree that he was irritable in the first place.

Aggressive behavior is, without a doubt, the most troubling for parents. If the teen is always irritable and angry, the parents may come to see their child as a bad kid. "He's just been a bad seed since the day he was born," said Sandy, the mother of 16-year-old Rodney. "Even when he was circumcised, he didn't cry. He just stared at us with a hateful glare." It's also hard to address aggression because it can be confused with the irritability that goes along with depression. One mother told us that her son had been struggling with depression for months. When the son was asked about his mother's impression, he said that he was not depressed at all but that he was always "antsy" and "angry." In many cases, a parent's misinterpretation of mood states irritates the teenager further and causes yet another outburst.

If you have other children, the effect of irritability on them can make your life even more difficult. Many parents report severely ruptured relations between siblings that will be difficult to repair. "He's always mean to me," said Josh, the 12-year-old brother of a 14-year-old with bipolar disorder. "Even when I'm not doing anything, he's making fun of me. If I do get tired of his attitude and try to tell him to back off, he gets physical. If I get physical back with him, he always pushes it farther and hurts me. Now, I just avoid him and can't wait to leave home so I don't have to deal with him anymore."

The problems that irritability and aggression can cause are heartbreaking for families. We offer lots of advice for reducing the damage that irritability can cause in Chapter 9.

Increased Energy and Activity

I know I'm going into an up phase when I want to clean my room. No, dude, you don't understand. I can't just straighten it up—it has to be spotless. If I start this at 11:00 at night, which is usually when I feel this way, it will be hours before I get to sleep.

—Maya, a 17-year-old with bipolar disorder

The energy level of a manic or hypomanic adolescent is something to see. We have seen kids visibly fidget, walk around the room, hide behind chairs, and fiddle with everything in the office. Many need to go outside and run around the block, roller skate, or skateboard in the midst of a therapy session to burn off energy. Many cannot tolerate sitting in the office and talking for a 50-minute session. This energy level rarely seems to bother the adolescent, despite the fact that it causes a lot of trouble at home and in the classroom. Many bipolar teens have a provision in their individualized education plan (see Chapter 14) to take frequent breaks to walk or run around so that they can tolerate a full day of classroom activity.

This hyperactive symptom is often one of the more obvious symptoms in younger children diagnosed with bipolar disorder. But since it's a symptom that bipolar and ADHD kids have in common, the younger child with this symptom is often diagnosed with ADHD before bipolar disorder. Younger children with bipolar disorder may have high energy most or all of the time, but in adolescence the teen's energy remains high during mania but so low during depression that she may not even be able to stay awake in class.

When teens are in the manic or hypomanic phase, they may channel this energy into doing chores to the point of perfection, like Maya, after a long period of having done no chores, or they might get motivated about a school project or take a special interest in a hobby. The volume of output these kids can produce in a short time and the level of creativity involved can be quite impressive. Unfortunately, the output can also be directed toward unrealistic tasks or things that have nothing to do with school assignments. For example:

"Well, Frank [father] and Evan [16-year old son] got into another fight yesterday. Evan got into one of his manic phases and decided to build a catapult. He went to Home Depot, got all of the parts, came home, and built this huge catapult. Frank came home and blew up because his tools were strewn all over the garage. I understood his frustration, but I tried to point out to him—he built a catapult from scratch that could launch 50 feet."

The same boy spent hours with little pieces of metal making a link shirt of armor. He laboriously sat for hours, bending and connecting the small pieces of metal. The same boy, however, could not complete his homework. He also went through numerous periods of depression during which his parents would feel ill-equipped to get him out of the house or engage him in any activities.

Poor Judgment and Impulsivity

We have had the worst weekend in our life as adults. On Friday afternoon we told Mariah she was not going anywhere over the weekend and was grounded for her disrespectful attitude toward us that morning. She laughed in our faces, said that we couldn't stop her, and ran out the door. We followed her outside, only to discover that she was getting on the back of a motorcycle with a man who appeared to be about 30 years old. We pulled her off the back of the bike and had quite a tussle while trying to restrain her. A neighbor noticed the scene and called the police. When the police arrived, Mariah was bleeding from a cut on her cheek that must have occurred during the scuffle. The police are reporting us to child services and have suggested that maybe Mariah live in someone else's home for the time being. We are completely overwhelmed and don't know which way to turn anymore. We never imagined that this would happen to us.

—Parents of 14-year-old Mariah

Over 90% of youth with bipolar disorder exhibit poor judgment of the kind that Mariah did. During a time when kids are trying to assert their independence, pushing the limits is expected, but hypersexuality, daredevil acts, and excessive socializing or "people seeking" can put teens with bipolar disorder in real danger. As with other behavior, bipolar teens and their parents rarely see these acts the same way. When Justin's parents took him to the emergency room for a safety evaluation, he was livid because, as he described it, "I was just drunk and my parents were completely stupid and overreacting." Ideas for protecting your teen during manic escalation are in Chapter 11.

Alcohol, Drug Abuse, and Other Self-Destructive Behaviors

She told us she was just going over to a friend's house to spend the night. We normally check with the other parents, but she is 16 and we decided that we should trust her. We didn't realize that the other girl told her parents that she was spending the night at our house. The girls met up with some boys who had a bunch of alcohol. They said that Freda took a bottle of gin and drank the whole thing in 5 minutes. We got a call at around 11 P.M. that they were worried about Freda because she had passed out and they couldn't wake her. Our daughter's alcohol experimentation almost killed her. How can we ever feel comfortable letting her go out alone again?

—Parents of 16-year-old Freda

Teens with bipolar disorder—like Freda—often seek out harmful behaviors to take away their emotional pain or to accelerate the highs. As many as 40% of teens with bipolar disorder also have a substance abuse disorder. Some teens have described using cocaine to raise their mood or using marijuana, alcohol, or painkillers (also called "pharmies") to bring them down if they feel too hyper or revved. In other cases, the teen is impulsive and gets into trouble with substances without thinking about consequences. Bipolar teens may try to outdo their friends' consumption—often with a sense of toughness or bravado rather than a sensible modicum of fear or caution. Kids whose onset of bipolar disorder began in their teen years are at especially high risk. One study reported that risk of substance abuse is 8.8 times higher in adolescent-onset bipolar disorder than in bipolar disorder that began in childhood.

In addition to substance use, kids can use self-cutting, binge–purge cycles (eating large amounts of food in one sitting [bingeing] and then purging), or even relationships with other people who are destructive forces in their lives to attempt to regulate mood states. For example, your bipolar teen may return to an abusive romantic relationship time and again because it is more exciting and shifts her out of depression. She may argue that these behaviors do not pose a problem for anyone, or that the romantic partner improves her mood much more than her medications do.

Changes in Thinking and Perception

Distractibility

You may have noticed that your teen is easily distracted. This plays out most obviously in situations that require the most concentration, such as the classroom or while doing homework. Any commotion in the classroom, another teen clearing his throat, someone slamming a book, or a bird chirping outside are all likely to pull the teen off task. Unfortunately, it's hard then for the teen to get back on task.

Distractibility is also a primary symptom of ADHD, and, in fact, in 60–90% of cases, kids with bipolar disorder also have ADHD. This diagnostic overlap will be discussed in the next chapter.

Delusions and Hallucinations

> I know there is someone in the house coming to get me. I noticed that the people across the street were looking at me in a weird way earlier today, and now that my parents are gone I know they are coming for me. I thought I saw someone tied up in my neighbors' front room. I hear the doorbell ringing and ringing. Why won't they go away? You have to help me.
> —Mandy, age 17, in an emergency call to her therapist

Symptoms of psychosis sometimes occur in teens with bipolar disorder, but they are not usually symptoms of the illness itself. The incidence of hallucinations and delusions has varied widely in research studies, from 16 to 60%. Adolescents with mood disorders appear to suffer from higher rates of bizarre delusions and hallucinations than adults. Many of the parents we've met describe a psychotic break in early childhood as the first mental health symptom their child had. Young people with psychotic depression appear to have a substantially increased risk (20–40%) of developing bipolar disorder. So it's wise to be familiar with these symptoms. In the next chapter, we'll explain how bipolar disorder differs from other disorders characterized by psychosis, like schizophrenia.

Delusions and hallucinations are particularly scary for parents who believe these symptoms signify that their child is beyond hope of having a normal life. Moreover, the bipolar teen may fixate on a certain member of the family who is "evil" or "dangerous." "He won't eat with the family," said 14-year-old Joe's mother. "He's fearful that the food is poisoned. He's also convinced that his father is evil. He won't use the computer if his father has used it, he won't take his shoes off in the house because his father has walked there, and won't come out of his room because he doesn't want to interact with his father at all."

Unfortunately, the teen with such symptoms often doesn't know that his ideas are not based in reality. Sometimes the adolescent's delusional system has been such a part of how he makes sense of the world that it can take months after mood episodes abate for him to question his beliefs. "When my moods were really off," said 15-year-old Matt, "I thought there was this huge government plot to program all of us through the television. I also thought that the government was controlling our minds with the fluoride they were putting in the water supply. Since I've been better, I question these things a little more, but I am still pretty sure that the government is trying to control us in some way."

When compiling your observations of your teenager, it's important to understand that psychosis does not always take extreme forms. Mindy described the delusional behavior of her 16-year-old this way: "I haven't been able to work a full day this entire summer. Although he is more than old enough to stay home, his fears keep him from being able to be alone for more than a few hours. By noon I get a call from him that a storm is coming, or he heard a noise, or any other little thing that signifies that the world is coming to an end and that I must come home and protect him. If I do not go home, he will call me so often that I can't work anyway."

In later chapters, we talk about the pharmacological (Chapter 6) and psychosocial strategies (Chapter 7) for managing these symptoms.

The Hallmark Symptoms of Depression

> *Everything is so boring. People are stupid, school is dumb, my friends are boring. Nothing is fun anymore.*
> —Stacy, age 15, during the depressed phase of bipolar disorder

> *I just want everyone to leave me alone. Everybody pisses me off, and I just want some quiet. It takes so much energy to have to deal with everyone else's stupid demands. Can't they see that I just want to be by myself?*
> —Matt, age 15, during the depressed phase of bipolar disorder

Depression in teenagers (whether part of bipolar disorder or major depression) often doesn't fit the image that adults have of this emotional condition. Many teens describe depression not as feeling sad or down but as feeling bored or withdrawn and taking little pleasure in the things they used to enjoy. Other teens experience more anger then sadness. If the irritability appears to be within the context of other symptoms of depression (decreased activity, fatigue, feelings of guilt, low self-esteem—see Chapter 3), then chances are that it is part of the depressed cycle as opposed to the manic cycle. We often see irritability in mania as being a "get out of my way" or "give me what I want or else" kind of irritability. In depression, the irritability takes the form "leave me alone."

You may feel at times that the withdrawal or boredom you witness represents typical teen behavior rather than bipolar depression. Because kids often express little or no emotion during depressive phases, it can be more difficult for parents and siblings to see this behavior as being part of the disorder. "We can't get her to do anything anymore," said the mother of a 14-year-old. "All she wants to do is play neo-pets or watch TV. She doesn't have any friends, she doesn't exercise, she won't eat, or even come out of her room."

Siblings may feel abandoned by the depressed sibling's withdrawal. If sibling relationships have survived the manic phases, then the sibling may be distraught over the bipolar sibling's sudden withdrawal. "She used to be fun," said the younger sister of a girl with bipolar disorder. "She used to come to my room and ask me how things were going at school and with my friends. Now all she wants to do is hang out in her room and sleep. I don't understand what I did to make her not want to talk to me anymore. I miss her."

Decreased Energy and Activity

It is so frustrating. He just lies around the house all day while his mother, brother, and I are doing chores or cleaning up after him. He is so lazy and I just can't stand how he expects the rest of us to pick up his slack.

—A father describing his frustration during his teenage son's depressed phase

Although manic activity and creativity can be very frustrating for parents, the lack of motivation and productivity during a down phase can generate considerable parental anger and criticism. This is why it's important to learn how these patterns of decreased energy and motivation occur in cycles with other symptoms of depression (see Chapter 3). Understanding these cycles will allow you to separate a depressive symptom from an annoying garden-variety teenage behavior.

Insomnia

I am so exhausted all the time. I lie in bed for hours and can't fall asleep. Sometimes it seems just as I am starting to drift off that my alarm clock is ringing for me to get up to go to school. I'm so out of it at school that I can't pay attention and am exhausted all day.

—A 17-year-old in the depressive phase of bipolar disorder

Unlike decreased need for sleep, teens with insomnia typically never feel rested and have compromised functioning as a result of sleep deprivation. There are several types of insomnia. Some teens have difficulty falling asleep, some wake in the middle of the night, and others wake up too early and can't fall back to sleep. These can all be signs of depression. The person with insomnia desperately wants and feels the need for sleep, but it eludes him.

Fatigue and Agitation

He just sits on the couch all day. When I ask him to get up and wash up for dinner, it takes 15 minutes for him just to get to the bathroom. He tries to follow through with what we require; he just does it at a snail's pace. I almost don't have the heart to ask anything of him anymore.
—A father observing his 15-year-old son's depressive symptoms

Another behavior you may observe in your teen is extreme fatigue. Often, teens with bipolar disorder appear to be so low energy that they can't even have a conversation. A symptom called *psychomotor retardation* may accompany depression. Psychomotor retardation is present when the teen experiencing depression feels so slowed down that he has the perception of being stuck in mud or that his limbs are very heavy. This symptom may appear to family members as slow movement, constrained conversation, and decreased productivity.

In addition to noticing fatigue, you may observe agitation or restlessness that takes shape as fidgeting, pacing, pulling on clothes, pulling on hair, biting nails, and general squirminess. These behaviors may also occur with the hyperactivity that accompanies mania, but with depression these behaviors will have a different feel. For example, the fidgeting will not appear as too much energy and an inability to sit still; rather, the teen will appear visibly distressed and agitated, and the movement will appear to be a product of this internal discomfort.

Suicidal Thoughts and Impulses

I wouldn't kill myself, I wouldn't do that to my family, but I don't want to live anymore. I lie in bed at night and pray to God to let me die in my sleep. I feel so sad and miserable. Each morning that I wake up and I'm still alive I just feel more depressed.
—Lucy, age 15

Sometimes I have thoughts of stabbing myself when I see a knife or taking all of my pills when I open my pill bottle. These are just flashes that I don't think I would act on. But other times I can sit for hours and contemplate, plan out exactly how I'm going to do it. I've tried to hang my-

self, and I've taken an overdose of pills. I'm not scared of death. In fact,
I'm kind of curious about it. I think that's the way I'll eventually die.

—Jami, age 16

Suicide is one of the most frightening things that parents can imagine. There is no doubt that it is a real risk for teenagers with bipolar disorder. In one study, 44% of adolescents with bipolar disorder had made a suicide attempt. They also had more thoughts about suicide, a younger age at the first attempt, a higher percentage of multiple attempts, and more serious suicide attempts than adolescents without a psychiatric disorder. Considering the impulsivity of behavior during adolescence and the mood dysregulation associated with bipolar disorder, the increased risk of suicide in these teens is not surprising. Suicide in adolescents with bipolar disorder is a very real phenomenon about which all parents should be educated. Trudy Carlson, in her book *The Life of a Bipolar Child*, talks about her son Ben's completed suicide. She shares her experience and hopes that her loss will help parents prevent a loss of their own.

> "I could have decided to blame myself for Ben's death. It was I who had spoken to him about his eating habits, producing his angry reaction and creating an argument between us. . . . Although my actions would not have triggered suicidal behavior in a child without a bipolar (manic–depressive) illness, it could in a youngster with that disease. . . . There is an important distinction between triggering something and causing something. Ben's bipolar illness was the cause of his suicide." (pp. 87–88)

Fortunately, there are ways to help your teen manage his or her suicidal impulses. Some of these interventions are behavioral and practical (for example, removing weapons from the house), some are pharmacological, and some involve enhancing your teen's connection to major sources of support. Chapter 13 discusses the risk indicators and prevention and response plans for this frightening symptom of bipolar disorder.

A Typical Day in the Life of a Teenager with Bipolar Disorder

Now that you have a grasp of the individual symptoms of bipolar disorder and how they may appear in your teen, it may be helpful to have a sense of how they appear together during a typical day. If you've been exposed to the "textbook" depictions of adult bipolar disorder, you may have the impression that your teen will be either discernibly depressed or obviously manic at any one point in time. Actually, though, teens often experience their symptoms continuously. The different subtypes of bipolar disorder are described in Chapter 3, but for now it's important to know that a teen with bipolar disorder is likely to have frequent episodes during a year or even to cycle continuously, with no real breaks dividing the symptoms into episodes.

During a single day, however, we've observed moods cycling in a fairly predictable pattern. Teenagers typically describe a pattern of early-morning sluggishness. Parents say that it is difficult to get them out of bed and that it's not unusual for them to need to be shaken awake. Once they're up and at school, they often describe feeling "out of it" and "drugged" all morning, a state that can be exacerbated by nighttime medications. These kids usually do not perform well in morning classes, particularly those that require sustained attention (such as math). Around 11:00 in the morning or noon the adolescent's mood starts to perk up a bit, just in time for the lunch hour. Kids usually seem to enjoy the classes they have at this time. Then they describe getting more and more excited as the day progresses. By the time they come home they are exhausted and irritable but too revved and overstimulated to rest. Usually there are severe angry outbursts and conflict with family members right after school. After these outbursts the teen typically crashes and is sluggish through the dinner hour. He may want to lie around and watch TV or nap. For suggestions on how to help your teen find his optimal daily routines, and capitalize on his best hours of school functioning, see Chapters 10 and 14.

After dinner the adolescent's mood surges again and he gets excited and creative. Late in the evening he often finds the desire and energy to do homework and complete projects. Unfortunately, this increase in activity usually leads to a very difficult time winding down. As a result, the teen may end up staying up later than he should (3:00 or 4:00 in the morning in some cases), only to be dragged out of bed the next morning (if the parents are able) to start the whole routine over again. Typically, the week ends with a complete meltdown, which may be the end result of physical exhaustion, irregular schedules, and sleep deprivation (note that teens who are manic or hypomanic say they don't need sleep and don't feel tired, but lack of sleep is still taking its toll on their physical functioning). This pattern has been reported so often by teens and parents that we have started using it as an informal diagnostic indicator of bipolar disorder.

We hope this chapter provides a framework for discussions between you and your teen about what she is experiencing and a guide for communicating with others about what you're noticing in her. If what you've learned here confirms your suspicions about bipolar disorder, your informed observations will do a great deal to ensure that a professional evaluation (Chapter 3) is accurate and leads to quick and appropriate treatment.

3 Getting an Accurate Diagnosis

Arlene, the 40-year-old mother of 13-year-old Wyatt and 16-year-old Tabitha, had had it with psychiatrists and psychologists. The last 3 years had been nothing but frustrating wrong turns and dead ends. Tabitha had been depressed since she was in her early teens and had cut her arms and legs with razor blades. Mental health professionals had given her various diagnoses over the years, including recurrent major depression, borderline personality disorder, reactive attachment disorder, and oppositional–defiant disorder. She finally was diagnosed with bipolar II disorder and treated with oxcarbazepine (Trileptal), but Arlene was never fully convinced of the diagnosis and even less convinced that the medication was working.

Her worries multiplied when Wyatt starting developing problems with his temper. When he entered middle school, his grades slipped and he became unusually moody. His teachers said he wasn't paying attention and seemed preoccupied. On several occasions at home, he burst into inexplicable rages, threw things, broke lamps, and tormented the family dog. Arlene couldn't help thinking it had all started with her divorce from her second husband (not the children's father), but Wyatt wouldn't (or couldn't) talk about it.

Her first stop was Wyatt's pediatrician, who diagnosed him with ADHD, combined type (hyperactivity and inattention), and recommended the stimulant Adderall. The pediatrician also recommended a full evaluation with a psychiatrist. Wyatt took the medication, and, while it seemed to improve his attention, it also made him even more irritable and agitated.

Arlene finally located a child psychiatrist who claimed to specialize in "behavior problems of teens." Arlene and Wyatt spent most of the 2-hour initial appointment with a medical student, who, Arlene complained, was "about as green as could be." The psychiatrist then performed a very quick and routine evaluation that ended with "a few very formulaic interpretations," such as that Wyatt had ADHD and was probably reacting to the divorce. She questioned why, if he had ADHD, it hadn't been recognized when he was a child, since he had always done reasonably well in school. The doctor shrugged and said that ADHD often had a late onset. To help him control his rages, the psychiatrist started Wyatt on an antidepressant and also switched him to a different ADHD medication.

Wyatt became more and more agitated and angry in the coming weeks, seemed highly anxious and overreactive, and slept less and less. He started talking in a wild, disconnected manner. Arlene took him back to the doctor, who stopped all his medications. But his symptoms continued for another week, and then he threatened to hang himself. She finally took him to the emergency room at a local hospital, where he was admitted with a new diagnosis of bipolar I disorder, mixed episode.

Perhaps this is your first attempt at getting a diagnostic evaluation for your child. You may have recognized your teen's problems only recently, and the process of evaluation and diagnosis may be new to you. Or you may have initially had your teen evaluated when he was 8 or 10, which may have yielded a psychiatric diagnosis. But as your child ages, enters the stresses and strains of adolescence, and shows new symptoms, you may begin to wonder if that original diagnosis was accurate, or whether your teen has two disorders instead of just one ("comorbidity").

Like many parents of bipolar teens—including Arlene—you may have been given many inaccurate and meaningless diagnoses, and your teen, despite your best efforts, may have been treated for the wrong condition for many years. *If any of these situations applies to you, we suggest that you obtain for your teen a comprehensive diagnostic evaluation from a board-certified child psychiatrist or psychologist who knows (and, preferably, specializes in) mood disorders. If nothing else, the results of this evaluation will set your mind at ease that the original diagnosis your child received years ago was probably accurate. In the best-case scenario, your teenager may finally obtain the proper treatment for a previously unrecognized condition.*

TYPES OF BIPOLAR DISORDER

Bipolar I disorder: The teen has had at least one lifetime episode of mania or mixed disorder (typically lasting at least one week); he may or may not have ever had a depression.

Bipolar II disorder: The teen has had at least one full episode of depression lasting at least two weeks and at least one lifetime hypomanic episode lasting at least four days.

Bipolar disorder not otherwise specified (NOS): The teen has had at least four distinct lifetime episodes of mania, with elation and at least three mania symptoms (four if mood is only irritable), but these episodes have only lasted 1–2 days and have never lasted as long as 1 week or required hospitalization. She may or may not have had a severe depression.

Cyclothymic disorder: The teen has had mood swings from brief hypomanias to mild depressions on an ongoing basis for at least 1 year; she has never had a full manic or depressive episode.

Bipolar disorder with rapid cycling: The teen meets the criteria above for bipolar I or bipolar II disorder and has had four or more distinct episodes of mania, depression, hypomania, or mixed disorder (meeting the duration criteria above) in a single year, and/or has had multiple swings from manic episodes to depressive or mixed episodes within a continuous period of illness.

The Importance of Diagnosis

If you've been put through the wringer the way Arlene and her kids were, you may be wondering why you need to keep putting yourself through it. The answer is straightforward: diagnosis is absolutely essential to developing an effective treatment plan. A misdiagnosis of depression with ADHD led to Wyatt's being treated with medications that may have set off an episode of the bipolar disorder to which he was genetically predisposed. But the opposite situation can be just as problematic: a teen who should be diagnosed with depression might benefit most from a serotonin reuptake inhibitor like Prozac or Zoloft, but a misdiagnosis of bipolar disorder might lead to treatment with mood stabilizers like Depakote instead. Medications prescribed for bipolar disorder also have side effects. If your teen experienced adverse effects without getting any benefits, it wouldn't be unreasonable for him to start resisting treatment. An inaccurate diagnosis could, in fact, lead to complicated, multiagent medication regimens that make your teen feel discouraged with mental health treatment in general and deny himself the help that treatment based on an accurate diagnosis could provide.

The teen who receives an inaccurate diagnosis may also get discouraged about herself. It's normal to react to a diagnosis with self-questioning. However, your daughter may feel that her difficulties are being "explained away" by a label that doesn't fit her. Inaccurate labels can, in fact, interfere with a teen's development of a healthy sense of self and her acquisition of social skills.

Besides delaying effective treatment, failure to diagnose bipolar disorder can worsen your teen's condition exponentially. Through a phenomenon called "kindling," mood episodes increase in frequency over time when not treated appropriately. Early in the illness, episodes are often triggered by some major environmental stressor (such as the death of a loved one). But the more episodes a person has, the more these episodes can be triggered by minor environmental stressors, or even triggered spontaneously, without any stressor.

Besides leading to the right treatment and preventing an increasing number of episodes, proper diagnosis can give you a sense of your teen's prognosis, or expected symptom course over time. A teen who is diagnosed with bipolar I disorder will have manic or mixed episodes that alternate with severe periods of depression, but he may also just have manic episodes with no depressions. If your teen has bipolar II disorder, as Tabitha did, she will probably have lengthy periods of debilitating depression that alternate with brief bursts of hyperactivity and elation or irritability that may not seriously interfere with her day-to-day functioning. If the real diagnosis is ADHD, you should not expect to see wide mood swings over time, and it's even less likely that your teen will develop the hypersexual impulses, elation, grandiosity, or depression described in Chapter 2. If he has both bipolar disorder *and* ADHD (comorbidity), then the course of illness will be more complicated (for example, it will be difficult to tell when your teen is in remission) and the treatment regimen may include mood stabilizers and psychostimulants like Ritalin.

Finally, diagnoses are the language doctors use to communicate with each other. We can be reasonably sure that any doctor who ends up treating a teen labeled with, for example, "depression with mood-incongruent psychotic features" or "substance-induced mood disorder" will know what that term means. That does not mean that the other doctor will prescribe the same treatment, but at least we can be reasonably sure that both doctors are talking about the same disorder.

Don't Be Satisfied with Just a Label

A proper diagnosis should lead to effective treatment and also give you and your teen an idea of what to expect in the future. It should never produce just a dead-end label. The diagnostic evaluation should indicate whether your teen has any additional comorbid conditions; evaluate the roles of environmental factors, personal risk factors, and important developmental events; assess your family's history of psychiatric disorder; and, ideally, assess your teen's strengths as well as difficulties. All of this information will increase the chances that her treatment will produce as much improvement as possible.

Not all evaluations will cover the same ground, however. The breadth of the evaluation depends on why the teen was referred for an assessment in the first place. Marla's daughter, Erin, was having significant problems passing her classes at school. Her teen's school required a psychiatric evaluation to justify developing an individualized education plan (IEP; see Chapter 14) for Erin. Marla had to be sure the evaluation not only covered Erin's diagnosis but also included neuropsychological testing to rule out learning disabilities or attentional problems, assessments of developmental events (for example, she was of low weight at birth), and family history. In contrast, Allie took her son Kevin to an evaluation primarily because she did not believe his original diagnosis of separation anxiety disorder—and the psychotherapeutic treatment he had received for this condition—had led to any meaningful changes. So, Kevin's psychiatric evaluation concentrated on getting an accurate diagnosis with the aim of developing an appropriate medication treatment plan: the degree to which his anxiety symptoms were truly related to separation experiences, the extent to which he experienced depression and hypomania or mania, and the potential role of mood-stabilizing medications in controlling his symptoms.

How a Diagnosis Is Made

As a parent, you can't be expected to diagnose your own child. But if you understand how diagnoses are made, you'll know if the clinician is asking you the right questions and whether your questions are being answered appropriately. You and your teen may have gone through many evaluations before and may have been confused about why certain questions were asked over and over again, whereas some seemingly important questions were never asked. For example, Arlene was confused as to why the first doctor she saw was so preoccupied with Wyatt's inattentive school behavior and never seemed interested in his rage attacks or sleep problems. She was also frustrated that her child's doctor spent so much time talking about Wyatt's "early childhood traumas," which he defined as Wyatt's parents' divorce and his having had to change schools.

Part of the reason that parents get so frustrated is that bipolar disorder is diagnosed in a fairly subjective way. There's no lab test, as there is for many medical disorders. Bipolar disorder in teens is diagnosed by interviewing you and your teen and determining if your teen meets certain diagnostic criteria, which are usually behaviors like sleep disturbance, irritable mood, or any of the symptoms we discussed in Chapter 2.

A typical diagnostic session will consist of interviews with your teen, with you, and often with other family members. The doctor may also see the two of you together. A difference between diagnosing children and diagnosing teens is that the input of your teen will probably be given more weight than the responses of a younger child. For this reason, it will be critical to get your teen's "buy-in" to the process (see the discussion of how to get your teen involved below).

A diagnosis of bipolar disorder is based on the criteria listed in the *Diagnostic and Statistical Manual of Mental Disorders,* fourth edition, text revision (DSM-IV-TR), which is the manual all mental health professionals in the United States use to diagnose mental disorders. This means your teen must have been exhibiting a minimum number of symptoms on a criterion list for a certain period of time, causing a degree of functional impairment (problems in social, school, or family functioning, or the need for hospitalization, residential care, jail, or other restrictions of one's life). Unfortunately, there are no separate diagnostic criteria for children; they are diagnosed using the same criteria as for adults. As you read through the complexities of these criteria, you'll get a sense of why the diagnosis is so hard to make.

The Diagnostic Criteria for Mania or Hypomania

Knowing how doctors classify teenage mood episode as manic, hypomanic, depressed, or mixed will help you inform your doctor of what symptoms to look for in your teen (even if she is not displaying them in the office). Understanding what a manic or depressive episode looks like will also enable you to report the symptoms to your teen's doctor before they get out of hand. You began collecting data on your teen's symptoms through your observations on the Mood Disorder Questionnaire in Chapter 2.

The criteria for mania are in many ways the most straightforward. *To be classified as having a manic episode, your teen must have had a week or more of feeling euphoric, elevated, or irritable nearly every day for most of the day, or less than a week if he had to be hospitalized for it.* So sporadic rage attacks without any other symptoms of mania probably don't signify a manic episode. It may be something else: temporary stress, anxiety, depression, or even the teen's natural temperament (see also Chapter 4). But being angry every day for most of the day for a week or more, when the teen isn't usually like this, is evidence for mania.

An important thing to remember about mania, though, is that it involves changes not only in mood but also in thinking and behavior. So, in addition to looking for elation or irritability, the practitioner assessing your teen must see three of the following before making the diagnosis (and four if your teen's mood is only irritable):

- Inflated self-worth or grandiosity
- Decreased need for sleep
- Racing thoughts
- Pressure of speech or flight of ideas
- Increased activity (including hypersexuality)
- Distractibility
- Involvement in activities with a high probability of having dangerous consequences, such as driving recklessly, impulsive spending, or indiscreet or unsafe sexual activity

You know what these symptoms look like from the descriptions and first-person accounts in Chapter 2. But along with these symptoms, there has to be evidence that the symptoms have caused functional impairment (for example, a drop in school performance) and are not directly caused by ingestion of an illicit substance. When Wyatt was admitted to the hospital, he showed many of these symptoms. In addition to his intense irritability, he felt like his thoughts were going a mile a minute, he was agitated and full of energy, and he spoke rapidly and hopped from one topic to another.

The criteria for mania have to be distinguished from the criteria for hypomania. To be hypomanic, your teen needs to have only 4 days of symptoms, but still must meet the criteria above (elated mood with three symptoms or irritable mood with four). *What is more important to remember about hypomania is that it is not associated with functional impairment: whereas the symptoms are a noticeable change to others (for example, his friends may say, "You're really hyper today"), they will not cause your teen to miss a significant amount of school and do not require hospitalization or residential treatment.*

Why are these seemingly academic distinctions so important? For one, if your child has only hypomanic episodes and not manic episodes, he may have bipolar II disorder instead of bipolar I. Bipolar II, while not necessarily less debilitating than bipolar I, is often treated with different medication combinations, and the psychotherapy used may differ. Perhaps even more important, hypomania can progress into mania, and if you catch it early, you can sometimes stave off the negative effects mania can have on your teen's long-term development.

The Diagnostic Criteria for Depression

The DSM-IV-TR has some strange rules that can be hard to remember or put into context. For example, even if your child is diagnosed as bipolar, she may never have had a depressive episode. Daria, for example, had a severe manic episode when she was 10 and then a hypomanic episode when she was 14. She never had significant periods of depression but was still diagnosed with bipolar I disorder. The presumption is that your teen will eventually have some form of depressive episode (another reason future *prognosis* is so important).

What symptoms classify a person as having a major depressive episode? First, your teen must show sad mood and/or loss of interests in activities nearly every day for at least 2 weeks. Many teens get sad for a period of time or suddenly lose interest in their friends, activities, sports, or church/temple. But most of the time this lasts for only a short time and is usually replaced by other interests. Kids who get depressed seem to lose interest in everything.

Depression is a disorder of mood, thinking, and behavior. So, in addition to depressed mood and loss of interests, your teen must show at least five of the following symptoms to be classified as having major depression (see examples in Chapter 2):

- Fatigue or loss of energy
- Moving very slowly ("psychomotor retardation") or nervously agitated and restless ("psychomotor agitation")
- Insomnia nearly every night (inability to get to sleep or stay asleep)
- Loss of appetite (or weight loss) or significant increase in appetite (or weight gain)
- Inability to concentrate, difficulty making decisions
- Feelings of worthlessness or guilt
- Suicidal thoughts, plans, or actions

As was true for mania, your teen must show evidence of functional impairment to be diagnosed with major depression. Teens who get depressed usually stay in their room, sleep a great deal, withdraw from their friends, and neglect their schoolwork.

The Diagnostic Criteria for a Mixed Episode

As we talked about in Chapter 2, teens can be manic and depressed at the same time, though to meet the full DSM-IV-TR criteria for a mixed episode the teen must meet the full criteria for both mania and major depression during the same week. This is different from being a *rapid cycler*, which means that your teen has had four or more distinct episodes of mania/hypomania or depression (meeting the full DSM-IV-TR criteria) in a single year, or significant mood changes from mania to major depression to mania and back to major depression again, all within the same mood episode. Knowing about mixed episodes is important because kids may recover more slowly from them than from manic episodes and may need more aggressive pharmacological treatment.

Wyatt met the criteria for a bipolar mixed episode on his admission to the hospital. He was irritable, had racing thoughts, increased energy, and distractibility (all manic symptoms), but he also felt uninterested in things, suicidal, fatigued, worthless about himself and his future, and couldn't sleep even though he wanted to (all depressive symptoms).

Teenagers with Brief But Frequent Episodes: Are They Bipolar?

Many clinicians and researchers argue that there is a "bipolar spectrum" along which bipolar disorder appears. Children with bipolar spectrum disorders may have very brief episodes that resemble the full disorder but do not meet the 1- or 2-week time requirements. University of Pittsburgh psychiatrist Boris Birmaher and his colleagues diagnose children with brief recurrent episodes as having bipolar disorder not otherwise specified (NOS). These kids have distinct periods of abnormally elevated, expansive, or irritable mood plus two (three if irritable mood only) DSM-IV symptoms of mania that cause a change in functioning, last for at least 1 day, and have been present for a total of at least 4 days in the teen's lifetime.

Is this really bipolar disorder? Will kids with this symptom course really grow up to be bipolar? We don't know at this point, although we do know that these kids have a tough time. Dr. Birmaher and his colleagues followed a large number of kids for up to 3 years and found that about one in three children with bipolar NOS and a family history of bipolar disorder were likely to develop bipolar I disorder or bipolar II disorder at the follow-up (for example, they developed a full manic episode that lasted a week and was highly impairing). Also, kids with bipolar NOS had significant difficulties with both school and social functioning and often needed many psychiatric, school, and counseling services.

How Do You Tell Teenage Bipolar Disorder from Other Disorders?

As Arlene's family discovered, distinguishing bipolar disorder from other disorders is very difficult and frustrating for all. Even with well-defined diagnostic criteria, it's not always easy to answer questions like "Are his attention problems due to his bipolar disorder or his ADHD?" or "Could his paranoid beliefs be early signs of schizophrenia?" As you read the fol-

---

COPING "MANTRAS" WHEN TRYING TO OBTAIN A DIAGNOSIS FOR YOUR TEEN

- Have patience: diagnosis is an evolving process and can change as your teen ages.
- Accept ambiguity: many disorders have similar symptoms and can be hard to tell apart or can occur together.
- Be prepared for uncertainty: you may not be sure of your teen's diagnosis even after a full evaluation.

lowing descriptions of disorders that can occur along with bipolar disorder or be mistaken for it, consider whether you think any of them describe your teen. If so, ask the teen's doctor whether these disorders should be codiagnosed, or why the doctor thinks the bipolar diagnosis fits better.

Attention-Deficit/Hyperactivity Disorder

ADHD is codiagnosed in 60–90% of children and teens with bipolar disorder. It's characterized by difficulty paying attention to details, impulsiveness, distractibility, hyperactivity, making a lot of careless mistakes, trouble listening while others are talking, problems with organization, and forgetfulness. ADHD starts earlier than bipolar disorder, on average by age 7. As mentioned in Chapter 1, bipolar disorder begins on average between the ages of 15 and 19, although it can occur much earlier or much later. It is fairly rare to see ADHD develop for the first time in adulthood, although it may be *diagnosed* for the first time then.

> *I always related to that idea that my son had a motor attached. It seems like someone just pulls the ignition string and off he goes, like a rocket. Forget trying to talk to him when he's like that. He's like the Tasmanian devil.*
> —Mother of a 13-year-old boy with bipolar disorder and ADHD

How can one possibly tell the difference between bipolar and ADHD? The box on page 54 should help give you some clues, although the reality is that the only way to be sure may be to have the same doctor follow your teen and manage her medications over time to see what kinds of cognitive and behavioral problems she has in different mood states.

Knowing whether your child has ADHD as well as bipolar will help you and your doctor decide whether a psychostimulant, like Ritalin, Adderall, or Concerta, will help improve his attention. Stimulants are generally to be avoided if your teen does not have ADHD because they can be activating and cause sleep disturbance. However, if your teen has both bipolar and ADHD, it may never be entirely clear which disorder is causing which behavior, and his doctor may recommend a stimulant. The current thinking about giving stimulants to bipolar children or teens is that the mood episode (depression or mania) has to be controlled with a mood stabilizer like lithium, carbamazepine, or valproate for at

DIFFERENCES BETWEEN BIPOLAR DISORDER AND ADHD

Bipolar disorder	ADHD
Mania symptoms: distinct periods of elated mood, grandiosity, and hypersexuality, along with decreased need for sleep, excessive sociability, and silliness	Hyperactive and impulsive behavior but not usually accompanied by elation
Problems with attention, distractibility, and impulsiveness primarily along with other signs of mania	Relatively constant problems with distractibility, attention, organization, and memory regardless of mood state
Depressive symptoms: loss of interest, fatigue, feelings of worthlessness, and suicidal thoughts or actions	Sadness is transient, and suicidal thinking or attempts are rare
Rapid cycling of moods from one extreme to another	Moods do not cycle widely
Family history of mood disorder	No more likely than healthy children to have mood disorder in the family
Age of onset typically in mid- to late teens	Age of onset before age 10
Equally common in teenage boys and girls	More common in boys
Irritability, accelerated speech, and increased energy occur, but typically reflect a change from his or her usual state	May also have irritability, accelerated speech, and increased energy, but these are fairly stable attributes

least 6–8 weeks, after which giving a stimulant as an adjunct to the mood stabilizer is safe and won't cause a resurgence of symptoms.

Oppositional Defiant Disorder

Does your teen consistently:

- Have tantrums?
- Argue with parents and/or other authority figures?

- Refuse to comply with even the simplest of requests?
- Seem to enjoy annoying or upsetting people?
- Blame others for his problems?
- Seem unusually touchy or easily annoyed?
- Seem angry, resentful, mean, or hateful when talking?
- Tend to seek revenge?

Oppositional defiant disorder, or ODD, frequently appears along with bipolar disorder. The key difference is that the behaviors characteristic of ODD stay relatively constant in kids with that diagnosis, whereas oppositionality appears in bipolar teens mostly when they are manic or hypomanic. This distinction can be tough to make, however, since many teens with bipolar disorder are continuously cycling in and out of episodes of mood disorder. Your teen may have to have several discrete mood episodes before you or the doctor will be able to tell whether ODD is present. In any case, there are no medications specifically for the treatment of ODD, though there are psychotherapy options (see Chapter 7).

Conduct Disorder

Does your teen often:

- Bully or threaten others and/or provoke physical fights?
- Use weapons to intimidate or hurt others?
- Exhibit physical cruelty to people or animals?
- Steal, lie, or destroy property (for example, by setting fires)?
- Break into buildings or cars?
- Run away from home, repeatedly break curfews?
- Skip school frequently?

Although this kind of behavior speaks more of criminality, it's surprisingly common among bipolar kids and teens. One study reported that 69% of children with bipolar disorder had also at some point met the diagnostic criteria for conduct disorder. Another found a comorbidity rate of 40% for bipolar disorder and conduct disorder.

The reason this is such an important distinction is that your teen may have developed a style of moral reasoning that leads to consistent violations of the rights of others. Kids with conduct disorder often end up in jail. What is most difficult about this diagnosis is that teens who become manic sometimes do illegal things, but only when manic, not when feeling healthy or when feeling depressed. So, for example, a manic teenager can become violent, run away from home, become truant from school, and lie about all of it, but would not do any of these things when healthy. In fact, he may feel extreme remorse for his behavior later. This teenager probably would not be diagnosed with conduct disorder because the conduct problems are only episodic and characterized by remorse or regret.

If your teen has conduct disorder, you may have to seek additional treatments such as parent management training (for example, training in how to set appropriate rewards and consequences), cognitive-behavioral therapy, or medications to reduce aggression (which can include stimulants like Ritalin or atypical antipsychotics like Zyprexa). For more information on resources for parents with conduct-disordered kids, take a look at *www.aacap.org/publications/factsfam/conduct.htm.*

Anxiety Disorders

There are many different kinds of anxiety disorders:

Separation anxiety disorder: extreme distress about being separated from home, parents, or other close relatives, often accompanied by school refusal, unwillingness to be alone, sleep disturbance, nightmares, and physical complaints

Obsessive–compulsive disorder: recurrent thoughts or images that cause anxiety, usually leading to repetitive behaviors designed to neutralize the thoughts (for example, checking, hand-washing)

Generalized anxiety disorder: excessive worry and anxiety about a number of issues—such as school, work, or social expectations—along with restlessness, fatigue, difficulty concentrating, irritability, muscle tension, and sleep disturbance

Posttraumatic stress disorder: severe anxiety following a traumatic, life-threatening or personally violating event (for example, a car accident, a rape), which can include intrusive recollections of the event, feeling as if the event were recurring, avoidance of stimuli that remind one of the event, and high physiological arousal.

Most teens with bipolar disorder have a certain amount of anxiety, even when manic. As we said earlier, untreated anxiety can sometimes be the root cause of oppositional or angry behavior, although the teen is unlikely to be aware of this. If the anxiety disorder is not treated adequately, the course of the bipolar illness can get worse and increase the chances that the teen will attempt suicide. Kids with comorbid anxiety disorders are also at greater risk for substance abuse and dependence, to "self-medicate" the underlying anxiety.

The good news is that we have many new and effective treatments for anxiety, which we'll say more about in the treatment chapters. For example, there are now effective cognitive-behavioral treatments for panic disorder, obsessive–compulsive disorder, and posttraumatic stress disorder. Some of these treatments may be available from practitioners in your community. A good place to start is the treatment provider directory of the Association for Behavioral and Cognitive Therapies at *aabt.org/members/Directory/Find_A_Therapist.cfm*.

Alcohol and Substance Use Disorders

My parents say I'm bipolar, that I'm freaked out and have bad brain chemistry, and maybe all that's true, but the real thing is that I've got to stop gettin' stoned.
—An 18-year-old with bipolar disorder hospitalized for a manic episode brought on by cocaine use

Bipolar disorder and substance misuse disorders may co-occur in as many as six of every 10 people with bipolar disorder at some point in their lives. Most teenagers experiment with alcohol or drugs at some point, but kids with bipolar disorder are unusually sensitive to substances, and their mood symptoms can be provoked by their use.

To be diagnosed with a substance abuse disorder, your teen must show a "maladaptive pattern of use" along with symptoms such as:

- Recurrent use that interferes with her ability to attend school or complete schoolwork
- Recurrent use in hazardous situations (like driving)
- Legal problems (for example, being thrown out of school, DUI [driving under the influence] violations)
- Continued use despite losing friends or after-school jobs, or severe family conflicts

Your teen would be diagnosed with "substance-dependence disorder" if she showed evidence of tolerance (need for larger and larger amounts of the substance to get high), withdrawal (for example, the shakes if she hasn't had a drink), use of more of the substance than planned (for example, one beer always turns into 10), and the seeming inability to quit.

Your teen may be using substances to alleviate internal feelings of depression or anxiety, although alcohol usually *worsens* these symptoms over the long term. In contrast, people with bipolar disorder may be more likely to use marijuana when feeling high than when feeling low. Cocaine and other stimulants are often used to accelerate a high period, but they may also be used to alleviate internal feelings of distress.

If you know or suspect that your teen is using drugs, be sure to inform the psychiatrist conducting the diagnostic evaluation because he may miss it if your teen denies it. Some doctors will ask for a urinary drug screen, which is designed to pick up metabolites of drugs like cocaine and marijuana. It won't help identify alcohol use, though.

In Chapters 7 and 10, we'll deal more with how to address substance misuse in your teen's treatment, but for now, let's just consider the diagnosis. The only real way to tell if your child has both bipolar disorder and a substance misuse disorder is to observe her mood states for long enough (at least a year) when she is "dry." If she has been abusing substances all along, and you've never seen her manic or depressed without drugs playing a role, you won't know whether she has one disorder or both. The good news is that many people with bipolar disorder, both young and old, show a much milder course of their illness when they stop using substances.

Unfortunately, many teens learn the hard way. They finally quit when they realize that their substance use is hurting their friends or romantic partners or endangering other people (for example, they have a car accident). Sometimes it's a valued person outside the family—a girlfriend, boyfriend, or coach—who plays the central role in getting them to stop.

Schizophrenia and Other Psychotic Disorders

Last, bipolar disorder can be very hard to tell apart from psychotic disorders like schizophrenia. A teen with schizophrenia would experience some of these symptoms:

- Delusions, or false beliefs, like thinking his food has been poisoned, that some person or members of an organization are following him and want to kill him, or that his thoughts are being controlled by an outside force

- Hallucinations, which involve hearing voices or seeing things that aren't there
- Loss of motivation and withdrawal from people
- A "flattening" of emotions, such that she no longer laughs, cries, or communicates emotions through facial expressions
- Speech containing ideas that are jumbled, confused, and disconnected or that may contain made-up words or words used in odd ways
- Disorganized or bizarre behavior, such as forgetting to bathe, making rambling and incoherent public speeches, or rummaging through garbage cans

It's particularly hard to tell schizophrenic psychosis from mania, because mania can be accompanied by any of these symptoms. Usually, manic delusions have a grandiose quality, like when a teenager thinks he has superpowers, believes he is connected to some famous person, or thinks he can change the course of human events. Hallucinations can be grandiose too (for example, one manic teen we worked with heard voices telling her "You're doing great . . . just keep it up, everyone loves you").

If your teen shows some of the symptoms listed above, her psychiatrist will diagnose her with schizophrenia or schizoaffective disorder (a combination of the schizophrenic and mood disorder categories) only if she has delusions or hallucinations outside the context of mood episodes. That is, if she feels she is being followed or hears voices even when not manic or depressed, and these are significant and not just transient symptoms (and not obviously brought on by illicit drugs), she may have a psychotic disorder like schizophrenia or schizoaffective disorder rather than a mood disorder. If she has delusions and hallucinations that always coincide with being manic, and they go away as soon as the mania subsides, the diagnosis will probably be bipolar I disorder with severe psychotic features.

Why are these distinctions important? The main implications have to do with prognosis and treatment. The prognosis for people with schizophrenia is generally not as good as for people with bipolar disorder, although with new treatments for schizophrenia, more and more people are leading stable lives despite the illness. Also, for schizophrenia the psychiatrist is likely to start treatment with an atypical antipsychotic medication like olanzapine (Zyprexa), risperidone (Risperdal), quetiapine (Seroquel) or aripiprazole (Abilify) rather than starting with a mood stabilizer like lithium or Depakote. Even that treatment trend is changing, however. More and more doctors are treating bipolar kids with atypical antipsychotics, especially if they haven't done well with mood stabilizers (see Chapter 6).

Recurrent Major Depressive Disorder

The diagnosis of bipolar disorder is being thrown around a lot these days and sometimes given to kids who really just have recurrent bouts of major depression—despite the fact that the diagnostic criteria for bipolar disorder include mania or hypomania. This misdiagnosis may be occurring because some kids just feel better and more lively after their depression clears. They get more interested in romance, sports, hobbies, and even school. This is not the same as hypomania—though, as we mentioned in Chapter 2, it's equally important not to assume that hypomania is simply relief from depression.

Some of these kids who are treated as if they are bipolar (even though they've never had a hypomanic or manic episode) have a family history of bipolar disorder. Having a first-degree relative with bipolar disorder *is* important to point out to the doctor because it means that your teen is vulnerable to developing bipolar disorder (though the chances of developing a depressive disorder with this history are just as great). A doctor who doesn't know about this vulnerability and wants to diagnose your teen with major depressive disorder might recommend an antidepressant like Prozac when starting on a mood stabilizer first may in fact be preferable. As you'll learn in Chapter 6, drugs like Prozac—if administered alone—can cause a manic or mixed episode (or rapid cycling) in a kid who is depressed and vulnerable to bipolar disorder.

Asperger Syndrome

Can your teen be described as:

- Socially isolated?
- Lacking social skills, seemingly unable to interact constructively with peers?
- Unable to communicate nonverbally, lacking facial expressions or having peculiar nonverbal gestures?
- Likely to get obsessively fixated on one interest or activity to the exclusion of almost everything else?
- Engaging in repetitive, ritualistic behaviors?
- Physically awkward or uncoordinated?

Asperger syndrome is one of a group of pervasive developmental disorders considered part of the "autism spectrum," characterized by impaired social skills and highly repetitive patterns of thinking and behavior (see *www.ninds.nih.gov/disorders/asperger/detail_asperger.htm*). Typically, children with Asperger syndrome are considered odd by their peers because of their peculiar way of speaking (for example, in a monotone or in an overly formal way), their narrow interests, and their apparent disinterest in others. Unlike children with autism, children with Asperger's do not have impairments in language. About 2 in 10,000 children have the disorder, and it is more common in boys than girls.

> Alex, age 16, had few friends. When he spoke to someone, he would turn his head from side to side and had a fixed, glazed look in his eyes. He became so fixated on a modem he wanted to buy for his computer that he didn't seem to be able to talk or think of anything else. He would occasionally laugh to himself, but his humor seemed idiosyncratic—no one else got the joke.

Why is this disorder confused with bipolar disorder? Because when teens get depressed, they get socially withdrawn and seem unable to communicate—they may seem emotionally flat. Likewise, for some teens, mania takes the form of becoming obsessed with a certain idea (for example, the occult) and frantically pursuing it to the neglect of everything else. In both cases, however, these symptoms usually disappear when their mood returns to normal. In contrast, teens with Asperger's have had social skill problems since early childhood and usually reached other developmental milestones late, such as crawling or walking. Their deficits in social and emotional skills do not fluctuate along with their mood states.

Nowadays, some teens get diagnosed with both bipolar disorder *and* Asperger syndrome. We don't yet know from research how often the two disorders occur together, or whether Asperger's can predispose kids to getting bipolar disorder later. Like all the disorders described here, you shouldn't accept this diagnosis from a clinician without a thorough assessment of your child's long-term developmental history.

As you learn more about these different diagnoses and how they may or may not apply to your teen, keep in mind the mantra that diagnosis is an ongoing, evolving process and is rarely finalized in a single visit. Diagnoses can be changed as your teen matures and new symptoms (or new skills) develop. Most bipolar kids, in fact, get diagnosed with ADHD or depression well before they get diagnosed with bipolar disorder.

The First Step: Finding a Doctor You Can Trust

How do you choose a doctor when you've been going from doctor to doctor for many years and keep getting different diagnoses? This can be extraordinarily frustrating for you, your teen, and other members of the family. Nothing can seem as much of a setback as finding a doctor you really trust and then having him or her make an inaccurate diagnosis followed by ineffective treatment.

If your teen has never been to see a psychiatrist, it's probably a good idea to start with your pediatrician, whom your teen knows and probably will resist seeing less than an unknown psychiatrist. Second, your pediatrician may want to recommend biological tests to rule out purely medical conditions such as the low levels of thyroid hormone that cause some types of depression. Third, your insurance may be set up in such a way that you can see a psychiatrist only if one is referred by your general practitioner.

If your child has seen many psychiatrists over the past few years and never became fully stable, you may be angry at the thought of taking her to see one more. *If, however, she has never been seen by a board-certified child psychiatrist, especially one who specializes in mood disorders, it's definitely a good idea to arrange such an evaluation.* Finding a doctor who meets these criteria in your area can be very difficult. Good starting places are the excellent websites of the Child and Adolescent Bipolar Foundation (*www.bpkids.org*) or the Juvenile Bipolar Research Foundation (*www.jbrf.org*). These sites contain information on how to find psychiatrists with expertise in childhood mood disorders. You can also search directly for a psychiatrist in your area through the American Academy of Child and Adolescent Psychiatry (*office.aacap.org/eseries/ScriptContent/custom/member_search.cfm*). You can call the American Psychiatric Association's referral line (1-888-35-PSYCH or send an email to *apa@psych.org*), although they may not have information about an individual psychiatrist's area of specialization. When you identify a doctor who seems like a good match, ask questions such as: Have you treated teens with the same kinds of problems in the past? Do you consider teen mood disorders to be one of your areas of specialty?

Depending on your child's needs, you may also want to seek a separate evaluation from a child clinical psychologist. Whereas a child psychiatrist will usually be the one to conduct an evaluation leading to a diagnosis and a pharmacological treatment plan, a psychologist may be able to conduct a neuropsychological testing battery to determine whether learning, reading, or speech difficulties affect your teen's school performance (see also Chapter 14). The psychologist may also be able to help you develop a behavioral plan for the home setting, such as choosing effective rewards and consequences for appropriate and inappropriate behaviors (psychosocial treatments that effectively augment medicine are discussed in Chapter 7).

Unfortunately, finding an appropriate psychologist can be as difficult as finding a good child psychiatrist. The person should be licensed as a clinical psychologist and have a PhD or a PsyD (doctor of psychology) degree and should specialize in neuropsychological evaluation (if that's what you're looking for) and/or mood and behavioral problems of adolescents. For information on referrals, go to the American Psychological Association's website (*www.apa.org*) or the Association for Behavioral and Cognitive Therapies website (*www.abct.org/members/Directory/Find_A_Therapist.cfm*), both of which have lists of practitioners. The child bipolar websites mentioned above can also be helpful here.

How Does the Doctor Make the Diagnosis?: The Initial Evaluation

Arlene was excited to find a good child psychiatrist to treat Wyatt after his hospitalization. Unlike previous doctors, this physician read through Wyatt's medical records even before he met with Wyatt. He asked extensive questions of Arlene and Wyatt about when his symptoms started, how long they lasted, whether they occurred across different settings, and to what extent the mood and ADHD symptoms co-occurred or happened at different times. He asked about symptoms beyond bipolar disorder, such as anxiety, eating problems, bedwetting, and nightmares. He took a fairly thorough developmental history, including asking questions about Arlene's pregnancy, Wyatt's birth (which had been complicated), and when he had reached various developmental milestones. He wanted to know how Wyatt was doing in school and what kinds of friendships he had. The evaluation took two full appointments, but Arlene left feeling that his bipolar diagnosis was now justified.

There are certain things you can expect from a good initial evaluation. The box on page 64 lists key components of a comprehensive diagnostic interview for a teenager or child. Your teen's doctor may not do all of these, but you should expect most of these areas to be covered.

COMPONENTS OF A COMPREHENSIVE DIAGNOSTIC INTERVIEW FOR TEENS SUSPECTED OF HAVING BIPOLAR DISORDER

- A complete *developmental history*, including your teen's prenatal or peri-natal complications, infant temperament, achievement of developmental milestones, and social or mood problems during childhood
- *Clinical interviews* with you and your teen to identify the primary diagnosis and any comorbid conditions, usually consisting of questions about the frequency, severity, duration, and functional impairment associated with specific symptoms, both current and past
- A *family history* interview to identify persons in your son's or daughter's family tree who had mood, anxiety, or substance misuse problems
- *Rating scales* that you or your child fill out either before or during the session, which may cover manic or depressive symptoms, mood charts covering the prior 1–2 weeks, or questionnaires about school or social functioning

Source: Quinn and Fristad (2004).

Knowing about these will enable you to prepare some of this background material before the evaluation. In the following paragraphs, we'll talk about how you can prepare for the initial interview, which will probably consist of interviews with yourself, your child, another parent or stepparent in the home, and a review of medical records. But before we talk about these issues, let's address an issue that comes up frequently: What if your teen won't go?

Preparing Your Teen for the Interview

After Wyatt's evaluations were completed, Arlene decided she wanted to have Tabitha evaluated by the same doctor and arranged an appointment. When she told Tabitha about it, however, Tabitha flatly refused to go. Tabitha told her, "Psychiatrists are all idiots, and this one's no different. Besides, you can't make me go."

Your teen may have been through many psychiatric interviews before. If she's had trouble since early childhood, the psychiatrist's office and the questions asked will be nothing new to her. If she's developed problems only recently or had ongoing problems for some time but seen no mental health professional (or perhaps saw only pediatricians or school counselors), the psychiatrist will be new and often very frightening. In either case, your teen may oppose your decision to have a thorough evaluation. It can be hard to distinguish this kind of teenage oppositionality from the kinds of noncompliance your teen shows on a day-to-day basis (for example, coming home at agreed-upon times, doing homework, or doing household chores). But it can be especially infuriating to go to the extensive trouble of finding an appropriate doctor, only to have your teen sabotage the whole thing.

Presenting the Idea to Your Teen

Of course, your first step is to tell your teen that you want her to see a new doctor. There is no perfect way to do this, but the main rule of thumb is, don't make it seem like too big a deal. Avoid statements like "I haven't been satisfied with your doctors, and you've been getting worse" or "This is absolutely critical to your future." Instead, take a low-key approach. Consider the way Nancy broached the topic with 15-year-old Ben.

NANCY: Guess what? I think I've found you a new doctor who could be of help.

BEN: (*sullen*) What do you mean?

NANCY: I found this guy named Doctor Gutierrez, who is an expert in mood problems in kids and teens. He was recommended by Mrs. Oslander, Jessie's mom.

BEN: Not this again.

NANCY: Yup, I'm sure you're not thrilled, but I think we should be getting a second opinion. I'm not sure we've got the nature of these problems pinned down yet.

BEN: So I have to get all those stupid questions all over again? I did that already! Why can't he just talk to Dr. Rudolph?

NANCY: I'm sure he will talk to Dr. Rudolph, and I think that's a good idea. But each doctor does things differently, and he'll want to talk to you and then me, and ask questions about your moods, your background, and my background.

BEN: And then give me a whole bunch of new f**king medications.

NANCY: Well, that may be jumping ahead. I don't know if he'll change your medications or not. It's just a second opinion, kind of like I had for my back problems.

BEN: Forget it. I'm too busy.

NANCY: I know doctor's appointments are annoying, but this is one I want you to make time for. Let's look over your school schedule and see what times we could do it.

Nancy's approach was low-key, informative, but not overly detailed. She validated Ben's immediate reactions but forged ahead. She avoided getting into long back-and-forth discussions with him about the wisdom of doing this or making a point of asserting her parental authority. Bipolar teens can beat anybody at the argument game, which can go on indefinitely and just generate further resistance.

Try to Find Out What Your Teen Views as Problems

Many parents regularly have heart-to-heart discussions with their teenagers about their problems and where they think they need help. Others rarely talk to their teens for fear of upsetting them. If you encounter resistance to the idea of going to see a psychiatrist—whether for the first time or the one-hundredth time—try to get him to see the appointment as to his advantage as well as yours. Start with a question like "What do you think you might get out of this?" or "What would you like to see changed?" He may say "Nothing" or "I don't want to talk to you about it." If so, leave things be, but you may want to raise these questions another time when he's more receptive.

Explore Your Teen's Fears

A theme you'll hear repeatedly throughout this book is that oppositionality from a bipolar teen often hides anxieties and fears about what will happen to him. If he is currently symptomatic (and, of course, most teens who are in need of rediagnosis are symptomatic), these fears may be exaggerated or even delusional. Nonetheless, to gain his buy-in, you may have to address these underlying anxieties. Use our I–A–V–R four-pronged rule for addressing anxieties and fears:

- Identify what the anxiety is about.
- Address underlying assumptions ("self-talk") about what terrible things might happen.

- Validate the reasonableness of the fears.
- Reassure the teen that things won't turn out as badly as he fears.

One of Tabitha's fears was that a new psychiatrist would make her move out and go to a residential treatment facility, which other doctors had "threatened" before. She thought that her lack of improvement with previous treatments meant that "I'm a sicko, a wacko, a hopeless case." Seventeen-year-old Denise feared that she would have to switch schools or be forced into special education classes for "retards like me." Sixteen-year-old Ben feared that he would be given drugs that would dope him up and make him physically uncoordinated on the basketball court, and others would think he was a "spaz."

You can't always assure the teen that none of these things will happen. It's better to be honest about what outcomes are possible, but reassure her that she will have plenty of input into whatever decisions are made. A key difference between teens and children is that teens are more oriented toward autonomy and will feel better about most decisions if they feel that their point of view—however irrational to you—has been taken into consideration in the final decision making.

Normalize Your Teen's Responses

Teens generally respond well to statements that make them feel like they're no different from their peers. Try to normalize their responses as much as you can: "I think most kids would feel that way," "I would probably want to do the same thing," or "Most people feel nervous when they go to see a new psychiatrist." Be aware, however, that many teens will be on to your game and may even say, "Stop being my therapist." Try to take these responses in stride—your teen may feel analyzed from all sides, so try not to overreact to her rejection of your supportiveness.

Bring in Other Family Members or Trusted Professionals

Discussions between you and your teen about psychiatric matters may have become so toxic that you dread even bringing up the possibility of seeing a new doctor. If this is happening, it may make sense to have your spouse or the teen's other joint custodial parent (assuming he or she is on board with the plan) present the idea. If none of these persons are available, consider grandparents, school counselors, or the teen's therapist. Talk to this person about what you have in mind first (for example,

"I want him to see Dr. Gutierrez, but I know he'll say no if I ask. If you pave the way, I think he'll be more cooperative").

The Foot-in-the-Door Technique

Salesmen are famous for getting you to sign on for things by getting your compliance on some minor issue before moving on to larger ones. Sometimes parenting a teen can feel like being a salesman. The foot-in-the-door technique means getting your teen to agree to nothing more than just going to the appointment and answering the questions being asked. Make it clear that whatever follows from that—changes in medications, more appointments, new therapies—will require a new discussion between you and her. Statements like "All I want you to do at this point is to go and meet her and see how the two of you like each other" or "It's just a doctor's appointment; I don't even know if I'll want you to go back" can help alleviate anxiety.

Emphasize Your Teen's Strengths

When you discuss with your teen her need for psychiatric help, try to emphasize her strengths at the same time. If she is creative, artistic, athletic, good in school, or socially adept, make sure you show an awareness of these abilities and that you know they haven't gone away just because she needs an evaluation. If it seems appropriate, show your awareness of her attempts to better control her anger, work harder at studies, or be more respectful at home.

Let your teen's new doctor know of these strengths as well. It may influence what kind of psychotherapy, school assistance, or skills groups he or she recommends.

Addressing Concerns about Confidentiality

A teenager who has been to many psychiatric appointments before is unlikely to be concerned about whether the doctor will keep the content of the session secret (unless, of course, there have been major breaches of confidentiality in previous treatments). This is more likely to be an issue for teens who are seeing doctors for the first time. When exploring your teen's fears, you may want to ask him directly whether he thinks his friends will find out. It's equally important to find out what he thinks will happen next ("They'll 'dis' me; they'll think I'm crazy").

Consistent with our I–A–V–R rule, start by validating these concerns. For example, say "I can understand why you'd be worried about that. Adults worry about that too." Then reassure him about the rules of confidentiality: no information can be released by the doctor without express written consent from the parent, and typically the teen as well. The school guidance counselors may find out if the information gleaned from the diagnostic interview is essential to setting up an IEP. But even this disclosure requires written consent.

In our experience, though, concerns about confidentiality don't usually disappear with a few reassurances. More often, the teen needs to feel that the doctor is caring, compassionate, and trustworthy. So it may help to say "It's up to you what you do and don't want to tell her. You may want to wait to see how comfortable you are first."

What If Your Teen Agrees to Go but Then Clams Up Once There?

Be ready for this, especially if getting your teen to the appointment has involved considerable argument and negotiation. Clamming up is usually due to anxiety or in some cases resentment of the parent and the doctor. It can be a way of regaining some sense of control over what feels like an uncontrollable situation.

Most parents worry that the teen's unwillingness to share information will lead the doctor to make the wrong diagnosis and prescribe the wrong treatment. Responsible physicians, however, will wait to make a diagnosis until relatively sure of what they're dealing with, so don't push your teen to talk or disclose any more than she seems willing to do. If it seems right, ask her later why she was being so quiet and see if you can identify what fears were operating. It may be something minor (for example, "I hated his stupid bow tie") or more serious ("She's going to make you send me away if I tell her what's really going on"). Try to be patient with her as the diagnostic process unfolds, even if this requires several extra sessions because of her reticence.

What If Your Teen Goes but Then "Snows" the Doctor?

Like many parents, you may have taken your teen to the diagnostic interview with the expectation that he would burst forth with all of his teenage angst to a sympathetic ear. Instead, the teen insists that nothing is wrong, chats amiably, denies that major conflicts between him and parents or teachers have occurred, says he's not having sex when you know he is, or denies that he's doing drugs or drinking. You may worry that the doctor won't be able to see through all of this.

The doctor might think you're exaggerating your teenager's problems, but his or her view and final diagnosis are unlikely to be dominated by such a perception. In fact, discrepancies in reports are why most doctors will see you and your teen separately. Teens have been known to underreport depressive symptoms and especially manic symptoms. One recent study found that parent reports of bipolar symptoms were more valid than either teen or teacher reports. Thus a competent psychiatrist is likely to base her diagnostic judgments on the whole picture, not just your teen's report. Preparing materials like the Mood Disorders Questionnaire in Chapter 2 will help to assure that the psychiatrist has the complete story and knows why you think your teen might have bipolar disorder.

In the End, Stick with Your Position

No matter what happens, stick to your position that going to see a psychiatrist is what's best for your teenager. She doesn't have to buy into the idea just now, but she does have to go. Think about a psychiatric evaluation in the same way you might view a trip to the dentist: you would probably not give in to canceling your teen's dentist appointment because she didn't want to go. Also, don't postpone the evaluation to give your teen more time to think about it. It may be harder to arrange the appointment later, and her oppositionality may build rather than decrease over time.

Preparing Yourself for the Interview

Preparing Yourself Emotionally

If you've been to many psychiatric evaluations for your teen (or other children in your household), you probably have a sense of what to expect. If this is only your first or second time, the procedures may be new and frightening to you. Keep in mind that no doctor can tell you what you have to do with your child. That will be your (and your spouse's) decision, ideally with input from your teen. Taking your teen for a psychiatric evaluation does not mean you are consigning him to a life of medications and therapy. Think of the evaluation as information gathering: a way to consolidate a lot of disparate information into a diagnosis and, hopefully, a well-conceptualized treatment plan.

It is reasonably likely that the psychiatrist will not issue a diagnosis or prescribe medications at the end of this first evaluation. She may want to schedule a second interview, or have your teen also see a psychologist to obtain neuropsychological testing, or arrange a complete medical evaluation from a general practitioner. She may want to schedule a separate time with just the teen (especially if your teen hasn't been forthcoming) or another session with you and your spouse, if there is a spouse in the picture. The length and comprehensiveness of the evaluation can vary with the setting and also, unfortunately, with what insurance will and won't cover.

Many parents become frustrated by this lack of immediate resolution. They desperately want answers to their questions and dread the idea of trying to talk their teen into yet another appointment. But generally, you will appreciate the doctor's thoroughness later. It is better to wait for an accurate diagnosis—and the treatment plan that follows—than to rely on a diagnosis given quickly and without the necessary information in hand.

Things to Take Along

The best way to prepare yourself is to assemble the following information into a binder and have it available at the first appointment. You may even want to mail it to the doctor before the first evaluation, but don't be too surprised if he or she hasn't looked at it before you start talking.

First, put together a written timeline showing when your teen's problems first began. For each interval of her life (for example, 0–2 years, 2–5, 6–10, 11–14, 15–18), list the symptoms (for example, depression, irritability), functional impairments (for example, school refusal, couldn't be left alone), key events in her life (for example, parents' divorce, medical illnesses, moves, deaths in the family), and any diagnoses or medications that were prescribed. Try to be as succinct as possible (for example, avoid writing extensively about life events).

Second, make a list of the symptoms your child is having now, but make clear, perhaps in a table, which ones occur only at home (for example, rage attacks), only at school (for example, inability to concentrate with other kids around), or in both settings.

Third, make a list of all first- and second-degree relatives in your and your spouse's family, their relationship to your teen, their current age, and any problems they've had with mood, anxiety, psychosis, or substance/alcohol abuse. Note if any of them have been in a psychiatric hospital or made a suicide attempt. If your child was adopted, share this with the psychiatrist and recount as much information as you have about the biological parents.

Fourth, keep a mood chart on your teen that covers the prior 2 weeks, or even the prior month. Mood charts track the up-and-down fluctuations of your teen's moods on a day-to-day basis, and will give the doctor a sense of how unstable her moods are. You may also want to record her medications and any life events that have occurred over the prior weeks. There are good examples of downloadable mood charts on the Internet (for older adolescents, go to *www.manicdepressive.org*, click on "Resource Center," and then click on "Tools for All;" for more simplified versions for younger teens and children, go to *www.gcbf.org/resources/ moodcharts.html*). We'll say more about the pros and cons of mood charts in Chapter 10.

Finally, fill out the Parents' General Behavior Inventory on pages 73–74. This scale has been found to be helpful in distinguishing children and teens who are and are not bipolar. Like the Mood Disorders Questionnaire, it is not a diagnostic instrument, but it will help you and your doctor to distill a lot of information down to measurable amounts. This scale, along with the mood chart, can be a useful index of progress once your teen enters treatment.

Some Questions to Prepare For

The material above should give you a pretty good idea of what kinds of questions the psychiatrist will ask. Most of her questions will be about symptoms and functional impairments, and whether these coincide in time. But she may also ask a few questions that will surprise you. These questions may not be asked by every doctor. For example, consider the case in which your teen is being seen by a psychologist for therapy, and the psychologist refers her to a psychiatrist solely to reevaluate her medications. The new psychiatrist may be less interested in environmental factors that may be affecting your teen, and more interested in her current symptoms, history of medication usage, adverse side effects, medical history, or family history. In contrast, a psychiatrist evaluating a teen referred for "problems in the home" may proceed quite differently.

Most doctors will take a developmental history, including questions

GENERAL BEHAVIOR INVENTORY
Parent Version, Short Form

Here are some questions about behaviors that occur in the general population. Think about how often they occur for your child. Using the scale below, select the number that best describes how often your child experienced these behaviors **over the past year**:

0	1	2	3
Never or hardly ever	**Sometimes**	**Often**	**Very often, almost constantly**

Keep the following points in mind:

Frequency: you may have noticed a behavior as far back as childhood or early teens, or you may have noticed it more recently. In either case, estimate how frequently the behavior has occurred **over the past year.** For example: if you noticed a behavior when your child was 5, and you have noticed it over the past year, mark your answer **"often"** or **"very often, almost constantly."** However, if your child has experienced a behavior during only one isolated period in his/her life, but not outside that period, mark your answer **"never or hardly ever"** or **"sometimes."**

Duration: many questions require that a behavior occur for an approximate duration of time (for example, "several days or more"). The duration given is a **minimum** duration. If your child usually experiences a behavior for shorter durations, mark the question **"never or hardly ever"** or **"sometimes."**

Changeability: what matters is not whether your child can get rid of certain behaviors if he/she has them, but whether these behaviors have occurred at all. So even if your child can get rid of these behaviors, mark your answer according to how frequently he/she experiences them.

Your job, then, is to rate how frequently your child has experienced a behavior, over the past year, for the duration described in the question. Please read each question carefully, and record your answer next to each question.

(cont.)

Source: Depue, R. A., Kleinman, R. M., Davis, P., Hutchinson, M., & Krauss, S. P. (1985). The behavioral high-risk paradigm and bipolar affective disorder: VII. Serum-free cortisol in nonpatient cyclothymic subjects selected by the General Behavior Inventory. *American Journal of Psychiatry, 142,* 175–181. Adapted with permission from E. A. Youngstrom, personal communication, February 1, 2007.

0 1 2 3

❏ ❏ ❏ ❏   1. Has your child experienced periods of several days or more when, although he/she was feeling unusually happy and intensely energetic (clearly more than your child's usual self), he/she was also physically restless, unable to sit still, and had to keep moving or jumping from one activity to another?

❏ ❏ ❏ ❏   2. Have there been periods of several days or more when your child's friends or other family members told you that your child seemed unusually happy or high—clearly different from his/her usual self or from a typical good mood?

❏ ❏ ❏ ❏   3. Has your child's mood or energy shifted rapidly back and forth from happy to sad or high to low?

❏ ❏ ❏ ❏   4. Has your child had periods of extreme happiness and intense energy lasting several days or more when he/she also felt much more anxious or tense (jittery, nervous, uptight) than usual (other than related to the menstrual cycle)?

❏ ❏ ❏ ❏   5. Have there been times of several days or more when, although your child was feeling unusually happy and intensely energetic (clearly more than his/her usual self), he/she also had to struggle very hard to control inner feelings of rage or an urge to smash or destroy things?

❏ ❏ ❏ ❏   6. Has your child had periods of extreme happiness and intense energy (clearly more than his/her usual self) when, for several days or more, it took him/her over an hour to get to sleep at night?

❏ ❏ ❏ ❏   7. Have you found that your child's feelings or energy are generally up or down, but rarely in the middle?

❏ ❏ ❏ ❏   8. Has your child had periods lasting several days or more when he/she felt depressed or irritable, and then other periods of several days or more when he/she felt extremely high, elated, and overflowing with energy?

❏ ❏ ❏ ❏   9. Have there been periods when, although your child was feeling unusually happy and intensely energetic, almost everything got on his/her nerves and made him/her irritable or angry (other than related to the menstrual cycle)?

❏ ❏ ❏ ❏   10. Has your child had times when his/her thoughts and ideas came so fast that he/she couldn't get them all out, or they came so quickly others complained that they couldn't keep up with your child's ideas?

such as: Was the birth a difficult one? Was it a C-section? Was she premature? What was her weight and length at birth? If you are the mother: Did you take any drugs/smoke/drink while you were pregnant? Did he reach the developmental milestones (crawling, walking, talking) at the expected times?

Some parents are put off when the doctor hints around, or asks directly, whether their teen has ever been abused, sexually or physically. Many persons with bipolar disorder have a history of sexual or physical abuse, although not necessarily by their biological relatives. Knowing this part of your teen's developmental history will influence what kind of treatment is recommended (for example, treatment for posttraumatic stress disorder). Try to answer this question as honestly as you can, even if you find it insulting.

The doctor will probably ask, "Why now?" Why are you bringing in your teen today, especially if she has been having problems for a long time? This is a chance for you to expand on recent symptoms your teen has been showing, some of which may not have appeared until he became a teenager (for example, preoccupation with the occult; excessive cursing and swearing; downloading pornography from the Internet). The doctor may ask about any recent stressors to which you think your teen may be reacting (for example, a recent marital separation or troubles; an aging grandparent who has moved into the house). Stressors can also be good things: your recent job promotion, for example, may be bringing in more money and making you feel rewarded in your career, but may also make you less available to your teen.

You may also be surprised at how many questions the psychiatrist asks about your teen's medical health. As we said above, some will refer your teen back to his pediatrician for a complete physical exam to rule out medical causes of symptoms like nausea, headaches, weight gain, or low energy. In addition, the doctor may order certain blood tests, which, depending on your teen's health status and the medications she is taking, could include a fasting blood lipids panel, thyroid tests, a chemistry panel (sodium, potassium, glucose, electrolytes), a urinary drug screen, a pregnancy test, or blood cell counts.

Expect the doctor to ask something about family history. This could be as simple as "Does bipolar disorder run in your family?" or "Does anyone else in the family have a psychiatric disorder?" Other doctors will be more thorough and go through each person in your teen's family tree, asking questions like: Was she ever in the hospital? How did she die? Any reason to think it was a suicide? If he drank, how much? Was he ever arrested/sent to jail? Was she ever treated for depression or any medical problems? Try to be as honest as you can about your own history, your spouse's history, or any illness in your brothers, sisters, parents, or other children. As we'll talk more about in Chapter 5, having mental illness in your family doesn't mean it's your fault—your teen may or may not have inherited the predisposition from your family, and besides, none of us can control the genes we pass on to our children (see the box below).

Finally, and depending on whether the psychiatrist plans to do therapy with your teen and family, she may ask about the current family environment. This may include questions about your marriage (for example, how conflicts are handled, how autonomy battles are addressed, whether the teen sides with one of you against the other, or, if there is split custody, whether the teen feels caught between the two parents or families). The doctor may ask about your own psychiatric functioning, whether you are in therapy yourself, and how you, personally, have been affected by conflicts with your teen. Again, try to answer these questions as honestly as you can.

Getting the Diagnosis: Where Do We Go from Here?

The endless questioning finally ended. My psychiatrist looked at me, there was no uncertainty in his voice. "Manic–depressive illness." I admired his bluntness. I wished him locusts on his lands and a pox upon his house. Silent, unbelievable rage. I smiled at him. He smiled back. The war had just begun.
—Kay Redfield Jamison, *An Unquiet Mind* (1995)

FEELING BLAMED: A COPING MANTRA

Many parents feel blamed by doctors for the occurrence of bipolar disorder in their teen. Unfortunately, there is a long history in psychiatry of parents being blamed for the psychiatric disorders of their children, a trend that fortunately is changing. Nonetheless, doctors sometimes ask questions that seem to imply blame. Try to answer the questions as nondefensively as you can, keeping in mind that none of us can control the genes we pass on to our children. If you continue to work with this doctor and continue to feel blamed as a parent, bring that issue up with him or her so that you can get clarification on where he/she is going with these questions.

If you have been to many diagnostic evaluations with your teen, getting a new diagnosis will not be a shock. You may have even guessed the diagnosis yourself, and the purpose of the meeting might just be to make sure you're right. But if this is your teen's first evaluation, or the first time you've heard the term "bipolar" applied to her, you may feel upset by the blunt terminology. Your teen may also feel upset that a new label has been applied to her, that annoying siblings seem to be getting away scot-free, and, if she is forward-looking, that she might have to revise her view of her future.

If the meeting (or meetings) actually end with a diagnosis of bipolar disorder, ask some questions to help get clarification as to why this disorder applies. Ask the psychiatrist to clarify which symptoms apply to your teen, why she doesn't think another disorder is more accurate, and also what comorbid conditions she thinks are present. Ask her how severe your teen's bipolar disorder is compared to other kids she's seen. Ask what treatment seems reasonable at this point (see further discussions of treatment in Chapters 6 and 7). If you think your teen can handle it developmentally, we would suggest including her in this discussion and encouraging her to ask her own questions.

Of course, the diagnosis may be wrong. You may feel unconvinced that your teen really has grandiosity, hypersexuality, or elated mood, or that her depressions are any worse than the kid across the street's. Share these concerns with your doctor, and ask your teen to share hers as well. If you really feel the doctor is off-base or hasn't been listening to you, you may decide to try again with another doctor. Ask the first doctor to issue a diagnostic report to whomever you decide to see next. This will speed up the next diagnostic evaluation and help you to feel that your time and money and your teen's time and motivation have not been wasted.

Finally, remember that a diagnosis is only a first step in your teen's treatment. It is not a life sentence, and it doesn't carry with it a definitive prognosis or invariant treatment plan. It assembles a lot of complicated information into a single label, which, of course, doesn't say everything about who your teen is or who she will become. We will say more about coping with the realities of the disorder in the next chapter. But first, here are some of the realities of adolescent bipolar disorder that you may find encouraging:

1. *It's more likely to get better than to get worse.* Most adults with bipolar disorder say that adolescence was a time when their symptoms were at their worst and their resources for managing the illness were at their least

effective. Research bears this out, showing that the long episodes with rapid cycling and mixed mania that are typical of teenagers apply to less than 20% of adults with the illness. Over time, your teen's mood swings may get less challenging, and at the same time she will develop strategies to manage the disorder and life stressors more effectively.

2. *Many teenagers with bipolar disorder appear to stabilize when they become adults.* A follow-up of adolescents into young adulthood showed that many teens who are diagnosed with a milder form of bipolar disorder do not appear to keep that diagnosis into young adulthood. Although these teens struggled during adolescence and even those with a milder form of the illness had school and social difficulties, some appeared to "outgrow" the more classic bipolar symptoms. It may be helpful to tell your teen about this.

3. *Many teens and adults do quite well despite having the disorder.* Many teens in our treatment program at the University of Colorado have thrived in school, with friends, and with their families despite the illness. It appears that with good medication management, family support, and psychotherapeutic treatment, many teens can do quite well as they mature.

4. *Your role as caregiver will diminish over time.* Having a son or daughter with bipolar disorder does not have to mean that you will always be in a caregiving role, or that her and your lives will always be tied in with hospitalizations, trips to doctors, emergencies, and crises. As they matured into adulthood, many bipolar teens in our treatment program became more responsible about their own care. Some even expressed admiration for the parents who had stuck with them through the bad times, and wanted to give back to them in some way.

5. *Early detection helps with prevention.* Because you are catching the bipolar disorder now, there are many things you can do to ameliorate the negative effects of the illness. Strategies for preventing relapses of the symptoms will be discussed in more detail in Chapters 11–13, and throughout the book.

4

Living with Bipolar Disorder
What Your Family Can Expect

When Mark and Jennifer made an appointment for family therapy, they said their daughter's illness was steadily destroying their family. Sixteen-year-old Alicia was constantly flipping between giddiness and anger, being verbally abusive and even violent toward her parents and her 12-year-old brother, Seth. According to Jennifer, Seth was starting to "act out in response to Alicia's torments." Alicia's parents had no idea what to do—despite the fact that Jennifer, as Mark reported only half-jokingly, had "become so obsessed with this bipolar stuff that it's become a second career for her."

Alicia's psychiatrist prescribed Depakote and Risperdal to control the mood swings that had become more and more dramatic and intense as Alicia entered adolescence. However, 2 months ago, Alicia had decided on her own to stop taking them. "No one is ever going to pour that shit down my throat again," she had sworn. But in recent weeks, she had become increasingly agitated and irritable. Her parents watched Alicia start choosing provocative clothing and knew she had gotten involved sexually with at least one boy. On two recent occasions, she hadn't come home at night at all. When she was home, she was up late almost every night.

"She can't control her impulses," explained Mark. Jennifer shot him a resentful look and countered that bipolar disorder ran in her family (her sister was diagnosed at age 25) and that she understood it to be a "brain disorder" where "kids can't control the things they do." Mark said nothing to this but later burst out angrily, "I'm really starting to hate Alicia. Bipolar or not, she is incredibly mean-spirited."

Jennifer and Mark were now thinking of separating. They strongly disagreed on how to manage Alicia. Mark had begun to wonder, out loud, whether Alicia would do better if he and Seth moved to an apartment. Mark feared for Seth's safety. Jennifer announced she was not going to "stand around and watch the destruction of my family." They had consulted another family therapist 2 weeks earlier, who had explained that "your daughter is picking up on your marital troubles, and she's acting out to try to bring you together. Maybe she feels she needs to sacrifice her own health for the good of the family unit. You should show more physical affection toward each other when she's around so she sees that you're a united front, and then she'll stop." Both felt insulted by this interpretation and did not go back.

Nowhere will you feel the damage caused by bipolar disorder more than in your family life. Nearly all of the families we've worked with over the past 25 years have expressed a great deal of sorrow and pain over the stress and burden caused by the illness. Marriages are stretched, parent–child relationships suffer (both those involving the bipolar teenager and those involving unaffected siblings), and relations with extended family members like grandparents are harmed. Siblings struggle with the emotional pain of trying to grasp the nature of their brother's or sister's disorder, wondering whether they will get it, and even concluding that the sibling is "faking it" to get attention. They often end up resenting their parents for not gaining better control over their sibling's disorder. It's no wonder that a study by Deborah Perlick at Yale University found that those who take care of people with bipolar disorder often seek treatment for their own depression and anxiety.

When you feel highly burdened and distressed, you're more likely to express your anger and resentment than when everything seems under control, and as a result, conflict and emotion can run high in your home. Unfortunately, people with bipolar disorder who live in high-conflict environments have more frequent recurrences of the illness than those who don't. On the positive side, we've seen families who have learned to keep conflict to a minimum even in the worst of circumstances. There's a lot you can do to help your family cope, which you'll learn about later in this book (see especially Part III). But first, it will help if you understand how parents generally experience the bipolar disorder of their teenager.

What Will My Family Go Through?

Whether your son or daughter has not yet been diagnosed, has just been diagnosed, or was diagnosed long ago, your family has probably gone through a number of stages, and many stressful emotional reactions, on the way to accepting the diagnosis and learning to cope. At each of these stages, most families experiment with different styles of parenting, from "hands off" to overprotectiveness to "tough love." No one style of parenting is right for all bipolar teens, but some strategies work better than others. Here we'll describe the goal that most families are after—what we call the "balanced style" of coping—and in Chapter 9 we'll offer some specific strategies for achieving that style.

You and your spouse or partner are bound to disagree with each other when trying to cope with the ups and downs of the disorder. *A significant part of couple conflict comes from different perceptions of the causes of the teen's behavior.* Let's say you think your daughter's behavior is driven by hormones. Maybe your spouse believes she is just spoiled and overindulged. The outcome is bound to be conflict. You'll feel particularly disturbed by these conflicts if you're the natural parent and your spouse is a new stepparent. Even if any couple problems you have are independent of your kids, having a bipolar teen whose moods are not well controlled by medications can certainly bring out and worsen preexisting conflicts. We'll help you start to think about how to separate the problems generated by your teen's disorder from the problems in your marriage or relationship in this chapter and pick up the theme again in Chapter 9.

You're probably also concerned about the effects of your teen's bipolar disorder on your other children, and in turn, how the behavior of your other children can affect your teen with bipolar disorder. Special issues arise in sibling relationships, as in the case of Mark and Jennifer's family. We'll start to look at them here, and again, we'll return to the subject with more detailed practical advice in Chapter 9.

How Do Parents Usually React to Their Bipolar Teen's Disorder?

It's like an abusive relationship, only she's the abuser and I'm the victim or abusee or whatever it's called . . . parenting is a 24/7 job with no holidays or breaks. I have to lie down with her at night, get up with her in the middle of the night, be there to wake her in the morning . . . get calls

from the school that I need to pick her up because she's had a meltdown in class, and then get verbally assaulted when she comes home from school because she thinks I don't care enough.
—Mother of a 15-year-old with bipolar disorder

Your reactions to your teen's bipolar disorder may vary depending on when the symptoms arose and when (or if) your teen has been diagnosed—just as the teen's experience will vary depending on this history. It may help you to know, however, that many other parents are feeling, thinking, and behaving the same way you are. The box on page 83 lists some of the emotions, thoughts, and behaviors we've seen among parents. Some of these thoughts and feelings cause parents to feel shame and to silently boil away on their own. This is why it can be helpful to join a support group for parents of kids with mood disorders, such as those offered by the Depression and Bipolar Support Alliance (*www.dbsalliance.org*) or the National Alliance on Mental Illness (*www.nami.org*).

Notice how certain feelings and beliefs lead to particular behavioral strategies, some of which are more effective than others. As you'll learn throughout this book, some of these beliefs are realistic, whereas others don't take into account what we know about the causes, prognosis, and treatment of the disorder in teenagers. Identifying the thoughts that lead to certain reactions to your teen will help you change them and try out new behavioral strategies.

When Emotions Run High

Although Mark understood that his daughter had a biologically based psychiatric disorder, he also believed she wasn't trying hard enough to control her behavior, which understandably made him angry and frustrated. Like Mark, you or your spouse may feel that, biological or not, there's an element of purposefulness in your son or daughter's behavior. In fact, you may be right—teenagers have certainly been known to manipulate illness situations to their own advantage. Believing your teen is hurting others on purpose is infuriating and can make you say things you don't really mean. Parents we've worked with have said things in anger to their children like "I wish you were never born" or "I hate you" or "You're a loser."

There is quite a bit of research on parents' emotional reactions to a child with a psychiatric illness, summarized under the term *high expressed emotion,* or "high EE." This term glosses over the many complexities of

FEELINGS, THOUGHTS, AND REACTIONS AMONG PARENTS OF BIPOLAR TEENS

Feeling	Associated thought	Behavioral reactions
Anxiety	"What if he stays ill and doesn't get any better?" "What if she kills herself?" "What if he never has a career, family . . . spends his life in mental hospitals?" "What will happen if I don't watch her closely?"	Overprotectiveness, overconcern, extreme self-sacrifice
Anger	"She's doing this on purpose to hurt me." "He doesn't care about anybody but himself." "She manipulates everyone with her problems." "He's ruining our family . . . my marriage . . . hurting his brothers and sisters."	High conflict, criticism, hostile interchanges
Guilt	"I made her this way . . . it was my genes." "He never would have been this way if I hadn't worked so much when he was little." "I took her to the wrong doctors." "I should've been more on top of this."	Overindulgence, giving the teen what he wants, not holding him responsible for his behavior
Despair	"Nothing I've tried works." "There is no future for her." "Nobody can help him."	Giving up, not trying things that might help, avoiding the child
Acceptance	"I'm doing my best, and so is she." "We have to work together to tackle this." "The disorder is unfair, it's cruel, but we have to learn to live with it." "The illness is not the sum total of who she is."	More positive interactions with child, lower family tension

83

the family situation and can imply that you're to blame for your reactions. You're not. But high EE is a useful concept to understand, because *numerous studies have shown that recurrences of psychiatric illnesses are more frequent for those who live in high-emotion, high-conflict households than for those who live in lower-key, less critical or hostile "low-EE" households.*

Virtually all the parents we've met are doing their best to take care of a very difficult teen and to cope with an extremely demanding and unpleasant situation. They get frustrated that the teen isn't doing more to control herself and are often provoked by aggressive or insulting behavior like Alicia's. So it's no surprise that you can end up being critical or even hostile toward your teenager.

You could also quite easily become overprotective or overinvolved. Many parents naturally feel considerable anxiety about what will happen if they don't watch their teen closely, especially if they have spent years taking care of a child with many symptoms and poor social functioning. Some parents get so wrapped up with the teen's care that they give up their own personal lives and do things for the teen that he could do for himself. Jennifer might be seen as overinvolved, whereas Mark might be seen as critical. Other parents keep an emotional distance from their child's problems—not because they don't care or because they aren't upset, but because they've learned to accept them and live with them.

You may feel like the last thing you need right now is to label yourself as critical, hostile, overprotective, or overinvolved. But again, knowing whether you're succumbing to the pressures of raising a bipolar teen in any of these ways can be essential to your teen's improved health. In one of our studies, we found that young adult manic patients who returned following a hospitalization to parents who expressed many criticisms of them were five times more likely to have a manic or depressive relapse in the next 9 months than those who returned to parents who were less critical and low in EE. The implication of such studies is pretty clear: bipolar teens do better in households where family members are low key, conflicts are held to a minimum, routines are structured, and boundaries between people are clear. In later chapters (particularly Chapter 9) you'll get some concrete suggestions for how to reduce the level of conflict and criticism or hostility in your family relationships. But first, it might help to see how your emotional reactions are a part of the stage of acceptance and coping that you and your family are in.

Five Stages of Accepting Bipolar Disorder in a Teenager

Many kids exhibit symptoms when young but aren't diagnosed accurately until adolescence. Alicia, for example, was diagnosed with ADHD and oppositional defiant disorder at age 7 but it took many years for her to be diagnosed with bipolar disorder. This delay can cause a lot of confusion about what's going on and why, and delay your acceptance of and adaptation to the disorder. Reading about the five stages we see parents experience on their way to a balanced attitude and parenting style may help you determine where you stand and help you to move forward.

Stage I: "It's Probably Just Growing Pains"

If your family is at this stage, you probably have an adolescent who has severe mood volatility but may not be fully bipolar yet. Your family may have gone through this stage a long time ago, before you knew your child had a disorder. During this phase, you may have taken a passive stance and given in to your child's outbursts or tolerated his demands, irritability, or aggression.

Pros: In the short run, your family tension may have been temporarily diminished; your child or adolescent may have viewed you as compassionate.

Cons: With time, your child or adolescent can come to see you and your spouse as "pushovers" and learn to take advantage of you; she becomes a bully, takes on the parenting role, and attempts to exert control over others. She may become irritable and testy because of the lack of boundaries.

Alicia's problems became more evident to Mark and Jennifer around the time of Alicia's 8th birthday party, during which she had been especially revved up and then threw a tantrum in front of the other kids and hit another girl. She raced off to her room and slammed the door as the other children left, then started crying inconsolably.

At this early stage her parents had thought of Alicia as "hot-blooded" and "something of a drama queen," but didn't think she had anything like a psychiatric disorder. When she had meltdowns, Jennifer usually dealt with them as many parents do, by reflecting back Alicia's anger to her, as in "You seem really angry right now. Use your words to express it, not your fists." But when Alicia began a full tantrum, Jennifer usually let it go and then tried to talk with her later about why it had happened. In many cases, she gave her daughter whatever she wanted to calm her down. Mark would yell at Alicia, but she would ignore him and escalate her tantrum, at which point he would leave the room and avoid her. Her aggressive outbursts became more frequent over time.

In the earliest stages of coping with bipolar illness (which can be in the childhood or teen years), most parents don't know what to do when typical parenting techniques only seem to make things worse, and tend to explain away their child's behavior with beliefs like "She's just going through growing pains," "She's eating too much sugar," or "It must be something going on at school [or with her friends] that she's not talking about." The risk of continuing in this path of least resistance is that your teen won't learn that there are consequences for her behavior and she'll keep testing the boundaries. Much like the rat that presses a bar to get a food pellet, a child learns that having a tantrum eventually gets rewarded.

Falling into the Trap of Rewarding Aggressive Behavior

Avoiding the trap of inadvertently rewarding behavior like tantrums is, of course, commonsense parenting, but bipolar teens (and younger kids) have rages that escalate and get out of control very quickly. If your teen simultaneously learns that explosive outbursts yield useful results, they can increase in intensity and frequency. If this happens enough times, you'll be ready to ship him off to a desert island.

If your teen is being rewarded for undesirable behavior in one setting or with one parent, there's a pretty good chance he will try the same tactic in other settings. Worse yet, if this pattern of coercive interaction continues, the teen's initially innocuous behaviors can escalate to more aggressive behaviors, like kicking, punching, or other forms of violence.

It's important to understand that, if your teen has a bipolar-related meltdown and gets what he wants—even if the meltdown was the product of a biological process—he will learn that meltdowns are a way of getting rewarded in the future.

The take-home message from stage I is: keep firm limits even if (1) your child is fighting you on them, (2) they do not appear to produce any change in the number of difficult encounters you and your child have, and (3) you are clearly observing symptom-driven behaviors. Make it clear to the teen what you do and don't find acceptable. This is the only way she will learn that her behaviors—even those that clearly have a basis in biology—have consequences.

Stage II: "I'm Going to Put My Foot Down"

I get tired of walking on eggshells, trying to keep him from getting angry,
and then being told I'm a lousy parent. Sometimes I just lose it.
—Mother of a 13-year-old boy with bipolar disorder

Parents at stage II usually have preteens or teens who have short episodes of mania or depression (even though these may not meet the DSM-
IV-TR diagnostic criteria yet). If you're at this stage, you may take the
path of least resistance toward your teen's dysfunctional behavior most of
the time, but then abruptly, unpredictably, and harshly punish transgres-
sions. Typically, the punishment does not fit the crime.

Pros: In the short run, the teen usually stops the behavior, in part out
of surprise.

Cons: The adolescent doesn't develop a clear sense of rules or boundaries; views his parents as crazy, unfair, unstable, untrustworthy, or "bipolar"; and does not develop a sense of responsibility for his behavior.

At this stage most parents have become angry and fed up with their
teen's repeated meltdowns, disrespect, inability to follow routines, and
poor school performance. If your family is in this phase, you probably
know that something is seriously wrong but you may not yet have consulted a mental health professional.

For Alicia and her family, this stage lasted from about age 8 until she
was in her early teens. When she reached adolescence, Alicia developed
even more severe temper outbursts, some of which were related to her
menstrual period. Most of the time her parents ignored her, but on one
particularly difficult day she snapped at her father when asked to take out
the garbage. He lost his temper, dragged her into her room and slammed
the door, and took away her privileges for a week. The next time she had
a temper outburst, he did nothing. Alicia later wondered aloud why this
one particular episode had been punished so harshly.

Inconsistent discipline—or no discipline at all—has long been identified as a primary risk factor for later delinquency among youth. Of
course, it's hard to be a consistent disciplinarian all the time, and brief
periods of inconsistency won't send your child on a dangerous developmental trajectory. Prolonged periods of inconsistency, however, may contribute to mood instability, especially if major explosive outbursts are
punished only some of the time whereas seemingly minor infractions are
punished harshly.

The take-home message from stage II is: your teen must develop the

sense that the world around him has a structure with predictable rules. The availability of consistency and structure in the environment will help him regulate the chaos of his own internal state. In Chapter 10, you'll learn some strategies for increasing consistency and structure in your home environment.

Stage III: "Tough Love"

If you're at stage III, your teen has probably been seen by a mental health professional and medications may have been recommended, although not necessarily for bipolar disorder. You or your spouse may have undertaken autocratic means to assure your teen's compliance with recommended psychiatric treatments or family rules or routines.

Pros: Your adolescent's compliance may be assured in the short run, and you may have the temporary feeling of being back in control of your family life.

Cons: Your adolescent may be losing her temper or acting out more; she can start to become more aggressive in school and may start to spend less and less time at home; when at home, she may push limits. Pushing limits may have dangerous consequences. For example, the teen may refuse to take medications if medications are associated with giving up independence. This style of parenting usually becomes less effective as the teen ages and gains more autonomy.

When Alicia hit puberty at age 13, an endocrinologist recommended she begin taking birth control pills to diminish the irritability she showed prior to her menstrual periods. Things stabilized for a short time. But when she turned 14, she began to spend more and more time at her friends' houses and rarely told her parents where she was going. Her irritability and explosiveness erupted again, but were now accompanied by a slide in her grades and complaints from teachers about her disruptiveness. She began to cut school and often overslept. She started dressing and acting provocatively around her father's friends and coworkers. Mark, who was having trouble at his job, began to blame Alicia for a number of his own and his family's problems. He and Jennifer were starting to grow apart. They spoke of little other than managing the kids and the household.

After reading an article in an airline magazine on "tough love," Mark decided he had had enough and that his house was going to be run "like a military academy" from now on. He decided that both children should be assigned household tasks and were to report back to him every night about their completion. He came into Alicia's room in the morning and angrily demanded that she get up, and twice he lifted her out of bed and carried her into the shower. He behaved similarly when she was to go to bed at night. Even though these strategies temporarily assured her compliance, the net effect was to make her worse: her aggressiveness, irritability, and outbursts increased in other settings, and she desperately avoided her father at home.

If you're at this stage, you may be convinced that your child has a psychiatric problem, although what kind of problem may still be unclear. Various diagnoses may have been offered by doctors, including ADHD, oppositional defiant disorder, intermittent explosive disorder, conduct disorder, separation anxiety, personality disorder, or reactive attachment disorder (see Chapter 3). In the face of these diagnoses and the often chaotic array of recommendations you may have received, you or your spouse may have decided to take the tough love approach. You may believe (or have been told) that your child is spoiled, you've been too soft, and it's time to lay down the law. These reactions are understandable— many parents of healthy teenagers have them at times, believing that with good and strong limits the teen will fall in line like a good soldier.

This set of emotional reactions usually stems from the belief that the teen could control these behaviors if he tried harder. You may find yourself being highly critical, occasionally verbally hostile. You probably feel increasingly frustrated when your attempts to take over and make your teen behave appropriately have failed.

Setting limits with a bipolar teen—or any teen—involves a fair amount of negotiation. As you probably know, the key drive in adolescence is striving for independence. As a result, attempts at overcontrol are bound to be ineffective. *Moreover, a key attribute of people with bipolar disorder is a strong desire for autonomy and control, even though their behavior often seems to lead to the opposite result.* This desire may stem in part from the lack of control they feel in their own internal world. You can help your child by acknowledging this need for independence and being willing to negotiate on things that do not involve his immediate safety or health.

The take-home message from stage III is: it's important to allow your teenager, no matter how disruptive, to have a degree of autonomy and independence in making decisions and determining her own fate. This doesn't mean you shouldn't set appropriate limits, especially where his health or safety is at stake, but you may have to pick your battles. As

Ross Greene explains in his book *The Explosive Child,* you can distinguish between circumstances in which you have to set limits, those where you should negotiate, and those where you should just let things go.

Stage IV: "It's a Brain Disorder"

Most teens aren't diagnosed with bipolar disorder until adolescence, though they have often been diagnosed with many other disorders before then. Those diagnosed as children usually have a strong family disposition toward the illness. When you finally hear of this diagnosis, it's easy to slip into thinking that most or all of your adolescent's behavior is disorder-driven, including many behaviors that are perfectly normal for her age. If your teen is receiving medications, it's understandable to be confused about when to request medication adjustments from the psychiatrist to control fluctuations in her day-to-day moods. You may run into frequent conflicts with your teen's doctor or other providers in the mental health system.

Pros: For the first time, your teen may get the treatment she needs. She may feel supported by your interest in the illness.

Cons: Adolescents usually rebel against labels, especially if parents become preoccupied with them. If you get too involved with your teen's mental health care, he may not invest in it emotionally, may not take responsibility for getting to treatment sessions or taking pills according to schedule, and may believe that the disorder and its treatment are "my parents' thing." Some teens come to believe that they can't have normal emotions without being labeled as "acting bipolar." Your child's psychiatrist may resent your many phone calls.

Shortly after Alicia turned 15, she made her first suicide attempt and landed in the hospital. She had gotten into a severe argument with her boyfriend and then with Seth and had gone up to the roof and cut her arms with a potato peeler. When Mark and Jennifer took her to the emergency room, she reported feeling relieved and temporarily better, as if the self-cutting had released an evil force inside her.

During the hospitalization, the psychiatrist and social worker explained that Alicia had bipolar disorder. This was not a surprise to Jennifer, who had noted the similarities between Alicia and the children she had seen interviewed on a PBS special. Mark knew of this possibility as well, but the diagnosis was one more in a set of psychiatric terms that meant little to him. For the first time in a long time, however, he admitted feeling compassion for Alicia, and shed tears when asked what he wanted to do next. He said, "I want her to get better, no matter what it is she's got, before she kills herself."

When Alicia came home from the hospital, things were peaceful for a short time, but Jennifer, as Mark described it, "went to work on the bipolar thing." She read every book she could find, joined several online chat rooms, read books about suicide and bodily harm, and started attending conferences regarding bipolar disorder in children. She began introducing herself to others as "a parent of a child with a brain disorder."

Jennifer and Alicia's relationship problems took on a different form. Alicia started resenting being "put in a box," her problems explained away with a label. Her arguments with her mother now centered on whether she had taken her medications or whether she had talked about X or Y issue in her psychotherapy. She got annoyed that typical teen behaviors—such as spending a lot of time on the computer or talking loudly on her cell phone—were now viewed as signs of depression or mania.

When Seth heard about the diagnosis, it meant little to him. He said ruefully, "Does that mean she can do whatever she wants now?"

When you first learn of the diagnosis, or have it confirmed, you may feel relieved that a lot of your questions have been answered, as they were for Jennifer: Why had Alicia had so many good periods of attention and concentration if she had ADHD? Why was one day so different from the next? Why were there periods of good functioning followed by sudden deteriorations? Having the answers summarized by a single label can lead to an "Aha!" experience, a mild sense of elation that a lot of disconnected threads have been woven into a unified whole.

Having a teen with bipolar disorder also may open up a new kind of community. You may meet other parents (say, at meetings of the Depressive and Bipolar Support Alliance) who've gone through the same things you have. Hearing their stories can feel incredibly supportive. Likewise, being a member of a listserv (for example, *www.bpso.org*) or spending time on informative websites (for example, *www.bpkids.org*, *www.jbrf.org*) feels fulfilling, validating, and helpful. For the first time, you may feel like you're doing something positive for yourself and your family.

These activities, although certainly therapeutic for you, your family, and your teen, do carry one potential side effect: the ease of overidentifying with the diagnosis. If you get too preoccupied with the diagnosis, you can also become emotionally overinvolved (overconcerned, overprotective, or inordinately self-sacrificing) in the care of your teen. Interactions become increasingly focused on your teen's emotional health or medications rather than the healthy activities of daily living.

For some parents, the diagnosis brings a great sense of loss and deep sadness. This is called "grieving over the lost healthy child." It's the feeling that you've lost hopes and aspirations for your teen and that he is now nothing but a label with diminished potential. These reactions can bring about sadness, guilt, and the intense desire to help in whatever way you can, sometimes to an extreme.

Another sign of the "brain disorder" stage is frequent frustrations with the mental health system. You may begin to think that every emotional outburst, episode of silliness or giggling, pessimistic thought, night of poor sleep, or evening of hyperactive behavior is a sign of an oncoming episode that calls for a change in medications. You can easily get in the habit of calling the physician too often. And even when you're not calling to ask for medication changes, many doctors will try to help by raising dosages and adding new medications (for example, for sleep, anxiety, or agitation). This is one of the reasons many bipolar teens end up on so many different medications. A survey by the *New York Times* found that in 2005 more than 500,000 American children were receiving at least three psychiatric medications, and more than 160,000 were receiving four or more. We don't know whether such complicated medication regimens are really necessary to maintain mood stability among bipolar teens. We do know that any benefits of such combinations can be offset by their substantial side effects.

Some physicians stop returning phone calls, believing parents are "crying wolf." Then they become less available when you have a true clinical emergency. If this happens to you, especially if you also feel unsupported by your spouse or believe nobody else cares about your child's health, you may feel you should redouble your efforts, taking your teen to a different psychiatrist or combining psychiatric appointments with primary care doctor appointments. Your teen could end up getting several different prescriptions from doctors who may not even know about each other.

The bottom-line message from stage IV is: take the diagnosis seriously and get necessary treatments for your child, but avoid letting the diagnosis rule your lives. Keep in mind that your teen, however dysfunctional, is *affected* by a disorder but *is not the disorder herself.* She undoubtedly has strengths and personality characteristics that transcend the diagnosis. Your teen will be grateful when she perceives that you recognize this continuity in her strengths and assets even after the diagnosis has been given.

Working with the mental health system deserves a chapter in itself. There are effective and ineffective ways of communicating with doctors, as you'll see in Chapters 6 and 8.

Stage V: Balance

With a firm understanding of the disorder and some life experience, you can begin to combine compassion with appropriate limit setting. Learning specific communication and problem-solving strategies to collaborate with your teen in developing behavioral plans (earned privileges and rewards for adaptive behavior, and consequences for aggressive or disrespectful behavior) makes family life go much easier. Most parents don't reach this stage until the teen is in late adolescence or even young adulthood and they've lived through several different episodes. If you've achieved a balance in your approach to the disorder, you have learned to adjust your expectations to take into account the cycling of the illness and to take care of your own emotional and physical health and that of other family members. You and your spouse may disagree on how to manage the disorder, but you present a united front to the child and discuss your disagreements in private.

Pros: In the long run, the illness is better managed and the teen develops a stronger sense of personal responsibility in managing it.

Cons: In the short run, the implementation of behavior plans and communication or problem-solving strategies takes considerable time, practice, and effort. You may at times feel guilty about imposing consequences on the symptom-driven behaviors of your teen.

Learning to cope with bipolar disorder is an evolving process. With time, you'll learn the strategies that work best with your teen—from working collaboratively with your spouse, from other parents, and from your own experiences. Achieving this state of balance helps you combine ideas that may seem at odds with each other: (1) your teenager has a biologically based illness that requires acceptance and understanding from all family members, but (2) he also needs to take responsibility for his own behavior. *In other words, you need to adjust your expectations to what your child can tolerate given his bipolar condition, but at the same time provide the structure to allow him to function at his highest level.*

If you're at this stage, you've probably developed some effective behavior management plans. Maybe you've agreed to make desired privileges (for example, use of the car, time with friends) contingent on the teen's treatment adherence (going to treatment sessions, staying compliant with medications) or doing his best to contain explosive outbursts. One 15-year-old learned to ask her mom to take her for a drive around the block when she felt like her rage was getting out of control. One mother–son pair agreed to call a close relative to come over when he was on the verge of having a meltdown.

Achieving this balanced state requires understanding not only the teen's illness and her particular needs, but how the disorder has affected family relationships and how family members' behaviors and attitudes affect the teen.

Now that you've learned about the five stages, use the form below to think about where your family fits now and what stages it has gone through in the past. In the third column, write examples of experiences you had at that time that did or did not fit with each stage.

YOUR FAMILY
When Did It Go Through the Various Stages of Coping, and What Stage Is It in Now?

Stage	Age	Things you remember from that interval
I.	_____	_____
		_____
II.	_____	_____
		_____
III.	_____	_____
		_____
IV.	_____	_____
		_____
V.	_____	_____
		_____

The Effects of Bipolar Disorder on Your Marriage or Romantic Relationship

Mark and Jennifer's marriage had been "going south" (his words) for several years. He blamed it on their growing disagreement about managing Alicia's illness. Jennifer said their problems predated Alicia's and, in fact, that Alicia had become a scapegoat.

Mark said Jennifer "blames everything Alicia does on bipolar disorder, even stuff that's clear manipulation." Alicia would, he said, spend most of her Saturday "lollygagging" about the house, saying she was depressed, being irritable and snappy with others, sleeping on the couch while others cleaned up around her, and complaining that she was too depressed and exhausted to move. Then, around 6:00 P.M., she would "kick into high gear, go into the bathroom, and get all dolled up to go out for the evening." She would then go out with her friends and stay out until 1:00 A.M. or later. The next day she would sleep until noon and again be too depressed to help out in the house. Jennifer saw this as "evidence of her mood cycling. . . . I've read about how cortisol levels can change and how teenagers can rapidly cycle even within 1 day." Mark saw it as Alicia's "using her psychiatry problems to get out of facing life's demands." In turn, Alicia would rage at her father, saying that "only Mom understands what I'm going through . . . you don't care!" Mark would respond angrily to Jennifer, "Don't you see how she's using our disagreements to get her way?"

Bipolar disorder places incredible pressure on marital or romantic relationships. However, it's essential that you distinguish such pressure from relationship problems you had before symptoms appeared and those you still have when your teen is doing well. This distinction, although not always clear, will help keep you and your spouse from "triangulating" your child—getting her involved as a combatant in a marital battle. Mark and Jennifer fundamentally disagreed on the causes of Alicia's problems, and this disagreement caused Alicia to ally with one of them against the other, which then further fueled their marital conflicts. The worksheet on page 96 may help you keep these issues separate in your mind.

We've seen couples divorce over problems related to managing their bipolar child. We're repeatedly struck by the fact that it's more often severe disagreements over how to handle the behavior than the behavior itself that causes the rift. These disagreements are most likely to occur

DISTINGUISHING RELATIONSHIP PROBLEMS THAT ARE AND ARE NOT RELATED TO MY TEEN'S BIPOLAR DISORDER

How much distress is your relationship in now, compared to the other couples you know?

1	2	3	4	5	6	7

Less distressed　　　　　About the same　　　　　Much more distressed

Below is a series of relationship problems people often have. Circle the problems that you think your relationship has. Then, in the middle column, rate whether the problem is unrelated (1), somewhat related (2), or completely related (3) to your son's or daughter's mood problems. In the third column, check any problems in your relationship that *predated* his or her problems— that were present even before he or she was born or developed significant mood problems.

Problem area	Related to disorder?	Check (✓) if predated teen's problems
Conversation/communication	_____	_____
Sharing household chores	_____	_____
Sex/intimacy	_____	_____
Agreeing on parenting strategies	_____	_____
Problem solving	_____	_____
Shared activities/recreation	_____	_____
Planning	_____	_____
Money/finances	_____	_____
Managing the other kids	_____	_____
Sharing parenting duties	_____	_____

when one spouse attributes the teen's aversive behavior to the diagnosis and the other to the teen's dysfunctional personality.

Chapter 9 offers strategies such as communication and problem-solving skills that can help you resolve such disagreements. For now, keep in mind that you and your spouse should have frequent conversations to develop coordinated behavior management plans. This requires agreements such as:

- Who will work with the child on keeping her consistent with recommended medications?
- What kinds of behaviors are obviously mood symptom-driven, what behaviors seem independent of symptoms, and for which is it unclear?
- Who will make sure she gets to therapy or medication appointments?
- What rules are reasonable for him to follow, in terms of household tasks, bedtimes, wake times, and other responsibilities?
- If there are disagreements between us, how will they be discussed and resolved?

You may need a therapist to help you work through these issues, but start with these ideas:

1. *Choose a half-hour at the same time each week to talk, away from the kids, about problems—as well as successes—in managing your teen's bipolar disorder.* Difficult topics seem more manageable in a positive environment, so consider meeting during a walk together or over coffee. You'll be surprised by how helpful it is to just share your perceptions with each other. Don't try to convince each other of your point of view about your teen's behavior and what causes it, just let each other air your views without interrupting. If you're going through this book together, you'll probably find that your opinions become more similar as you have these collaborative discussions.

2. *Set aside time for each other.* Aim for an evening together without the kids each week—or at least reserve some private time at home a few times a week, watching a movie, reading together, or doing something non-child-related that you both enjoy. Some couples agree not to discuss the children but stick to talking about books, ideas, work life, and all the other things that remind them they were a romantic couple before they became parents.

Most of all, we want to leave you with the message that *relationship problems between parents are quite common when dealing with a major illness in a child, whether psychological or medical.* Parents coping with a child with juvenile-onset diabetes also have conflicts about the medical management of their son or daughter's illness, which is typically more straightforward than the medical management of bipolar disorder. Things may have gotten quite tense, but you can still rediscover the strengths of your relationship if you make time to communicate and collaborate with your spouse.

The Effects of Bipolar Disorder on Siblings

A quiet boy who liked baseball, hockey, and video games, Seth had always seemed unflappable and uninterested in emotional topics. But as Alicia's disorder got worse, particularly after her hospitalization, his grades dropped, and he started smoking cigarettes. He expressed considerable resentment about Alicia, whom he felt was putting on a big show for his parents' attention. At one point, when Mark and Alicia had argued heatedly over her coming home late, he angrily said, "Maybe I should slit my wrists, and then maybe you'd notice when I come home too." When his mother talked to him about it later, he said, "My whole life goes around her, I have to do all the work to keep her from getting mad, and she doesn't have to do a damn thing."

Like many parents, you may feel that the experience of having a bipolar teen has been hardest on your healthy children. Depending on their age and level of independence, some siblings are unaffected, but this is quite rare. At the other end of the spectrum, some siblings find the situation intolerable. On more than a few occasions we've heard siblings threaten, "Get her out of here, or I'm going to go live somewhere else."

There is virtually no research on how best to help siblings of bipolar children and teens, but in one study children with bipolar disorder and depression said their relationships with their siblings were not as good as between healthy siblings. In another study, healthy siblings of those with severe mental illness reported considerable emotional distress and practical problems from taking care of their ill sibling. Interestingly, the heaviest burden was felt by those who thought that the ill sibling could control the disorder if she wanted to.

Siblings aren't always innocent bystanders, by the way. Many bipolar children say they're continually provoked by their siblings and certain looks, words, or intrusions by siblings can trigger mood swings. You may have seen your healthy children deliberately provoke the ill brother or sister into a rage and then act as if they had nothing to do with it. No one has yet studied whether conflictual sibling relationships make bipolar people worse, but it seems likely that if high conflict with parents is associated with a poorer course of bipolar disorder, so too is high conflict with siblings.

Siblings may have a different reaction to your bipolar child when she is manic or hypomanic than when depressed. Some siblings, especially older ones, feel responsible for taking care of their younger siblings and that it's somehow their fault that their brother is depressed or suicidal. They may wish they could do more to help. Younger siblings who admire the older sibling may start to model some of the bipolar teen's unhealthy behavior, as did Yolanda in Chapter 1.

It's important to keep track of how your healthy children are reacting, especially when your bipolar teen gets worse. Healthy children often get neglected when the bipolar child is ill, because everyone assumes they'll take care of themselves. Make doubly sure you pay attention to their needs at these times: that they don't miss their soccer games, aren't alone on weekends, and are getting to school on time. *Most of all, explain to them what's going on, that things will not always be this way, that it's not their fault, and that you love them.* The box on page 100 provides some suggestions for helping your healthy children, a topic we'll return to in later chapters.

Preserving Your Teen's Place in the Family

There's no doubt that bipolar disorder in a teenager poses numerous challenges for everyone in the family. Recognizing these is the first step toward overcoming them. But it's also important to remember that your teenager is a person first, not an illness. He has strengths and other positive characteristics that make him a loved and valued member of your family. When you remind yourself of those qualities, you'll all be motivated to work empathically and cooperatively at the problem solving you need to do. Just as important, your teenager's management of the illness gets a significant boost from this more humanitarian perspective from her family.

As explained earlier in this chapter, most parents go through a phase where they see their teen only through the lens of bipolar disorder, attrib-

HELPING WELL CHILDREN COPE
WITH THE TEEN'S BIPOLAR DISORDER

- Talk to them about how they understand the problems their bipolar sibling is having.
- Educate them about what you know about the disorder so that you're on the same page (see Chapter 9).
- Remind them that your bipolar child is not just being manipulative; explain that the teen may not be able to help the way he acts.
- Do what you can to make sure their lives go on normally.
- Coach them on ways to avoid provoking the bipolar teen.
- Make special efforts to check in with them when your bipolar child is having significant mood swings.
- Try to allay their fears that they'll become mentally ill like their brother or sister.
- In sibling conflicts, avoid siding with the bipolar teen just because doing so makes him or her calm down more quickly.
- Make sure your well children feel like they have allies in the family, especially when problems with your bipolar child are most severe.
- Spend alone time with your healthy children, including going on special outings that involve only them.
- Get help for your well children if they're having problems, including looking into individual or group treatment.
- Try to maximize the times that your healthy children have positive experiences with the bipolar sibling.

uting all behavior to the illness. Although this is quite understandable, some families get stuck at this stage. The teenager becomes the scapegoat for everything that goes wrong at home, and bipolar symptoms are seen as the cause of every problem the family faces. This perspective can be very damaging to the teenager, whose healthy development depends on having a self-image that encompasses more than illness ("You wouldn't say 'I'm a heart attack,' " said one teen we know, "but lots of people say 'I'm bipolar' "). It also prevents you both from developing the crucial ability to recognize recurring mood symptoms. If you and your teen can't tell when she is showing the signs of mania or depression and when she is just, well, being a teen, you won't know when to take action to head off a mood episode. Therefore, it's important to resolve now, before you launch into the treatment and coping strategies in Part II, (1) to learn to distinguish between symptom-driven behavior and normal behavior and (2) to keep uppermost in your mind who your teenager is as a unique person and valued member of your family.

When Is It Bipolar Disorder and When Is it Just My Teenager?

Jokes abound about the challenges parents face when their kids enter adolescence. Although there's growing evidence that this phase of development isn't as chaotic or troublesome as conventional wisdom says, there's no question that teens exhibit some new troublesome behaviors and attitudes as they make the transition from childhood to adulthood. If your teen was diagnosed with bipolar disorder as a child, you may mistakenly view these new developments as bipolar symptoms. When bipolar symptoms and adolescence make an appearance at the same time, it can be even more difficult to distinguish the two. Teenagers typically start taking more risks, get moody, get embroiled in family conflicts, become excitable, have bad days, and get expansive, impulsive, and unrealistic. We see the same kinds of things emerging—albeit in more dramatic form—when teens start to develop bipolar disorder.

It's important to avoid overlabeling your teen's behavior as bipolar for a number of reasons:

• It sometimes leads to excessive medication changes. When you call your teen's psychiatrist or general practitioner frequently to report new symptoms, the doctor is likely to address the problem through medication. If the behavior wasn't actually a symptom to begin with, medication changes or additions probably aren't necessary.

• If you see most or all of your teen's behavior as being bipolar-driven, you may stop imposing consequences for the teen's manipulative or rebellious behavior. As mentioned, this may lead to more acting out by your teen and more overlabeling by you. Teens usually learn fairly quickly how to manipulate a situation, and bipolar teens have been described as being especially proficient in this area. If a teen learns that being hostile will get him out of chores or keep him from being grounded, he will continue to do what will get him what he wants. One family described being unable to make any request of their son because he would begin yelling and banging on the walls or kitchen counter in response. Interestingly, this teen seemed pretty asymptomatic much of the time, but his parents backed off from setting any consequences for fear of "making his symptoms worse."

• Continually seeing a teen's behavior as bipolar may make your teen resist observing symptoms in herself. If every time she has a mood swing or gets angry or emotional you tell her she's symptomatic, she'll learn to resist the notion that she has bipolar disorder. This can be a dangerous power struggle given that individuals with bipolar disorder need to learn to accurately track their early warning signs to prevent relapses. (Relapse prevention will be discussed in more detail in Chapter 11.)

• Your teen may begin to feel that nothing he does is mainstream or normal and may doubt his ability to fit in with other kids his age and society in general. This could rob him of hope and make him give up doing what he needs to do to manage the illness. Your teen has his own personality, likes and dislikes, strengths and weaknesses, and ways of looking at the world. When all that an adolescent hears is a commentary on whether his symptoms are occurring or not, the teen may begin to lose his sense of himself as well.

Given these risks, how can you learn to distinguish your teen's personality from his disorder, and how can you encourage others to do the same? Ask yourself the following questions to determine whether any behavior that concerns you is normal teenager behavior or driven by bipolar symptoms:

• *Do most teenagers act this way?* If your teen has received five traffic tickets, and every other teenager you've run into has had no more than one or two, your teen may be driving under the influence of mania or hypomania. If your teenager shocks adults with sexually precocious behavior, maybe she's demonstrating the hypersexuality of mania. Social and cultural customs are familiar to everyone; deviation from them is a good indication that something may be wrong, especially if that deviation is sudden and significant.

• *Is your teen acting her age?* If your teenager suddenly acts much younger than her age (for example, getting very anxious or whiny, withdrawn, and dependent when you leave the house), and this behavior is not typical of her, she may be experiencing mood symptoms.

• *Is your teen's functioning impaired?* If your son suddenly can't go to school, eat meals with the family, concentrate enough to watch a TV show, or otherwise go through his normal routine, bipolar symptoms might be at work.

- *Has something happened recently to get her distressed?* Teens live in a swamp of life events, family conflicts, risk taking, and peer pressure. Sometimes what look like bipolar symptoms can be temporary reactions to events at school, conversations on the Internet, or altercations at some social activity. Emotional reactions that extend well beyond an event and seem to get worse with the passing days rather than better are more likely to be bipolar symptoms.

Know Who Your Teenager Is

Many teens with bipolar disorder have been described by their parents as having been the best and brightest—precocious and smart as children, meeting their developmental milestones earlier than others, more creative than their peers. Kids at risk for bipolar disorder demonstrate innovative thinking, high productivity and energy, a merging of grandiosity and optimism, and verbal fluency. There also appears to be an interpersonally gregarious and sensitive side to individuals with bipolar disorder: they have a desire to be with others and an ability to engage, persuade, and inspire people. There is no research on whether kids with bipolar disorder are especially gifted, but we have observed—and many of our observations are shared by teachers—that bipolar kids have features in common with kids who are identified as gifted and talented in the school system: superior vocabulary, creative, imaginative, questioning, advanced ideas and opinions, consuming interest, problem-solving ability, wide range of interests, sophisticated sense of humor, and resourcefulness.

Pride can make it difficult for parents to accept that their son or daughter, who may have had these talents, now has a debilitating illness. But it's critical to remember that this talented and creative person still exists and that the bipolar disorder is just one aspect of your teenager. Finding a pathway to success that maximizes use of these traits while avoiding the destruction brought about by the disorder is the challenge.

It's easy to equate your teen with the bipolar disorder because there is evidence that people with the disorder have mood swings or "temperamental disturbances" that date back to childhood. You may have noticed moodiness in your child early in his development (relative to his peers or siblings) and even during times when he was apparently well. You may have thought of them as part of your teen's personality, but in fact they may have been milder symptoms of the illness. In other words, teasing apart what is your teen's personality and what is his bipolar disorder is usually a matter of nuance and degree. The following exercise may help your thinking about who your son or daughter is aside from having a mood disorder.

The following is a list of personality attributes that many teens possess. Take a few moments and check the traits that seem to fit with your teen's basic personality. It may help to think back over his whole life to attributes that have seemed fairly consistent over time. Does his personality consist of certain traits that go together (for example, shy, serious, pensive, analytical, curious, talkative, humorous, bright)? It may be helpful to think about feedback you've received about your teen over the years from teachers, coaches, religious teachers, or friends. Try asking yourself, "Is this who my teen always is, or does it wax and wane with her mood swings?" If you would answer that the trait is a defining characteristic of your teen, then it would fit with what we mean by personality.

Traits like "perceptive" or "curious" or "pensive" are probably not bipolar attributes. Traits like "strong-willed" and "withdrawn" and "humorous" can be, but only if they appear during mood episodes and then disappear once she is stable. Keep in mind that personality is *stable*, but bipolar disorder is *cyclic*.

Strong-willed	___	Analytical	___
Outgoing	___	Pensive	___
Withdrawn	___	Serious	___
Shy	___	Sensitive	___
Talkative	___	Quiet	___
Self-assured	___	Judgmental	___
Physical	___	Perceptive	___
Emotional	___	Curious	___
Humorous	___	Innovative	___
Affectionate	___	Passive	___
Bright	___	Unmotivated	___
Interpersonally savvy	___	Impulsive	___
Finicky	___	Hard working	___
Perfectionistic	___	Reliable	___
Indecisive	___	Open	___
Gentle	___	Optimistic	___
Competitive	___	Reserved	___
Apprehensive	___	Full of life	___
Defiant	___	Unpredictable	___
Destructive	___	Inspired	___
Aggressive	___	Communicative	___

Being able to distinguish your teen's personality from her symptoms will help you identify when your teen is having an increase in symptoms rather than just going through a rough time. For example, if your teen is gregarious by nature, the fact that she has planned activities with friends from Friday afternoon until Sunday evening may not be cause for worry—unless you simultaneously start to notice that she also isn't sleeping and is more irritable. However, if your teen is more shy and withdrawn by nature, this level of increase in social engagements may be a sign of the illness.

Teenagers, who are going through the process of identity development, want to feel that they are being seen for themselves aside from their symptoms and biochemical imbalances. We've heard numerous teens describe with great emotion how their parents don't see them or relate to them as who they really are. One girl we know said that her parents only saw her as a crazy person and so, according to her, she had begun to act the part.

Of course it doesn't have to be that way. You can learn more and more about the symptoms of bipolar disorder and what they look like in your teen, always keeping a handle on who your teenager is, what you value about her, and how she can use her personal strengths to battle the illness and help set herself on a proper developmental course.

As we go forward in this book, you'll get a better sense of how you can help your teen stay stable and how this stability can translate into better family relationships. Some of these interventions involve medications, some behavior modification plans, and others strategies to communicate and solve problems as a family, while building acceptance of your teen's disorder in yourself and other family members. In the next part, you'll learn what causes the disorder, and what pharmacological and psychosocial treatments are available to help manage it.

PART II

Treating Adolescent Bipolar Disorder

5 "How Did My Teenager Get This Illness?"

By age 15, Lola had already been hospitalized several times, most recently for a suicide attempt following bouts of rage, sleeplessness, and the kind of "wild ideas" that her mother, Karen, had come to associate with bipolar disorder. Apparently this latest mixed (depressive and manic) episode had been triggered by a breakup with the classmate Lola referred to as her "boyfriend" even though she had only gone out with him a couple of times. Karen couldn't understand how the disintegration of this fledgling relationship could have caused such a severe bipolar episode, but every time she tried to sort through the possible causes of this episode—or, for that matter, her daughter's illness in general—she ended up baffled and immersed in self-blame.

Karen knew that bipolar disorder was heritable, but no one on either side of Lola's family had had it. Karen had grown up with a volatile, angry father and a mother prone to bouts of depression, and her ex-husband's father had been an alcoholic. But she could find no one on either side of the family who had manic episodes, and no one who had even received any psychiatric treatment.

In her darker moments, Karen blamed herself and the environment in which her daughter had been raised. After Karen's divorce when Lola was 4, Lola's father had moved to another state and started another family. Karen had raised Lola with little help. Lola had been volatile from early on, but Karen couldn't piece together whether it had gotten worse after the divorce. What if all of this was brought on by the divorce and her father's absence afterward? Had Lola been abused by someone, perhaps a babysitter? Should Karen have done more to shield Lola from her own problems, such as her depression and loneliness? Understandably, she had relied on Lola for companionship after the divorce—did this emotionally harm her in some way?

Karen knew from her reading that bipolar disorder had a biological basis in most cases, but this wasn't much comfort. Even with the medication treatment designed to recognize that fact, Lola was struggling with a troubling array of symptoms. If Karen could really pinpoint what was causing those symptoms, would she be able to get her whatever help she needed?

As we'll explain in this chapter, there are many causes of bipolar disorder, and different factors play a greater or lesser role at different points in a teenager's development. You've probably asked yourself the same questions that Karen is asking herself:

- How did my teenager get this illness?
- Did I pass it on?
- Did I cause it with my parenting?
- What can be done to treat it?

You're wise to gather as much information as you can about what causes bipolar disorder in teenagers. Not only will it alleviate the guilt that many parents adopt so readily but it will also, as Karen intuited, help you arrive at the best possible treatment for your son or daughter. Knowing that biology is so intricately involved in the onset of bipolar disorder will help you see that your parenting isn't to blame; your teen was already predisposed to the illness. But looking into the environmental and psychological factors that contribute to the illness and play a big role in triggering episodes will steer you to the best approach to managing symptoms: both psychotherapy and medication together, rather than as substitutes for one another.

The Biopsychosocial Model of Causes and Treatments

What every parent of a teen with bipolar disorder wants is to stabilize the child's symptoms, avoid triggering new episodes, and enhance the teen's life functioning. We've found those goals eminently achievable when you use (1) medication treatment to control biological vulnerabilities, (2) psychotherapy to teach coping skills to lessen the impact of stress, and

(3) family communication and problem-solving skills to enhance the protective effects of the family environment. This three-pronged approach is called *biopsychosocial* because it helps us grasp how biological, psychological, and social (or environmental) factors all contribute to the disorder and then how to address each of these factors—with medicine (*bio*), therapy (*psycho*), and interpersonal and coping skills (*social*). This three-pronged model is even more effective than the sum of its parts because each facet is designed to reduce illness cycling from a different angle and to strengthen the contributions of the other facets. Together, they form a pretty powerful intervention package. In Chapters 9–13 you'll see this multifaceted approach in action, where we'll give practical suggestions for minimizing stressors that trigger mood episodes and maximizing the protective effects of your teenager's environment.

Vulnerability and Stress

One way to understand teenage bipolar disorder is to think of genetic inheritance combined with environmental triggers. A child can come into this world with a predisposition to bipolar disorder—a disordered set of genes, a frontal cortex that does not adequately inhibit emotions, a neurological system that overproduces the neurotransmitter dopamine—but a set of environmental circumstances may set it off. For example, some kids with a genetic predisposition may develop bipolar disorder only if repeatedly and severely abused sexually or physically in the context of a highly stressful and unsupportive family environment. But that doesn't mean all teens with bipolar disorder have been abused— far from it. Parents like Karen need to understand that many teens with bipolar disorder have had a relatively healthy upbringing but are strongly genetically wired to develop the disorder, such as having first-degree relatives (parents, siblings, or children) with bipolar disorder on both sides of the family. Apparently this wasn't the case in Lola's family, which is not unusual. The combination of factors that can cause bipolar disorder can be much more complicated.

Vulnerabilities can be genetic (inherited), biological (disordered brain chemistry or brain structure or neural circuitry that has changed in some way), or psychological (problematic coping mechanisms, such as the tendency to blame yourself every time something goes wrong). Stress can be caused by factors entirely outside the person, such as negative life events, or it can be brought about through the teen's own behavior (for example, initiating stressful family arguments, rejection by peers). You

111

may have noticed how your teen seems to create stressful situations and then react to them. For example, Lola would have temper tantrums at her friends' houses and often run away crying, one time in the middle of the night. It wasn't surprising that friends on the receiving end of this behavior stopped calling her.

In one way of thinking, vulnerability and stress interact with each other so that when vulnerability is high (for example, multiple members of a teen's family pedigree have the disorder) only a small amount of stress will result in a mood disorder. When vulnerability is low (for example, only an aunt or an uncle had depression but not bipolar disorder), the teen may not get the disorder unless a major stressor hits (a severe car accident, a natural disaster like 2005's Hurricane Katrina). We really don't have enough studies to know whether this theory is valid, however. For example, we don't know if a stressful event can cause bipolar disorder when no genetic history is present.

We do know that there are factors that affect teenagers more than other age groups. For example, teens are more likely to use stimulating drugs like cocaine, which can activate biochemical imbalances. They are more strongly affected by peer pressures and rejection by peers than younger kids. A first attempt at a romantic and sexual relationship may end badly, leading the teen to question her worth, develop depressive symptoms, and make a suicide attempt (which is what happened to Lola). And, as you well know, family conflict often reaches a peak during the teen years. It is important to keep these age-related issues in mind when trying to understand how your teen developed symptoms.

Risk and Protective Factors

In our view, it's more useful to ask, "How did my teen develop symptoms this most recent time?" than "How did he or she develop the disorder?" You may never arrive at a conclusive answer to the second question, but investigating the first can give you valuable information that will make it easier to prevent future episodes. This is not to say that all the same factors will be at work in triggering each episode. One of your teen's episodes could be related to a relationship breakup and another to the death of a grandparent. Yet you may be able to identify some common precipitating element—in this case, the loss of people close to her—that will help you predict and protect your child from future episodes.

Risk factors are events, situations, dysfunctional coping mechanisms, or biological factors that increase the chances that your teen will develop the illness or experience a recurrence of it. So a teen who has had one manic episode is vulnerable to another but is especially vulnerable if she's using drugs. Alcohol or drug abuse is just one risk factor; others can include sudden disruptions to the sleep–wake cycle, conflict-ridden interpersonal situations, and intensive family conflict. Protective factors are health habits that decrease the chances of illness when a child is predisposed to it. These can include regular daily routines and sleep–wake cycles, supportive friendships and family relationships, and good relationships with treatment personnel.

How Bipolar Disorder Develops among Teens: The Kindling Theory

The theory of kindling, although controversial, is important to understand when trying to make sense of why your teen needs treatment sooner rather than later. According to this theory, a combination of stress and genetic vulnerability causes the nervous system to get more and more unstable, eventually provoking a full mood disorder episode. Then the brain becomes increasingly sensitized with each later manic or depressive episode, until episodes occur with only minor stressors or without even being triggered by environmental stress at all. In other words, stressful events like relationship breakups can play a more powerful causal role early in the illness than later. Over time, teens who are not getting adequate treatment for bipolar disorder can have recurrences closer and closer together and with increasing severity, leading to more episodes and resistance to treatment. Conversely, early intervention aimed at controlling symptoms may slow down or even stop this process.

In making sense of the kindling theory, consider first the prefrontal cortex, a part of the limbic system of the brain. The limbic system is involved in mood, emotion perception and arousal, sleep, motivation, and the associations between emotions and memories. One study found that bipolar children misclassified faces with neutral expressions as more hostile and fear-producing than did healthy children. Misclassifications of faces as hostile were related to increased activation of key structures in the limbic system, notably the amygdala, the nucleus accumbens, and the ventral prefrontal cortex. The prefrontal cortex is important in problem solving, decision making, planning, and deciding whether to express strong emotions (like rage). It's also involved in sustaining attention and concentration. Think of it as the "executive" of your teenager's brain.

Prolonged bipolar illness is believed to cause the prefrontal cortex and other areas of the limbic system such as the hippocampus and amygdala to suffer the gradual loss of nerve cells. This loss in turn (1) reduces the ability of this part of the brain's circuitry to regulate moods, (2) makes it harder for the teen to plan and problem-solve (executive functioning), and (3) increases the teen's resistance to treatment. A child or teen's developing juvenile brain may be especially susceptible to neuronal cell loss with repeated manic episodes. It's like a tire that runs over a nail: you can repair it, but the tire will be weaker where the nail damaged it and more susceptible to a blowout when the next nail comes along.

The good news is that interventions that decrease stress and improve the teen's ability to control mood could preserve both prefrontal function and the integrity of the brain cells. Learning to deal with peer pressure, for example, may render these kinds of pressures less likely to provoke mood swings, kind of like swerving your car to avoid hitting a nail. Likewise, taking medications regularly makes episodes less likely to occur, leading to less loss of brain cells in the limbic system.

Not everyone subscribed to the kindling theory as of this writing, and not all research studies have found it a valid explanation for the progressive nature of bipolar illness. Nevertheless, one review of bipolar studies found that people who've had multiple episodes benefit less from drug treatments, suffer more disability, and have more changes to the brain. *The key point is that effective treatment early in the illness may protect teens from a worsening course of the illness.* Research has shown that this treatment should be both pharmacological (for example, mood-stabilizing medications) and psychosocial (for example, individual or family therapy). We'll say more about these treatments in subsequent chapters, but keep the kindling model in mind as we talk about the individual roles of genetics, biology, and stress.

Where Is the Evidence That My Teen Inherited the Disorder?: Constructing Your Family Pedigree

When Lola was diagnosed, her psychiatrist asked Karen to bring in information on Lola's family pedigree. Karen's conclusion was that several family members were moody and that Lola's grandmother was "depressive." But no one in the family tree seemed to have bipolar disorder: no one had had a manic episode, spent a lot of money in one place, had multiple marriages and jobs, or moved about from place to place. This raised a question in her mind: If no one else in the family had the disorder, could Lola have been misdiagnosed?

There is little question that bipolar disorder runs in families, but people differ considerably in how many of their relatives are affected and with which disorders. To see if your teen is genetically at risk, start with the following exercise: complete the family pedigree chart on page 116. Circles are female relatives and squares are male relatives. Consider your teen's siblings, both parents, grandparents on both sides, and aunts and uncles. Make a list of everyone in the tree, their relationship to your teen, their age, and, if they have passed on, how they died. Ask yourself questions such as: How did this person die? Any possibility it was a suicide? Was he able to work consistently, or did he jump from job to job? Was she moody, temperamental, angry or violent? Did he have a drinking or a drug problem? If hospitalized, what was it for? Did she take antidepressants or lithium? Did he shut himself up in his room for long periods of time, unable to get out of bed?

Your teen may have inherited a vulnerability to the disorder from your side or her other biological parent's side of the family. If possible, ask the other parent to fill out the chart as well, or fill it out with what you know about his or her lineage.

Mark on the chart any person in the family tree you think may have had the disorder or some form of it. When considering other forms of bipolar disorder, we think of a spectrum of disorders: the genetic predisposition to bipolar disorder may be reflected in depression without mania, suicidal attempts or completions, alcoholism or drug abuse, hyperthymic personalities (a person who is constantly running, agitated, aggressive, and over the top), and cyclothymic temperaments (people who cycle back and forth between high and low moods without ever getting seriously manic or depressed).

When filling out your chart, keep in mind that many of these disorders do not strike until after age 18 and even in the late 20s or early 30s. This is particularly true of depression, which often affects men and women in middle age. Don't be surprised if many of your teen's first-degree or second-degree (aunts, uncles) relatives have disorders that don't seem related in any obvious way to bipolar disorder. These can include anxiety or panic symptoms, obesity or eating disorders, alcoholism, aggression that has led to legal problems, or ADHD. As we discussed in Chapter 3, these disorders often occur along with bipolar illness. In addition, the illness can get worse with successive generations and have an earlier onset. For example, the bipolar genes may have manifested as

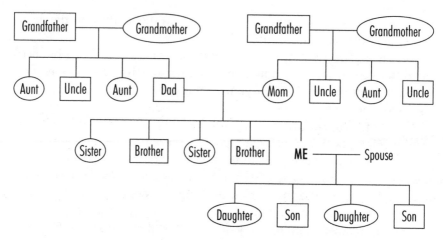

Family Pedigree Chart

mild depression in your parents' generation, which did not hit until after they had had their own kids; more severe depression and moodiness in your and your spouse's generation, which may have been noticed first in college; and full bipolar disorder in your own children during the teen or late childhood years.

Don't be surprised if you see a variety of family members affected by disorders that are considered to be within the bipolar spectrum. If so, you should have some confidence that your teen has been diagnosed correctly. (Also keep in mind that the family pedigree can aid your teen's treatment: if a first-degree relative also has bipolar disorder and has done well on lithium, for example, your teen may do well on lithium too.)

Family and Twin Genetic Studies

Most of the studies of bipolar disorder and genetics have asked a very simple question: What percentage of the first-degree relatives of bipolar individuals had the disorder or some form of it? These studies are often flawed because we can't interview these relatives directly. The rates from these studies probably underestimate how prevalent the illness is in family pedigrees. But one thing is clear, no matter what the methodology: bipolar illness is highly heritable, much more a matter of genetics than environment. This is not to say that the environment is not important: It is incredibly important when we try to understand why certain kids relapse very frequently and others don't. As we've said, it's best to understand the illness as a combination of genetics and environment. But in terms of the strength of various causes, genetics trumps the others.

The rate of mood disorders (including bipolar disorder and various types of depression) in the parents, siblings, and children of people with bipolar disorder averages about

The heritability of bipolar disorder is between 59 and 87%. This means that the original cause of the illness is related more to genetics than to environment. Recurrences of the illness can be strongly affected by stress, even if the original onset was not stress-related.

20–25%. Think about what this statistic means for your teen: if he has five first-degree relatives (for example, two parents and three siblings), on average, one will have a mood disorder. Of this 20–25%, about 14% will develop just depression and about 9% will develop the full highs and lows of bipolar disorder. So even though there is an elevated risk to family members, the greater probability is that first-degree relatives won't be affected at all.

When you complete your and your spouse's pedigree, you may notice other psychiatric problems besides mood disorders. The offspring of any adult with bipolar disorder have a fourfold greater chance of developing a mood disorder (depression or bipolar disorder) than the offspring of parents without psychiatric illness. But they are also at a 2.7 times higher risk of developing *any* kind of psychiatric disorder. In fact, between 50 and 60% of the offspring of parents with bipolar disorder have some type of psychiatric disorder, especially mood, anxiety, ADHD, and disruptive behavior disorders. So the more you see these illnesses appearing in your and your spouse's family tree, the more likely it is that the diagnosis of bipolar disorder your teen has received is correct.

Studies of identical twins consistently show that when one identical twin has bipolar or another mood disorder, the chances that his or her cotwin has bipolar disorder are high, averaging 57%. So, there is a greater than 50/50 chance that identical twins will both have mood disorders. If twins are nonidentical, meaning they are as similar genetically as any other siblings, the risk goes down to 14%.

What Does the Genetic Evidence Mean for My Child?

This can be a very emotional question for parents. Most of us would like to be grandparents one day, and it's understandable to worry that your bipolar teen will pass on his genes to the next generation. Our position on this is more practical: a teen who grows into a stable adult and has a strong partnership or marriage should be able to have children. Again, the risk of mood disorder to offspring is about four times higher than average, but the odds are still against your grandchildren developing the illness. We're not aware of any evidence that people with bipolar disorder do not make good parents, and, in fact, many of the people we work with are excellent parents. But everything rides on mood stability. Understandably, the children of a parent who is in and out of hospitals, on and off medications, or abusing substances will undoubtedly be affected negatively.

If your teen is the first in your family to develop the illness, her diagnosis may cause you to ask whether your other children will develop bipolar disorder. It is impossible to say in any given case, but the chances are relatively low that a full sibling will develop bipolar disorder (estimates of risk range from 7 to 10%) or major depressive disorder (15 to 25%). If one or more parents also has bipolar disorder, the chances that additional children will get it go up proportionately. If you see signs like irritability, overly silly or giddy moods, inappropriate displays of sexuality, rapid mood swings, or progressive social withdrawal in your teen's siblings, you may want to have them evaluated (as in Chapter 3). But keep in mind that your other children may be reacting to the stresses and strains of having a bipolar sibling, and/or may be vying for attention by displaying the same symptoms. This is more likely if the sibling is younger than your bipolar teen.

What If My Teen Has No Family History?

If your family tree shows no family history of mood disorders and you really want to get to the bottom of this, consider asking your siblings, parents, or grandparents for information about relatives you don't know much about. The ill person could have been several generations back and may never have been diagnosed or treated. Sometimes, though, there really is no history of bipolar illness. In this case the illness could have been brought on by a neurological problem (for example, a blow to the head as a youngster) or hidden drug abuse. A current theory of schizophrenia is that some cases of the illness can be attributed to viruses the mother contracted while pregnant or birth complications like low birth weight, anoxia, or preeclampsia. Research by Mani Pavuluri and her colleagues at the University of Illinois showed that pregnancy and birth complications were important risk factors in the onset of childhood bipolar disorder as well.

A teen who has no family history may still respond well to the medications typically used for bipolar disorder, such as lithium, divalproex sodium, lamotrigine, or atypical antipsychotics (see Chapter 6).

What Role Does Stress Play in Bipolar Episodes?

We really don't know if bipolar illness can be brought on by severe stress when there is no genetic vulnerability. We do know that depression can be brought on by stress, as can posttraumatic stress disorder, but the severe mood swings characteristic of bipolar disorder have a more strongly genetic and biological basis.

Nonetheless, stress can play a significant role in triggering your teen's recurrences or periods of symptom worsening. Think about the last time your teen had an episode of rage, or became giddy and silly and began sleeping less, or became depressed, suicidal, and morose. In most cases, you'll be able to identify stress triggers that played a role in the development of the episode. Some of these stressors will have been directly caused by the teen, and others will have arisen independently. To help you think this through, complete the exercise on the following page.

We have filled out the first two examples. You may want to substitute an event like Christmas, end of school, or Thanksgiving for a particular date, since reliably charting the onset of episodes can be difficult. Try to distinguish manic and hypomanic from mixed or depressed episodes. List all events and family conflicts, even if you aren't sure if they played a significant role in your teen's episode, or even if you're fairly certain your teen caused them. If you have a number of examples, you may be able to identify stress triggers that routinely precipitate episodes. For example, for the 14-year-old girl in the examples above, losing the structure of the school day was consistently associated with a worsening of her symptoms.

Stress triggers aren't always bad things. For example, some teens have hypomanic "blips" when they meet new potential romantic partners, do well in sports or drama, or earn some kind of public recognition. Some kids get depressed when positive things happen. For example, moving to a newer, bigger house may seem like a positive event for all, but it can also involve the loss of friendships or the comfort of a well-known neighborhood.

WHAT ROLE HAVE STRESS OR LIFE CHANGES PLAYED IN YOUR TEENAGER'S RECURRENCES?

Date of last episode	Type (manic, hypomanic, mixed, depressed)	Type of stress (describe)
March (spring break)	Mixed	School break; conflict with teacher prior to break; arguments with siblings
Mid-June (end of school)	Hypomanic	End of school; dating new guy

From *The Bipolar Teen* by David J. Miklowitz and Elizabeth L. George. Copyright 2008 by The Guilford Press.

What Kinds of Stressors Affect Bipolar Teens?

Surprisingly little research has been done on stress in bipolar teens. Most of the research concerns bipolar adults, although many of the findings probably apply to teens as well. We know that life events such as significant losses can set off depressive episodes. Research by our group found that stress plays a strong role in bipolar disorder among teens. Not surprisingly, the kinds of stress teens identified most often were those related to families (for example, parents undergoing a separation) and events involving peers (for example, romantic conflicts). Teens with high life-stress scores—particularly stress in intimate relationships—showed less improvement over 1 year in depressive and manic symptoms. Chronic strains in family and other close relationships took their greatest toll on the mood states of older adolescents (16- to 17-year-olds).

Sleep–Wake Cycle Disruption

Of course, any adolescent—bipolar or not—will be affected by peer or family stress. What is unique about the role of stress in bipolar illness is its effects on the sleep–wake cycle. A study by Susan Malkoff-Schwartz and her colleagues at the University of Pittsburgh found that bipolar manic episodes among adults were often preceded by events that disrupted people's sleep–wake cycles. In the 8 weeks before mania began, vulnerable people had at least once stayed up late (for example, to care for a sick child), experienced a change in time zones, or shifted job hours.

Part of being a teenager is staying out late with friends, going to parties, or being "wired" before going to bed. This means that teens with bipolar disorder have to take extra measures to keep very regular sleeping routines, even on the weekends. Going to bed at the same time, waking up at the same time, and not dramatically shifting routines like eating or exercising can all be important to maintaining mood stability. We will talk more about how to actually put this into practice in Chapter 10.

High Conflict in the Family

As explained in Chapter 4, we've found in several studies that teens in families high in "expressed emotion" tend to do worse than those who live in calm, low-conflict households. So negative back-and-forth interchanges between parents and teens and intense conflict or competition between siblings can serve as stressors that activate underlying biological

121

vulnerabilities. Consider this exchange between a mother and her 14-year-old daughter with bipolar disorder:

> MOTHER: I told you it was time to shut down the computer and head off to bed.
>
> DAUGHTER: (*angrily*) I will!
>
> MOTHER: That's what you said the last four times. I don't want to come in here again.
>
> DAUGHTER: (*defensive*) Would you get out of my room?
>
> MOTHER: Terri, I will *not* tolerate that tone of voice in this house!
>
> DAUGHTER: OK! Just leave me *alone*!
>
> MOTHER: You are being very disrespectful!
>
> DAUGHTER: I said I'd go to bed! Now will you get out of here!?
>
> MOTHER: I will after I see you turn off the computer.
>
> DAUGHTER: (*enraged, agitated, throws book off desk, throws pencils on floor*) There! Satisfied?

Sound familiar? The mother's point of view is understandable, and she was clearly tired of having to nag her daughter and be shouted down in the process. But notice how the teen is escalating in this encounter. Bipolar kids' mood swings can easily be triggered by these interchanges, much more than ordinary teens. Cognitively, they have trouble shifting their attention immediately and can get frustrated when such a shift is demanded by the situation. Terri's mother would have been better off ending the conversation at "I don't want to come in here again," and, if necessary, imposing consequences later.

Protecting against the stress of volatile family relationships requires families with a bipolar teen to have better communication skills (see Chapter 9) than other families. Both you and your teen will have to practice these skills to make them work for you in day-to-day life.

How Do Stress and Biological Vulnerability Interact to Become Bipolar Episodes?

Knowing that your teen has certain biological imbalances that are set off by stress can help you understand why, for example, she might fly into an uncontrollable rage when she can't watch her favorite TV program. Bipolar teens get upset by the same things that ordinary teens do, but because of their unique biology they react much more strongly. Missing a TV program is not enough to set off a manic or depressive episode, but if the teen is already starting to cycle, little things like this can accumulate and worsen symptoms.

The reason it's so important to avoid stress and thereby avoid triggering these mood swings is not just to make your life easier on any particular day—though that's certainly a valuable benefit. As we said earlier, with more and more of these episodes, the brain begins to suffer damage that, in turn, makes moods harder for the teen to regulate. In kids with mood disorders, stress can lead to the overproduction of the hormone cortisol. When cortisol is continually overproduced, cells in the hippocampus eventually can be damaged or destroyed. The hippocampus has many functions, but most importantly it is part of the limbic system, as discussed earlier.

Stress hormones are, however, only part of the picture. We know that among bipolar adults too much or too little of certain neurotransmitters is produced at different phases of the illness—which is why you may have heard bipolar disorder called a "biochemical imbalance." These neurotransmitters include dopamine, serotonin, norepinephrine, and gamma-aminobutyric acid (GABA). The nerve cells also have receptors for neurotransmitters, kind of like a lock that's activated by a key. These receptors can become over- or undersensitive to certain neurotransmitters like dopamine or serotonin, which can cause cells to fire either too often or too seldom.

Whether such imbalances are causing your teen's bipolar symptoms is difficult to say because they are very hard to measure directly (and even if we could do so, some of the same imbalances are associated with ADHD, schizophrenia, and other childhood psychiatric disorders, not just bipolar disorder). But if you view stress hormones and neurotransmitters run amok as part of the biological aspect of the cause of bipolar illness, you'll understand why medications intended to correct these biochemical imbalances are often prescribed. Divalproex sodium (Depakote), for example, enhances the action of GABA and inhibits the activity of the protein kinase C pathways. Atypical antipsychotics like quetiapine (Seroquel) block the action of dopamine and serotonin. Unfortunately, these mechanisms of action do not come without costs in the form of side effects. We'll tell you more about each medication and what it does in Chapter 6.

From Seeking a Cause to Seeking Treatment

No one can say what combination of factors produced bipolar disorder in your teen or any other. In fact, these biology–environment "equations" can change at different points of development, with biology playing a stronger role at some stages and environment at others. What's important to know is that genetic, neuroanatomical, biochemical, and stress factors all combine to produce episodes of bipolar disorder, and that means the more you respond with a multipronged treatment plan, the greater your teen's chances of managing symptoms and preventing recurrences.

Karen took heart in knowing that "bad parenting" doesn't cause bipolar disorder. Lola did not become bipolar because her parents divorced. Teens do not develop this illness because their parents were immature when they got married or didn't give them enough love and understanding. Nor is Lola or your teen doing this on purpose. On some conscious or unconscious level, all teenagers with bipolar disorder want to have better control over their mood states, if for no other reason than that their home environment would be more peaceful and they'd have more friends. But they are fighting with their own brain and brain chemistry. Try to keep this in mind when you find yourself getting understandably angry at your teenager's arrogance, hostility, oppositionality or disrespectfulness.

In the next chapters, we'll make these recommendations more concrete. Karen's understanding of the biology behind bipolar disorder strengthened her conviction that her daughter needed the help of medications. But which ones? Chapter 6 explains which medications are most helpful to teens with bipolar disorder and the evidence for their effectiveness. She also decided Lola needed to have the benefit of individual therapy so she could learn to manage stress and take responsibility for her own health as she matured. Family counseling sounded like a good idea as well, not because she and Lola had a bad relationship but because they were up against a lot more than most mother–daughter pairs. What kinds of therapy are available and how to decide what you need are the subjects of Chapter 7. Finally, Karen and Lola and all parents of bipolar teens need ways to cope and manage in the family environment so the teenager has a better chance of sustaining recovery. You'll find out how in Chapter 9.

6　Medications for Bipolar Disorder in Teens

Sixteen-year-old Tyrone had been given "one useless medication after another," according to his mother, Harriet. He was being treated at an outpatient mental health center by a psychiatric nurse. She originally diagnosed him with conduct disorder and ADHD because of, as she put it, his "strong tendency toward juvenile delinquent activities" like breaking into an abandoned house. The nurse gave him a stimulant, Adderall. When he responded poorly and became increasingly aggressive, she added Haldol, a traditional antipsychotic medication that made him feel numb, dull, and restless. He stopped taking this medication against the nurse's advice and sank into what Harriet called a "combative depression." His nurse didn't agree that he was depressed and could only see the aggression and disruptive behavior, so she switched him to Topamax, a new anticonvulsant that has a record of treating impulse control problems in adults. That seemed to calm down his agitation for a while, but the depression continued. When Harriet finally convinced the nurse that Tyrone was also depressed, she prescribed Celexa, an antidepressant. This made him nervous, anxious, agitated, irritable, and sleepless.

Harriett decided to have Tyrone reevaluated by a child psychiatrist who specialized in mood disorders. This required a series of negotiations with Tyrone, who had lost much of his faith in doctors and medications. In fact, she discovered he had stopped taking the Haldol on his own and took the Topamax inconsistently.

The new psychiatrist recognized Tyrone's underlying bipolar disorder almost immediately and decided to start him on Depakote as well as an atypical antipsychotic, Seroquel. Over the next several weeks, he slowly tapered Tyrone off the Topamax and Celexa and lowered his dosage of Adderall. Within 2 months, Tyrone was more stable than Harriett had ever seen him; he had a more positive attitude about school, household chores, homework, and even his psychiatric treatments. His blood levels indicated he was taking his Depakote regularly, and the Seroquel was clearly helping with his agitation and sleep problems. He even agreed to try a session of psychotherapy with a psychologist recommended by the psychiatrist.

One of the biggest issues you may be facing is whether to give medications to your teenager. But even if you have decided on this course of treatment, which medications should your teen take, in what order, in what combinations, and at what dosages? This is a very complex illness. How do you treat the manias, the depressions, the psychosis, agitation, and any comorbid conditions? Does each problem require a separate medication? And what about side effects? How will they affect your child over the short and long term?

This chapter gives you some of the "brass tacks" information about how bipolar disorder in teens is treated with medications. Medication recommendations from a physician or psychiatric nurse can seem haphazard or even random (as illustrated by the twists and turns of Tyrone's treatment), but there is usually an underlying logic to them. You'll come away from this chapter knowing what medications are available (and their supporting evidence from research), how treatment of a manic or mixed episode differs from treatment of a depressive episode or from treatment for comorbid conditions, how "acute" treatment is different from "maintenance" treatment, and under what conditions medications may be switched, adjusted, or supplemented with other medications. We'll talk about how to identify and monitor the side effects of these medications and the importance of blood level monitoring. Chapter 8 is devoted to talking to your teen about medications and helping assure her consistency with them.

You will immediately be struck by a couple of things. First, teenagers usually require several different medications, and these may change at different phases of the illness. Research by Boris Birmaher and his colleagues at the University of Pittsburgh found that kids with bipolar disorder typically receive four or five medications! Second, you'll come to understand the trial-and-error process of choosing medications. Manic or depressive episodes often require a first-line treatment, a second-line treatment, and even a third-line treatment before stabilizing. There is a certain amount of research on what works for whom, but to date most of this has been on adults. Nonetheless, big strides are being made. As you'll learn in this chapter, we now have practice guidelines for psychiatrists to follow when treating children or adolescents with bipolar disorder. The psychiatrist who treated Tyrone had knowledge of these guidelines, and his success in treating Tyrone reflected it.

Why Medication Treatment?

We want to be very clear on our position regarding this aspect of treatment: *medication is an absolute necessity for controlling the mood swings and comorbid conditions of bipolar teens (and we wish to make clear that neither of us is associated with or funded by drug companies!).* You cannot substitute psychotherapy, alternative treatments (for example, vitamins, acupuncture, cranial–sacral therapy, omega-3 fatty acids [fish oil], St. John's wort, reiki, yoga) for any of the traditional medications we're about to discuss—there simply is no evidence for their effectiveness. Yes, medications come with risks. But so does not taking medications, whose risks include increased mood cycling, more recurrences, deteriorated school performance, and more treatment resistance. The cell loss that can occur in your teenager's developing brain can be minimized by early intervention, in the form of both medication and psychotherapy (see Chapter 7). Most teens have only a partial response to medications alone and need psychotherapy to help them accept their illness and gain coping strategies to function at their best level. So medications are only one part of a comprehensive treatment plan for a bipolar teen, but they are an indispensable part.

Many parents are hesitant to have their teen take medications, because little is known about their long-term effects. For teens who have mild symptoms that do not meet the diagnostic criteria for bipolar disorder, some parents opt for family or individual therapy first and medication only if symptoms worsen. At this stage, the purpose of therapy is preventive—to keep a difficult situation from getting worse. Nonetheless, we strongly recommend that you initiate medication if your teen is (1) symptomatic to the extent that he has difficulty functioning at school, home, or with peers, (2) at risk for harming himself or others, or (3) using illicit substances regularly.

To get an idea of what your teen's doctor might prescribe, review the box on page 128. It lists the drugs that are usually first, second, and third choices for treating mania or depression, plus ADHD or anxiety for teens with these common comorbid conditions.

127

MEDICATION CHOICES FOR THE MANAGEMENT OF CHILD AND ADOLESCENT BIPOLAR DISORDER

Episode type/ comorbid disorder	First line	Second line	Third line
Mania/ hypomania, moderate severity, *without* psychosis	Lithium or divalproex "monotherapy" or atypical antipsychotic	Alternate monotherapy, or augment first-line choice with lithium, valproate, or carbamazepine	Alternate monotherapy from (2), or use combination therapy with different mood stabilizer or SGA
Mania/ hypomania, severe, and/or *with* psychosis	SGA, lithium plus SGA, or divalproex plus SGA	Augmentation: two mood stabilizers (for example, lithium plus divalproex or carbamazepine), plus SGA	Lithium plus divalproex or carbamazepine plus different SGA from (2)
Depressive episode	Lithium or lamotrigine	Augment with quetiapine	Augment with citalopram (SSRI)
Comorbid ADHD	Long-acting methylphenidate stimulant compound (for example, Concerta)	Long-acting amphetamine compound (for example, Adderall)	Augment with bupropion (Wellbutrin)
Comorbid anxiety	Augment with divalproex	Augment with quetiapine	Augment with citalopram

Therapeutic serum levels for lithium are 0.8–1.2 mEq/L; for valproate, 85–110 mcg/ml; for carbamazepine, 8–11 mcg/ml

SGA = second-generation or "atypical" antipsychotic agent: risperidone, olanzapine, quetiapine, ziprasidone, or aripiprazole

Mood stabilizers = lithium, divalproex sodium (valproate), carbamazepine, lamotrigine

Stimulants = methylphenidate in all forms (for example, Concerta, Ritalin LA, Ritalin SR, Metadate), or amphetamine (for example, Dexedrine or Adderall)

Antidepressants = SSRIs (selective serotonin reuptake inhibitors)

Source: R. Kowatch and M. DelBello, personal communication, February 3, 2007.

General Principles of Medication Treatment

Whenever medication is prescribed for any illness, the doctor should choose a medication regimen that balances the benefits of the medicine against the side effects and economic costs. For teenage bipolar disorder, the goal is to achieve mood stability and better school, home, and social functioning with the least possible short- and long-term side effects and at the lowest cost to your family. If your teen has been medicated for bipolar disorder for many years, you're probably familiar with the importance of this balance. But there are other principles that underlie medication treatment, and it will help if you learn them and remember them—whether medication is new to you or familiar.

First, good pharmacotherapy begins with a thorough evaluation and diagnosis, not only of the mood disorder but also of any comorbid conditions. Because early-onset bipolar disorder can look just like ordinary depression or ADHD, the wrong medications, such as antidepressants alone, can be prescribed. A careful evaluation (see Chapter 3) can reduce this likelihood. Likewise, if a teen doesn't respond well to a medication, that doesn't mean the bipolar diagnosis is wrong or the wrong drug was chosen. It may mean that comorbid disorders haven't been identified or treated adequately. Dora did not know that her son, Allen, had ADHD as well as bipolar disorder or that he had ongoing, untreated anxiety that led to rage outbursts. Martha did not know that her son, Brad, was using cocaine so often that his divalproex (Depakote) was ineffective. So be patient with the sometimes lengthy and repetitive diagnostic process; it will save you and your teen much anguish later.

Second, you have to give medications a chance to work. The teen has to get up to a therapeutic level of the medication (more on this soon) for at least 4–6 weeks before we can know whether it's working. Lithium and the antidepressants can take as long as 8 weeks. So if your teen takes a new medication and you don't see benefits right away, it doesn't mean the medication trial has failed and a new medication should be tried. He may need a higher dosage to get to a therapeutic level, or it may be too soon to tell.

Third, most bipolar kids need several medications to get stable. Modern psychiatrists follow treatment algorithms or "drug decision trees" (see box on page 128). Because of the trial and error inherent in these algorithms, it won't be unusual for a teen who has just had a severe manic episode to be on a mood stabilizer (for example, lithium) and an atypical antipsychotic (for example, Seroquel), and maybe even another mood stabilizer as well (for example, Depakote). Kids who have se-

129

vere, unremitting depressions may need a mood stabilizer, an atypical antipsychotic, and an antidepressant. Kids who have mania and comorbid ADHD may need a mood stabilizer, an antipsychotic, and a stimulant like Ritalin.

Fourth, poor medication responses can mean that your teen is not taking the medications with enough regularity. Kids and adults with bipolar disorder often discontinue their medications without telling anyone. Doing this suddenly increases the likelihood of a recurrence. Even if a recurrence doesn't occur right away, ongoing mood symptoms won't stabilize. Cheryl was confused as to why her 16-year-old, Marissa, never seemed to fully stabilize—she was always somewhat hypomanic or dysthymic. When Cheryl learned that Marissa had been regularly missing her mood stabilizers on weekends, and never took them on days in which she was planning to see her boyfriend, it became clear why she never achieved an adequate therapeutic blood level.

Fifth, effective medication treatment requires an ongoing, solid relationship between you, your teenager, and your teen's psychiatrist. It's not enough for your teen to go in every 3 months for a 15-minute checkup. Your teen needs to feel comfortable calling the psychiatrist if she's having a crisis or a recurrence of symptoms, if she feels suicidal, or if she is having significant side effects. It will be much harder to do this if she doesn't feel comfortable with her doctor.

Sixth, your teen's doctor will need to see him often enough to monitor his blood levels. For example, if he's taking lithium, his doctor will want to conduct a blood test every month or so when the treatment is started to make sure your teen is within the established therapeutic range. If your teen is experiencing disturbing side effects (for example, poor balance, extreme nausea), his doctor will want to make sure he's not getting toxic blood levels. If your teen is taking olanzapine (Zyprexa) or another atypical antipsychotic, his doctor will want to test his blood lipid profiles—at least once a year and probably more frequently at the beginning of treatment—for evidence of metabolic dysfunction and to reduce the risk of diabetes.

With these principles in mind, you can see how drug treatment can go awry even when the right medications have been chosen. Many parents report that their child has tried various medications but still has not improved. This occurs because medication is one part of a larger puzzle, which includes a supportive psychiatrist, psychotherapy, family encouragement of medication adherence (Chapter 8), and your teen's appreciation of the nature of the disorder she is fighting. The "coping mantras"

COPING MANTRAS: MAXIMIZING THE CHANCES OF YOUR TEEN'S SUCCESS WITH MEDICATIONS

- Make sure your teen has had a thorough diagnostic evaluation.
- Be aware of how changes to medications affect your teen during the transition from acute to maintenance treatment (see below).
- Give medications a chance to work before changing them.
- Accept that your teen may need several medications to become stable.
- Make sure your teen is taking medications regularly and on schedule.
- Make sure your teen is having regular blood tests.
- Encourage a solid relationship between your teen and her psychiatrist.

listed in the box above should help you maximize the likelihood of success with drug treatment.

Acute versus Maintenance Treatment

Your teenager's doctor may want to change her medicines after she has been doing consistently well. You might find yourself asking, "Why fix it if it ain't broke?" It's important to understand that the treatments for the *acute* episode of your teen's mania or depression are different from *maintenance* treatment. The purpose of acute treatment is to stabilize an existing episode: to bring a manic child back to normalcy (euthymia) or to bring a depressed child back to feeling healthy, if not always positive or upbeat. It can also mean bringing a rapid-cycling or mixed teen to a stable mood state. So acute treatment means treating the symptoms that are present. Usually, the number of medications needed and the dosages required will be highest during this phase.

During maintenance treatment, the purpose of medications is to keep your teen's mood stable and to prevent future recurrences (or at least to minimize the severity of the episodes that do occur). It aims to reduce "subthreshold" symptoms like irritability or mild depression, reduce the risk of suicide, reduce your teen's problems in the academic and social milieu, and generally promote her long-term health. Also called *preventative treatment,* maintenance treatment can often mean discontinuing one or more medications (for example, stopping an antidepressant), lowering dosages, or otherwise simplifying the regimen. For some teens, it can mean continuing the same medications they were on during the acute phase. Tapering or stopping medications has to be done gradually in an environment that is safe and calm.

As we'll talk more about in subsequent chapters, you have to be especially attuned to early warning signs of recurrence during maintenance treatment. Psychotherapy is of greatest value during the maintenance phase because the immediate crisis has passed and your teen can begin to develop coping skills for preventing future episodes.

The Mood Stabilizers

The main classes of medications for bipolar disorder are mood stabilizers and atypical antipsychotics. The major medications in these classes, their generic and trade names, and their side effects are listed in the box on page 133. The two most commonly used mood stabilizers for teens are lithium and divalproex sodium (also called valproic acid or valproate, and usually dispensed as Depakote), and more recently lamotrigine. Other mood stabilizers include carbamazepine and, possibly, topiramate.

What distinguishes mood stabilizers from other medications are their targets. They each aim to stabilize manic or depressive symptoms (and sometimes both). Some of them (notably lithium) have a record as maintenance agents (preventing future episodes) as well as acute agents (controlling the current episode), at least in studies of adults. Moreover, none of them *cause* mania or depression. Whereas this last point may seem obvious, there are medications used regularly for bipolar disorder— like the selective serotonin reuptake inhibitors (SSRIs)—that sometimes alleviate depression at the cost of initiating new manic symptoms.

Lithium

Lithium, the "old standby," has been in regular use for bipolar disorder since the 1960s. It has the largest research base supporting its use. Lithium's discovery is a story of scientific serendipity. Although in the 1800s "lithium bromide" had been in use for stress, agitation, and overexcitement, its use in bipolar illness began in 1949 by a psychiatrist in Australia, John Cade. Dr. Cade found that injecting guinea pigs with lithium calmed them down and made them less active. He then gave it to one of his manic–depressive patients, who recovered from his illness very quickly and was able to function outside of the hospital for the first time. Unfortunately, the man later went off his lithium, perhaps presaging the

SPECIFICS ON THE MOOD STABILIZERS AND ATYPICAL ANTIPSYCHOTICS PRESCRIBED FOR CHILDREN AND ADOLESCENTS WITH BIPOLAR DISORDER

Generic name	Brand names	Tablet sizes (mg)	Blood levels	Major side effects
Lithium carbonate	Lithonate Eskalith Lithotabs Lithane	150, 300, 600	0.8–1.2 mEq/L	Thirst, hypothyroidism, nausea, acne, weight gain, excessive urination
Lithium carbonate (slow release)	Eskalith CR Cibalith-S	300, 450		
	Lithobid (slow release)	300		
Lithium citrate	Liquid form	5 cc = 300 mg		
Divalproex sodium	Depakene	250, 500, 50 mg/ml	80–120 mg/L	Elevated liver enzymes, menstrual and/or hormonal irregularities, hair loss, weight gain, sleepiness
	Depakote	125, 250, 500		
	Depakote ER	250, 500		
	Depakote sprinkles	125		
Lamotrigine	Lamictal	25, 100, 150, 200	N/A	Rash (with varying degrees of severity)
	Lamictal chewable	2, 5, 25		
Carbamazepine, Carbamazepine XR	Tegretol	100, 200	8–11 mg/L	Elevated liver enzymes, aplastic anemia, rash
	Tegretol XR	100, 200, 400		
	Tegretol suspension	20 mg/ml		
	Equetro	100, 200, 300		
	Carbatrol	100, 200, 300		
	Atretol	200		

(cont.)

133

SPECIFICS ON MOOD STABILIZERS AND ATYPICAL ANTIPSYCHOTICS (cont.)

Generic name	Brand names	Tablet sizes (mg)	Blood levels	Major side effects
Topiramate	Topamax	25, 50, 100, 200	N/A	Word-finding problems, decreased appetite, nausea, diarrhea, vision problems, tingling sensations, kidney stones
	Topamax sprinkles	15, 25		
Olanzapine	Zyprexa	2.5, 5, 7.5, 10, 15, 20	N/A	Weight gain, sleepiness, elevated prolactin levels
	Zydis	5, 10, 15, 20		
Quetiapine	Seroquel	25, 50, 100, 200, 300, 400	N/A	Weight gain, dizziness, sleepiness
Risperidone	Risperdal	0.25, 0.5, 1, 2, 3, 4	N/A	Muscle stiffness and rigidity, leaky breasts, abnormal menstrual cycle in females, sleepiness
	Risperdal-M	0.5, 1, 2, 3, 4		
	Risperdal oral solution	1 mg/mL		Elevated prolactin levels
Ziprasidone	Geodon	20, 40, 60, 80	N/A	Sleepiness, dizziness, muscle stiffness
Aripiprazole	Abilify	2, 5, 10, 15, 20, 30	N/A	Restlessness, nausea, insomnia, sleepiness
	Abilify discmelt	10, 15		
	Abilify oral solution	1 mg/mL		

Source: Adapted and updated with permission from Kowatch and DelBello (2003).

unwillingness of many patients with bipolar disorder to continue taking lithium because of its side effects.

Lithium is the only medication that has been approved by the U.S. Food and Drug Administration (FDA) for the treatment of mania among adolescents (although most of the medications you'll read about in this chapter are prescribed by doctors "off-label," without FDA approval; see the box below). It has a long record of support for the treatment of adults. About 65% of bipolar adolescents show a positive response to lithium (for example, their manic or mixed symptoms decrease). Kids who have the classic symptoms of mania, like elated mood, grandiosity, and hypersexuality, are the most likely to respond well. Unfortunately, only about half of manic children or teens respond to lithium by itself—most need other medications like Depakote or Seroquel as well to fully control mania.

Lithium is also a good preventive agent, although it hasn't been studied adequately among teens. Research by Michael Strober and colleagues at UCLA found that, over 18 months, only 35% of teens who started off in a manic episode had a recurrence if they stuck with lithium. Among those who did not, the rate was 92%. The effects of continuous lithium treatment in preventing recurrence were less impressive in a controlled treatment trial of teens with mania conducted by Vivian Kafantaris and her associates at the Zucker Hillside Hospital in New York.

What about depression? There's not much research on it (unfortunately, a phrase you'll hear frequently in this chapter). One 6-week study of 27 bipolar teens found that half showed a good response to lithium when it was being used alone to treat depression. Lithium has a reasonably good record of treating depressive episodes, suicidal thinking, and

WHY IS MY TEENAGER BEING GIVEN MEDICATIONS NOT APPROVED BY THE FDA?

Most of the psychiatric medications prescribed for kids with bipolar disorder have not been approved by the FDA. This is not a cause for alarm—it doesn't mean they are dangerous or ineffective or that the doctor is behaving inappropriately. It also doesn't mean that your teen is sicker than other children. It typically means that the controlled experimental studies with children and teenagers that would lead to FDA approval have not yet been done. If you are concerned about this, ask your teen's psychiatrist to explain why she prefers to prescribe a medication that is off-label instead of lithium.

suicidal behavior among adults. These are important considerations because teens are prone to impulsive suicide attempts (see Chapters 12 and 13).

Lithium is a reasonable first option for a teen who is manic, depressed, or mixed. Tyrone might have responded well to lithium if in fact his conduct problems were masking an underlying mania. Lithium does not work immediately—most treatment guidelines suggest waiting 6–8 weeks for a full response. You will probably start seeing beneficial effects within the first week or two after your teen starts the drug, but be patient. Your teen may show rapid improvement from mania once the proper blood level of lithium has been reached but still have depressive symptoms. Lithium may stabilize the depression later on, or your teen may need to take a second medication with antidepressant properties, like lamotrigine or quetiapine.

Lithium Dosing and Side Effects

Lithium is usually dispensed under names like Eskalith, Lithonate, Lithobid, or Cibalith-S (see the box on page 133). It comes in 300-mg or 450-mg tablets, and the typical teen takes about 25 mg per kilogram of weight per day. That means a teen who weighs 65 kg (about 143 pounds) will take somewhere between 1,200 mg and 1,600 mg of lithium. Younger, smaller children can often get by with less than that. When mania is not severe, the doctor may recommend a low dose (for example, 600 mg) and increase the dose later if there's a recurrence.

We usually suggest having blood drawn to determine lithium levels every week or two for the first 1–2 months of treatment and then every month for the next 3 months. After that, blood levels may need to be taken only every 3 months or so. When the teen is ill, the physician usually tries to obtain a blood level of 1.0–1.2 milliequivalents per liter. Sometimes kids and teens need higher dosages than adults to make sure the concentrations of lithium in their brains reach therapeutic levels.

If your teen's blood test comes out too low or too high, you'll want to advocate for him with the physician. If the blood level falls below the therapeutic level, lithium may not be effective. If it rises above this level, he will probably have to take a lower dose. High doses put him at risk for *lithium toxicity*, in which the blood accumulates lithium at high levels. A teen who has become toxic will usually have problems with balance and coordination, severe stomach pains and diarrhea, blurred vision, severe shaking of the hands, slurring of speech, nausea and vomiting, and general disorientation or mental confusion (for example, not knowing where he is or what day it is). *If your teen shows these signs, get him to a doctor (either his psychiatrist or his general practitioner) immediately so that his blood level can be checked.* If he has lithium toxicity (as revealed, for example, by a level of 1.5 milliequivalents per liter or higher), he will need to stop taking lithium or drastically drop the dosage.

Your teen also has to be cautious about taking other medications that might interact poorly with lithium. For example, she should discuss the use of antibiotics or regular use of nonsteroidal anti-inflammatory medicines (such as Advil) with her physician. She should also not change her level of salt intake when she starts lithium. In addition, during the summer months your teen's lithium dose may need to be increased if he is more physically active and perspiring more regularly.

Don't be too surprised if your teen refuses to get her blood drawn. Many children and teens are afraid of having blood taken, and often this fear will color their feelings about the medications they take. Although having blood drawn is a minor issue for most adults, it can seem like a huge deal to a teen. If you feel strongly that your child should take lithium and have blood tests, try to get her desensitized to needle pricks. Some parents give their teen a cold soda to hold on their arm where the blood draw will occur. The teen's arm becomes numb, and then she gets to drink the soda as a treat after the blood draw. Ice could also numb the arm but isn't as much of a treat. Some clinics offer a cream that numbs the skin so the teen won't feel the needle. Treatments like behavioral exposure or systematic desensitization also may ease your teen's fears of needles. For a helpful online article on overcoming needle phobias, see *www.diabetesselfmanagement.com/article.cfm?aid=1702.*

Other side effects that are annoying to teens and adults include thirst, frequent urination, weight gain, fatigue, sedation, stomach irritation, diarrhea, shaking of the hands, acne, and memory problems. Long-term effects, although they are by no means inevitable, include hypothyroidism and kidney clearance problems. Some of these side effects can be controlled by lowering the dosage and by conducting regular thyroid and kidney functioning tests.

Divalproex Sodium (Valproate)

Divalproex sodium (valproate or valproic acid), usually dispensed under the names Depakote or Depakene, is an *anticonvulsant*, meaning it's one of the drugs whose main purpose is to treat epilepsy and other seizure disorders. Many but not all anticonvulsants also effectively stabilize mood. Divalproex is prescribed seven times as often as lithium for children and teens, probably because it seems to have more benign side effects, and people take it more regularly than lithium. Also, divalproex doesn't seem to have the stigma that lithium carries (some teens will automatically believe that taking lithium means you're crazy), perhaps because divalproex hasn't been around as long.

Divalproex works just as well as lithium in treating mania and may even work a bit faster. One 6-week trial involving children showed that 53% got better on divalproex, a rate significantly higher than lithium (38%). A study of prevention of recurrence among bipolar kids (average age 11) over 18 months indicated that the two medications were equally good at preventing recurrences once kids had been stabilized during the acute phase. Among adults, divalproex may work better than lithium in the treatment of mixed episodes and rapid cycling although this is controversial.

Like lithium, about half of teens who are manic will respond to divalproex when given by itself. Often, however, they will need adjunctive drugs. Research by Melissa DelBello and her colleagues at the University of Cincinnati School of Medicine found that the combination of divalproex with quetiapine (Seroquel), an atypical antipsychotic, was more powerful than divalproex alone in stabilizing manic episodes among adolescents. It may simply be that two medications are better than one, but this combination will probably be increasingly recommended for teens who become manic. It's not clear how good divalproex is at treating depression among youth—as of this writing there are no controlled studies.

Divalproex Dosing and Side Effects

Our 143-pound teenager would get about 1,300 mg of divalproex; a 110-pound teen would get about 1,000 mg (see the table on page 133). The 125-mg tablets can be obtained as "sprinkles" that your teen can put on his cereal. This preparation, along with a 500-mg extended release form, can reduce stomach irritation, which is one of divalproex's side effects.

Divalproex is not without its problems. Kids may feel nauseous or start vomiting at first, have stomach aches or irritation, or get shaky hands. These side effects usually disappear quickly, but over-the-counter nausea aids like ranitidine (Zantac) can help. Some teens experience hair loss (alopecia) or the growth of facial hair (hirsutism), which can be treated with vitamins containing selenium or zinc.

Because divalproex is metabolized by the liver, some people develop elevated liver enzymes, which can lead to liver inflammation and may require them to discontinue the drug. Some people develop thrombocytopenia, which is decreased production of blood platelets (cells in the blood needed for clotting). Your teen's doctor will want to prevent these conditions by conducting regular liver enzyme and blood platelet count tests.

As with lithium (and many of the other drugs discussed in this chapter, notably the atypical antipsychotics), the biggest problem for teenagers is usually weight gain. As you know, weight gain is a risk factor for many other diseases, such as diabetes, high blood pressure, and heart disease. The average teenager will gain approximately 5–6 pounds in the first 6 weeks of taking divalproex. Needless to say, teens—both boys and girls—are mortified by sudden weight gain, especially if they don't expect it. As a result, weight gain can be a major cause of nonadherence to this medication. The treatment for medication-induced weight gain, assuming the medication has been effective and warrants continuation, is usually just nutritional counseling and exercise. Your teen's psychiatrist should monitor your child's body weight and lipid profiles (which requires blood testing) and will probably switch to a different medication if her weight gain continues. He may also suggest adding a medication like metaforim or topiramate to help your teen lose weight.

A less likely although worrisome side effect of divalproex is an increased risk of *polycystic ovary syndrome* (PCOS) among girls. PCOS is a disorder of the endocrine system that goes along with lack of ovulation, overproduction of male hormones, and infertility. It carries a high long-term risk for coronary disease. Its symptoms are irregularity or absence of menstruation, weight gain, development of unwanted facial hair, and acne. Research in adult bipolar women by Hadine Joffe and associates of the Systematic Treatment Enhancement Program found that divalproex was associated with a 7.5 times greater rate of oligomenorrhea (infrequent or light menstruation) and hyperandrogenism (overproduction of male hormones) than other medications. This did not mean that all of the women in the study had PCOS, but they were at risk for developing it. To prevent PCOS, your daughter's doctor will need to regularly evaluate her menstrual regularity and look for the other symptoms. She may then refer your daughter to an endocrinologist.

This side effect profile may make divalproex seem like too much of a risk. Most of these side effects are, however, rare and can be controlled once they appear. Rather than rule out divalproex, talk to your teen's psychiatrist about how likely she is to develop these side effects. Not surprisingly, a teen with a history of menstrual problems is more likely to develop endocrine problems; kids with weight problems are more likely to gain weight rapidly. Be sure your teen's medical history is taken into account in medication decisions.

Lamotrigine (Lamictal)

Another anticonvulsant, lamotrigine (Lamictal), is increasingly being used to treat bipolar depressions and rapid cycling. As many as 50% of adults with bipolar depression respond to lamotrigine with improved mood. An 18-month relapse prevention study by Charles Bowden and colleagues of the University of Texas Health Science Center compared lamotrigine to lithium and found that lithium worked better than lamotrigine in preventing manic episodes, but lamotrigine was somewhat more effective in preventing depressive recurrences. It has some effects on preventing manic recurrences as well, although not as strong as its effects on depression. In fact, it seems to work well for depression when other medications have failed, sometimes when given by itself or when added to other medications.

Lamotrigine is one of the few medications that had received FDA approval for long-term maintenance treatment of bipolar disorder in adults as of this writing, although it had not yet received approval for the treatment of bipolar teens or children. In fact, to date it hasn't been studied in children much at all. One trial found an 84% response rate among children with bipolar depression, but because the study didn't compare the drug to a placebo, we don't really know exactly how effective it is.

Lamotrigine is one of the medications mentioned in Chapter 5 that seems to help regulate mood by correcting imbalances in neurotransmitters. It inhibits the release of neurotransmitters like norepinephrine and, like the SSRIs, blocks the reuptake of serotonin into the cells. Unlike lithium or divalproex, lamotrigine does not apparently cause weight gain, even among people who have weight problems. Unlike the SSRIs, lamotrigine does not seem to cause mania, hypomania, or rapid cycling, which is perhaps its biggest advantage over the other antidepressants.

What's the bad news? About 6% to 10% of people who take lamotrigine develop a skin rash. In rare instances (about one in 300), this rash can progress to Stevens–Johnson syndrome, a potentially fatal skin condition involving blistering or burning of the skin tissues or lining of the mucous membranes. If your teen develops a rash within the first 2–8 weeks of starting lamotrigine, her doctor will probably discontinue it. Those most at risk for the rash are younger, being treated simultaneously with divalproex, or those who abruptly discontinue their oral contraceptive medication. Starting at a high dosage or increasing the medication too quickly may lead to a rash as well.

Other side effects can include sleeping too much, problems with physical coordination or shakiness, nausea, vomiting, dizziness, headaches, or problems with vision. These usually don't last long, however, and can usually be controlled by adjusting the dosage. Finally, if your teen is taking birth control pills, she will probably need a higher dosage of lamotrigine because estrogen can induce the metabolism of this drug. Because of these complications, your teen's doctor will probably adhere to the "start low, go slow" principle—she will start with a low dose and adjust it upward slowly until your teen is responding with a minimum of side effects. There are no blood tests of therapeutic levels required for lamotrigine.

Other Anticonvulsants

Carbamazepine (Tegretol)

The anticonvulsant carbamazepine is an alternative for teens who don't do well on other mood stabilizers. When people don't respond to lithium or other treatments for bipolar depression, there is about a one in three chance that they will respond to carbamazepine within 1 month. A bonus is that carbamazepine doesn't cause much weight gain. Nevertheless, it's rarely prescribed these days because of its other difficult side effects.

Carbamazepine is usually marketed under the names Tegretol, Carbatrol, Equetro, or Atretol. It has a substantial record of effectiveness for adults who are manic, but there is virtually no research on it in kids. A study by Robert Kowatch and colleagues at the University of Cincinnati School of Medicine found that carbamazepine worked about as well as lithium for controlling mania in children. It may be useful among people with bipolar disorder who haven't done as well on lithium, including those with psychotic/delusional mania, mixed episodes, and rapid cycling, but again, this indication is based on studies of adults, not teens.

A typical dosage of carbamazepine for a teen weighing 143 pounds would be about 450 mg, which would be dispensed in 200- and 100-mg tablets. Your teen's doctor will probably keep adjusting the dosage until he has found a good balance between effectiveness and side effects. Typical blood levels for people who have achieved a therapeutic dosage are between 4 and 12 micrograms per milliliter.

This is not an easy drug to take, which is probably why it has fallen into disfavor. The most common side effects are nausea, dizziness, sedation, and mild problems with memory such as difficulty with word finding. Other people develop blurry vision, constipation, or problems with muscle coordination. As with most of the mood stabilizers, these side effects are worst at the beginning and may be prevented by the "start low, go slow" approach to dosing. Some people develop elevated liver enzymes. Your teen's doctor will discontinue her carbamazepine if she shows signs of hepatitis, including feeling tired and having stomach pains or other gastrointestinal symptoms. Some people develop hyponatremia (low sodium). Like lamotrigine, carbamazepine carries about a 10–15% risk of a skin rash, which in rare instances can develop into Stevens–Johnson syndrome.

The most worrisome side effect is a bone marrow reaction called *agranulocytosis* or *aplastic anemia*. This is a sudden and dramatic drop in white blood cells, accompanied by fever, infection, sore throat, sores in one's mouth, or bleeding or bruising easily. Your teen's doctor should watch for this set of side effects by monitoring the teen's blood count and stopping the medication if necessary.

Oxcarbazepine (Trileptal)

A newer anticonvulsant, oxcarbazepine, looked initially quite promising as an antimanic agent, without all the complex side effects of carbamazepine. Many clinicians assumed that it would work just as well because it has a very similar chemical structure. That didn't turn out to be the case, however. A recent large-scale clinical trial found no evidence that oxcarbazepine worked better than placebo in controlling mania among children. There may be some use for it as an add-on to other antimanic agents, but currently the evidence is sparse.

Topiramate (Topamax)

Somewhat more promising is the anticonvulsant topiramate, which is reasonably effective among adults with mania and rapid cycling. It may stabilize mania among bipolar children and teens as well, although few controlled studies have been done. It's particularly useful in treating disorders involving impulse control (for example, sudden, angry outbursts; aggression or violence; substance abuse).

There was much excitement about topiramate when it first appeared because it caused weight loss rather than weight gain. However, it causes other side effects, including blurred vision, eye pain, and most disturbingly, mental sluggishness (word-finding difficulties, problems concentrating, memory problems). Some people develop tingling sensations, sedation, fatigue, nausea, dizziness, and rarely, kidney stones. It also can be associated with the failure of certain oral contraceptives. Topiramate is not considered a first-line treatment option: most psychiatrists use it as an add-on to other drugs rather than by itself.

Atypical Antipsychotics: The New Approach to Bipolar Treatment

Increasingly, psychiatrists are turning to the class of medications called the *atypical antipsychotics* (also called "second generation" antipsychotics) to treat symptoms of childhood bipolar disorder. In many ways these drugs are misnamed, because most have mood-stabilizing properties as well as antipsychotic properties. Several are effective in treating mania as well as depression. Six atypicals are available in the United States: quetiapine (Seroquel), olanzapine (Zyprexa), aripiprazole (Abilify), risperidone (Risperdal), ziprasidone (Geodon), and the rarely used clozaril (Clozapine). All have FDA approval for the treatment of mania in adults, and two (olanzapine and aripiprazole) have been approved for the maintenance treatment of bipolar adults. Once again, however, none have been FDA-approved for childhood for adolescent bipolar illness and are therefore used off-label.

More and more, doctors are beginning with an atypical antipsychotic—either alone or in combination with lithium, divalproex, or lamotrigine—in treating mania. Atypicals may result in better response rates than lithium or the anticonvulsants during the acute phases of mania among young people. Depression may also be treated with atypicals (for example, with quetiapine or the combination of quetiapine and lamotrigine). The atypicals can stabilize mood but also reduce anxiety, agitation, and psychotic thinking, as well as enhance sleep.

To give just a brief sampling of the research relevant to atypicals for children and teens, a recent study showed that the combination of quetiapine and divalproex was more effective than divalproex alone in stabilizing mania among hospitalized teens. When compared head to head, quetiapine worked faster at stabilizing mania than divalproex.

Studies of adult and teen patients find that atypical antipsychotics—notably quetiapine—are effective in treating depression among both bipolar I and bipolar II patients. They can be effective in treating rapid cycling and comorbid anxiety disorders as well. Among 110 kids with disruptive behavior disorders, risperidone was much more effective in stabilizing mood disorder (including bipolar) symptoms than placebo pills.

A large-scale, 3-week trial found that olanzapine (Zyprexa) stabilized mania better than a placebo among children and teens. The combination of olanzapine with fluoxetine (Prozac)—which can be administered in a single pill called Symbyax—is more effective than olanzapine alone in stabilizing depression among adults. Symbyax worked faster than lamotrigine in stabilizing bipolar depression among adults, but also had more side effects.

So, why don't we just put all of our teens on atypicals? Because all of the atypicals (except for ziprasidone) cause weight gain, and weight gain can lead to the "metabolic syndrome" characterized by abdominal obesity, hypertension, dyslipidemia, and insulin resistance. These are very troublesome side effect for teens, who have been known to "balloon up" rapidly on these drugs. For example, in the 3-week study of olanzapine, 42% of the children and teens gained more than 7% of their weight in 3 weeks. They also showed abnormal blood lipid profiles (a risk factor for diabetes) and elevated prolactin levels. Risperidone and quetiapine cause weight gain as well, although less than olanzapine. Ziprasidone (Geodon) seems to cause less weight gain than any of the others, but it hasn't been studied adequately. Moreover, it has its own side effects (headaches, fatigue, nausea, and dizziness). Cognitive side effects (for example, word retrieval difficulties, problems concentrating), restlessness, and sedation can also occur with many of the atypicals.

That said, weight gain, cognitive problems, and sedation can often be controlled by adjusting the dosage, taking a single dose at bedtime, or switching to a different atypical agent. Your teen's doctor will want to monitor his weight and body mass index, as well as his lipids and triglycerides while he is taking atypicals. Often, exercise regimens and nutritional counseling must accompany these medications. Despite these disadvantages, atypical antipsychotics represent an important advance in the treatment of teen bipolar disorder.

What about Antidepressants?

If your teen has ongoing symptoms of depression or has a comorbid anxiety disorder (for example, panic disorder or obsessive–compulsive disorder), there is a reasonably good chance that her doctor will prescribe an antidepressant medication. There are too many antidepressants to discuss fully here. The most common are bupropion (Wellbutrin or Zyban) and the host of medications known as the SSRIs: fluoxetine (Prozac; currently the only FDA-approved antidepressant for depressed teens), sertraline (Zoloft), paroxetine (Paxil), citalopram (Celexa), and escitalopram (Lexapro). Other (non-SSRI) antidepressants include venlafaxine (Effexor) and the monoamine oxidase inhibitors (tranylcypromine or Parnate; phenelzine or Nardil). These will be recommended for your teen when drugs like lithium, divalproex, or quetiapine have failed to control depressive, mixed, or anxiety symptoms. They are not used to treat mania, and they should never be given alone without an accompanying mood stabilizer or atypical antipsychotic.

If given alone, all of the antidepressants can set off mania, hypomania, mixed episodes, or other types of mood destabilization, particu-

THE USE OF ANTIDEPRESSANTS

Antidepressants should be considered when your teen has a persistent, unremitting depression or severe anxiety that hasn't responded to mood stabilizers or atypical antipsychotics. The following caveats usually apply:

- Your teen should never take an antidepressant alone without an accompanying mood stabilizer or atypical antipsychotic.
- When your teen starts an antidepressant, be on the lookout for agitation, restlessness, irritability, suicidal thoughts (for example, "I'm worthless ... nothing matters"), deliberate self-harm, aggressiveness toward others, anxiety or panic, insomnia, impulsiveness, recklessness, or unusual thoughts (for example, preoccupations with death, paranoia) or unusual behaviors (for example, writing long letters to people she hasn't spoken to in years).
- Inform your teen's doctor as soon as these signs appear; distinguish them from behaviors or thoughts shown before taking the medication.
- Antidepressants should be stopped slowly, not all of a sudden.
- If your teen responds well to the antidepressant, it should be continued for at least 8 weeks after the depression has gone away.

larly in a teen who has a history of rapid cycling. Moreover, the FDA recently issued a "black box" warning of the increased risk of suicidal thinking and behavior during the early phases of antidepressant treatment. The increased risk is not large (4% of kids on antidepressants developed new suicidal ideas, threatened suicide, or made an attempt, versus 2% with placebo), but nonetheless it is to be taken seriously.

You can help minimize these risks by closely monitoring your teen's behavior and mood. Regular communication between you, your teen, his psychiatrist, and other members of the family about any changes you observe will help tremendously. Chapter 13 describes how you can help your teen develop a safety plan to combat suicidal thoughts (identify triggers for suicidal thoughts or actions; who the teen will call if he feels suicidal; which mental health professionals you should get in touch with and what to do if they are unavailable).

Won't your teen react negatively to all of this extra monitoring? Yes, he will probably complain about it and express resentment, but you should do it anyway. This is a significant health issue, and you should approach it the same way you would approach care of a severe physical illness like asthma or diabetes. Explain to your teen that these medications are relatively new in their use with kids and we don't yet know how individual kids react; that your watching over him reflects your caring for him; and that he can let you know how he feels in other ways than talking (for example, sending you an email or a cell phone text message).

Supplements

You should ask your child's doctor whether she is a candidate for thyroid supplementation. As we mentioned, drugs like lithium can suppress the production of thyroid hormones. Also, people with bipolar disorder sometimes have thyroid abnormalities, particularly during the mixed episodes, which are common illness states among kids. Even if your teen does not have a hypothyroid condition, a simple thyroid supplement (for example, Synthroid) can make the difference between a teen who does and does not respond to mood stabilizers.

Other supplements that are recommended "over the counter," like omega-3 fatty acids, should be taken only once you have discussed them with your teen's doctor, to make sure there are no drug interactions. Certain of them (for example, St. John's wort) should not be taken alongside of SSRIs; Valerian root should not be taken with Valium. There is currently no convincing evidence that these agents are helpful for bipolar disorder in kids. In fact, they can be dangerous if taken without monitoring by a physician.

What If My Child Has Another Condition Too?

Comorbid conditions can worsen the course of bipolar disorder and also make functioning at school or at home more difficult, so they are usually treated separately. ADHD usually requires a psychostimulant (for example, methylphenidate [Ritalin]) or an amphetamine (e.g., Adderall), particularly one of the sustained-release varieties; a nonstimulant like atomoxetine (Strattera) or bupropion (Wellbutrin); and/or behavior therapy or a specialized school program. Psychostimulants have side effects including insomnia, reduced appetite, jitteriness, and headaches. The drug Wellbutrin may be effective both as an antidepressant and as a treatment for ADHD. Some teens with ADHD respond only to stimulants, however.

Anxiety disorders may require the use of benzodiazepines like Valium, Xanax, or Ativan, along with behavioral treatment for anxiety (for example, exposure and response prevention) or, in some cases, the anticonvulsant gabapentin (Neurontin). Benzodiazepines carry a risk of addiction and can also produce headaches or lethargy. Paradoxically, some kids become impulsive and overactive when they take these drugs.

Aggression and impulse control disorders (conduct disorder, oppositional defiant disorder, and substance misuse disorders) can respond to lithium, divalproex, an atypical antipsychotic, or topiramate. Your teen's doctor should rule out stress factors that may cause these symptoms (for example, reacting to a change in family circumstances) rather than immediately treating your teen with additional medications.

Treatment for comorbid conditions usually has to follow an algorithm. First the mania or depression symptoms need to be stabilized; then the comorbid conditions can be treated. So, for example, your teen needs to be relatively free of mood symptoms for 6–8 weeks before Ritalin or Adderall can be introduced (if she was not already taking them). Then her doctor will try to stabilize each comorbid disorder (for example, ADHD) before moving on to the next one (for example, social anxiety disorder). The good news is that some comorbid conditions that were originally diagnosed tend to disappear once the mood symptoms have stabilized.

For more information on drugs for comorbid conditions, take a look at the Child and Adolescent Bipolar Foundation website (*www.bpkids.org*) or *www.healthyplace.com/communities/bipolar/toc_gary.htm*.

How Will the Doctor Make the Right Choice?

Reading about all the medication options may have made you wonder how the doctor can possibly figure out which options are best for your son or daughter. In fact, the science in this field is so new that most doctors use a lot of trial and error to find the combination that works best.

It's not snake oil, though. As mentioned earlier in this chapter, the best doctors use *treatment algorithms* or *drug decision trees* to figure out what medications to try and in what order (see the "Medication Choices" box, page 128). There are algorithms for kids and adults. Psychiatrists usually start with monotherapy (one medication), and if the first medication doesn't work, they adjust dosages, switch to a different class of medications, or combine the first medication with a second one. Each of these trials takes time (often 6–8 weeks), so that each medication has been given enough of a chance to work.

Doctors are likely to start teens who are manic and not delusional on lithium, divalproex, an atypical antipsychotic, or less frequently, carbamazepine. If the teen doesn't show a good response within 6–8 weeks, the doctor will probably increase the dosages or, alternatively, combine two agents (for example, Depakote with Risperdal). She may also suggest a different mood stabilizer or atypical not used in step one. If your teen still doesn't respond, the doctor may recommend two mood stabilizers (for example, lithium with Depakote) plus an atypical (for example, Risperdal) or maybe switch to a different atypical (for example, Abilify). If your teen is severely depressed, the doctor will probably start with Seroquel (an atypical with antidepressant properties) or perhaps lithium, or perhaps the combination of Seroquel with lithium or Depakote. If there is an inadequate response within a month or two, she may add Lamictal. An antidepressant like Wellbutrin is usually considered a third add-on option because of the risks outlined above.

Tyrone, the 16-year-old discussed at the beginning of the chapter, underwent numerous changes in medications before he and his doctor found a combination that worked. Tyrone's doctor first took him off of Celexa and Topamax and lowered his dosage of Adderall. Then the doctor gave him Depakote and Seroquel and allowed him the time to stabilize on these medications. Later, when Tyrone became depressed, his doctor tried him on Lamictal. His dosages had to be adjusted several times along the way.

You should feel free to discuss these treatment algorithms with your teen's doctor. To what extent is he following a decision tree? Where in the process is your teen at any given point? What options follow the one he is now using? Many teens end up on a combination of medications. As we've said before, don't assume that being on several medications means your teenager is sicker than a teen who is taking only one.

Explaining Medications to Your Teenager

As you'll learn more about in Chapter 8, medications are a choice for your teenager. Although you can force him to take them for the short term, over the long term he will have to "buy in" to the idea. As we'll explain in some detail in that chapter, he will have a variety of emotional reactions to medications. He will complain of their side effects, their effects on his mood states or energy level, and the stigma among his friends of being on psychiatric medications. He may dislike taking a medication that takes away his high moods without alleviating his lows. He may view the medications as one more attempt for you to control him. He may fear going into the future on these medications. In Chapter 8, you'll get some good ideas for how to address these issues and obtain your teen's acceptance. A preview of the main point of that chapter: *teens need to feel that medications are important to achieving their own long-term goals, not the goals stated for them by other people.* A successful collaboration with your teen requires acknowledging her life goals and framing the medications as a way of getting there.

Remember, medications are indispensable to controlling bipolar disorder, but they are not the only treatment that will be important to your teen. The medication regimens we've described will work much better, and faster, if they are accompanied by family, individual, or group psychotherapy. As explained in Chapter 5, the biopsychosocial model leads to effective treatment because it calls for attacking bipolar disorder from different angles. Medication can't do everything. Psychotherapy, when it's the right type for your teen and your family, can do a lot to improve your lives.

7

How Psychotherapy Can Help Your Teenager and Your Family

For parents who have gone through the trial-and-error process of finding the right medication for their teen, the notion that medicine might not be enough can be disheartening. Yet many parents say medication doesn't resolve many of the issues their teens have—and the research agrees. Whether you're struggling with typical teen behavior problems that predate the illness or unresolved issues related to the ongoing symptoms of (or fallout from) your teen's bipolar disorder, your lives can be greatly improved if you take advantage of therapy in addition to filling your teen's prescriptions. Psychotherapy can, in fact, support medication treatment so that your teen will stay with it and get the most out of it. It can also help with psychological and social problems that biological treatments can't address.

How Your Teen Can Benefit from Psychotherapy

According to the biopsychosocial model introduced in Chapter 5, it makes perfect sense to address psychological and social factors that contribute to your teen's bipolar disorder. But it makes even more sense to maximize the effectiveness of the medication that's the first line of treatment. This is one important place where psychotherapy can help.

Using Psychotherapy to Boost Medication Efficacy

Does your teenager know why he's taking medication? Is he on board with the regimen? Many are not, at least at first.

Psychotherapy Can Help Your Teen Accept the Diagnosis and the Need for Treatment

Often when we ask adolescents why they think they're in therapy or taking medications, they shrug and mumble some form of "I don't know." All too often, parents and doctors decide what type of treatment a teen should have without ever fully explaining the rationale for it to the teen. This makes some teens resistant, while others follow along obediently. The problem with this latter group is that they will most likely stop taking medications when old enough to be on their own because they've never appreciated why they were taking medications in the first place. Seventeen-year-old Peggy had been taking medication since she was diagnosed with bipolar disorder at age 14, but when asked what medications she was taking and whether they were helping, she said she did not know and that she only took them because her parents insisted. She also said that as soon as she left home she wasn't going to take the pills anymore because "It's my parents' thing, and besides, I won't have time for doctors."

Psychotherapy can help teens become active participants in their own treatment. Through therapy a teen becomes educated about bipolar disorder, draws connections between symptoms and negative life events, and identifies the benefits of medication. Peggy's therapist helped her recognize that the erratic mood swings she had experienced before taking medication had consequences she didn't like, such as getting kicked out of school and losing many friends. He also helped Peggy see that since she had started medication she had more stable moods, had been successful at a new school, and had a new group of friends. Making the connection between medication and stability in her life showed Peggy that medication wasn't her "parents' thing" at all but in fact a necessity to making a successful transition out of her parents' home.

Psychotherapy Can Help Maintain Open Communication and Good Relations with the Teen's Prescribing Psychiatrist

Teens with bipolar disorder can be extremely sensitive and finicky about other people and their behavior. Many parents have said that their teen seemed to be doing fine with a doctor and then refused to return for further appointments because of a single negative comment the doctor made. It's not unusual for teenagers to have many psychiatrists and therapists over the years. Switching doctors frequently can add to your stress and may not even be feasible for your family.

Unfortunately, most psychiatrists today don't have the time to address with teens the complex issues related to the therapeutic relationship. A therapist who has a good connection with your teen can encourage communication and resolution and mediate the relationship between your teen and the prescribing psychiatrist.

Thirteen-year-old Jeremy had rejected many psychiatrists since his diagnosis during fourth grade, saying that he could read people within 2 minutes of meeting them and tell if they were "real." He had a good relationship with his current psychiatrist, but whenever his symptoms recurred he'd get suspicious of the doctor's reserved style. Eventually, he announced during one of these episodes that he wanted to leave this psychiatrist because he didn't talk much and Jeremy didn't think the doctor liked him anymore. Jeremy's therapist helped Jeremy identify the ways in which the psychiatrist had been helpful and also set up a meeting among the three of them to discuss Jeremy's resentments. The meeting left Jeremy reassured that his doctor was on his side and kept a valuable treatment team intact.

Calling in Psychotherapy Where Medication Can't Help

Psychotherapy Can Help Your Teen Keep His Mood Grounded

Teens who have bipolar disorder may resist giving up the pleasant high of hypomania. Some discover that they can create mania by manipulating their sleep, engaging in daredevil activities during the day, or using illicit drugs to re-create the false sense of well-being that often accompanies hypomania. Therapy can provide a rationale for why the teen must not fall into this trap.

Sixteen-year-old Bruce was an avid rock climber, long skateboarder, and snowboarder. When he realized that medication was taking away his highs, he began to resent it. When high he felt like he was superhuman and immune to social insecurity. Without the highs, he was afraid that he wouldn't be as good at climbing or boarding. Although he did not quit taking his medications, he started staying up late and spending hours on end in his favorite high-adrenaline activities to keep his mood elevated.

Bruce's therapist showed him that although medications would probably mean giving up the highs, it also meant preventing or at least diminishing the lows that followed, which had become longer and more severe over time. Also, though he felt great when he was high, his girlfriend had broken up with him due to his flirtatiousness when he was in this state, and his friends had told him that his behavior had become impulsive and dangerous. As the realities of the impact of his highs on people outside the family became clearer to him, Bruce started acknowledging to his therapist that it was better for him to work toward mood stability, even if it meant sacrificing his superhuman feelings.

Psychotherapy Can Enhance Your Teen's Independence and Functioning at School

Teens with bipolar disorder often seem much younger than they are, appearing stunted in the physical, social, emotional, and academic realms. They may be overly dependent on their parents in some ways—the young adolescent who still sleeps in a parent's bed when afraid, the many teens who depend on their parents to hand out their medications—yet seek independence in others, such as wanting to stay out all night or have their own car. Therapy can steer your teen toward developmentally appropriate behavior, while at the same time helping him develop strategies for getting back on track academically if bipolar disorder has disrupted his education.

Shawn was 15 years old but looked and acted more like an 11- or 12-year-old. He was very thin, small, and, when he was hypomanic, silly, goofy, and hyperactive. He would hold hands with his parents in public, hop or skip, and wear costumes that made him look odd. When he was depressed, he would avoid new people, refuse to help out with chores, and avoid going to routine places like the post office or the grocery store. When his mood was up, he was unable to focus, sit still, or follow directions, and his "goofy" behavior alienated kids at school. When he was down, he withdrew completely and avoided school altogether or, if he attended at all, would crawl under his desk. His teachers had no idea how to respond. As a result he was behind other kids in age-appropriate behavior, friendships, and academic achievement.

Shawn's therapist helped him identify what he was doing to alienate others and how to behave like other teens. Following a series of behavioral homework assignments, Shawn began spending more time with his peers doing the typical things that 15-year-olds do (for example, playing sports, going to the mall). He got more interested in moving forward with independence from his family (for example, getting his driver's permit, having a girlfriend) when he noticed that his friends were doing these things. The therapist also met with Shawn, his parents, and his teachers to develop a plan for Shawn in the classroom. As a result, Shawn started to perform better academically (specific school strategies will be covered in Chapter 14).

Psychotherapy Can Help Your Teen Develop Coping Strategies to Manage Age-Relevant Stressors

As we explained in Chapter 5, typical teenage stress can completely destabilize a teen who has bipolar disorder. Bipolar teens who suffer chronic relationship stress tend to improve more slowly during depression. Stressful events like moving, changing schools, or divorce, as well as the amount of social support a teen gets and how critical or controlling the family is, influence how well she is likely to manage the illness. It's impossible to avoid all stressful life events. But therapy can teach teens to develop effective coping strategies to manage stressors and prevent destabilization. Specific strategies for staying well will be discussed in Chapter 10.

Suzette had been taking Depakote for several years. Although the medication had made a huge difference in preventing her sleep difficulties and rage, Suzette remained extremely sensitive to stressful life events. When she was 16, she had a particularly difficult mood episode. Over the course of a week she and her best friend had a fight, her boyfriend broke up with her, and her parents grounded her for being disrespectful. By the end of the week Suzette wasn't sleeping, was raging every day, and was making plans to run away from home. Her psychiatrist increased Suzette's Depakote and suggested she begin individual therapy. With her therapist's help, Suzette pinpointed the most problematic stressor—seeing her boyfriend at school—and discussed coping strategies (acknowledging him but not initiating conversations; use of adaptive self-talk such as "I can get through this"). The next time she saw her boyfriend at school, she used those strategies and reported that her anxiety went down as a result. Although change was slow, and many other social and family conflicts had to be addressed, Suzette gradually felt more confident about her ability to cope with stress.

Psychotherapy Can Help Teens Repair the Damage after a Manic or a Depressive Episode

There is a high quality-of-life cost to those who have bipolar disorder. Your teen may have said or done things during an episode that have alienated family or friends or led to social, legal, or academic troubles. Teens often benefit from examining and exploring the regret, grief, and low self-esteem flowing from these consequences. Some teens also need help defining what they should take responsibility for (for example, creating drama in relationships that trigger more mood swings) and what they should not—things that are really out of their control (for example, having friends whose after-school plans may not include them).

Becky's parents and friends urged her to break up with a boyfriend who had become physically abusive, but Becky blamed herself for the abuse, saying that if she had been a better girlfriend this wouldn't have happened. She seemed unable to end the relationship. Two weeks later her boyfriend broke up with her, saying she was too moody. Becky became fixated on causing the boy as much pain as he had caused her by spreading degrading stories about him. As a result, he began threatening her life. The drama culminated with Becky making a very serious suicide attempt.

Afterward, Becky began grieving the loss of the relationship and seeing the situation as all her fault. Becky's therapist helped her group events in the relationship into those for which she was responsible and those for which she was not. Although they talked about choices that Becky had made that worsened an already tough situation, the clinician avoided placing any blame about her suicide attempt, making clear that the clinician viewed it as a symptom of Becky's depression. Through therapy, Becky came to see that, although her behavior and the symptoms of her illness were certainly related to the breakup, she was actually better off—and safer—in the long run.

Psychotherapy Can Help Your Teen Cope with Ongoing Symptoms

Studies consistently show that medications can't eradicate all of the symptoms of bipolar disorder. The majority of children with bipolar disorder (55–70%) have recurrences within a 2- to 4-year period even when taking mood stabilizers, and many continue to have significant symptoms between major episodes. On the hopeful side, you'll find that psychotherapy is an effective way to help your teen manage ongoing symptoms of depression and anxiety, without the risks associated with antidepressant and antianxiety medications (see Chapter 6).

Fifteen-year-old Lynette took her Depakote and Risperdal every day, but she still seemed listless and unmotivated, had few friends, struggled to keep up with her schoolwork, had low self-esteem, and had lost interest in her hobbies. Her parents said that she didn't seem depressed so much as "lost." Lynette's psychiatrist offered to switch her to a different medication, but neither they nor their daughter liked that idea. Lynette said she was already considering quitting her medications because she felt they were making her worse.

Individual therapy helped Lynette put some strategies in place to combat her low mood. Specifically, her therapist developed a behavioral activation plan with her (see Chapter 12). Lynette started making sure she got no more than 8 hours of sleep a night, performed one pleasurable and one productive activity a day, kept in contact with her friends even when she didn't feel up to it, and got sunlight and limited exercise each day. Although these changes felt like significant struggles at first, they did help her confront the depression, and gradually her symptoms began to abate.

In the best-case scenario psychotherapy should help your teen (1) manage the mood symptoms she is experiencing, (2) understand and accept the rationale for her medicines, (3) identify and reduce stressors that may negatively impact her symptoms, and (4) move toward higher functioning and greater productivity between episodes. Psychotherapy can be a way of "resetting the developmental clock" so that your child can progress through the teenage years at a more typical rate.

If you still have questions about whether your teen might benefit from psychotherapy, see the box on page 157.

What's the Right Psychotherapy for Your Teen?

The psychological treatment of bipolar disorder has changed drastically over the past 20 years. Long ago, treatments were based on a psychoanalytic (Freudian) interpretation of the illness, which viewed mania as a more severe form of depression and a defense against feelings of abandonment. In the last 20–30 years it has become apparent that bipolar disorder has strong genetic and biological underpinnings. We now know that psychotherapies that focus on the day-to-day management of symptoms are the most effective. Mental health professionals now take a collaborative, teaching, coaching, and advising approach that helps people with the disorder build skills for mood management.

The new form of therapy that has revolutionized the treatment of bi-

It might be a good idea to consult a therapist if . . .

- Your teen is continuing to have symptoms even with medications.
- Your teen continues to struggle with day-to-day functioning (getting to school on time, personal hygiene, taking care of basic life demands).
- There is ongoing family conflict that never seems to resolve.
- There is a major life change on the horizon (divorce, move, etc.).
- Your teen is struggling academically.
- Your teen seems unable to cope with the stressors that life presents.
- You suspect your teen has started using alcohol or drugs.
- Your teen struggles socially (has no friends or is teased by peers).
- Your teen asks you if he can see a therapist.
- Your teen's psychiatrist recommends that she see a therapist.

polar disorder is called *psychoeducation*—literally, psychological education, in this case about coping with a biologically based illness. Psychoeducation has been used for some time with adults with bipolar disorder, but its use with teens is new. The therapist and teen (and in many cases, family members) work together as a team to:

- Improve functioning through a better understanding of the disorder and its biological underpinnings.
- Develop strategies for managing symptoms and stressors.
- Make clear that much of the teen's behavior is beyond her control, but that certain behavioral techniques can increase personal effectiveness.
- Teach new skills for communicating with family members or other important people in the teen's life.
- Take a structured approach to problem solving.

The family's functioning is seen as central to the teen's improvement over time. Your family isn't causing your teen's problems, but a supportive and structured family environment is considered instrumental in improving your teen's course of illness—and helping your family cope.

Our clinical experience and research has shown that psychoeducation is crucial to understanding the nature of bipolar disorder and managing the illness. So, be sure that any individual or family therapy you decide to pursue includes some form of psychoeducation that addresses the biopsychosocial model described in Chapter 5; otherwise, the treatment may not be effective.

Individual Psychoeducational Treatments

Several treatments are being developed to help adolescents cope with bipolar disorder (based on effective treatments for bipolar adults). Each treatment goes about developing these coping skills in a different way, but they all focus on helping your teen understand the nature, causes, and management of bipolar disorder; maintain stable moods; improve family and peer relationships; stick to regular sleep–wake and day-to-day schedules; and solve problems more effectively. The individual treatments that have shown promising results for bipolar adults are cognitive-behavioral therapy and interpersonal and social rhythm therapy.

Cognitive-Behavioral Therapy

Cognitive-behavioral therapy (CBT) addresses errors in thinking (cognitions) and problematic actions (behaviors) that may increase your teen's depressive or manic symptoms. Teens often get trapped by distorted thinking—depressive, negative thinking such as "Nothing ever works out for me" and "No one likes me" or manic, hyperpositive thinking like "I'm in charge; I can do no wrong." Ruth's parents noticed that right before she became manic she always seemed to develop a defiant and haughty attitude, which in turn caused her problems at home and at school. Ruth's CBT therapist helped her to recognize these distorted thought patterns as they were occurring and to be on the lookout for other symptoms of mania.

As for behavior, CBT can help your teen increase activity during a depressive phase (as in Lynette's case) or decrease activity and stimulation during a manic phase (as in Ruth's case). Bryan's parents knew he was getting depressed because he spent increasing amounts of time lying on the couch watching TV or disconsolately playing video games. As part of his CBT he worked up a list of pleasurable and productive activities to do each day to ward off depression, and kept track of his moods during and after each activity.

CBT typically is given in weekly individual sessions and requires your teen to chart his moods, keep track of his distorted thinking and attempts to modify it, and carry out behavioral exercises. If your teen is going to pursue CBT, it is important to understand that doing this homework is essential to its success.

How Well Does CBT Work?

CBT is the most well-known and well-established treatment for depression. Several groups have developed different forms of CBT for bipolar disorder. Several but not all published studies on CBT report that people with bipolar disorder who undergo CBT while on medication have fewer relapses. Two groups have adapted CBT for adolescents, and the initial results appear promising.

Interpersonal and Social Rhythm Therapy

Interpersonal and social rhythm therapy (IPSRT) can help your teenager figure out how his mood is affected by two major categories of stress: chaotic sleep–wake cycles and irregular daily routines. This therapy can help your teen establish a consistent schedule for going to bed and getting up and also set a stable pattern of daily habits, both of which can decrease mood symptoms and cycling. Hank, who called himself a "night owl," would stay up until 2:00 A.M. working on art projects. During the school year, when he couldn't sleep in, he got irritated, agitated with his friends, and highly distractible at school. His IPSRT therapist helped him see the benefit of going to bed earlier so that he got 9 hours of sleep. The fact that extra sleep eased Hank's symptoms convinced him to stick with the mood charting that he described as "lame" but that he eventually found could get done in about 5 minutes a day (see Chapter 10).

IPSRT also helps teens see how various relationship and social matters affect their moods and how their moods affect relationships. Kids

---

SIGNS THAT CBT MAY BE A GOOD FIT FOR YOUR TEEN

- Your teen thinks and solves problems on an intellectual or analytical level.
- You've identified negative thought patterns in your teen (for example, "I'm at fault, I'm worthless") that are associated with depressed moods.
- Your teen blames himself for most negative events and predicts that nothing will ever change.
- You've noticed that your teen seems to feel better when able to shift her negative thinking.
- You've noticed that small behavioral changes—such as exercising or interacting with favorite people—are helpful to your teen's mood.
- Your teen is not averse to doing homework.

with mood disorders often have conflicts with others, have trouble making transitions in their roles (for example, accepting that they may not be able to attend a public school), and lack social skills. They also may have had to deal with the loss of personal life goals. IPSRT helps them here too. Rita, 17, had been on the gymnastic Olympic development track since age 5. But then medication side effects and the stress of elite athletic competition made it necessary for her to cut back. Not surprisingly, Rita became depressed. Her IPSRT therapist helped her work through her grief and accept the illness and its associated losses. He also helped her deal with the role transition this change caused. Rita started focusing on areas of interest that she had neglected in favor of gymnastics, which helped her make necessary shifts in her sense of self and her expectations and gradually eased her depression.

Like CBT, IPSRT typically requires weekly individual meetings with a therapist. The meetings will continue as long as there are problem areas to address. As mentioned, your teen will be asked to complete daily charts recording sleep and stimulation levels throughout the day; you'll learn how these simple records work in Chapter 10.

How Effective Is IPSRT?

In a large study conducted at the University of Pittsburgh, IPSRT was found to be effective in preventing recurrences among bipolar adults followed over 2 years. It was most effective when patients received it when they were stabilizing from an acute period of illness. Patients in IPSRT were also able to stabilize their daily schedules and sleep–wake cycles.

SIGNS THAT IPSRT MAY BE A GOOD FIT FOR YOUR TEEN

- Your teen consistently struggles with maintaining regular sleep–wake schedules and daily routines.
- Your teen has been destabilized by grief, relationship conflicts, role transitions, and/or social skills deficits.
- Your teen has chronic problems with authority figures or peers.
- Your teen has already had losses related to bipolar symptoms in important relationships or life goals.
- Your teen has verbalized the loss she feels related to the illness.

Family Psychoeducational Treatment

Only one family treatment has been shown to be effective for adolescents with bipolar disorder. This is the treatment developed in our laboratory at the University of Colorado: family-focused treatment.

Family-Focused Treatment

In the family-focused treatment (FFT) for bipolar adolescents, parents and teens are first educated about the symptoms and causes of bipolar disorder, stressors that elicit symptoms, strategies the teen and family can use to decrease the risk of relapse, the distinction between bipolar behavior and ordinary teenage behavior, and medication and psychosocial treatment options. Then FFT focuses on improving the family's communication and problem-solving strategies. Families are taught how to listen, give and receive feedback, and negotiate and resolve conflicts within the family.

The Parker family said that almost every night Rick would ask his son Jake to do some chores and Jake would get agitated and refuse. Rick would get annoyed and threaten Jake with consequences for not complying. Jake would begin yelling at his father, which only made Rick angrier. Lately the fights had taken a physical turn (Jake had shoved his father once), and Jake's mother, Leslie, was worried about both her husband's and her son's safety.

Through FFT the family discovered that Rick's tone of voice was triggering Jake's hostility and rage. Through communication and problem solving the family decided that Leslie would make the work requests of Jake and check with Jake on his follow-through. The family also decided that his noncompliance would have agreed-on consequences, such as losing his phone privileges. Rick and Jake were encouraged to spend more time together doing things that didn't involve household chores, such as watching sports on TV or playing basketball in the driveway. This set of solutions didn't erase all the conflict in the family, but it made a big difference in its intensity.

FFT is traditionally a 9-month treatment that involves 21 family sessions, which can include siblings. FFT requires the teen and family to have weekly family meetings to complete homework and practice the skills learned in each session. Both the homework and the family meetings are essential to the treatment's success.

Can FFT Help?

Our research—as of 2006, six studies involving nearly 300 patients— has shown that FFT combined with medication greatly reduces the risk of bipolar relapses and symptom severity. FFT also improves the emotional atmosphere in the family and increases the likelihood that patients will stay on medications. FFT may also prevent rehospitalization by teaching family members to recognize relapses early and get emergency treatment. *Our most recent work shows that FFT helps teens with bipolar disorder stabilize their manic and depressive symptoms as well.*

Dialectical Behavior Therapy

Another treatment that may be helpful for bipolar disorder is dialectical behavior therapy (DBT). To date, there are no studies of DBT for bipolar patients, but it has been shown to be effective in reducing suicidal behavior among those with personality disorders.

DBT focuses on developing and practicing skills for the management of distorted thinking, difficulty with relationships, intense emotional experiences, and self-injurious or suicidal impulses. DBT holds promise for the treatment of bipolar adolescents given that these teens struggle with suicidality, interpersonal deficits, and treatment adherence. A modified version of DBT for bipolar teens, developed by Tina Goldstein and colleagues at the Western Psychiatric Institute and Clinic in Pittsburgh, involves individual sessions and family groups. It includes a psychoeducation component for addressing symptoms specific to adolescent bipolar disorder.

SIGNS THAT FFT MAY BE A GOOD FIT FOR YOUR FAMILY

- Your teen has more conflict in the home than in other settings.
- Your teen is "triggered" by negative interactions with parents or siblings.
- Your teen has just had an episode or is continuing to have severe symptoms.
- One or more other members of your family have mood disorders.
- You are concerned about your other children as well as your bipolar teen.
- Your bipolar teen is agreeable to family treatment.
- You are concerned about the health and functioning of your family.
- Your bipolar child is having trouble accepting the need for medications.
- Your bipolar teen is unlikely to open up in individual therapy.

THE SYSTEMATIC TREATMENT ENHANCEMENT PROGRAM

An important study of psychotherapy for bipolar adults was recently published. Funded by the National Institute of Mental Health, it examined 293 bipolar adults who were in a depressed phase and were treated in one of 15 participating university clinics. All patients received mood-stabilizing medications and one of the three treatments described in this chapter: CBT, IPSRT, or FFT. The treatments consisted of up to 30 sessions over 9 months. A subset of the patients (40%) got a control treatment called "collaborative care," a brief psychoeducational treatment consisting of three individual sessions. All three intensive treatments led to more rapid stabilization of depression than the collaborative care condition. The intensive treatments also kept patients well for more months of a year-long study period.

Source: Miklowitz, D. J., et al. (2007). Psychosocial treatments for bipolar depression: A 1-year randomized trial from the Systematic Treatment Enhancement Program. *Archives of General Psychiatry, 64,* 419–427.

Mary was able to function fairly well in the face of continuing symptoms of bipolar disorder. However, when she got extremely upset, she resorted to cutting herself with scissors and abusing alcohol. Her DBT therapist helped her learn "distress tolerance" skills, which included distraction, self-soothing, and improving the moment through relaxation (see also Chapter 13). Practicing these skills helped Mary focus her attention elsewhere. Ultimately, she was able to quit injuring herself and using alcohol as an escape.

Traditional DBT can be provided in either peer groups or individual sessions. DBT for bipolar adolescents requires 24 weekly sessions—12 with the family and 12 with the teen—over 6 months. During the next 6 months there are biweekly sessions for the first 3 months and monthly sessions over the next 3 months. DBT involves practicing the skills in and out of sessions.

Psychotherapy to Support Other Members of the Family

Separate from the psychotherapies that may benefit your teen, you should consider therapy, counseling, or support for other family members who are under stress. If multiple members of your family have psychiatric symptoms, family treatment may be the most cost-effective option; however, there will be times when their issues are best dealt with individually.

Individual Therapy for Siblings

We've talked elsewhere in this book, particularly in Chapter 4, about the challenges faced by siblings of teens with bipolar disorder. If you have other children, you already know that your teenager may take out her frustrations on her brothers or sisters and that these other kids may struggle with anger, fears about developing bipolar disorder themselves, or even guilt for being the "normal" ones in the family. These issues are hard for parents to address. They're also hard for siblings to bring up in family therapy out of concern for making the bipolar teen feel stigmatized and even more alienated from the family.

Individual therapy offers a neutral setting for siblings to discuss these concerns and examine their own feelings about family relationships. Sometimes so much of the family's attention and energy is focused on the teenager with bipolar disorder that the other kids don't have a chance to deal with their own problems. Lisa, for example, knew very well what would set her younger bipolar sister off, what made her happy, and how her parents interacted with her sister during mania or depression. But she had no idea how she contributed to family conflicts or how they in turn affected her. In individual therapy, Lisa described the various conflictual interactions that occurred at home along with her thoughts and feelings about them. Gradually she started to see how her sister sometimes used her illness to manipulate the family and began to set firmer boundaries in response (for example, having friends over when planned even if her sister was having a "meltdown"). She also acknowledged that she had gained satisfaction from thinking of herself as the good child of the pair, which had kept her from admitting to her own emotional struggles with her parents.

When Are Family Support Groups Useful?

Many support groups and conferences are available to parents and family members of individuals with psychiatric disorders, including bipolar disorder. These groups are usually run by the Depression and Bipolar Support Alliance (DBSA), the National Alliance on Mental Illness (NAMI; especially the "Family to Family" program), or parents who have a child with bipolar disorder (see the Resources section at the back of this book). Many parents find it comforting and informative to get involved in a family support group. It can be a relief to be with parents who understand what you're going through and don't judge you or impose a typical outsider's misconceptions on you. You may find that other parents of bipolar teens make good friends and help you expand your social network.

Don't be immediately discouraged if you try out a group and find it doesn't meet your needs. You may have found a group that does not specifically address adolescent bipolar disorder or that focuses on kids who are much younger or older than yours. The parents may be dealing with much more severe problems than what you experience with your teen. So consider trying a group a few times before committing to it. If the group in your immediate area is not adequate, call the local DBSA or NAMI office to see if other groups exist.

How to Find a Good Therapist for Your Teen

Once you make the decision to have your teen see a therapist, you have to find the best practitioner in your area and navigate logistics like costs and insurance.

Locating an Appropriate Therapist

Start by knowing the differences between the various health care providers and which type of provider is most appropriate for your teen's needs (see the box on page 166).

Any of the following can be a useful lead in finding a good therapist for your teen:

- Ask family and friends. Has a particular therapist been helpful to them, or have they heard good things about one in the area?
- Ask other health care professionals—your pediatrician, general practitioner, other therapists, or psychiatrists—for referrals.
- Ask your insurance company for a list of providers.
- Ask professional organizations such as the American Psychological Association or the American Psychiatric Association (see the Resources). These organizations can also tell you if any complaints have been filed against this person.

THERAPIST DEGREES AND WHAT THEY MEAN

PhD   This means the therapist is a clinical psychologist with a doctor of philosophy degree, usually from a fully accredited university. Clinical psychologists are well trained in assessment, research, and therapy. The term *psychologist* indicates that the therapist has a state license to practice psychological assessment and therapy. It's a good idea to see licensed providers because they are held to certain minimum legal standards for training, supervision, and ethics.

PsyD   This degree means that the therapist is a "doctor of psychology." Therapists who have this degree may provide assessment or therapy but are generally not as well trained as clinical psychologists in research methods. This may not be an important consideration if the therapist specializes in childhood mood disorders (which you can ask about).

MSW   A therapist with a master's degree in social work is usually skilled at matching families with social services. These therapists most often work in hospitals and clinics but may also provide services in a private practice setting. They have less formal training than PhDs or PsyDs but also usually charge less.

MFT   A therapist with a master's degree in marriage and family therapy usually focuses on helping families and couples improve relationships. These therapists are unlikely to specialize in particular psychiatric disorders, but they may help your family communicate and get along better.

LPC   A licensed professional counselor has a master's degree in counseling. LPCs usually focus on wellness and normal human development as opposed to more serious emotional difficulties. They may be of assistance in helping you and your teen negotiate the school setting.

- A local college or university can be a great resource for finding knowledgeable treatment providers in your community. Ask for the on-campus student health service.
- Go to a website for bipolar disorder and see who is recommended.

Once you've identified a few therapists, make sure anyone who looks like a good candidate has a state license, either by asking directly, checking credentials online, or contacting the state psychology or social work boards that issue licenses. Then interview each of them and ask questions such as:

- How many years have you practiced psychology or social work?
- What are your degrees, and what treatments are you trained in?
- What are your areas of expertise?
- What experience do you have in working with bipolar disorder in kids?
- How do you typically approach teens with these problems?
- How much contact do you typically have with a teen's parents or other doctors and school personnel?
- What is your policy about confidentiality with a minor?

During these interviews you should be trying to get a good sense for whether the therapist meets the criteria listed below. But always remember that essentially you are employing the therapist and have the right to "fire" a therapist and look for another if you don't feel comfortable with him or her, you feel that the therapy is not helpful or is making things worse, or the therapist hasn't established specific treatment goals. Your choice of a therapist is never irrevocable, so your goal is just to do the best you can to find a good fit.

The therapist is someone with whom your teen—and you—are likely to be able to have a good relationship. Therapy in general will go better with a therapist that you, your teen, and other family members respect, trust, and feel genuinely cares about you. If you feel comfortable with a therapist and your teen does not, you'll have to rely on your parental instincts to tell you whether the therapist is not a good fit or your teen would be resistant to anyone.

The therapist should be able to demonstrate a commitment to expanding his knowledge of bipolar disorder over time. You'll get an idea of how knowledgeable the therapist is from asking the preceding questions, but you also should ask how he stays informed about the latest advances. A therapist who attends conferences and reads journals and/or books about bipolar disorder should be up on the most current information and able to share the latest research and treatments with you and your teen. Ask what the therapist's theories are about how teens come to have bipolar disorder and what the family's role is in the illness. If the therapist tells you something very different from what you have read in this book (such as that your teen is just being manipulative, your teen is expressing the family's dysfunction, or bipolar disorder is a fad and just today's way of labeling "acting-out" kids), be wary about how knowledgeable he truly is.

Finally, you may want to share a few examples of your teen's behavior or your family's problems with the therapist and observe his response. Does he appear to understand, and does his response seem knowledgeable and supportive? Lucy explained to her daughter Samantha's therapist that she had given in to Samantha's extreme temper tantrums out of fear for her and her other children's safety. He offered the opinion that maybe Samantha didn't have bipolar disorder at all but had just been conditioned by Lucy to behave aggressively. Feeling blamed, Lucy decided to find someone who would be more compassionate, understanding, and helpful.

The therapist should agree to have regular contact with you and your teen's psychiatrist. All members of your teen's treatment team—psychiatrist, school counselor, teachers, tutors, mentors, and possibly others—need to communicate regularly with each other. A therapist may be able to help your teen communicate and resolve problems with her psychiatric and school personnel and gain a sense of competence in doing so. Although open communication is essential, the therapist must be sensitive to confidentiality issues and not breach trust with your teen. Be sure to discuss how the therapist will handle confidentiality so that you, the therapist, and your teen are all on the same page.

Your teen's therapist should be able to tell you how she will work with your teen, define treatment goals, and observe the process of change. Make sure that the therapist believes bipolar disorder is a treatable (not curable) illness, that stabilization is the first goal, and that good maintenance treatment can reduce the frequency of relapses and improve functioning. A therapist who believes, for example, that cases of bipolar disorder are really cases of posttraumatic stress disorder or reactive attachment disorder and would benefit from immediate trauma treatment will probably not set treatment goals that fit with your teen's needs.

Once you've identified a therapist you'd like to work with, you need to make sure that you can afford to pay for the therapy. See the box on page 169 for the various ways to make treatment affordable.

How to Motivate Your Teen to Attend and Engage in Therapy

Teens who are in the midst of identity development and moving toward independence usually resist parents' attempts to have them "get their

NAVIGATING THE FINANCIAL COSTS OF TREATMENT

- Find out what most therapists and psychiatrists charge in your area and resolve all payment issues before you begin treatment.
- Ask what types of insurance the therapist accepts, if he belongs to any managed-care companies, or if he accepts Medicare or Medicaid.
- You may still be able to see a therapist who doesn't participate with insurance or managed-care companies. Ask your insurance company about out-of-network benefits for a specialist for a child with a biologically based psychiatric illness.
- Ask if the therapist would consider joining your insurance network. If not, ask if she would be willing to be a one-time provider. Some insurance companies will contract with a therapist for one client.
- Ask the therapist about reduced or sliding scale fees. It's better to negotiate an affordable fee than to accrue debt and pay over time.
- Find out about resources for your teen in university psychology departments, university hospitals, or community mental health centers. They may have specialty clinics or research programs that offer reduced fees for therapy.
- Ask if the therapist will contract with you for a limited number of therapy sessions to address just one or two specific goals (for example, to get your teen to accept a medication regimen).

head shrunk." If you're wondering how you can possibly get your teen to attend therapy sessions, here are some strategies you can use.

How to Make It to the First Session

Your teen might have a number of reasons for resisting therapy ("I'm not the problem," fear of being teased by friends, fear of the unknown, "I can do it on my own," etc.). There are several avenues for motivating your teen. First, although teens may resist going to therapy for themselves, they may be open to the idea that the whole family needs therapy. Many teens will go to therapy for a parent or other family member.

Second, you can try offering rewards. For example, some parents make therapy part of the required weekly responsibilities for a teen to get an allowance or to use the car. Michelle allowed her 13-year-old son, Alex, to go on sleepovers if he would first see a therapist to address not only a plan for getting more sleep at sleepovers but also how to manage his irritability the next day. The therapist then helped Alex identify an extended list of goals to work on. You may want to have a discussion with your teen about potential reinforcers for attending therapy.

You may have to be creative to get your teen to the first session through enlisting the help of a school counselor, best friend, coach, or peer support group. Jackson, age 17, had been suspended from school on a number of occasions and made several trips to the emergency room because of his impulsive and risky behavior. He denied any need for treatment, arguing that "if I need therapy, then so do all my friends." He finally compromised by attending a peer support group. When he recounted to others in the group some of the things he had done (for example, getting thrown out of a shopping mall for disruptiveness; cursing at a teacher who had asked him to settle down in class), he was surprised that several group members considered his behavior "over the top" and "uncool." This feedback helped convince Jackson to see his own therapist and, eventually, a psychiatrist who diagnosed his bipolar disorder.

Parents will often go to a therapist by themselves to strategize how to get their teen into treatment. Unknown to Maria, her mother and father attended therapy for months before they were able to get Maria to go to her first session. They spent their time discussing (1) various tactics for having Maria attend therapy and the pros and cons of each plan and (2) ways to support healthy change in the home in the meantime. She finally agreed when a respected and trusted family friend told Maria that she had been helped by seeing a therapist during her adolescence.

Finally, some parents get so frustrated with their teen's behavior that they resort to ultimatums. Although we generally discourage this tactic, some families decide that their teen is either going to therapy or to a therapeutic boarding school. A teen who is faced with these choices typically opts for going to therapy and continuing to live at home.

How Will We Know If Therapy Is Helping?

The success of therapy depends on your teen and your teen's therapist, but some basic guidelines will help you know whether to stick with it or try something (or someone) else. The first sign that therapy is helping is that your teen likes the therapist and is becoming less resistant to going. Second, if you start to see a reduction in symptoms, the use of adaptive coping strategies like good communication, and/or moving forward with age-appropriate developmental goals (for example, appropriate moves toward independence like getting an after-school job), this treatment has been helpful. With successful therapy many teens become less resistant to parental demands and behave more responsibly. Third, if you get outside feedback from teachers, coaches, or family members that your teen seems to be doing better, this therapy is probably on the right track. Finally, even if you aren't noticing any mood improvement but your teen seems to be more aware of and willing to work on his problems, therapy may be enhancing his self-monitoring and insight.

When evaluating the success of your teen's therapy, don't assume it hasn't been helpful just because she still has symptoms of depression or mania. Therapy take times to stabilize the illness, and the medications she is on may not be adequate. Nonetheless, symptom stabilization should eventually occur if the drug treatment and psychotherapy are being done well. A good rule of thumb after a depressive episode is to wait at least 6 months for a significant mood stabilization, after which you may want to reevaluate your teen's treatment plan. After a manic episode, you should see stabilization sooner, perhaps in 2–3 months.

As we said at the beginning of this chapter, one important benefit of psychotherapy is in keeping your teen on track with taking medications. But your teen's psychotherapist doesn't live with you, so it will be largely up to you to monitor whether your teen is being adherent. Because medication is such a critical part of treatment and there's a lot you can do to ensure that your teen gets all the benefits it offers, we've devoted the entire next chapter to this subject.

8 Helping Your Teen Accept Ongoing Medication Treatment

Sarah described her 18-year-old son, Bart, as a "trickster." He had never been fully on board with his diagnosis or treatment, although he had gone along with his regimen of lithium (1,200 mg) because it allowed him access to the family car. He had had two major manic episodes that landed him in the hospital, one of which resulted in an assault charge.

He began dating a 17-year-old, Estela, with whom he described having "nights of nonstop passion." Sarah felt he was still manic and that this relationship was making him worse. She became preoccupied with whether her son had truly been taking his lithium and started asking him about it daily and then several times a day. She began labeling their arguments over his privileges as signs of his untreated mania and demanded that he go in and get his blood tested. Bart would have no part of this. In fact, he started needling his mother by saying things like "Wild night at Estela's last night . . . good thing I didn't bring my lithium." Then he started leaving lithium tablets around the house. He left them on the kitchen counter, behind the toilet, and finally underneath her pillow. He was amused at how upset she got, until she threatened to kick him out of the house. When he finally did get his blood level tested, it came out low, meaning he had missed a number of doses.

In a family therapy session, Sarah described her frustration with the Catch-22 she felt she was in: it annoyed Bart when she reminded him to take the medication, and yet if she didn't, he wouldn't take it as prescribed. She railed at her husband, who seemed to be siding with her son. He responded by laughing at her: "You just said, 'We didn't take the lithium last week.' Got a mouse in your pocket?"

Bart complained that "I can't take them [the pills] if I'm doing it for her. I just can't do it." He admitted his mother's attempts at monitoring were making him want to resist while, at least on some level, he knew he needed to take lithium. In a problem-solving discussion with their family therapist, Sarah and Bart agreed on the following solution: she would leave his four tablets on a plate for him in the morning. He would agree to take them at their scheduled times, but the topic was off-limits for discussion unless there were pills remaining at the end of the day. In addition, he agreed to let his mother have access to his monthly lithium lab report. If pills were remaining or the blood levels were low, his father was to approach him about what had happened. Sarah had to "bite her tongue" when she felt the impulse to check on his lithium usage.

After 2 months, Sarah reported that Bart was taking his medication more regularly. She was relieved to have given up the nagging role. Even more surprisingly, Bart had independently asked his psychiatrist whether his lithium dosage should be upped to help control his mood and impulsiveness. His breakup with Estela, who had become afraid of his loud, aggressive manner, convinced him that he had problems to address.

What happened in Bart's family illustrates some important points about teens taking—or not taking—medications for bipolar disorder: they usually don't want to take medication and often don't at some point. Their reasons for not "following doctor's orders" are complex and may not be the ones you think are at work.

Although few teens accept medications from the outset, their eventual cooperation and buy-in is absolutely critical to the success of treatment. This is why we advocated getting help from a psychotherapist in Chapter 7 and why we're devoting a whole separate chapter to the subject of medication consistency.

Your family can help your teen get the most possible out of the medical part of his treatment, but unfortunately, trying to help can also backfire. Your teen's medication can become an issue tied up with family dynamics and the teen's ongoing striving for independence, as it did in Bart's case. Encouraging consistency is more difficult with teens than younger kids because they won't want you to watch them and may not even let you attend their medication appointments. It's important for you to understand the nuances involved in medication treatment if your teen is to benefit from it.

Some kids refuse to take their pills altogether. Some take only half of the prescribed dosages or only certain of the pills (which can be dangerous, such as if they take only the Ritalin without the recommended mood stabilizer). Some teens seem to "mess with it" enough that you wonder whether blood levels are adequate. A teen can be on board when the medications are first prescribed and then drop them when she experiences the first side effects.

If you haven't experienced any problems with your teen's taking medications as prescribed, you may be wondering why we're making such a big deal of the possibility. The fact is that lots of research shows that nonadherence with medication is a big problem. About 60% of adult bipolar patients stop their medications against medical advice or take them inconsistently and miss dosages in the year after being hospitalized for a manic episode. The rate seems to be a little better in kids—between 25 and 44%. In the two studies that have focused to date on whether bipolar adolescents take their medications, one study found that teens missed only 2.3 medication doses per month on average but that only 35% took all the prescribed doses. Even more telling was the fact that most of the kids who did take their medications consistently had just been diagnosed. This may mean adolescents are more at risk for nonadherence as they age and progress through treatment—hardly surprising, since as they age, adolescents are at risk for just about everything! The second study found similar results: only 35% took all their medications during the first year, and almost 25% did not take their medications at all.

For a lot of people, taking medication inconsistently is part of the process of coming to accept the illness. After taking medications for many years and being relatively free of symptoms, nearly anyone would wonder whether it was possible to get along without them. Unfortunately, many people learn the hard way and have several episodes involving hospitalization or incarceration before the reality of their illness sets in and they come to accept their mood stabilizers as a medical necessity. Most people with bipolar disorder who stop their medications, especially if they do it suddenly, are at high risk for having another recurrence. Discontinuing medications also slows down the recovery process after an episode. As if these were not reasons enough, discontinuing medications contributes to suicide attempts and suicide completions. When people stop suddenly, they shock their own system and often experience a sudden return of depression, mania, or severe anxiety. Immediately going back on their medication does not necessarily make the drug immediately therapeutic: it takes time to build up to an adequate level in the brain.

The take-home message is that your teen is more protected from illness episodes and suicide if she is protected by medications. However, teens do not usually think in terms of the future. They know they feel bad now and believe it's the medication that's causing it. They may argue that the statistics tell you nothing and that they will be the one exception to the rule. The role of a parent in this situation is very tough. How do you deal with refusal to take medication when it occurs, and how do you prevent it from ever even occurring? This chapter offers ideas that we've seen work in a variety of settings.

Strategies for Encouraging Your Teen to Take Medication

If you know your teen isn't taking medications as prescribed, try to find out why not. We know quite a bit about why adults with bipolar disorder stop their medications, but we don't know much about teens. One of the main reasons that adults stop taking lithium or other mood stabilizers is that they miss their high feelings and resent having their moods controlled by a drug. The highs feel good, so why stop? When you combine this with the fact that mood stabilizers erase the highs more than the lows, you can conclude, as one of our patients did, that "medications take away all the good parts of the illness without touching the bad." This reasoning, however, oversimplifies things. Mania can feel good, but it quickly feels like a merry-go-round that's running off its tracks. Most of the mood stabilizers and atypical antipsychotics do alleviate depression even if they don't fully eradicate it. The dosages of lithium, Depakote, or other medications can be adjusted so that teens don't feel so devoid of emotions.

Side effects also contribute to nonadherence, especially when problems that can make a teen feel different from peers arise, like weight gain, jitteriness, cognitive problems, acne, or shaky hands. Codiagnosis (comorbidity) with other disorders can contribute too. In one of the studies mentioned above, the teens who didn't take their medication were most likely to be those who also had ADHD (who might have been more likely to forget their medications), those who abused alcohol, or those from a lower socioeconomic background (which may mean less money to pay doctors and buy medications and less access to health care in general). To determine exactly what is at work in your teen's case, you need to take a collaborative approach and communicate openly with your teen.

How to Discuss Medications with Your Teen

The best time to have an open discussion with your teen is at the beginning of her medication treatment or when medications have changed substantially because of the new bipolar diagnosis. Some parents had their first discussion with their children at age 7 or 8. If the first onset is during the preteen or teen years, you will usually have to do a fair amount of explaining, coaxing, and compromising to make the treatment plan work. Encourage your spouse to do the same.

Start by asking yourself a question: How strongly do I feel that my teen should take medications? Be very clear about your position on this—if you're not sure, your teenager will pick that up and run with it; see the box below.

If you're sure your teen should be taking medications, then ideally discussions with your teen will end with her assuring you of her intention to stay with the regimen. However, you may eventually have to insist in the same way you insist that she go to school or complete her homework. We hope it won't come down to your having to say "You'll do it or else" because then your teen will stop taking medications as soon

HOW DO YOU FEEL
ABOUT YOUR TEEN'S TAKING MEDICATIONS?

None of us wants to put our kids on medications unnecessarily. But if you're convinced that your teen has bipolar disorder, you should know that medication is going to be necessary. You should also know that kids tend to miss more doses when their parents don't believe the drugs are effective. This suggests that parents may directly or indirectly communicate their disbelief in the treatment regimen to their children. Alternatively, parents who don't view medications as effective may refuse to give them to their kids.

You may be less likely to feel this way if your teen has been ill for a long time or if you take medications for a mood disorder yourself. But even then, it's not uncommon for parents to raise questions. Or maybe your spouse has doubts and you feel like getting your child to adhere to a medication regimen involves convincing two people, not just one. If you're not convinced your teen needs the medication prescribed, review Chapters 3 and 4 to see whether your attitude is based on reasonable doubt about her diagnosis or an emotional reaction to accepting the realities imposed by the disorder.

as she is out of your reach. The goal is to get her on board with the treatment plan and the importance of taking care of her own health.

Talk with your teen about the pros and cons of taking medications, the fact that it is really a cost–benefit decision (and how you—and she—would weigh the pros and cons), the side effects she might expect, your awareness that medications make her feel different and perhaps stigmatized, what the future may hold, what your own experiences have been with medications, and similar issues. These talks usually go along with some discussion about the bipolar illness itself (along with any comorbid conditions), a diagnosis your teen may or may not agree with. Show your awareness and understanding of the kinds of issues that may be running around in her head but that she can't articulate ("This means I'll never be independent"; "I'll never have kids"; "Boys won't find me attractive"; etc.). If you want to read more, we highly recommend Tim Wilens's book *Straight Talk about Psychiatric Medications for Kids*.

Finding the Right Tone

Seventeen-year-old Tashi admitted she had bipolar disorder with wide mood swings, but her consistency with her Depakote and Seroquel was spotty at best. She reacted angrily when her mother asked her if she had taken her pills on any particular day. Nonetheless, during a family therapy session she had this to say: "I think it's a good idea that Mom reminds me to take it, and I want her to, especially when I'm getting manic. I know I need to. But I can tell you now I'll hate it when she does." Her mother had learned to raise the issue cautiously and with an easygoing tone of voice.

Consider Tashi's example in contrast with one described by Kate Millet, the author of the well-known book *Sexual Politics*, who also wrote an autobiography of her experiences with bipolar disorder (*The Loony Bin Trip*). She describes her interactions with her family members like this: "Accusing me of mania, my elder sister's voice has an odd manic quality. 'Are you taking your medicine?' A low controlled mania, the kind of control in furious questions addressed to children, such as 'Will you get down from there?' "

Note the central issue of personal control. While your teen may indeed need reminding, the act of being reminded makes her feel small, dumb, and dependent, all the things that teens hate to feel. So, approach her in a low-key, nonaccusatory way, even when you have doubts about whether she is sticking with an agreed-on treatment plan.

If your teen is taking medications on his own, you may suspect that he's cutting corners or lying about taking them. There are good and bad ways to ask if he's following through. We prefer questions like these: "Are you having any trouble taking all of your pills?" "Do you ever find yourself forgetting? It's easy to do so." "You know, most kids miss their pills once in a while—what about you?"

Lastly, as you'll see in numerous examples in the next section, we prefer the "motivational enhancement" approach to encouraging healthy behavior. This means avoiding an overly directive, authoritarian, commanding approach in favor of a lower-key stance in which you ask questions that tap into the goals your teen has set for herself. Instead of "You'd better take those pills if you want to avoid going to the hospital," ask a question: "How do you see your life changing if you stop taking the pills?" "How could taking them potentially help you?" "What do you want to have happen in the next school year—will the medications help you or hurt you in getting there?"

Some parents feel it's really up to the teen's psychiatrist or therapist to ask these questions. Maybe you don't feel comfortable in this role or you feel your teen wouldn't welcome such a discussion. That's understandable, but we also believe it's risky to assume that these issues are being addressed elsewhere. The "open door" approach, even if redundant with what your teen is hearing elsewhere, is more likely to yield positive outcomes than avoiding the topic.

Using the Best Term: Concordance, Compliance, and Adherence

We usually prefer to use the term *concordance* when talking about whether a teen is taking prescribed medications, rather than either *compliance* or *adherence*. *Compliance* assumes the doctor is in command and the patient must follow along without thinking for himself. *Adherence* conjures images of authoritarian doctor–patient relationships, which, needless to say, don't work well. People with bipolar disorder tend to dislike the term *adherence* (Paul, a patient of ours, when asked if he was being adherent with his Depakote, responded, "What am I? Glued to the stuff?"). Nonetheless, you may hear both of these terms in your teen's doctor's office.

Concordance refers to the congruence between the treatment plan recommended by the psychiatrist and the plan your teen actually carries out. It emphasizes that the teen has *agreed* to the treatment prescribed and is not just following it. A doctor–patient relationship ought to be a collaborative one, where the doctor takes in and actively considers the patient's (or his caregivers') input. The term *nonconcordant* does not have to imply that the teen or the parent is at fault; in fact, a teen can be nonconcordant because the doctor didn't explain the drug regimen, discuss the expected side effects, or treat him (or you) in a respectful, empathic, or collaborative manner.

Ultimately, what's important is not the term used but the concept. Your teen will be most likely to take medication as prescribed if he has agreed to the treatment plan, not had it foisted on him. This concept underlies the general principles that encourage many teens to take the medications that can help them.

General Principles for Encouraging Your Teen to Take Medications

Most people with bipolar illness will eventually commit to a program of medications if the conditions in the sidebar below are met. None of these will come as a surprise to you—naturally, teens choose to do something when they feel there's a good rationale for doing it. In reinforcing this rationale, you'll have to reach your teen on the *cognitive, emotional,* and *behavioral* levels.

Most people with bipolar disorder will commit to a program of medications if they . . .

- Receive information on what the drugs will do, how they will help, how they work, and what side effects to expect.
- See the actual evidence of benefits of medications, either through their own experiences or by observing their recovery on a mood chart.
- Are approached with compassion, emphasizing that taking medications doesn't change one's fundamental identity.
- Feel it is their own decision and not forced on them by others.
- Can communicate regularly with their physician about adjusting dosages or introducing other medications to reduce side effects.
- Are not given a "life sentence" but instead are given a hopeful and realistic view of the future, including the expectation that symptoms and side effects will eventually remit and life will improve.

Cognitive Level

Teens must have an intellectual understanding of what bipolar disorder is. They need to understand that medications don't change who they are but rather their symptoms; that depression or anxiety will not disappear right away but that they should be able to expect to feel better within a few months if they stick with it; and why it is important not to drop the medications if side effects are at first troubling and improvement is not immediate.

They need to understand that they can discuss their concerns with their doctor and the doctor will make adjustments. Many doctors communicate this directly to the teen: "Try the medications out for a couple of months and see if you feel better. If you don't, come in and talk to me and let's see what we can do to adjust it." Teens want to feel they have some control over their own fate, even if they know their parents can ultimately decide they must take it.

Understanding that the disorder has a genetic basis can also help here. Patrick, age 17, was reluctant to take medication because he didn't feel like being the "odd man out" in his otherwise healthy, wealthy, and athletic family. Learning that his father had had a psychotic episode in college involving a suicide attempt, which was subsequently treated successfully with antidepressants, made him feel less stigmatized within his own family and more willing to at least try medications.

Behavioral Level

Assistance on a behavioral level usually takes the form of reminders like weekly pill dispensers or watch alarms. It may also involve rewards for taking medications (for example, being able to stay out later on Friday night or gain access to the car) or consequences for not taking them. It involves designing the regimen (with the doctor's help) so that taking pills fits in with other routines like eating, showering, homework, or bedtime. It involves making regular trips to the psychiatrist's or general practitioner's clinic to get his blood level tested or to get prescriptions adjusted and filled.

Emotional Level

Medications make teens feel creepy and stigmatized, as if they've turned into old people overnight. They feel sick, different from their friends, or crazy (or, as one teen put it, like I'm "going postal"). The pills make them nauseous, give them headaches, make them gain weight, and above all, *make them feel different.* Tanya, age 16, thought, "If I could go off them and do OK, I could show everyone that they were wrong, that I wasn't crazy after all."

Addressing emotions means being compassionate and validating your teen's reactions, even if they are irrational. She may strongly resent taking medications but then panic when she realizes she didn't take them to her friend's house. She may accuse you of drugging her and threaten to stop taking them, and then brag to her friends that she needs to take "mood pills because I have a bipolar brain." She may resent your reminding her to take pills but then blame you for not reminding her if she forgets to take them. Some teens have a love/hate relationship with the pills, as these examples illustrate.

Talk to your teen about her painful emotions about being ill and different from others, fears about what this means for her future, and the eventual need to revise her life goals to take into account the cycling of the illness. These emotional reactions and worries have been summarized as "grieving over the lost healthy self" and involve the fear that one has fundamentally changed or left an earlier, happier life behind, that one must give up one's most important life goals, or that the future will be less hopeful and more painful than the past. There is nothing like having to take a medication every day to remind you of this conflict.

Matching the Strategy with the Reason for Nonconcordance

If your discussions about medication are fruitful, you'll emerge with an understanding of why your teen may choose not to take medications at different phases of his life. The following ideas will help you address each of these reasons as they arise.

"I Miss My High Periods"

Kay Jamison has written extensively about the strong pull of the manic high and how the stabilization offered by lithium or other drugs spoils the party. Not everyone experiences mania as a positive state, but the increased energy and speed of thinking can be a real draw. A teen who starts to experience the early signs of mania or hypomania may conclude that she doesn't need medications and that the fun has just begun.

If your teen expresses these thoughts, remind him of how prior manic episodes have disrupted his life, ruined friendships, gotten him into trouble at school or with the law, and possibly landed him in the hospital. Think of this as a cost–benefit analysis: If you go off, yes, you may feel better and happier temporarily, but what else can happen? What will you do if you start to get *really* high and can't slow down? You've said you want to get your learner's permit this summer, and we've said that requires you to get good grades this year; will going off of your medications increase your chances of making that happen?

If your teen never gets manic, only hypomanic, remind him of two things: first, being hypomanic is not the same as feeling good, and you can still feel good on medications, and second, "what goes up must come down." So, while medication may even out a relatively harmless high period, it may also prevent a more serious depression from following.

If your teen continues to yearn for her highs throughout several manic and depressive cycles, consider the potential utility of a support group with other bipolar teens. She may have to hear from other teens that being drawn in by euphoric feelings is dangerous. Your teen may have developed a type of amnesia for the events that occurred during her last manic episode, and other teens may remind her of what can happen—the arrests, the conflicts with school personnel, the unwanted pregnancies, or the hospitalizations.

"I Can't Deal with These Side Effects"

Many teens understandably find the weight gain, acne, shaking hands, headaches, and cognitive slowing caused by mood stabilizers or atypicals unacceptable. If they're athletes, they may feel like a "spaz" on the basketball court or soccer field. They may hate the way they look or the way they carry themselves. They may feel that their mind or memory is gone or that they constantly have a queasy or jittery feeling in their stomach. Some of the side effects are difficult to even talk about. One girl stopped taking her antipsychotic agent because it caused constipation that she was too embarrassed to discuss with her doctor. Another was having problems with the regularity of her menstrual period due to her Depakote. A 17-year-old boy who was sexually active was unwilling to take antidepressants because of the erectile difficulties they caused.

Side effects can be managed by developing a collaborative connection with the psychiatrist, with whom your teen can negotiate an acceptable treatment plan. ***There are four ways to adapt a medication regimen to minimize side effects: drop the dosages, change the frequency or time*** *of day of dosing, switch to another medication, or add a side effect medication.*

Here are a few examples: The sedation caused by Seroquel can sometimes be managed by taking the pills at night. Likewise, the agitation and insomnia caused by Adderall can be managed by taking the entire dosage in the morning. The mental sluggishness or "blunted" feeling on lithium can be addressed by reducing the dosage or by switching to Depakote, which is less likely to cause this side effect. The hair thinning that occurs with Depakote can be addressed by adding a zinc or selenium supplement (both available over the counter). If your child is still manic and gaining a great deal of weight on Zyprexa, her doctor may recommend Risperdal; likewise, if she's depressed and gaining weight on Depakote, lamotrigine can sometimes be substituted. Provigil is sometimes recommended for problems with mental slowing. Changing to extended-release forms of certain drugs (for example, Depakote) can reduce side effects like weight gain or stomach distress. Introducing drugs like metaforim or topiramate can also combat weight gain.

Of course, switching medications or lowering dosages can have its own risks. The new medication or lower dosage may not be as effective as the old regimen or may come with other side effects (for example, a rash on lamotrigine; cognitive slowing with topiramate). Nonetheless, side effects are a problem with a concrete solution.

One way you can assist in this process is to ask your child to record her side effects on a daily chart that she takes in to the psychiatrist during her weekly, biweekly, or monthly visits. One such chart is on page 184. If she won't or can't do this, try to do it with her every day or every few days. Star those side effects you'd particularly like her to talk about with her doctor.

Of course, problem solving with the doctor about side effects is most likely to be successful if you, your teen, and the physician have a good working relationship. Not surprisingly, medication concordance is higher among adolescents who like their physician and whose sessions are long enough to discuss any concerns. If your teen strongly dislikes the doctor, and/or you feel the doctor is not listening to the concerns raised, switch to another physician. Keep in mind, however, that teens often say they dislike their doctor when the doctor gives them information they don't want to hear.

As we've mentioned, certain medications, notably lithium and Depakote, require regular blood draws. Many kids and adults are afraid of needles, and this requirement can be enough to cause your teen to stop

Keeping Track of My Side Effects

Day of the week	Kind of medication	Number of pills	Side effects
Monday	_____	_____	_____
Monday	_____	_____	_____
Monday	_____	_____	_____
Tuesday	_____	_____	_____
Tuesday	_____	_____	_____
Tuesday	_____	_____	_____
Wednesday	_____	_____	_____
Wednesday	_____	_____	_____
Wednesday	_____	_____	_____
Thursday	_____	_____	_____
Thursday	_____	_____	_____
Thursday	_____	_____	_____
Friday	_____	_____	_____
Friday	_____	_____	_____
Friday	_____	_____	_____
Saturday	_____	_____	_____
Saturday	_____	_____	_____
Saturday	_____	_____	_____
Sunday	_____	_____	_____
Sunday	_____	_____	_____
Sunday	_____	_____	_____

Examples of side effects: Insomnia, headaches, fatigue, memory problems, low energy, hand shaking, weight gain, urinating often, constipation, dry mouth, rash, hair loss, restlessness, crabbiness, acne, diarrhea.

her medication. If your teen is needle-phobic, it's probably best to ask the doctor to switch her to options that don't require as many blood tests, such as lamotrigine or the atypical antipsychotics. If the doctor insists your teen continue on lithium and get blood levels, you may have to look into behavioral desensitization programs that reduce needle phobia (see Chapter 6).

"Medication Destroys My Creativity"

As you may have heard, bipolar illness has been linked with artistic, musical, and literary creativity. Kay Jamison wrote about this in her book *Touched with Fire: Manic–Depressive Illness and the Artistic Temperament*. Examples of historical figures with bipolar illness may have included Ernest Hemingway, Ludwig Van Beethoven, Vincent Van Gogh, Sylvia Plath, Delmore Schwartz, Robert Lowell, and Anne Sexton. A study at the Stanford University School of Medicine found that children of bipolar parents had higher creativity scores than children of nonbipolar parents.

Although your teen may complain that mood stabilizers affect her creativity, the data on lithium suggest the opposite: among artists and writers with bipolar disorder, more say that lithium enhances their creativity than detracts from it. Although mania can increase work *quantity*, it doesn't necessarily improve work *quality*. Artists, musicians, and writers with the disorder usually report that they do their best work when their mood is stable.

If your teen does artwork or plays a musical instrument requiring fine motor control, lithium or Depakote could interfere because of the side effect of shaking hands. If it does, ask the teen's doctor to reevaluate her medications and, if possible, lower her dosage or switch to another mood stabilizer. But in most cases, teens will not be more creative or produce better work off medications than on.

"There's Nothing Wrong with Me"

Teens who adhere to this belief usually think that the problem is those around them and there's a conspiracy to label them as crazy and make them take medications. This lack of insight can be a symptom of mania or psychosis.

Some teens will continue to take their medications while insisting there's nothing wrong with them. They may reject the idea that they have a biological vulnerability and believe that the illness was a one-time occurrence. These kids will often discontinue medications at some later point when they have more control over their day-to-day life. Others covertly believe they do have an illness but find it too painful to admit, so their compromise is to take medications and complain that they're being treated unjustly.

If your teen is using this argument to avoid taking medications, acknowledge that there may indeed be environmental stressors that are affecting him negatively, like heated family arguments, a recent relationship breakup, economic problems, or a difficult sibling. In language he can understand, make clear that you view bipolar disorder as the result of the interaction of life stressors with an individual's biological system. Say that you plan to help him address some of the issues that are serving as environmental triggers for mood episodes. In fact, if he has a therapist, ask him if you can talk to the therapist about the stressors you feel are weighing on him and contributing to his mood swings and nonconcordance.

Once again, reflect on the teen's personal goals and the ways in which medications can help her achieve things that might otherwise be impossible (for example, graduating from high school). Teens need to understand why they are being treated and how this is in their best interests. Help your teen see the link between therapy, concordance, and staying out of the hospital (if she has been in one before).

"My Medications Aren't Working"

In our experience, teens say this for one of two reasons: (1) the medications really aren't working, or (2) they define *working* quite differently than you would as a parent.

It's entirely possible that the medication is not effective, because between 30 and 40% of teens don't respond to drugs like lithium or Depakote. Teens tend to do better on combinations of mood stabilizers and/or atypical antipsychotics than on any single medication, but even complex regimens can be ineffective, especially if the diagnosis was done hurriedly and in such a way that comorbid conditions were missed. So, as a first step, determine if you agree that there has been *no* improvement. Your teen will almost certainly doubt the utility of his medications if he knows you have your own doubts.

As we discussed in Chapter 6, medications need to be taken for at least 6–8 weeks before determining whether they're ineffective. Keep a mood and sleep–wake chart to have a more quantifiable measure of your teen's success over time and encourage your teen to do the same (see the extensive discussion of mood charts in Chapter 10). Then set up a session with his psychiatrist to troubleshoot the regimen and see if it's time to make a switch. Avoid discussing your own doubts about the medications' efficacy with your teen before you've had a chance to share these perceptions with his doctor.

If you feel the medications are working but haven't been given enough time, explain the trajectory of improvement to your teen. Explain that depressive episodes sometimes take several months to stabilize and that your teen's cognitive or athletic abilities may take longer to fully return than her stable moods. Encourage her to remain hopeful and optimistic.

Your teen may admit that the medications have stabilized his mood but that other goals, like having a girlfriend or making the cut on a sports team, have not been achieved. Some teens believe a medication works if others are nicer to him and give him what he wants! So it's important to have a discussion about how he defines medication success and whether these are realistic expectations.

"Medication Makes Me Feel Different from Everyone Else"

Psychiatric disorders and the medications used to treat them continue to carry a stigma of personal or moral weakness, despite the best efforts of mental health professionals and groups like the National Alliance on Mental Illness to reduce this outdated view. Your teen will probably be acutely aware of this issue, especially if he was diagnosed recently. But stigma has a way of rearing its ugly head even for kids who got used to the diagnosis long ago and believed that everyone else understood and accepted them.

Teens often talk painfully of the way their peers use the term "bipolar" flippantly (for example, "Don't go all bipolar on me") or say of a person they dislike that "she should totally be on lithium." Your teen may admit to a trusted friend that she has bipolar disorder and takes medications, only to have that friend spread it over the Internet the next time they have a fight. Teens may also believe that people have learned of their illness even though they haven't disclosed it to anyone. One teen said, "They can tell there's something wrong with me just by watching me walk." The stigma can make a teen think about stopping medications, or even that medications are the real cause of his social problems. Alternatively, your teen may decide not to take them when spending time with friends, such as during summer camp or a weekend overnight. Of course, this kind of inconsistency can render the medications ineffective.

The first step is to acknowledge your teen's feelings about the disorder's stigma. Try to get into the mind-set of a teenager who is trying to make sense of the illness, doctors, blood tests, therapy, and pills, and what they mean for now and the future. Calmly say something like, "I think you're absolutely right. There's a lot of ignorance out there about mood disorders—I'm sure that's pretty upsetting." If you have a mood disorder yourself and take medications, share your own experiences of stigma (if you've had any) and how you came to terms with your own need for medications.

The other point to get across, however, is that combating the stigma by discontinuing medications is tantamount to giving up the battle and saying that others are right. If you refuse medications that could help you because others will make fun of you, you are essentially buying into their point of view. Teens want to feel that they are making decisions that are not forced on them by others, including their peers.

The feelings of stigma are often tied in to the teen's distrust of the diagnosis and the need for medications. Often the conversation about how *others* think it's weird has to start with the question "Do you agree with them?" Your teen may be shielding her own doubts by attributing the discomfort to other people. The real issue may be "I don't like that I *need* to take medications." Once again, a support group with other teens who have bipolar disorder will be helpful in reducing her denial, feelings of isolation, and doubts about the need for medications.

Some teens benefit from a problem-solving discussion about whom to tell about the disorder and how much. Some teens proudly tell everyone. Others keep it a closely guarded secret and worry constantly that others will find out. It's a good idea to draw out your teen's thinking about how to present it to people. What would she want others to know, and why? Can they help her in some way? Does she want to tell them about the disorder and the hospitalization, or only that she's taking medications? One teen described her mood disorder as simply a "problem with my chemistry that makes my moods go all over," which seemed adequate for her friends.

Ask your teen to identify when and in what situations she is most likely to feel stigmatized. For example, is she being called out of class to go to the nurse's office to take her pills? Does she have to take them in front of others at lunch? Taking longer-acting medications or medications that require fewer tablets (for example, Adderall XR, Depakote ER, Lithobid, or single daily dosing of Abilify) may reduce the likelihood of this kind of public discomfort.

Finally, try to get her to see the issue in a larger context. Yes, taking medications and experiencing side effects makes her feel different, or slow, or overweight. But the illness has its own negative consequences that are minimized by medications. Remind her that bipolar illness is a medical illness like any other and that most medical illnesses (diabetes and asthma, for example) require taking long-term medications.

"Taking Medications Means Giving Up Control in My Family"

As Bart's story at the beginning of this chapter illustrates, medications can easily get tied up with family dynamics. Many of the studies of children with medical illnesses find that concordance is intertwined with family cohesion, conflict, or communication. Few teens can say directly that they are refusing medications to gain their independence, but that's often the case, particularly among older teens. We've seen cases where a child has been concordant throughout childhood and then stops when he hits the teen years. What better way to assert your independence?

A sign that this issue is operating in the background is when, during battles over privileges, your teen says, "Okay! Then I won't take my medication either!" These situations have to be handled delicately. Rule one is to not play the game: *don't allow your teen to fight his autonomy battles by rebelling against his treatments.* A good first response is "That's your option, of course, and it always has been. But I don't see what that has to do with your going out tonight." Other responses, which may or may not feel appropriate at the moment, may include "That's not on the table for discussion right now—I'll be happy to talk with you about that at another time when we're not both angry," or simply "That's a very important issue. I can understand why you'd want to make you own choices about medications."

When you feel she's ready to discuss the issue in a rational way, examine the possibility that your teen can take more responsibility for her own regimen. Marla's daughter, Bernadette, age 13, said, "I'm not a kid anymore, so you don't have to feed me your little pills." Marla had been giving Bernadette her medications with breakfast up to this point. Could Bernadette take responsibility for dispensing them from the pillbox each morning and taking them? Marla challenged her to behave in a more adult way: adults would make sure they took their medications along to school, overnights, or sporting events, instead of expecting a parent to remind them.

You can make other valued teen privileges contingent on remembering to take medications and keep appointments. Get your teen to agree to a daily contract for a minimum level of consistency and, if she follows through, reward her by backing off, as Bart's story illustrates. These plans encourage your teen to view medications as one avenue toward independence.

Sabotage from Other Family Members

Earlier in this chapter we noted how important it is that you be on board with your teen's medications so that you don't unintentionally give "unstated permission" to stop taking them. But it's also possible that other family members will contribute to your teen's resistance to taking the pills. Siblings, for example, can make your teen feel like taking medications makes her the black sheep, the crazy one, the wimp, the less loved one. Your teen will particularly rebel against medications if there is an older, more successful sibling who is also moody but doesn't have to take medications. Does she believe that there are "sick people and well people" in her family and that she happens to be one of the unlucky ones? If you recognize these dynamics, have a long talk with her—and, separately, with her siblings—about what the diagnosis and medications do and don't mean and how sensitive these issues are for her. If it seems appropriate, say to an older sibling, "I know you want to be a good big brother [sister]. Making her feel okay about herself is one way."

An even tougher situation involves a spouse who is not on board with treatment. We've seen this issue crop up most frequently in divorced, coparenting pairs where one believes the child is ill and the other doesn't. Separated parents have been known to undermine the treatment arranged by the other parent through comments to the child such as "You were so much more agile/graceful/athletic/quick before you started taking that medication." One divorced father of a 17-year-old put it bluntly: "I think all these drugs and therapists are bullshit. The real problem is that she can't get along with her mother." Teens can easily exploit this situation to their benefit. They will learn that they can skip medication at Dad's house. They may say they prefer Dad's house because that's where they can forget about their illness.

It will come as no surprise to you that coparenting a bipolar teen requires a highly coordinated effort in which both parents follow the same health-related plans for their child. If you feel your ex-spouse (or your current spouse, for that matter) is interfering with your teen's treatment, clear this up through constructive discussion, without your teen present. You may need to educate the other parent about how you understand the teen's problems, why you think he has bipolar disorder, and what purposes the medications serve. A couple therapist or divorce mediator may be very helpful, as might be a support group oriented toward educating parents about the illness (see *www.ndmda.org* or *www.nami.org*). In the next chapter, we'll acquaint you with some skills you can use to facilitate communication with your current or ex-spouse.

"I Can't Remember to Take My Medications"

Nonconcordance is often related to simple forgetting. Teens with bipolar illness have problems with attention and memory, as well as other cognitive disturbances. Moreover, the side effects of lithium, topiramate, and other drugs can include mental confusion. Forgetting is most common among teens with comorbid ADHD or those who are abusing alcohol, both of which are associated with short-term memory impairment.

It's easy to forget to take medications. Think of the last time you took antibiotics, birth control pills, or blood pressure or cholesterol medications. If your teen is on several medications that have to be taken at different times of the day, the problems are compounded. Common memory disturbances related to pill taking include thinking you've taken them when you haven't and taking them again when you already have. People sometimes mistakenly take double dosages and then have more side effects.

The real dilemma for parents is determining whether their teen is really having trouble remembering to take medications or is just resisting taking them. How cognitively compromised is your teen? If he's having trouble with other kinds of recall, such as remembering homework assignments, bringing books or clothes home, keeping appointments, or doing chores, he may not remember to take medications either. Some parents take the safest route and simply dole out the medications and watch the teen swallow them. This procedure, while probably the most likely to yield consistency, will be less and less feasible—and less developmentally appropriate—as your child ages.

Your first stop in dealing with this issue is an open discussion with your teen. What does he understand of the reasons for the drug regimen and its daily dosing schedules? Many teens who forget their pills haven't been given good reasons for why medications should be a part of their daily routine. Do they understand why maintaining a therapeutic blood level is important (that is, to prevent recurrences)? If he understands all of this but still says he can't remember, get your teen into the habit of keeping a daily mood and sleep chart (see Chapter 10) or use the side effects sheet printed on page 184.

Your teen's doctor should be your next stop, to determine if there are ways to adjust the regimen to make it easier to remember. There is considerable evidence in the medical world that single dosing of medications—regardless of the illness—promotes better adherence than twice- or three-times daily dosing. The doctor may be able to change your teen's dosing frequency or even the medication itself (for example, changing from multidose Seroquel to single-dose Abilify, or switching her Depakote tablets to the 500-mg extended-release version).

The third stop is the drugstore. There you'll find memory aids such as clear plastic pill boxes with slots for each day of the week and even the time of day. They are about 4 inches by 6 inches and can come with different colored borders for the names of different children in your family. These boxes allow your teen to tell at a glance whether he has taken a pill on a specific day and time. If your teen is younger and/or has many cognitive problems, you may use the pillbox as a reminder to yourself or other family members (for example, grandparents) who become involved in your child's health care.

If pills are to be taken several times a day and don't necessarily coin-

---

REMINDING YOUR TEEN TO TAKE MEDICATIONS

- Explain to your teen the rationale for the regimen and how it should fit in with his daily routine.
- Ask her to keep track of her medication taking with a daily mood or side effects chart.
- Arrange with the physician to have dosing plans simplified.
- Buy him a pill dispenser or pill key chain with days of the week marked on it.
- Use watch alarms for twice- or three-times daily dosing.
- Use Post-It note reminders.
- Arrange medication to coincide with breakfast, dinner, TV time, bedtime.

WHAT TO TELL YOUR TEEN
TO GET HIM OR HER ON BOARD WITH MEDICATIONS

- Medications are not a "life sentence"; they are a means of improving your health and quality of life now.
- Side effects can be controlled.
- Medications can limit the fun and exhilarating features of the illness, but these features often have the most dangerous consequences.
- Medications don't have to mean giving up personal control or autonomy.
- Medications don't have to mean that you're crazy or dramatically different from your siblings or peers.
- If one medication doesn't work, another can be added or substituted.
- You have a greater chance of becoming independent if you take medication than if you let the illness run its own course.
- There are effective ways to remind yourself to take medications.

cide with events like breakfast, lunch, and dinner, make sure your teen has a watch alarm. If the pills coincide with going to bed or waking up, leave a Post-It note on the bathroom mirror. If you or other members of your family also take regular medications, make medication taking a family ritual and take your own pills at the same time she does.

Of course, all of this presumes that your teen's issue is forgetting, rather than resistance to the idea that she's ill at all. If your best attempts to structure her and remind her have failed, and she is otherwise functioning at a healthy cognitive level, you may be dealing with resistance to the diagnosis and its treatment rather than forgetting. Your teen may not have access to these feelings or beliefs, which may be entirely unconscious. Her therapist and psychiatrist should be involved in addressing these issues.

As you've noticed throughout this chapter, medication concordance is only one piece of the larger puzzle of effectively managing the disorder. Good communication and problem solving between you, your teen, and other family members is one of the keys to making the illness and its treatments go smoothly. In the next section of the book you'll learn about ways to promote long-term stability: how to manage family relationships, what strategies to use to maintain wellness, and ways to prevent the most severe highs and lows.

PART III

Helping Your Teen
Stay Well

9   Family Management and Coping

When we first started seeing the Martins in family-focused treatment, the family was on the verge of splitting up. Tara, their 17-year-old with bipolar disorder, was "wreaking havoc with our lives," according to her mother, Tess. She was disappearing at night and showing up early the next morning with no explanation of where she had been. She had been arrested for drunk driving several times and recently had taken the drug Ecstasy at a party. Without her parents' permission, she had invited her boyfriend to come and live with them, saying he would sleep in the basement. However, Tess woke up to find him in Tara's bed on several mornings. Tess's second husband, Chris, was shown little respect by Tara or by any of her siblings; they repeatedly told him, "You're not our dad, so don't act like you are."

Several times when they had been out, Tara had loudly called Tess a "bitch" when denied something she wanted. They would get into "screaming brawls" in public that continued until they got home. Tara would then threaten to kill herself and Tess would cry. Tara's other siblings did not have bipolar disorder but were "acting out in response to what they see in Tara," Tess said. Katy, age 13, had begun telling her mother to f**k off, wearing provocative clothes, and staying up unusually late on school nights. Bob, age 15, had been caught stealing a soda from a minimart, and his grades were dropping.

When we asked Tara for her side of the story, she angrily responded that she had become the "lightning rod" for all of her family's problems. Her mother was constantly angry at her and blamed her for things that her siblings had done. She felt no connection with Chris. She and her brother, Bob, had gotten into one physical scuffle where Bob had punched her. She cried and said that no one acknowledged anything she did well, such as baking a cake for her grandmother's birthday and cleaning the garage without being asked. Tess ignored these comments and kept coming back to "My family is falling apart. If she weren't bipolar, none of this would be happening." This enraged Tara even further, saying that "my supposed bipolar" had come to mean everything that her mom disliked about her own life.

We probably don't have to tell you that bipolar disorder can cause upheaval in families. To make matters worse, tension and conflict in the home can rob a teen of a major source of protection and support. When the teen's illness worsens as a result, the family is damaged even more. Fortunately, taking measures to reduce family conflict can help your teen gain control over the cycling of her disorder and make a more complete recovery.

This is, of course, easier said than done. What can a family do when there is constant mudslinging going on, much of which can be attributed to the bipolar teen's instability? How can communication be improved so that every encounter doesn't feel like an attack? *In our experience, parents of bipolar teens need to become extra skillful at communicating, solving problems, and managing their own emotions, far more so than is required of the parents of healthy teens.*

In this chapter, you'll gain some tools for enhancing your own coping skills so that you can more effectively manage a difficult family situation. The five techniques of the PEACE model (summarized in the box on the facing page) will help you preserve everyone's well-being and rights as well as provide tools for tackling the specific challenges of living with a bipolar teen. All of these skills require substantial practice, and even then they won't apply to every situation, but we're confident that if you regularly apply them, family life will be substantially better.

A Fine Balance

An important component of maintaining peace in your family life is negotiating the balance between being more involved when your teen is experiencing mood symptoms and less involved at other times. This is one of the biggest challenges for parents—figuring out when to step in when

FIVE PRINCIPLES FOR MAINTAINING
GOOD FAMILY RELATIONSHIPS
The PEACE Approach to Coping with Bipolar Disorder

- Problem solving
- Education about the disorder
- Acceptance of the disorder and its limitations
- Communication skills
- Escape from the situation when necessary

the teen is doing things that harm herself or others (for example, taking drugs or using alcohol, getting into brawls with siblings) and when to back off and allow the teen to be more independent. Three concepts are central to finding this balance: *support*, *structure*, and *setting limits*. We'll say more about each of these below.

P: Problem Solving

Tess had learned from parenting classes that "you always have to negotiate with teenagers." But she had begun to believe that negotiating with Tara was impossible: Tara seemed to expect Tess to give her everything she wanted. In fact, when Tess tried to meet Tara halfway, Tara became even more hostile and would not budge. As a result, Tess had stopped generating solutions to problems and would simply start shouting, which usually resulted in Tara screaming back. She had noticed, however, that before Tara became enraged, there was an interval when she seemed able to reason and think through a situation. Tess eventually learned that problem solving needed to occur before Tara's mood began to deteriorate and to exit the confrontation herself if this wasn't possible.

Problem solving involves identifying and defining problems as specifically as possible and then, with your teen, "brainstorming" solutions to these specifically defined problems. Bipolar disorder can seem like one big intractable problem, but it can almost always be broken down into smaller, potentially negotiable units. You'll find problem solving especially helpful with disagreements over practical problems where family life and bipolar disorder often intersect, such as how to deal with poor sleep–wake habits, use of alcohol or drugs, medication nonconcordance, school problems, and lack of respect for others. Your goal will be to help your teen choose among various solutions and come up with a two-person agreement ("I'll expect you to talk to me in a more civil tone when I ask you to do something, and I'll do my best to keep from losing my temper"). Then you'll need to discuss how to implement the chosen solution.

This system sounds straightforward, but remember that bipolar teens have problems with "executive functioning" that make it especially difficult for them to plan ahead even when their mood is stable (see Chapter 5, where we discuss prefrontal cortex functioning in the context of the kindling theory). In many cases you'll have to step in to provide structure for your teen. Once she begins to be unreasonable, you may have to delay problem solving until she's in a more rational frame of mind.

Find the Problem-Solving Window in Every Conflict

Many parents say they've come to recognize exactly when their bipolar teen is going to "lose it," which is usually when he is asked to do something different from what he is already doing or wants to do. Your teen may have trouble shifting to a new task or set of plans. Many parents feel that this is just willful disobedience or a sign that the child is spoiled. It's more likely, however, that the teen is *unable* to make this mental transition and gets angry when asked to try. But there can be a brief window of opportunity *before* the teen loses it during which collaboration and problem solving are possible.

If you observe your teen carefully, you'll probably find that such a "window of opportunity" exists. It may be short—maybe only a few minutes—but if you work effectively with your teen you may be able to extend this window. Consider the following interchange between Tess and Tara. Tara was on the computer and seemed fully locked into instant messaging her friends.

TESS: Time for dinner, honey.

TARA: Just a minute!

TESS: (*Waits several minutes.*) Tara, come on, dinner's getting cold.

TARA: (*Responds quickly, angrily.*) I will! Leave me alone!

This is a choice point, because Tara was starting to escalate into the hostile, rageful reactions that were typical of her responses to her mother's requests for change (and are typical of the reactions of most bipolar teens). Tess could (1) go into Tara's room and attempt some problem solving (for example, "We seem to be having a disagreement. You want to work on the computer and I want us all to have dinner. What do you think we should do?"). She could also (2) start dinner with the rest of the family and Tara could join when she pleased. Or (3) Tess could yell in frustration, which would cause Tara to yell back and probably precipitate full-scale family conflict.

Tess learned that alternative (1) was useful for the first few minutes after the request had been made (the window of opportunity) but that after repeated failed attempts, it was better to drop the issue and then address it with Tara *after* dinner, when Tara had fully shifted her attention to the family. Avoiding (3), no matter how provocative the interchange, was critical to family peace.

Break Down Big, Overwhelming Problems into Smaller, More Manageable Units

Bipolar teens can easily become panic-stricken at the prospect of changing some major aspect of their behavior, so breaking a big problem into smaller issues can help ease their anxiety. Take chaotic sleep–wake habits as an example. What are the components of this larger problem? Maybe your teen gets overstimulated in the evening talking to his friends on the phone, or puts off his homework until the last minute, or drinks coffee after dinner and then can't fall asleep. If you think he's overstimulated by the computer at night, define the problem as "You get wired at night when you sit at the computer and then can't get to sleep—how are we going to interrupt this pattern?" Likewise, rather than defining a problem as "disrespect for parents," specify the "tone of voice you use when I ask you to help me with housework" as the specific problem for resolution.

Brainstorm and Choose Solutions

Here's where you can engage your teen in an important process: having input into family decisions. As you've probably noticed, teens with bipolar disorder are exquisitely sensitive to control by others. In brainstorming, encourage your teen to generate as many solutions—whether realistic or not—to the specifically defined disagreements you've identified. Then help him choose the best solution, which could end up being a combination of different solutions or "quid pro quo" (you do X and I'll do Y) agreements, and discuss how to implement it.

Tess and Tara had been getting into fights about whether she should go back to public school. Tess wanted her to go to an alternative school, where the academic load was lighter and she would be less likely to be provoked into irritability by her teachers (for example, she had recently cursed at a teacher who asked her to stop talking in class). Tess also felt that the ready availability of drugs and alcohol at the public school was contributing to Tara's emerging problems with substance abuse. However, Tara did not like the stigma of an alternative school—she thought it made her look like a "retard" to her friends. This issue had become very volatile because Tess felt it was her duty to protect her daughter from provocative situations that could worsen her symptoms, and Tara felt that her mother's intervention invaded her space. To what degree should Tess take charge to help her daughter manage her school life, and to what degree should she back off and let Tara make her own decisions?

With some coaching from a family therapist on how to paraphrase and acknowledge each other's point of view, Tess and Tara had the following collaborative discussion:

TESS: Well, it sounds to me like you don't want to go to Raleigh High (*paraphrasing*). But what are we going to do then? You can't go back to East High.

TARA: I *will* go back to East High.

TESS: Well, let's throw out all the possibilities first.

TARA: I could go to East High during the morning and Raleigh High in the afternoon.

TESS: That sounds like a good idea. What about the reverse?

TARA: No way. I wanna go in to East on the bus.

TESS: Okay, then, what about mixing the day between the two schools?

TARA: You mean, like, one class at Raleigh?

TESS: If we can work it out.

TARA: (*hesitating*) Maybe. I'd rather do Tuesdays and Thursdays, though.

After considerable discussion, Tess and Tara agreed to investigate a school schedule that would allow Tara to attend Raleigh High on Mondays and Wednesdays and East High on Tuesdays, Thursdays, and Fridays. They also agreed to try to arrange for her to take certain classes that previously had worsened her mood (math, science) at the alternative school. They agreed this was the best solution and admitted that they had arrived there together. But implementing it raised other challenges.

Implement the Solution

In addition to supportive conversations like those above, bipolar teens need considerable structure to implement changes in their behavior or habits. So, after you've arrived at an agreeable solution, take some time to talk with your teen about how you will both implement it. It may require action items (for example, calling a school counselor) or additional research (such as finding out what courses are offered at which school and at which times). Problem solving often falls by the wayside because parents or teens neglect the legwork required to implement a promising solution or because implementation generates other disagreements.

Tess felt (wisely, we agreed) that Tara needed to do some of the information gathering required to construct a new school schedule. This showed an acknowledgment of her daughter's desire to feel competent, especially because the illness had made her feel so inadequate and dependent. Tara found, to her disappointment, that certain of the courses she wanted to take at the two schools occurred at the same time, and dividing up the week was not realistic. Tess assisted Tara in scheduling a meeting with Raleigh High's guidance counselor. This meeting led to other creative scheduling solutions, which were eventually implemented.

As you've seen in these examples, problem solving is less likely to work when your teen's mood is unstable, but even then, progress can be made. In fact, structured problem solving can contribute to your teen's mood stability. It will help him feel that the immediate environment is predictable and that he has some control over what will happen to him. So, even though you may feel like you're swimming upstream, it's best to forge ahead. If you're not getting anywhere due to your teen's mood reactivity, return to the problem topic at another time.

What about Imposing Consequences?

Problem solving can include agreements of the form "If you fail to do X, I will impose Y consequence." You can try these, but in our experience they rarely work as well with bipolar teens as with nonbipolar teens. Some parents, for example, have attempted to discipline their child's aggressiveness by taking away TV privileges or use of the home computer. However, these are short-term consequences that cannot be expected to arrest emotional escalations that may be beyond the teen's control. In fact, we've seen some teens get more aggressive when their parents impose consequences, until their parents run out of ideas. Moreover, parents often can't possibly implement all of the disciplinary actions they've threatened.

E: Education

As we've emphasized throughout this book, knowledge is power. If everyone in your family is on the same page about what bipolar disorder is and is not, what causes it, how to prevent new episodes, and how to create a less conflictual family environment, you'll have a much easier time creating a protective environment for your teen.

The "Frequently Asked Questions" sheet on pages 205–206 lists some of the key facts about early-onset bipolar disorder that you'll want your family to know. It's designed to be understood by younger siblings, but it will also be a useful introduction for a spouse, extended relatives (for example, grandparents), your ex-spouse, or even one of your teen's schoolteachers (see Chapter 14). Use it as a starting point for discussions of how best to handle your teen's disorder as a family and then encourage your family members to read other, more in-depth material about the disorder (see the Resources section at the back of the book).

Depending on the age of your teen's siblings, you may want to explain the disorder in your own words, with the sheet as a backup. The goals of this discussion are to get across that (1) a significant portion of the teen's behavior is out of his control and driven by biological factors, (2) it is not the siblings' or the parents' fault, and (3) siblings can help the family by not provoking the bipolar teen. This is not the same as saying the bipolar teen's rights prevail; you can have a similar discussion with your teen about how not to provoke her siblings. As we discussed in Chapter 7, you may want to get your teen's siblings into treatment if they're showing the early warning signs of a mood disorder or seem to be having a tough time adjusting to family life with a bipolar sibling (as in Tara's family).

A: Acceptance

Acceptance is partly a thinking process, the core of which is to recognize that your child's behavior is at least in part driven by an illness, even when it seems willfully contrived. This is the hardest thing to do when

FREQUENTLY ASKED QUESTIONS ABOUT ADOLESCENT BIPOLAR DISORDER

What Is Bipolar Disorder?

It is a medical illness involving severe mood swings from very high and energized (manic) to very low or sad (depressed), often rapidly alternating between the two extremes. It often starts in the teen years or earlier. It affects about one in every 25 people in the United States.

What Are the Symptoms of Mania?

During the manic periods, kids feel overly happy or very irritable and angry. They may feel like they can do things no one else can or that they are smarter than everyone else. They may be constantly active, busy, and full of energy. They often sleep very little or not at all, or have very chaotic sleep patterns (for example, they stay up all night and sleep all day). They may talk very fast and express a lot of ideas or big plans, many of which are unrealistic.

What Are the Symptoms of Depression?

During a depression, kids feel very sad, irritable, and uninterested in things. They may lose interest in sports, school, or friends. They may sleep too much or not sleep even though they want to, which may make them even more irritable and sad. Depression also makes kids uninterested in eating, bathing, or taking care of themselves. Kids who are depressed move very slowly, talk slowly, get tired easily, and feel very bad about themselves. Some even talk about dying or try to hurt themselves.

How Will Bipolar Disorder Affect the Family?

When a bipolar teen becomes ill, he will have a tougher time getting along with family members. He may be more irritable, angry, or easily provoked by things that ordinarily wouldn't bother him. Family life will probably improve as his mood improves, but you can help by being kind, avoiding getting into

(cont.)

From *The Bipolar Teen* by David J. Miklowitz and Elizabeth L. George. Copyright 2008 by The Guilford Press.

arguments or fights (even when you feel the teen started it), and giving him plenty of room to get better on his own. Bipolar teenagers get better faster when family members are supportive and encouraging and avoid being critical or judgmental. Some families get counseling to help them get along better.

What Causes It?

People with bipolar disorder have problems with their brain chemistry, such as their neurotransmitters or hormones. These chemicals are necessary for the cells in the brain to communicate with each other. Nobody chooses to become bipolar. A bipolar kid may inherit the disorder from a parent or another relative. Having a brother or sister with bipolar disorder does not mean you will get it also. Most bipolar kids have siblings who do not have the illness.

How Is Bipolar Disorder Treated?

Bipolar illness usually requires medication treatments, which can include drugs like lithium, Depakote, or other mood stabilizers. Some bipolar teens have to take several different medications at different times of the day. This is why they have to see a psychiatrist (a medical doctor) to make sure they are getting the right medications and not having too many side effects. It can help for parents to remind him to take medications if he is prone to forgetting.

Some teens need to be in a hospital periodically to help them become stable. A bipolar teen usually needs to see a therapist or counselor to help him cope with the disorder and deal with the things that set him off, like school or family problems. It's important not to make him feel bad about taking medications or getting therapy.

What Will Happen in the Future?

Kids with bipolar disorder usually continue to have highs and lows throughout their lives, but with proper medication, therapy, and support from family members, these episodes will become rarer and less extreme. Your teen can still go to college, get married, have kids, and work productively at a job.

your teen is screaming and cursing at you, but the stance of acceptance will help you not to overreact.

Acceptance involves gaining some emotional distance from the negative behavior you're observing. Try this mental exercise: How would a stranger from another planet describe a serious argument between you and your son, using as many objective, nonjudgmental adjectives as possible, and without implying that one of you caused it more than the other? How would he describe each of you? The tone, the logic, the emotions? Then describe this to your son: "We're getting into that pattern again where you get mad, I get mad, you get madder, and I get madder—how do you think we can get out of it?" Or "This is not something either of us likes; what do you think we can do differently?"

The other side of acceptance is reminding yourself that there are environmental factors—both within and outside of the family—that affect your teen's behaviors and are not caused by bipolar disorder. Sometimes parents exaggerate the contribution of bipolar disorder to their teen's behavior, or exaggerate its contribution to the entire family's state of well-being. This exaggeration makes them take unnecessary control of the teen when she is really not that ill. It is understandable to have this kind of confusion—bipolar disorder explains a lot of family problems that may have been mysterious earlier. But it can be tempting to blame everything on the illness (see the section of Chapter 4 titled Stage 4: "It's a Brain Disorder"). Tara was particularly sensitized to this issue, believing she was constantly being blamed for everyone else's problems.

In trying to determine whether the irritability you're observing is bipolar behavior versus some other issue, ask yourself whether the symptoms have been consistent from day to day and go along with other symptoms of bipolar illness, such as sleep disturbance, grandiosity, or pressured speech. If none of these symptoms are present (that is, your teen does not appear to be in an illness episode), but your family is still fighting, there may be other issues to consider. Are siblings angry that the teen has been getting too much attention and provoking brawls to draw more parental attention to themselves? Has the family been under stress for other reasons (like financial problems or unrelated but escalating marital conflicts)? Try to take a similarly nonjudgmental, accepting stance toward these alternative explanations: if you or other family members are under stress for any number of reasons, naturally you'll overreact to your bipolar teen at times.

Finally, you and your teen may be discouraged by the idea that "this is as good as it gets." Try to convey to your teen and other family members that they need to accept the limitations imposed by the illness on their individual and family lives, but that you also recognize their attempts to make things better. Your teen and other family members are probably trying as hard as they can and need to feel that they're making progress, even if it's not immediately obvious. Express confidence that things will eventually improve. Voicing this kind of acceptance, acknowledgment, and encouragement takes some of the frustration out of the present and offers hope for the future.

C: Communication

Due to their ongoing problems with frontal lobe functioning, teens with bipolar disorder need parents to deliver succinct messages with clearly stated expectations. Unclear communication can raise your teen's anxiety and cause her to react angrily without knowing why. Communication skill principles such as active listening and making a positive request for change (see the box on the facing page) can help you act on the principles of support, structure, and setting limits. Any family with teenagers would benefit from the use of these skills, but bipolar teens are especially likely to benefit because of their cognitive limitations and emotional reactivity.

Consider the use of communication skills in the following conversation between Kurt (age 17) and his father, Evan, within a family treatment session. Kurt divided his time between his father's and his mother's houses. Evan and Kurt had been embroiled in a series of arguments about Kurt's unheralded disappearances from home and reappearances at all hours. Evan associated this behavior with Kurt's mania, although Kurt argued that he was just being independent, like any teen. Evan was understandably confused about how to set limits: should he err on the side of interfering with Kurt's independence in an attempt to keep Kurt stable or back off and risk facilitating Kurt's mania?

> KURT: (*snidely*) So, I have a "clarifying question." Why is my coming and going a problem for you?
>
> EVAN: I understand that you want to come and go as you please [active listening]. But living together in our house requires consideration for others. Also, I'm concerned that if you get little sleep you'll start getting more irritable. So I'd appreciate it if you would tell me where you're going when you go out. Take your cell phone along [makes a positive request].

EFFECTIVE COMMUNICATION STRATEGIES THAT YOU AND YOUR TEEN CAN USE

- Active listening
  - Look at the person speaking.
  - Listen to what the person is saying.
  - Nod or say "Uh-huh."
  - Ask questions that clarify what the other person is saying.
  - Paraphrase or check out what you heard.

- Expressing positive feelings
  - Look at the person.
  - Say what the person did that pleased you.
  - Tell the person how it made you feel.

- Making a positive request
  - Look at your family member.
  - Say exactly what you would like the person to do.
  - Tell the person how it would make you feel.
  - Use phrases such as:
    - "I would like you to _____."
    - "I would really appreciate it if you would _____."
    - "It's very important to me that you _____."

- Expressing negative feelings
  - Look at the person.
  - Say what the person did that annoyed you and how it made you feel.
  - Say what you would like the person to do differently in the future.

Source: Adapted with permission from Miklowitz and Goldstein (1997). Copyright by The Guilford Press.

KURT: That is *not* happening.

EVAN: You're supposed to paraphrase me.

KURT: (*annoyed*) Okay, whatever, you're like, you want me to be considerate, you wanna know where I'm going.

EVAN: Because?

KURT: Because . . . you want to punish me.

EVAN: Hmmm . . . that's not quite what I said.

KURT: Because . . . well, you're worried about how I'm going to function, whether I'm gonna get manic and all that. But I get just as much sleep at Nathan's house as I do at home, maybe even more.

As this conversation progressed into problem solving, Evan and Kurt developed a contract: Kurt and Evan agreed that staying away overnight was acceptable, but only when Evan judged that Kurt's mood was stable. Kurt agreed to let his father know in advance if he hoped to stay overnight at a friend's house.

Importantly, the listening and validating that Kurt was required to do in his conversation with his father, and that Evan did in return, contributed to a sense of collaboration between them. It opened up a deeper conversation in which Kurt admitted to feeling inadequate that he was having trouble finishing high school and moving out on his own. He admitted, somewhat sheepishly, that he doubted whether he could take adequate care of his disorder (take his medications, stay away from alcohol) without his father's help. Structured, supportive communication with his father made it safe for Kurt to delve into these issues.

E: Escape and Exit Strategies

Tess told us that one of the most useful strategies she had learned in family-focused treatment was to exit unproductive interactions with Tara. When she "felt my own heat rising," she learned to leave the room and go to a part of the house that everyone knew was hers (a study), rather than exploding, yelling, or crying. When she gave herself time to breathe, think, and decompress, she often found that she could address problems with Tara more productively later on. In addition, Tess's leaving the room became a signal to Tara that she had pushed the envelope too far. She often apologized when Tess returned.

You'll find escape and exit strategies to be among the most useful of the techniques we recommend. They will help you manage your own reactive emotions, which in turn will promote a more protective atmosphere for your teen and other children. The "mantra" of escape strategies is to know when your own limits are being exceeded. There will be many times when you feel your buttons are being pushed and you know you're responding in unhelpful ways, as all parents inevitably do. When this occurs, exit the situation until you can regroup and examine your own reactions. This is also called giving yourself a time-out, although it may not have to mean going to your own room (and besides, your teen may follow you there!).

Don't Let Your Teen Determine Your and Everyone Else's Mood

I feel like a puppet. It feels like my son is dangling me and everyone else on a string with his vicious mood swings, and what's more he seems delighted that he can do it.
—Mother of a 14-year-old boy with bipolar I disorder

Many parents report that their bipolar teen feels overly powerful in the family context, as if he were running the show. This has led some to wonder whether bipolar disorder is really an illness or just a power game. Although the mood cycles of bipolar disorder unquestionably have biological underpinnings, it's also true that teens feel empowered when they believe they can control everyone else's emotions. When they get angry, everyone else gets angry; when they get anxious, everyone else gets anxious.

A useful piece of self-talk for parents is the statement "I don't have to let my teenager's moods control mine." If your teen is irritable, you or others in the family don't have to follow suit. Recognizing this is in itself an escape strategy, because you're not allowing yourself to become engaged in unproductive interactions. Backing off and emotionally disengaging can sometimes be the most helpful thing you can do.

The Three-Volley Rule

A related strategy is to count the number of negative "volleys" you've had in a specific interchange with your teen and then exit the conversation when it exceeds three. So, if you've made a reasonable request to which your teen has responded with hostility, and you've had two subsequent "volleys" in which you've restated your position and she has returned with another negative or hostile reply, your part of the conversation has ended. In one of our studies, we found that high expressed emotion and low expressed emotion families could be distinguished by whether they exceeded three volleys in their negative interchanges.

It's like refusing to hit the ball back in Ping-Pong: it's very tempting to keep the volley going to assert your authority, but your teen will become more emotionally activated, angry, and even verbally or physically assaultive if the conversation escalates. You can end an argument with a statement like "I think I've made my point" or "I'm sure you've heard me" or "I can't talk about this anymore now." If she insists on keeping the argument going, do your best not to respond.

Using Humor

It may be hard to believe, but sometimes the best thing to do when a bipolar teen is angry, speaking rapidly, or behaving in an inappropriate or grandiose way is to make a nonsarcastic joke or use irony. Usually, self-effacing humor works the best: "It was your bad luck to be born to a parent who can't think or talk as fast as you can"; "I can't come up with insults as fast as you can"; or "Slow down; I need to take notes." These statements, whether or not they seem funny to your teen, communicate that you're in a different mood from him and his mood will not take over yours.

One family we know had a weekly fight over the bipolar teen's running out of mousse for her hair. She would refuse to do anything or go anywhere until her mother bought her some mousse. In the midst of one fight over this topic, her mother said, "I wonder if they sell it in cases." They both began laughing, defusing what otherwise would have become a heated argument.

Improving-the-Moment Strategies

Many parents, including Tess, learn to use self-calming strategies to deal with their own negative emotional states. These can be highly effective in the moment, although sometimes you'll need to exit the room for them to work. These can include breathing (paying attention to the rhythm of your breath—see the box on the facing page), counting backward from 100 by 7's, or simply making self-statements like "I don't need to get into this now . . . I don't need to win."

Some parents use more elaborate self-calming strategies, such as yoga or relaxation. Exercise (going out for a walk, jogging, bicycling) can also be a way of burning off the tension engendered by stressful interactions with an unstable teen.

Finally, some parents have successfully used imagery as an escape strategy. For example, one parent reported that whenever she got into conflicts with her teenage son she would picture him as a toddler having a temper tantrum. This image helped her set aside her anger in the moment and feel more compassion for her son. It also helped her flip back into the parental role and not get drawn into reciprocating his negativity.

Relying on Social Supports

Having your own social support network and activities outside the home is, as you know, essential to your own mental and physical health. When you're getting repeatedly frustrated by your teen, rely more and

A 3-MINUTE BREATHING EXERCISE

- Find a comfortable chair to sit in; sit with your back upright and your hands on your thighs, not touching the back of the chair. You can also lie on your back.
- Close your eyes or stare at an object in the room. Spend 60 seconds being aware of noises in your room—the sound of the air conditioner or heating, sounds from the street, music, people's voices. Ask yourself, "What am I experiencing in my thoughts, my emotions, and my body?" Acknowledge each sensation, thought, or feeling, whether pleasant or unpleasant.
- Now, for the next 60 seconds, focus on your breathing. Keep focusing on your in-breath and out-breath, like you were riding on a wave. It's inevitable that your mind will wander. If your attention shifts to thinking of other things, notice what took you away but gently escort yourself back to your breathing.
- Now, for the next 60 seconds, shift your attention to your entire body— your belly, feet, legs, thighs, buttocks, stomach, chest, neck, and facial expression. Notice your posture and the sensations in different parts of your body as you breathe in and out. If your mind wanders, gently escort your awareness back to your body and breathing.
- Slowly open your eyes and come back into contact with the room.

Source: Adapted with permission from Segal, Z. V., Williams, J. M. G, and Teasdale, J. D. (2001). *Mindfulness-based cognitive therapy for depression: A new approach to preventing relapse.* New York: Guilford Press.

Note to the reader: If you'd like to learn more about using mindfulness meditation as a coping strategy, we recommend Williams, M., Teasdale, J., Segal, Z., & Kabat-Zinn, J. (2007). *The Mindful Way through Depression.* New York: Guilford Press. This book will take you through numerous meditation practices, of which the one here is just an example.

more on your friendships, church, temple, or other social connections for emotional and practical support. Tess began attending a support group for parents of kids with "brain differences." She found the support and new friendships from the group tremendously helpful. Other parents suggested strategies to try with Tara that had worked for them in similar circumstances.

When you have a strong social support network, it's easier to turn negotiations with your teen over to someone else. If you're getting repeatedly stuck in negative interactions that are destabilizing to you and her, and if your spouse has not been effective, ask a close friend or relative to step in. The success of this endeavor will, of course, depend on what kind of relationship your teen has with this person and how effective he or she is at communicating with your teen, but often it's the best option.

You can invite others over to your house when you feel you can't handle things with your teen. One parent routinely asked her 36-year-old brother, who lived nearby, to come over when her 16-year-old became verbally abusive. She knew that her son would be unlikely to rage and scream when her brother was there, if for no other reason than that he was afraid of him. This intervention was also effective when she tried to exit negative interactions and her son continued them by following her into her room. Simply picking up the phone to dial her brother ended the confrontation.

Tara: Epilogue

Tara is now 20 years old, and her relationship with her mother is much better. In fact, she's working in her mother's dry cleaning business and they have a much more civil relationship. She continues to have mood episodes and takes mood-stabilizing medications, but she has stopped drinking and using drugs. Her two younger siblings still have their own problems, but they seem less related to Tara's problems than before. Tess would never describe her family life as peaceful, but it's certainly more manageable. Her "mantra" for getting through the most difficult times with Tara has been "I didn't cause this, and neither did she. It probably will never go away, but we can both work together on it."

As you've seen, there are many useful strategies for maximizing the protective effects of your family environment to help your teen maintain stability. In the coming chapters, you will learn some tools for helping your teen manage the acute manic or depressive cycles of the illness. As you read these chapters, keep the "four C's" (from David Karp's *The Burden of Sympathy* [2002]) in mind to make these strategies work for you:

- You can't *control* it.
- You can't *cure* it.
- You didn't *cause* it.
- You can only *cope* with it.

Rehearse these statements to yourself when things are going badly and encourage your other family members—and most important, your teen—to do the same.

10

Tools and Tactics for Preventing Mood Episodes

The problem-solving and communication strategies in the preceding chapter will serve as a good foundation for keeping your teen well. In this chapter we'll show you how to adopt a variety of tools and strategies designed to prevent bipolar episodes as much as possible:

- Developing and maintaining regular sleep–wake cycles
- Keeping a mood chart
- Avoiding high levels of stimulation
- Creating and maintaining regular routines
- Avoiding alcohol and other mood-altering substances

These strategies work best when your teen is feeling well or experiencing only mild mood swings, and they may protect her from developing more severe mood episodes. But they do require a daily commitment. We think you'll find the effort worthwhile since the teens who use some of these strategies, as well as take their medications regularly and see their doctors, are the ones most likely to remain stable over time. Most parents find it takes less time to implement these steps toward promoting health than to manage a highly symptomatic teen. Also, you can customize the strategies to meet your family's specific needs.

Maintaining a Regular Sleep Schedule

Maybe your teenager resembles Nicole, who spent most of the school week feeling revved up, irritable, and explosive and then during the weekend being sullen, depressed, and withdrawn. When Nicole's parents pointed out this pattern to her, she said her friends were also busier during the week and took it easy on the weekend. Although they agreed, they were concerned that her activity cycles seemed to be growing more extreme each week. Her parents began keeping a mood chart (described in the next section) in which they recorded her sleep patterns and mood symptoms. Through mood charting they could see that during the school week Nicole was getting only 5–6 hours of sleep and during the weekend sometimes as much as 14 hours, including naps.

Though the connection between her sleep and mood swings was obvious, Nicole resisted making any changes. She already complained of not having enough time in the week to get everything done, saying the weekend was her only chance to catch up on sleep. Even if she tried to go to sleep earlier during the weeknight, she was too worked up from soccer, homework, and talking to her friends on the phone. Nicole's parents didn't know how to get beyond their daughter's resistance but didn't want to give up either, because her grades had begun to suffer, she was getting in fights on the soccer field, and her friends were calling her less frequently.

Some parents give up on establishing a regular sleep schedule because it may not seem like a high priority compared to, say, addressing alcohol use or oppositionality. We strongly suggest that you make sure your bipolar teen is maintaining a consistent sleep cycle because sleep deprivation can set off manic or hypomanic symptoms. Parents have told us that their teen has become irritable and hyperactive after even a single night of poor sleep. Alternatively, sleeping too much can precipitate or intensify a depression. One of the first signs of depression can be a strong urge to sleep more, which leads to a more depressed state and increases the desire for more sleep.

> **Maintaining a regular sleep–wake cycle is one of the most important behavioral changes your teen can make to manage a mood disorder.**

If your teen can learn to control his sleep patterns, he can reduce the frequency of his mood swings and reduce their severity and length. The more consistently you emphasize healthy sleep patterns, the more likely your teen will begin to see them as important to maintaining his health and independence.

Types of Sleep Disturbance in Bipolar Teens

The first step toward stabilizing your teen's sleep–wake cycle is to figure out exactly what kinds of sleep problems he has. Does he have trouble falling asleep, waking in the middle of the night, waking too early, and/or not feeling rested after sleep? There are unique strategies for each of these difficulties. Start by tracking when your teen goes to bed (you may need to ask him because you may be asleep long before he is), awakens, and the number of hours of sleep he seems to get. You can also help him identify the causes of his sleep problems (for example, late caffeine intake, sleep "bingeing" during weekends).

Typical Adolescent Sleep Deprivation

Adolescents need at least 9 hours of sleep, yet most don't seem to have the time to get it these days. Sleep deprivation affects all teens, impairing memory, inhibiting creativity, worsening stress management, making it hard to regulate emotions, causing or worsening depression, and making teens more susceptible to serious illnesses by weakening the immune system. Bipolar disorder compounds these problems. Sleep deprivation can directly affect mood cycling patterns and exacerbate manic symptoms. So, begin by assessing whether your teen is getting enough sleep—how far from 9 hours is she, on average?

Sleep Inertia

Sleep inertia is the feeling of grogginess after awakening and is common in bipolar teens (see the description of a typical day in Chapter 2). Sleep inertia can usually be reversed within 15 minutes by activity and noise, but it can last much of the morning if your teen has to wake before he has had the appropriate amount of sleep or if he is woken from a deep sleep stage. Because sleep inertia can cause impairment of motor and cognitive functions, it can affect a teen's morning school performance or make driving dangerous.

Decreased Need for Sleep

Getting less than the required 8–9 hours of sleep a night without feeling tired the next day is a hallmark symptom of mania (see Chapters 2 and 11) and usually requires medical intervention.

Insomnia

Unlike decreased need for sleep, insomnia will leave your teen feeling tired the next day and can take several forms: "initial" insomnia (trouble falling asleep), "intermittent" insomnia (waking multiple times in the night), and "terminal" insomnia (waking too early and not being able to go back to sleep).

Circadian Reversal

When your teen switches to being awake at night and sleeping during the day (for example, going to bed at 4:00 or 5:00 in the morning and sleeping until 1:00 or 2:00 in the afternoon), she may get enough hours of sleep, but this abnormal circadian schedule will certainly interfere with school performance.

Delayed Sleep Phase Syndrome

Bipolar teens often seem to be "phase delayed," meaning they go to bed very late—for example 2 A.M., even on weekdays—and then have trouble getting up on time for school. Their bodies naturally want to sleep for 8–9 hours after they go to bed, but they still have to get up for school. So, they spend their weekdays feeling tired much of the day, and then sleep excessively on the weekends to catch up. The pattern starts over again as the school week starts.

Strategies for Helping Your Teen with Sleep Problems

There are several strategies you can try to help a sleep-deprived teen. First, look at his schedule to see if he's overcommitted. If so, you may be able to help him choose the top priorities and quit the other activities. Problem solving (see Chapter 9) will help you and he make appropriate choices.

What Your Teen Can Do

A regular bedtime is essential to good sleep—encourage your teen to go to bed and get up at the same time every day, including weekends. If your teen has trouble unwinding at night, make sure her bedroom is comfortable (dark, quiet, cool). She may need earplugs, a noise machine, and/or a fan. Make sure she falls asleep in her bed rather than on a couch or chair. Next, taking a hot bath about 90 minutes before bed lowers body temperature at bedtime and leads to feeling sleepy. Eating a light snack before bed may help, especially foods that have tryptophan (for example, turkey, milk), a natural sleep inducer.

Anything stimulating within 2 hours of bedtime may make it difficult

EXAMPLE OF A SUCCESSFUL BEDTIME ROUTINE

8:00 P.M.	Turn off all media and begin the process of winding down
8:30 P.M.	Take a shower/bath or wash face and brush teeth
9:00 P.M.	Get things together for the next day (for example pack lunch, backpack, choose clothes)
9:15 P.M.	Take nighttime and sleep medications
9:20 P.M.	Get ready for bed (for example, put glass of water next to bed)
9:30 P.M.	Do a quiet activity in room (for example, relaxation, meditation, listen to calm music, read something low key)
10:00 P.M.	Lights out.

to sleep (for example, highly emotionally charged discussions, computer and television screens, video games, text messaging). Exercise can deepen sleep, but it can also be stimulating and may be disruptive if it is done within 3–4 hours of bedtime. Have your teen avoid stimulants (for example, caffeine and nicotine) and all products that contain stimulants (for example, energy and sports drinks, Sudafed) later in the day and at night. Avoid bright light in the evening, but you can expose your teen to bright light in the morning to help with sleep inertia (see discussion of light boxes on the next page). Try to prevent your teen from napping. If she must nap, keep it early in the day and less than 30 minutes. Finally, sleep bingeing (catching up on sleep on the weekends) confuses a teen's internal clock and could worsen depressive symptoms or cause more cycling.

If these strategies don't work or your teen resists trying them, consult your teen's psychiatrist about medications and other interventions for sleep.

How the Doctor Can Help

Your teen's doctor may want to order a thorough sleep exam to pinpoint the nature of your teen's sleep disturbance, which requires that your teen spend the night in a sleep laboratory. This exam will clarify such matters as the onset of rapid eye movement activity or disturbances in transitions from one sleep stage to another. In addition to assessing your teen's sleep, the doctor may recommend that your teen take a sleep medication. Various over-the-counter sleep aids (for example, melatonin,

Tylenol PM) may be helpful for initial insomnia but should be tried only on the advice of your teen's psychiatrist and/or pediatrician. These medications or supplements have pros and cons and should be taken only as recommended by a doctor who is knowledgeable about how they affect the symptoms of bipolar disorder. There are also stronger prescription medications for sleep (for example, Ambien, Lunesta, Restoril), which are typically prescribed for insomnia, decreased need for sleep, delayed sleep phase, or circadian reversal. Be aware of the addictive potential of these drugs. A downside of other medications used for sleep (for example, Seroquel, Risperdal) is that they may increase morning sedation and contribute to sleep inertia especially if taken later in the evening (after 9:00 P.M.).

For extreme cases of delayed sleep phase syndrome, circadian reversal, or sleep inertia, you may want to consult a doctor about the benefits and dangers of light boxes (a full-spectrum light used in the morning), dawn simulators (an instrument that gradually introduces light and simulates the sun rising), and/or chronotherapy (pushing your teen's bed and wake times a few hours forward around the clock until they approximate a typical sleep–wake cycle). These strategies may help reset your teen's sleep clock but carry certain risks, such as the possibility of inducing hypomanic or manic symptoms. Consult an expert in sleep problems to manage the difficulties these strategies present.

"I'll Go to Bed When I Feel Like It"

The biggest problem you may encounter with sleep is resistance from your teen. There's no simple solution, especially with older teens. You may find, however, that problem solving in which your teen develops his own solutions may make him a more willing participant.

Remember the value of compromise. Maybe if your teen is willing to be consistent during the week you could allow him to have a sleepover or later curfew for one night on the weekend. You two might also agree that there will be special occasions when he may stay up later or sleep in as long as the rest of the time he stays on a regular schedule.

We recommend having ongoing dialogues with your teen about the importance of sleep regularity for his general health (that is, not just about bipolar disorder), and offering praise and incentives (within reason) for following through. Some parents have successfully influenced their teen to develop better sleep habits by withholding certain privileges (such as video games) if the teen isn't willing to get the required amount of sleep and rewarding him with other privileges (for example, being driven to a sporting event) when he is. With your consistent stance and feedback, your teen may eventually prioritize sleep as a health habit.

Keeping a Mood Chart

A mood chart is a systematic way to bring together information about mood states (mania, depression, cycling patterns), medication adherence, sleep patterns (typically total number of hours, or bed and wake times), stressful life events, and, if applicable, alcohol and substance use. Mood charts can help you and your teen synthesize what is occurring in her life and how it is affecting (or is affected by) her mood.

Mood charts can be set up in a variety of ways. The example on page 222 shows how 16-year-old Nicole set up the chart that we use with the teens in our program (a blank mood chart that you can photocopy or use as a model to customize to your teen's particular symptoms is on page 223). We use the teen's own words to describe the mood states and symptoms that go along with a particular mood. This way the teen feels some ownership of the chart and there is no confusion about what she's recording. Second, this mood chart is not time-consuming: it takes about 1 minute to complete each day. Third, because teens' moods cycle frequently, there are two places to rate mood: morning (A.M.) and evening (P.M.). Finally, she can track any other important data such as when she falls asleep and wakes up, whether she takes her medications, what stressors have arisen and when (for example, Monday—exams, Wednesday night—family argument), and whether there's been any alcohol or drug use. A teen who wants to keep track of school attendance can add a line at the bottom of the chart similar to the wake and bedtime lines, recording "yes" if she attended school and leaving it blank if not.

Mood charts perform a number of functions that you should explain to your teen before asking him to create one so that he knows you're not just coming up with "busy work" for him. Most important, mood charts pick up on subtle fluctuations in mood, thinking, and behavior that tell you and your teen when his mood is worsening. This information can be critical to nipping in the bud an episode of mania or depression. But mood charts can also help you get the most possible out of your teen's visits with his psychiatrist. You may already know that these visits tend to be short and rushed. Mood charts kept in a binder can tell the doctor at a glance how your teen has been doing and whether any changes in

How I Feel

Week of __April 8__

	Mon A.M. P.M.	Tues A.M. P.M.	Wed A.M. P.M.	Thurs A.M. P.M.	Fri A.M. P.M.	Sat A.M. P.M.	Sun A.M. P.M.
Amped	X	X X	X X	X X	X		
Pumped					X	X	
OK	X						
Bummed						E X	X E X

	Mon	Tues	Wed	Thurs	Fri	Sat	Sun
I took my meds (Y = yes, N = no)	Y	Y	Y	Y	Y	Y	Y
I woke up at:	6:00 A.M.	5:45 A.M.	5:30 A.M.	5:30 A.M.	5:00 A.M.	11:30 A.M.	noon
I went to bed at:	midnight	1:00 A.M.	12:30 A.M.	2:00 A.M.	1:30 A.M.	10:00 P.M.	9:00 P.M.

Additional symptoms: __E = explosions and is charted on the mood bar__

(I = irritability, A = anxiety, SA = substance abuse, P = paranoia—you may need to add additional lines for these or other items)

Mood words (from above)

Amped	Pumped	OK	Bummed

Mood descriptors

Amped	Pumped	OK	Bummed
Irritable	Feel good	Present	Bored
Lots of ideas	Upbeat	Clear	Exhausted
Edgy	Rushed	Focused	Feel stupid and ugly
High energy	Snappy	Considerate	Feel like no one likes me
	Feel smart	Engaged	

Stressors—date when it occurred during the week

__Monday—test__

__Wed. night—family fight__

How I Feel

Week of _____

	Mon A.M. P.M.	Tues A.M. P.M.	Wed A.M. P.M.	Thurs A.M. P.M.	Fri A.M. P.M.	Sat A.M. P.M.	Sun A.M. P.M.

_____

I took my meds
(Y = yes, N = no)

I woke up at:

I went to bed at:

Additional symptoms:
(I = irritability, A = anxiety, SA = substance abuse, P = paranoia—you may need to add additional lines for these or other items)

Mood words (from above)   Stressors—date when it occurred during the week

Mood descriptors

From *The Bipolar Teen* by David J. Miklowitz and Elizabeth L. George. Copyright 2008 by The Guilford Press.

medications are needed. Finally, mood charts can remind you and your teen during an episode of depression or mania that things haven't always been this way. When your teen is depressed, it's easy for him to get discouraged and feel that he isn't getting any better. Mood charts will show him and you otherwise.

How to Create a Mood Chart

Step 1

The first step in creating a mood chart is to ask your teen to choose a word for each of her mood states—probably one for a manic or hypomanic mood, one for a stable mood, and one for a depressed mood. Notice that Nicole described her most manic mood with the word *amped,* her hypomanic mood with the word *pumped,* her stable mood as *OK,* and her down mood with the word *bummed.* Write the mood word your teen supplies on the left side of the chart.

Now look at the bars spanning the days of the week placed next to each mood word. This is where your teen will chart her mood by placing an X above the bar that best represents her mood that day. As a visual aid, we typically color the bar representing mania red, the bar representing a stable state black, and the bar representing depression blue. If your teen has mood states between stable and the most extreme manic or depressed states, you can use a lighter shade of blue or red. One teen said he had two depressed mood states: a milder "melancholy" mood and a worse "down-in-the-dumps mood." He made the bar for melancholy light blue and the down-in-the-dumps bar dark blue.

Step 2

Now your teen should list additional words ("mood descriptors") he would use for each mood at the bottom of the chart under the main mood-state headings. Nicole, for example, said that during her "amped" times she felt irritable, had lots of ideas and high energy, and was edgy.

Step 3

Decide with your teen which additional symptoms to track on a daily basis and how she will measure those. For example, if she wants to monitor her anxiety symptoms, she may want to use an "A" and chart them on an additional line at the bottom. Or she could put the A on one of the mood state bars to show that anxiety accompanies some mood states (such as depression) but not others (hypomania or stable mood).

The box below lists symptoms or other behaviors (for example, substance abuse) that you or your teen may want to track. Getting your teen involved in deciding which other symptoms to include and how to represent them on the chart will get her invested in using this important tool from the start.

Step 4

If you've read the earlier chapters of this book, you know by now that there's a direct correlation between stress and mood instability. Many teens can connect the onset of a major mood episode to a stressful life event. Knowing what kinds of stressful events affect your teen's moods will help you develop a plan for coping with these events before her moods get out of hand. For example, Amy and her son identified "midterms" as a stressor, which meant that it was particularly important for him to get extra sleep during those intervals.

EXAMPLES OF THE USE OF MOOD CHARTS TO GAIN SOME PREDICTABILITY OVER THE CYCLING OF BIPOLAR DISORDER

- *Suicidality*—Monitoring her son's depression helped Marilyn notice that within a week of the onset of depression, he developed suicidal thoughts.
- *Thought problems (paranoia)*—Henry noticed that his daughter started being afraid of him within days of becoming agitated and sleep deprived.
- *Outbursts*—After a missed night's sleep, Fran's daughter got severely irritable over imagined slights.
- *Side effects of medication*—Bob noticed that his son became listless and tired in the morning after starting to take an antipsychotic for sleep.
- *Stressors*—Amy noticed that her son was more mood-reactive during midterms.
- *Anxiety*—Tom realized that his daughter had considerably more anxiety than depression.
- *Irritability*—Hope found that her daughter's irritability usually went along with depression, not hypomania as she had presumed.
- *Substance use*—Nate observed that he smoked pot when he was hypomanic but not when depressed.

Have your teen brainstorm the one-time occurrences (for example, a move) and daily events (for example, math class) that he considers stressful. If the list looks incomplete to you, ask your teen if you can include some stressors you've noticed. However, your teen should take ownership of this mood chart, because some will reject the whole process if they think you're forcing your observations on them.

Now ask your teen to imagine a thermometer with 100 degrees at the top representing the hottest (most stressful) items and 0 at the bottom for the coldest (least stressful) items. Draw the thermometer if such visuals help or appeal to your teen, but be careful not to treat the teen as a child. Have your teen give you a number for each item that corresponds with how "hot" that item is for him. Record the stressors in order from most to least stressful.

Now you and your teen can look at the list of stressors everyday to see which (if any) have occurred and record them in the blank spaces at the bottom right of the mood chart along with the date they occurred. Over the next few weeks, you'll be gathering a picture of how these stressors are related to the mood fluctuations your teen experiences. You'll probably notice that some stressors produce an immediate mood reaction and others are less explosive. If you find that stressors rated hottest on your teen's original list don't have as big an effect as you thought, revise the list so that you and she know which stressors require your communication and problem-solving efforts (see Chapter 9).

Thirteen-year-old Ted's mood chart revealed that whenever his mother told him "No," he had an angry outburst. He and his mother brainstormed alternative solutions and came up with these possibilities: When Ted had a request (for example, "Take me to the mall"), his mother could ask him questions about his plan for the request (for example, "When would you like me to do that?" "Why is this important to you now?"), listen to Ted's request and let him explain his feelings about it before responding (active listening), and if her answer was still "No" she could offer a compromise (for example, "I'll be happy to take you when I'm not so busy"). Though Ted still became visibly upset when his mother didn't accede to his requests, his reactions became less intense over time.

Step 5

Now that you've created a mood chart, your teen needs to be sure to fill it in every day. At the end of the day, she should place an X on the bar where her mood was in the morning (A.M.) and in the evening (P.M.). She may need to look at the mood descriptors to remember what the mood state word represents. Then she will write in a Y if she took her meds and an N if she did not. In addition, she'll record what time she went to bed the night before and what time she awoke that morning. She'll also write in the letter for any other symptom that she's tracking that occurred that day. Finally, she'll record the stressors that occurred that day and put the date next to each.

The mood chart will help your teen not only pick up shifts in mood but also identify whether one of the other factors being measured is related to such mood shifts (for example, a missed dose of medication leading to a worsening mood). Nicole's chart showed that she had an "amped" mood through the week and a "bummed" mood on the weekend. Though she took her medication every day, her sleep–wake cycle was not consistent and was most likely responsible for her mood fluctuations. At times Nicole's irritability grew into full-blown anger; she charted her angry outbursts by putting an E (for explosion) on her chart on the line that denoted her mood state when explosive. Interestingly, although Nicole was more irritable during the week when she was amped, you can see from the chart that her explosions occurred only on the weekend when she felt bummed. In response to what Nicole and her parents discovered through mood charting, they began to put more effort toward managing her sleep problems: setting regular bedtimes and wake times, avoiding sleep bingeing, and arranging low-key activities—and avoiding family conflicts—during the hour before bedtime.

Step 6

Help your teen keep her weekly mood chart with her other treatment items. Some families designate a drawer in the kitchen or a space on a bookshelf in the teen's room. When the week is over, have your teen put her mood chart in a binder so that you and she can observe changes in her moods over time.

What If Your Teen Won't Participate?

Even when they're told how valuable the information charted can be, teens usually start out resistant. Typically, teens claim they're too busy to add this to their other obligations. If your teen claims she doesn't have time, tell her that the whole process will take 5 minutes a day once she gets used to it. If she still balks, try offering a small amount of money or something valued like an iTunes song card for each week your teen completes the chart. Most parents find that teens need these reinforcers for only a short time.

If your teen doesn't want to fill out the mood chart because she doesn't want to be reminded of her illness, try the reinforcers at first and keep pointing out to her that working with all elements of the chart (for example, sleep, medication, stressors) and devising strategies to gain more control over her mood fluctuations (for example, taking medication regularly, getting regular sleep) makes her more powerful in the face of her illness. Over time, developing a sense of mastery over her symptoms may help her feel more accepting of and less demoralized by having bipolar disorder.

What if she can't remember to do it? Ask her to put the mood chart with her evening medications so that when she takes them she is reminded of the chart. If medications have become a point of contention, ask her to keep her chart with a school planner or binder that she needs to access on a daily basis to remind her of this task. Some teens prefer to fill out an online version that they create and put on their "desktop"; this can be a good reminder also.

Finally, mood charts need to be tried on like a new pair of shoes. The first chart she tries may not fit. In this case you may want her to try each version for a week while making notes about how it could be improved, until it has been broken in. Then, at the end of the week, incorporate changes that make the chart more likely to yield the information you're seeking. Many families have gone through several versions until they found a chart that fit.

Avoiding High Levels of Stimulation

Because of the limitations imposed by their frontal-cortical functioning (see Chapter 5), people with bipolar disorder can easily get overwhelmed by various stimuli. Your teen may experience overstimulation as an escalating pressure that makes it hard for him to think straight, gives him a headache or stomachache, or makes him feel uncomfortably keyed up. Some teens don't have any physical symptoms but get very angry, anxious, and irritated.

Because the experience of overstimulation varies so much from person to person, this phenomenon can be confusing to family members. Teens with bipolar disorder can become completely overwhelmed by even ordinary life situations like going to the grocery store. Paradoxically, they are often drawn to other very stimulating activities (for example, video games) and don't want to give them up. To make matters even more confusing, you may have noticed that your teen gets overstimulated in settings that appear to offer little stimulation and is quite comfortable in settings that most people would find overstimulating.

It's important to identify what overstimulates your teen because many teens with bipolar disorder can't articulate the discomfort of being mentally challenged in this way and instead throw tantrums or get physically aggressive. Other teens turn to alcohol or drugs to control their reactions. Some teens have used marijuana to slow things down when overwhelmed. If you can help your teen identify what causes overstimulation and how to manage it, you may be able to help prevent these unhealthy coping strategies.

Be aware too that overstimulation puts teens at risk for mania. A feedback loop occurs in which stimulation leads to manic escalation, which drives the desire for more stimulation, which worsens mania symptoms even further. One of the more effective ways to manage mania is to have your teen avoid stimulation at the beginning of this feedback loop. If your teen has sleep problems, keeping the stimulation low during the day and evening may help him go to sleep at night.

An Overstimulation Inventory

Ask your teen which of the following items he experiences as overstimulating, rating each with a number from 1 to 5, 1 being "not stimulating at all" and 5 being "the most stimulating." Make sure he understands the word *stimulating* (arousing, intimidating, interesting, new, exciting). Pleasant or positive events may be experienced as overstimulating, and negative events may be experienced as understimulating.

____Spending time with family	____Spending time with friends
____Concerts	____School
____Church or other religious events	____Family-oriented parties
	____Talking on the phone
____Websites (for example, *Myspace.com*)	____Text messaging
	____Video games
____Instant messaging	____Being in trouble
____Difficult discussions	____Parental expectations
____Bright lights	____Traveling

___Vacation	___Taking lots of classes
___Tests at school	___Sporting events
___Movies	___Being overscheduled
___Being rushed	___Being the center of attention
___Interactions with boy-/girlfriend	

Once your teen has filled out the list, talk about when the items are or are not stress-producing and what strategies could reduce his reactions to them. Fourteen-year-old Beau said eating dinner with the family was overstimulating—that he'd feel a mounting internal pressure that usually ended with having to excuse himself from the table because he felt sick. Beau said one factor that created pressure for him was when his four siblings and parents were talking all at once. The next night Beau's parents instituted a rule that only one person could talk at a time at the dinner table and no interrupting was allowed. The family wasn't usually able to follow the rule, and Beau would sometimes still feel overwhelmed, but there were many nights when the strategy worked.

Strategies for Avoiding Overstimulation

Try cutting back on nighttime activities. Teens typically get overstimulated in the evening, so start by observing your teen's nighttime activities. A teen who watches a lot of TV, talks on the phone, plays video games, has friends over late, or text messages may get more revved up and irritated as the evening progresses. You might try limiting or prohibiting such activities after 8:00 P.M., which will not only reduce stimulation but also promote good sleep hygiene. Remember that you are the "keeper" of the modem or the TV remote.

Encourage your teen to start noticing when he's starting to feel overstimulated. It's much easier to manage the flow of stimuli before your teen gets overstimulated than to back off once he's already there. Suggest that your teen think of a "stimulation pie" with each potentially exciting event taking up a piece of the pie. Then ask him to monitor how the pie is getting used up during his day and at what point the pie is gone. If he learns to be aware of getting overstimulated, he may be able to remove himself from challenging environments before he gets anxious and agitated. Joseph, who was having trouble in math, noticed that he tended to feel overstimulated after he and his teacher met in her office with the fluorescent lights on, and once he felt this way, he could no longer communicate with her. At the beginning of their next meeting he mentioned his difficulty with the lights, and she agreed for them to meet in the classroom instead, where the lighting was less oppressive.

Remind teens who enjoy stimulation that it has its downsides. Teens who say they like "feeling alive" may resist efforts to control the stimulation level. You may have to remind them that there's a fine line between the enjoyable effects of mental or emotional challenges and the discomfort—feeling anxious or fearful, unable to stop racing thoughts—of overstimulation. There's a fine line here for you too: you don't want to nag constantly about this, but if you can help your teen realize that certain particularly exciting or novel activities tend to make him irritable, make it harder to go to sleep, and leave him less focused at school the next day, he may agree to put a time limit on some of them.

Consider medications that improve attention and concentration. Sometimes, overstimulation is caused by difficulty focusing one's attention or screening out relevant from irrelevant information. Because of their difficulty with frontal–cortical processing, some bipolar teens feel like they are sitting at an overloaded telephone switchboard. Certain of the medications used to treat ADHD, such as Ritalin or Adderall, and certain of the atypical antipsychotics can help teens focus and not become so agitated by multiple novel stimuli. If you're concerned about this set of symptoms, talk to your teen's doctor about the pros and cons of adding these medications to his regimen. Some of the medications prescribed for ADHD can *cause* agitation, so be careful to note whether his symptoms improve or worsen after initiating these drugs.

Maintaining Regular Routines

Bipolar teens often thrive on the chaos of being "overbooked" and running from one activity to the next. Therefore it's important to put into place some tools that keep your teen's daily schedule reasonable and predictable. So, help your teen construct an agreed-on list of target times for beginning and ending each daily activity. You may want your teen to eat dinner with the family, do homework, and then wind down before bed. Your teen may want to play video games until 9:00 P.M. and then begin his homework. Negotiating to come up with an agreed-on schedule

> **All teens resist structure to some extent, but regular routines are of paramount importance because irregular schedules and rapid transitions can cause mood instability.**

can keep your teen's moods stable as well as prevent conflicts between you over how to structure the day.

We recommend having a weekly meeting with your teen to discuss what's going to happen and when during the next 7 days. Nicole's family developed the plan depicted below for managing her irregular weekly schedule (and the power struggles that had developed over this). You can adopt the same format; be sure to include the activities you want to target and strategies your teen can use to ensure that these activities occur when planned.

	Target time	Actual time	Strategies
Wake up	7:00 a.m.	7:30 a.m.	Move alarm clock away from bed
Eat breakfast	7:15 a.m.	Didn't happen	If get up on time it won't be a problem
Leave for school	7:30 a.m.	7:45 a.m. — had to drive to school	
Arrive home	3:30 p.m.	4:15 p.m.	Need to remember to get book bag
Soccer practice	5:00 p.m.	6:00 p.m.	
Eat dinner	6:30 p.m.	6:30 p.m.	Mom gave positive feedback that we made our goal at dinner
Start homework	7:00 p.m.	7:00 p.m.	Because we had dinner on time we started homework on time. Good work!
Begin bedtime routine	9:00 p.m.	11:00 p.m.	Homework took longer than we thought. We need to add a time to do homework either at school or before dinner
Lights out	11:00 p.m.	midnight	Not bad considering we were late getting started

Nicole's Schedule

Some of the more important areas to consider in establishing regular routines include the following:

Extracurricular Activities

Identify how many of these should occur on any given day or week and when they should take place. Nicole had soccer practice three nights a week from 5:00 until 6:00 P.M. On those nights she and her mother agreed that mealtimes and homework would be a bit later. Nicole agreed to do as much of her homework as she could when she arrived home so that she could still get to bed at the agreed-on time of 11:00 P.M.

General Nutrition

Teens benefit from healthy nutrition and regular food intake. Teens with bipolar disorder often crave carbohydrates and sugar, which can destabilize their mood through blood sugar highs and lows. Encouraging your teen to eat regularly and stay away from caffeine and excessive amounts of sugar will help.

Exercise

When your teen's mood is escalating, exercise during the day can help him burn off steam and wear off some of his excess energy to focus on homework and help him sleep. Exercise can also help alleviate a depressed mood. However, avoid allowing him to exercise right before bed; this can keep him awake.

Bedtime

If the other activities on the schedule happen on time, bedtime has a much better chance of being regular. However, some families decide that no matter what else is going on, the bedtime ritual begins at a given hour. Although you will need to make allowances for special occasions (for example, parties, sleepovers), ideally your teen will be open to keeping the agreed-on time as the norm.

Transitions

Sometimes the problem isn't scheduling activities as much as transitioning between activities. Trying to switch gears without having transitions built in may make your teen resist changing activities and result in mood swings. So, for example, you could allow him to play video games for 30 minutes between the end of the school day and beginning his homework. He may need a similar amount of transition time to do a favorite activity between dinner and resuming homework. Video gaming or other stimulating activities are not good transition activities between homework and bed, however. Encourage a lower-key activity, like reading or playing a board game.

Predictability

A teen who knows what to expect each day will be less likely to resist moving from one activity to the next. Some parents say their teens' "meltdowns" are frequently precipitated by unexpected changes in plans. Of course, it's impossible to maintain complete predictability of routines, but the more regular they are, the more stable your teen will be.

Avoiding Alcohol and Other Mood-Altering Substances

Bill and his family had been in treatment for about a year. Despite the fact that his single dad had followed through with treatment, that the therapist was well trained and thorough, and that the psychiatrist had been attentive and responsive with changes to his medication regimen, Bill continued to have intense and debilitating mood swings. On many occasions, his dad came to treatment sessions frustrated that Bill was not getting any better; the therapist was equally confused. About a year after therapy began, Bill made a very serious suicide attempt in which he overdosed on his medication and was admitted to the hospital. The psychiatrist on call ordered a blood test to see if he had drugs or alcohol in his system. His blood test came up positive for marijuana and cocaine. It then became clearer why Bill wasn't benefiting from his existing treatments.

Unfortunately, Bill is not unusual among teens with bipolar disorder. As many as 39% of adolescents with bipolar disorder have a lifetime substance use disorder (drug or alcohol abuse or dependence) compared to 7% of nonbipolar adolescents. When your teen is evaluated initially, you may be surprised to find that his substance abuse problems are playing a major role in his mood instability. Teens most frequently use marijuana, but more and more are abusing street substances such as steroids, ephedrine, methamphetamine, crack cocaine, and narcotic pain medications.

Until your teen abstains from alcohol and other substances, it will be very difficult for her medications and/or therapy to be effective. Although you're likely to appreciate the risks to your teen of using substances, it's equally likely that she won't. You can start by explaining some hard facts: alcohol and drugs worsen the course of bipolar illness. Substance misuse brings about a number of neurobiological processes that can activate the imbalances in brain chemistry associated with bipolar disorder (see Chapter 5), so that she now has two sets of biological vulnerabilities instead of one. Worse yet, because of the bipolar teen's brain chemistry, drinking and drugs put her at greater risk for becoming addicted than if she did not have bipolar disorder. Drugs and alcohol may interfere with the teen's commitment to taking medication consistently or make it impossible for her to even remember to take them. And they put teens at risk for dangerous and impulsive behaviors, including suicide attempts. It's no surprise that teens who use and abuse substances continue to have debilitating symptoms and often wind up in the hospital.

Is It Drugs or Bipolar Symptoms?

An important component of substance abuse management for parents is to distinguish the signs of being high or drunk from the signs of mania, depression, and/or medication toxicity. This distinction is difficult to make. A teen who's been drinking may act giddy, silly, or belligerent or demonstrate poor judgment, which can mimic a mood swing. On the other hand, slurred speech, loss of balance, glassy eyes, dilated pupils, inability to focus, looking sleepy, a bobbing head, staggering, swaying, and inability to walk are signs of intoxication that typically don't occur during a mood episode, but they may occur as a result of toxicity with lithium or other psychiatric medications. *If your teen displays these symptoms, call his doctor or take him to the nearest hospital emergency room.*

The effects of cocaine and other stimulants are often confused with mania (and of course your teen can be using these drugs while manic). These drugs can cause euphoria, irritability, restlessness, anxiety, increased energy, grandiose thinking, and hyperstimulation. At higher doses and with prolonged use, these drugs can trigger paranoia. Withdrawal from these drugs can look like depression.

The short-term effects of marijuana can include problems with memory and learning, distorted perception, difficulty in thinking and problem solving, and loss of coordination. Long-term effects of marijuana use include depression, anxiety, and personality disturbance. Marijuana compromises the ability to learn and remember information, as well as other cognitive abilities.

If you're not sure whether your teen is abusing substances, it's better to err on the side of caution. You can ask her doctor to give her random drug screens (urine analyses, or UAs). If these tests come up positive, ask for a formal assessment to determine if your teen is merely abusing substances or has a chemical dependency problem. Your teen may be experimenting or trying to manage her mood with substances (that is, self-medicating). Outpatient alcohol and/or drug rehabilitation programs may help her quit using substances before a dependency problem develops. If she has a chemical dependency (for example, she has withdrawal symptoms when she tries to quit or desires more and more of the substance to get high), she will most likely need an inpatient detoxification and treatment program (see Resources).

What Can I Do to Help?

First, start by being a good role model. Many teens have said that it's okay for them to drink or smoke pot because their parents do. It will be important for you to abstain from illegal substances or excessive alcohol use if your teen is at risk for using them. In addition, don't have drugs and alcohol in the house and easily accessible.

Second, know where your teen is and who she is with as much as possible. Know the parents of your teen's friends and contact them when your teen is going to a sleepover or party at their house. If your teen and her friends know that parents are communicating with each other, they'll understand that they're being supervised and be less likely to do things that would get them in trouble.

Third, make sure your teen is getting good medication management. Some teens are able to quit using substances once their moods are well managed with medications. Medications can be effective in treating substance abuse if they alleviate the symptoms the teen is attempting to self-medicate. One study found lithium to be an effective treatment for substance abuse in bipolar kids, and another found divalproex sodium to have positive effects on managing alcohol withdrawal in bipolar adults.

The specific strategies covered in this chapter are most helpful when your teen is stable and functioning well. Although these strategies can go a long way toward preventing mood disorder episodes, they are not foolproof, and they can be harder—although not impossible—to implement when your teen starts to cycle upward or downward. The next three chapters will help you and your teen identify and intervene with the early warning signs of a developing mood episode.

11 | What to Do When Mania Begins

When Patrick and Wendy got the call asking them to come pick up their 14-year-old son, they leaped into action, calling Max's psychiatrist even before they headed for the high school. On the way, they agonized over the latest recurrence of Max's illness. Would he have to be hospitalized again? They had carefully monitored his Risperdal and Depakote, and he had been seeing a therapist. But now Max had gotten agitated and angry, withdrawing into a corner of the cafeteria and crying, saying he believed the food and water were contaminated and his teachers were trying to kill him.

Although Patrick and Wendy were upset and worried, they felt more prepared than they had been prior to Max's previous two manic episodes. They had noticed him getting more agitated, sleepless, and irritable over the prior 3 days while he was preparing for a big exam in math, his worst subject. When he started saying things like "I don't really have to study because I can read his [the teacher's] mind and I already know what will be on the test," they had asked Max whether he thought he needed more medication. Max had angrily responded, "It's my teacher who sucks, not me."

Max's prior episodes had been caught too late for him to avoid hospitalization, which lasted for over a month each time. This time Patrick and Wendy's watchful planning, good relationship with their son's treatment team, and quick action eliminated the need for hospitalization, though Max missed 2 weeks of school and had to drop his math class. An increase in his Risperdal plus Klonopin for sleep and daily sessions with either the psychiatrist or his therapist for the remainder of the week helped avert a major crisis.

Teens who are entering a manic episode may become violent, aggressive, promiscuous, and substance abusive. This behavior is highly disturbing to families, debilitating to the teen, and potentially embarrassing for all. Fortunately, there is much you can do to head off manic episodes, even though you can't fully prevent them in a bipolar teen. It's hard to identify the early warning signs and take action on them, but doing so makes a huge difference. Although Patrick and Wendy could have intervened even earlier, their awareness of the steps required to prevent further escalation did much to minimize the severity, duration, and impact of Max's episode.

Mania is like a train leaving the station. Early on, it's still possible to jump off without getting hurt. But once the train is barreling down the tracks, it's impossible to slow it down without some sort of emergency intervention. The early phase (the "prodrome") can be as short as a day or two or can last several weeks or more. *So your first step is to determine when the train has left the station because this is when you have the most control.*

By the time Max's parents were called, their son had already developed a full manic recurrence. If you haven't been able to catch the "train" in time, you'll need to know what to do when your teen develops the full syndrome: the need for emergency medications, when to call the police, the potential value of hospitalization, and what to do afterward. You'll also need to know about the reparations your teen may need to make in any relationships harmed by his behavior. But not all bipolar teens have full manic episodes. Some have bipolar II disorder and/or rapidly cycle between brief episodes of depression and hypomania or mixed states. This chapter focuses primarily on the prevention of full manic episodes, but much of what we say here applies to preventing hypomanic or mixed as well as manic episodes. There is value in learning to anticipate and intervene early with hypomanic episodes: if untreated, hypomania can bring on a depression in its wake and lead to an increased pattern of cycling.

Mania Prevention

> It's very difficult for me to tell when I'm getting high. I get sort of wired, I get these big movements, it's like Broadway versus the small screen or something. I start talking louder . . . and then I'm, like, totally pissed off at everything, like I don't want anyone to tell me what to do, even though they really should.
>
> —A 17-year-old girl with bipolar I disorder

Being alert to the early warning signs of mania can help you *prevent, minimize the severity,* or *shorten the length* of a developing episode. Even if you can't catch an episode right at the beginning, acting the minute you see the more blatant signs of mania will lessen the damage done. *A tool that we've found valuable is the Mania Prevention Contract, in which you identify the early warning signs and plan what strategies you'll use when you see them, to prevent a full-blown episode.* Some of these strategies require the doctor's assistance, and others can be used at home, even without your teen's assistance.

"When Should We Develop the Contract?"

Ideally, a mania prevention contract should be created when your teen is healthy and stable. Don't be surprised, however, if you encounter resistance from your teen and other family members. Your teen may deny that she has ever been manic and may not want to talk about it. Your spouse may fear that talking about it will make it more likely to happen. Present the task of developing the contract as if it were a fire drill and the early warning signs were like a smoke alarm going off: "We may never need to use the drill, and hopefully we won't, but it's better to formulate a plan when everyone's well and safe so that you know exactly what to do if we hear the alarm." Most teens really resent the idea of having to go to the hospital, so use avoiding hospitalization as an incentive for developing the contract. If it helps, you can remind your teen and other family members that this is a medical illness: people whose sons or daughters have insulin-dependent diabetes develop similar agreements about what to do when their children go into insulin shock.

Mania prevention requires four steps:

1. Identify the early warning signs ("prodromal" symptoms) of an episode.
2. Clarify the context in which they occur.
3. List preventive measures to keep the symptoms from escalating.
4. Create a contract detailing these prevention procedures, which you, your spouse, your teen, and her treatment personnel sign.

Step 1: Identify Early Warning Signs

When she starts getting manic, she appears to be doing well. She's happy, talkative, energetic, more engaged and positive about herself and her prospects. I feel like we're spoiling the party, but we know that the

LISTING YOUR TEEN'S PRODROMAL SYMPTOMS OF MANIA

All of the following items refer to *changes* in your teen's usual mood, behavior, or sleep, rather than typical behavior. Consult with others who have observed your teen's behavior during the prodromal period.

1. If your child has had a prior manic or hypomanic episode, or may be having one now, describe the symptoms during the buildup. For any prior episodes, how much time (for example, a few hours, 1 day, 1 week) passed between the first manic symptom (for example, sleep loss) and symptoms becoming out of control? _____

2. List adjectives describing the teen's mood when manic or hypomanic episodes begin (examples: irritable, cranky, moody, bouncy, cries easily, anxious, cheery, giddy, impatient, wired, pumped up, amped, happy, euphoric, overly reactive).

_____

_____

_____

_____

3. Describe changes in the teen's activity, energy, or physical behavior as the episode mounts (calls lots of people, takes on new projects, multitasks, spends inordinate time socializing, talks fast, gets physically intrusive, "invades my space," is hypersexual).

_____

_____

_____

_____

4. Describe your observations regarding the teen's thinking and perception (thoughts seem to be racing, driven; the teen thinks he/she can do anything and is better than others [grandiosity]; acts overconfident, paranoid, or suspicious ["someone has it out for me"]; says that colors seem brighter and sounds get louder; claims to be psychic; gets easily distracted; talks about morbid things like death or violence).

_____

_____

_____

_____

_____

5. Describe changes in your teen's sleep patterns (sleeping several hours less than usual, waking up multiple times at night, seems energetic despite lack of sleep, has a vastly different bedtime and wake time every day).

_____

_____

_____

_____

6. Describe any behavior that could threaten the teen's health or get the teen into legal trouble (buying or selling drugs, driving fast or recklessly, screaming obscenities in public, gambling, getting thrown out of school, having unsafe sex).

_____

_____

_____

_____

7. Describe any other circumstances that could have contributed to these symptoms (for example, stopped taking medications, changes in home environment, a new romantic relationship, a school failure, problems with a teacher or schoolmate, loss [by death or separation] of another family member, new use of a certain drug [either illicit or prescribed; include antidepressants], travel across time zones, more family conflicts, changes in financial circumstances).

_____

_____

_____

_____

longer it goes on, the more at risk she is for the really high periods that can last weeks. This we want to avoid at all costs.
—Mother of a 14-year-old with bipolar I disorder

Start by filling out the prodromal symptoms list on page 240. If your teen has been manic before, it may be hard to recall the exact sequence of events and mood changes, so try to collect information about this phase from the teen, the doctor, and any other caregivers, siblings, or relatives who were around at the time (for example, "I remember all that stuff about selling her art on the web"). If your teen has never had a full manic episode but is at risk (for example, she has bipolar II or bipolar not otherwise specified), making a list with the behaviors to look for will help stave off a full occurrence.

Think about the mania prodrome as involving *subtle changes in mood, behavior, thinking/perception, and sleep.* Typical early warning signs involve a decreased need for sleep (not just insomnia followed by being tired the next day), increased moodiness (for example, an increase in "cycling," or abrupt but frequent changes from sad to angry to anxious to giddy), more energy, more activities, or unrealistic plans (for example, "I'm going to move to New York City to become a dancer"). Some teens will do things that are clearly dysfunctional, such as have sex with strangers, run away from home, repeatedly come home drunk or stoned, or get into fistfights at school. Usually, however, these behaviors come later in the escalation and reflect the onset of the full manic syndrome.

For some teens, the buildup to a manic episode looks like the symptoms of depression, such as suicidal thinking, loss of interest in activities, or guilty ruminations. This is especially likely if the teen is developing a mixed instead of a purely manic episode. If you think your teen gets depressed before getting manic, be sure to record these signs and symptoms in the relevant places on the list.

Is This Something New or Just More of the Same?

It may be hard to tell whether you're observing a *change* in your teen's moods or behavior because many parents say their teen seems manic or hypomanic all the time. But if you look carefully—and especially if you're keeping a mood chart (Chapter 10)—you can observe even subtle changes that occur on top of your teen's ongoing hyperactive, hyperenergetic style. Catherine knew that 17-year-old Vanessa had been having sex with her boyfriend for at least a year. But when she began talking about wanting to have sex with other boys and using sex to make her boyfriend jealous, Catherine suspected she was having a prodromal manic symptom (hypersexuality).

"FIND" Out Whether You're Seeing Signs of Mania or Normal Teenage Behavior

How do you know whether this is a mania prodrome (and when you should let your teen's doctor know about it) and when it is just a single symptom or behavior that could occur in any teenager? Usually, the mania prodrome is a constellation of symptoms that go together (changes in sleep, thinking, behavior, and mood), but sometimes the prodrome is just a single symptom. It's not always possible to tell whether this symptom is just a passing phase, but *it's better to err on the side of caution, even if it means being wrong at times.* In our experience, parents are more often right than wrong when they observe subtle mood or behavioral changes in their bipolar teen. Always call your teen's psychiatrist and therapist if you think she's having a recurrence: at worst, they may think you're trigger-happy, but this is better than neglecting to let them know when there's a true emergency.

One method that doctors use to determine whether a symptom or constellation of symptoms is clinically significant is the FIND acronym:

- Frequency: Is the symptom (for example, irritability) new and occurring more and more often?
- Intensity: Is it increasing in strength (for example, arguments initiated by your teen are becoming increasingly volatile)?
- Number: Is there only one symptom or many? Does irritability coincide with decreased need for sleep, grandiosity, or talking faster?
- Duration: How long do these symptoms last—is it just a quick on–off expression of irritation, or does the teen seem to be irritated for the better part of a day?

As you judge these four features, consider also whether there is *functional impairment.* If your teen is irritable in ways that are getting her into trouble at school, home, in sports, or with friends, the symptom is probably clinically significant. If it's just more arguments with a sibling and doesn't occur anywhere else or with anyone else, it's probably not a prodromal symptom.

List all the new symptoms or behaviors (using the prodromal symptoms list) that you've observed during the buildup, whether or not you're sure they're clinically significant. Try to limit your observations to behaviors that clearly co-occurred during the same 1- to 2-week period, rather than, for example, sleep disturbance that occurred 6 months prior and then disappeared.

You may want to go back to Chapter 3 and rerate the Parents' General Behavior Inventory, only now rate it based on how frequently your teen has had each symptom over the past week. This scale should also help you (and her doctor) determine if her symptoms are clinically significant (How many items are rated 2 [often] or higher?).

Step 2: Clarify the Context

Equally important is to clarify the environmental circumstances that precipitated the symptom buildup, especially because some of these circumstances may be controllable (or their effects can be minimized) now or in the future. Has your teen stopped taking his medications, and if so, how long ago did that occur? Has he gone a long time without seeing his psychiatrist and/or therapist? Has there been a recent relationship breakup? Has there been more family discord—arguments with parents, siblings, or extended relatives? Some of these circumstances may have been caused by the teen's early mania symptoms (for example, irritability causes more family conflict), but record them nonetheless—they may be playing their own causal role in his mood escalation. Louise said she recognized when Sam was getting manic by how frequently she found herself getting angry at him and how many fights they had. They usually fought when Sam had become more reactive to minor changes in his environment. These arguments, in turn, contributed to Sam's escalation, substance misuse, and self-injurious behavior (such as hitting his head against the wall).

Sometimes changes in context and the associated prodromal symptoms are *seasonal* and therefore can be anticipated for treatment planning purposes. Nancy, an accountant, noticed that her daughter, Elise, got irritable, giddy, and energetic when tax season began and Nancy had to spend more and more time at the office. When Elise was younger, Nancy had assumed this was her way of garnering her mother's attention. After observing several manic episodes during this time of year for several years in a row, she concluded that Elise had episodes that were related to the onset of spring. She then made plans with Elise's doctor to increase her dosage of Seroquel as spring approached.

Step 3: Identify Preventive Measures

Preventive Strategies That Your Teen's Doctors Can Initiate

If you're observing an upward spiral, your most straightforward preventive maneuver is to call your teen's psychiatrist, describe what you've observed (perhaps with the prodromal symptoms list in hand), and ask him to either make a change in medications over the phone or arrange an emergency appointment. As we've said in other chapters, a good working relationship with the psychiatrist is critical to dealing with these emergencies: it's tough to call a doctor you don't trust or think doesn't care about you or your teen. You have to trust that the doctor will approach your teen compassionately and do things that will help her.

After reviewing your list, your teen's doctor will probably (1) evaluate the teen, either in the office or over the phone, (2) order blood work if your teen is taking a medication that requires blood levels (usually lithium, Depakote, or Tegretol), and (3) change the medications. Medication changes may include increasing the dosage of a mood stabilizer like lithium or Depakote; adding an atypical antipsychotic medication like Risperdal, Zyprexa, or Seroquel or increasing the dosage of one your teen is already taking; or adding another mood stabilizer (such as adding Depakote to lithium). The doctor may also suggest a faster-acting emergency "rescue" medication when the teen's behavior is out of control, such as a high dosage of the benzodiazepine (tranquilizer) Klonopin or Ativan.

Your teen's doctor may also decide to *discontinue* a medication. This strategy is most likely to be used with antidepressants, which can cause or worsen mania, or an ADHD stimulant, which can also worsen mania. These medications are typically discontinued when manic symptoms appear shortly after the teen has started taking them.

A separate phone call to your teen's therapist is also a good idea. First, the therapist may be aware of factors contributing to this episode (such as drug abuse or medication nonconcordance) and hopefully has communicated about these matters with the psychiatrist. Second, the therapist may want to see your teen on an emergency basis, especially if your teen seems to be responding to an event that has been addressed in therapy (for example, his relationship with a girl who has been rejecting him). Third, if your teen's symptoms are severe enough to require hospitalization, his therapist may want to continue their sessions on an inpatient basis (see the section on hospitalization later in this chapter).

PREVENTION STRATEGIES THAT CAN BE ARRANGED BY YOUR TEEN'S DOCTORS

- Making one or more emergency medical appointments with your teen
- Referring you to an on-call physician if the doctor is away
- Obtaining a blood level to see if the teen is getting appropriate dosages or has been taking them regularly
- Changing medications—adding a new agent, discontinuing one, or adjusting the dosage
- Arranging therapy sessions to address environmental events contributing to her symptoms

Finally, if your teen has been doing well with this therapist, they will want to continue sessions after the episode has cleared, and the therapist's knowledge of all that has happened will make their postepisode treatment more productive.

Strategies You, Your Teen, and Your Family Can Undertake

Fortunately, there are options you can pursue during your teen's prodromal phase other than just calling the doctor. It's best to involve your teen in developing these strategies when she's stable. Encourage her to make a list of the things she can do for herself when the mania is starting to escalate. Then consider the tasks she'll need your help to implement and those that involve the cooperation of other family members (see the box on page 247). Some of these tasks are elaborations of the strategies we described in Chapter 10. Others will be new to you.

Of course, implementing any of these preventive measures will be much easier if your teen believes he really does get manic and has bipolar disorder. As we've mentioned before, some teens will resist any intervention that smacks of attempts to limit their freedom or independence (for example, going out with someone they can trust, having to be in by a certain hour). Manic symptoms can drive teens toward unrealistic expectations of what they can accomplish solo. Your teen will not appreciate how upsetting, dangerous, or damaging his behavior has become. If you're like most parents, you probably feel very helpless when trying to negotiate with a teen who clearly needs help but can't see it.

This is why it's so important to encourage your teen to be involved in relapse planning when she's well. Say, "This is one of the few things you can actually do to control your life when your mood starts to change other than just take medications." Your teen may like the idea that these exercises will contribute to her ongoing quest for independence.

Staying Away from Drugs and Alcohol

The prodromal period is the most important time for your teen to stay clear of substances, as well as anyone who provides access to substances. The manic high produces an intense desire for substances that are likely to increase pleasure, notably cocaine, marijuana, and hallucinogens. Your teen may also abuse alcohol, which, while not a stimulant, will worsen sleep problems and interfere with the effectiveness of medications. Some people with bipolar disorder get into an unfortunate loop in which they use substances, skip their medications, get drawn into dangerous sexual or other high-risk situations, get more manic, and then use more substances.

Your teen's psychiatrist and therapist may have good ideas of what substance abuse prevention strategies will work for him when he's getting manic or hypomanic, which may involve teenage AA support groups, ad-

---

WHAT YOU, YOUR TEEN, AND YOUR FAMILY CAN DO TO CONTROL ESCALATING MANIC SYMPTOMS

- Call the psychiatrist and therapist.
- Assure that medications are being taken as prescribed.
- Make sure your teen is in the house by nightfall and maintains a regular sleep–wake cycle (even if prescription sleep medications are needed).
- Chart mood and sleep cycles.
- Encourage your teen to avoid any alcohol or drugs or anyone who could increase the teen's chances of using substances.
- Insist that your teen take along someone he trusts when going out at night.
- Demand that your teen give up her car keys.
- Advise your teen to avoid managing large sums of money.
- Insist that your teen avoid making major life decisions.
- Have your teen cut back on social activities.
- Reduce your performance expectations of the teen.
- Keep your teen's home environment structured and low in stimulation.
- Impose consequences on your teen for aggressive or abusive behavior.
- If all else fails, call the police.

ditional psychotherapy, Antabuse (a drug that makes you vomit if you drink alcohol), or mandated urine screens. Of course, hospitalization and detoxification should be considered if the teen is abusing substances and unwilling to stop. You may also have to call the police if your teen is a danger to himself or others (see more on involving the police below).

See That Your Teen Is Accompanied by Someone Trustworthy When Going Out at Night

The best way you can help your teen avoid risky sexual or drug-related situations is to limit her ability to go out, or at least make sure she goes out with a trusted, responsible friend or relative. When Camille, age 16, was getting manic, she would climb out her bedroom window in the middle of the night and meet her friends in a local park to smoke marijuana. Her mother threatened to hospitalize her or send her to a drug rehabilitation facility. After considerable negotiation, Camille agreed that until her lithium blood levels had reached a therapeutic level, and her doctor verified that she was stable, she would go out at night only with her cousin, Phil, who was 18, could drive, and was reasonably responsible.

Likewise, some teen girls are less likely to behave in a sexually inappropriate manner when with an older and more responsible girlfriend whose opinion matters to them. If your teen has such a friend, ask her to involve this friend in any nighttime social activities and tip off the friend that she needs monitoring. Insist that your teen take a cell phone with her and call you at least every 2 hours to let you know where she is and when she'll be home. You may decide to "ground" her if she doesn't comply with this simple request.

Giving Up the Car Keys

A teen who drives is at high risk for an accident during the prodromal phase (and worse yet when fully manic). If you think your teen's behavior has been irresponsible, take away his car keys or have the car locked with a "boot" for which only you have the key. Needless to say, he will stomp and scream and threaten, but his and others' health are the primary considerations. Once again, it's helpful to set this consequence in writing at a time when your teen is well (for example, "If you develop a high mood, a decrease in your sleep, and show poor judgment, we will take away the car keys"). Make it clear that he'll get them back when you decide he's been consistent with medications and his mood is stable.

Avoiding Handling Large Sums of Money

Some teens have problems with spending when in the prodromal phase. This is one of those behaviors that worsens with increasing mania—your teen may be prone to overspending anyway, but when he's getting manic he'll spend wildly, with no consideration of the consequences. If your teen has a history of this behavior, you may have to cancel any credit or ATM cards he has. Insist that he not leave the house with more than $40.

Avoiding Making Major Life Decisions

A similar issue has to do with decisions that will affect your teen's future. During the symptom buildup, some teens decide that now is a good time to sell their clothes, buy a motorcycle, quit the soccer team, change schools, or move to California. Mania and its prodromal phases are affected by "hyperpositive thinking," in which people underestimate the risks of taking chances and overestimate the benefits. For example, when Max got manic, he believed there was no chance his music would not make him famous. When he was stable, he felt his music was good but needed work before it could be performed. Ask your teen questions like "Is there any chance at all this won't work out the way you want? If so, what percent? 10%? 20%? Can you imagine anything that could go wrong?"

Some parents have successfully used the "48-hour rule" and the "two-person rule": Encourage your teen to wait 48 hours before acting on any idea, and during that time ask two other people she trusts whether they think it's a good idea. If it still sounds good after 48 hours and the other two people agree, maybe it's okay to act on it. When Max wanted to spend his limited savings on a water purification system for the house, Patrick and Wendy insisted that he wait 2 days and ask two people about it, one of them an adult. Although Max didn't let go of this idea until he had gotten through his manic episode, he did admit later that their requirement of the two-person rule had at least slowed him down.

Cutting Back on Activities

A teen who is escalating into mania is highly likely to oversocialize, spending hours on the phone calling long-lost friends or relatives she hasn't seen in years, often in the middle of the night. You'll probably want to limit her access to the phone (including text messaging), at least during certain hours. Likewise, don't allow your teen to schedule social activities every weeknight—teens need a predictable, low-stress routine during the prodromal phase.

As with all of these strategies, you'll encounter resistance from your teen. Explain your requirements as similar to what you would do if she had the flu—she needs a period of convalescence to restore her health, with the expectation that normal patterns of socializing can resume once she is well (by your and the doctor's standards).

Reducing Performance Expectations

When your teen is getting manic (or has developed a full recurrence), it's critical to your family's stability to stick to your routines, such as when you eat, sleep, and clean house. However, your teen will probably not be able to meet your expectations for "pulling his weight" when he's escalating. He may be too cognitively disorganized to remember chores or too overstimulated to sit at the dinner table. Some teens have been known to focus their manic energy on housecleaning (to their parents' delight), but this is usually short-lived and may not be done ideally—such as scrubbing the insides of cabinets with toothbrushes late at night.

Your teen's school performance is likely to slip, and he'll probably need to miss classes. It's best not to overreact to such decreases in day-to-day functioning—when becoming manic, teens get confused, disoriented, and inattentive and can't perform at their usual level. Wait until your teen's mood has stabilized before expecting him to carry on with family and school routines. Make arrangements for him to get extra tutoring when he goes back to school and arrange for extensions on the deadlines of school assignments, in the same way you would if he were recovering from any medical illness (see also Chapter 14).

Keeping the Environment Structured and Imposing Limits

In Chapter 10, we emphasized the importance of low-key, structured routines, supportive interactions, and keeping family conflict to a minimum. At no time is this more important than when your teen is escalating, but this is also when it will be most difficult. His irritability will precipitate family arguments. These arguments will worsen his irritability and aggressiveness, which in turn will worsen the arguments in a vicious cycle. He will benefit most from low-intensity interactions with family members, even if he tries to "up the ante."

Nonetheless, that doesn't mean you have to put up with verbal or physical abuse or aggression from your teen. Even though his behaviors are illness-driven, he needs to know there are limits. Tess, the mother described in Chapter 9, felt it was important not to tolerate her daughter's verbal obscenities and physical taunts. If Tara got out of control while in the car, Tess drove to the nearest police station or hospital emergency room. As she approached the station, Tara tended to rein herself in. In other cases, you may decide, as Tess did, that simply exiting the confrontation is more effective than staying and taking the verbal abuse.

Calling the Police

When should you call 911? Calling the police is a very important option to consider, especially if your teen has become physically assaultive, is damaging your home, or you feel you or others are unsafe around him. The police will usually come and question the teen, who may be able to pull it together and look very innocent. There is the potential for you to feel embarrassed by this event if the neighbors are watching or if the police imply that you should have been able to handle things without their help. But they may also take your teen in for a psychiatric evaluation at a local hospital (which sometimes opens up other treatment options), and they will almost certainly make a report.

You may not be satisfied by what the police end up doing, but their involvement can be a strong deterrent for your teen's most aggressive behavior, as it was for 16-year-old Trey, who was usually quite gentle but when escalating would stand in his mother's way and not let her leave the room. He would also burst into Nan's room whenever he wanted and aggressively "get in her face" when she tried to avoid him. On one occasion Nan called the police. Trey retreated to his bedroom in the basement, but when the police arrived, they went down to question him. He was terrified by this experience, even though no arrest was made. The next time Nan felt bullied by Trey she threatened to call the police, and he backed down.

Some parents feel it's unfair to exercise this option because the teen's behavior is based on disordered brain chemistry and beyond his control. *It's important to enforce limits even on symptom-driven behaviors.* Even if such limits don't help derail your teen's oncoming episode, he'll probably be more aware of your boundaries the next time he develops symptoms.

When he was getting manic, Jordan wrecked his family's car after taking it out joyriding. The police gave him a ticket for reckless driving, but his parents thought this penalty was inadequate. Once they had gotten him stabilized, which required a brief inpatient hospitalization and a renewed medication regimen involving lithium, Depakote, and Abilify, they set up a plan for him to earn the money to pay the deductible on the insurance claim. This took him over 4 months, but it made the accident a learning experience for Jordan, and he agreed that giving up his car keys was a good idea if he escalated again.

Putting It All Together: The Mania Prevention Contract

Now, put together all of the strategies you've learned into one place, type it up as an agreement, and ask your teen, your spouse, and the therapist and psychiatrist to review it (see page 253). If they agree on its contents, they should sign it and have their own copies. Keep the contract in a readily accessible place.

"What If My Teen Has a Recurrence of Mania Anyway?"

Despite your careful planning and prevention efforts, your teen may still develop a full recurrence of mania. Some teens' manic episodes develop so quickly (within a day or two) that no one sees them coming, making relapse prevention ineffective.

If your teen does develop a full recurrence, the doctor may recommend hospitalization for the teen's own safety. Try to be as open to this option as you can, because it may be the safest and most time-efficient way to interrupt the mania cycle. It doesn't mean your prevention efforts have failed. About one in eight bipolar teens need to be hospitalized in any given year of their illness, usually for manic or mixed episodes. It's a good idea to be aware of hospital resources in your area even if you never have to use them. When inpatient stays are arranged early in the episode, the length of stay is usually shorter than when arranged later.

Safety is the primary concern in whether hospitalization is recommended. It will usually be necessary if your teen behaves such that:

- His or someone else's life is in danger (for example, he makes suicidal or homicidal threats).
- He can no longer function at school, at home, or out in public.

CONTRACT FOR PREVENTING MANIA

Your teen's psychiatrist's name _____

Phone number, office _____ Emergency # _____

Your teen's therapist's name _____

Phone number, office _____ Emergency # _____

Name of local hospital _____ Emergency # _____

Your insurance carrier _____

Agent's name _____ Phone number _____

Group number _____ Policy number _____

List your teen's prodromal signs of mania (from the form on page 240)

_____

_____

_____

_____

List the circumstances in which these prodromal symptoms are most likely to occur (for example, when your teen refuses medications, in the spring, after a relationship breakup, during finals week, or after intense, prolonged family discord).

_____

_____

_____

_____

List what you or members of your immediate family can do when your teen has prodromal symptoms (for example, call the psychiatrist, arrange an emergency medical appointment, arrange a hospitalization, renew prescriptions, chart the teen's moods, take away car keys or credit cards, call the police, keep the environment low in stimulation, keep family conflict to a minimum, adhere to regular family routines, take care of yourself and other family members). After each item, list the initials of each person who has agreed to do each one.

_____

_____

_____

_____

_____

List what behaviors you would like your teen to perform (take medications as prescribed, avoid alcohol or drugs, go to see the psychiatrist or therapist, go to bed at an agreed-on time, keep up with schoolwork, avoid making major life decisions, agree to seek others' advice, take along someone you and she trust when she goes out at night, refrain from obscene language or taunting siblings).

_____

_____

_____

_____

List what you would like the psychiatrist and therapist to do (arrange an emergency meeting, evaluate the teen's clinical state, order a blood level, revise the medication regimen as appropriate, prescribe an emergency supply of antipsychotic medications or benzodiazepines, call the hospital and arrange admittance, counsel you on how to handle things at home, arrange a family therapy session).

_____

_____

_____

_____

Signatures   Dates

_____   _____

_____   _____

_____   _____

_____   _____

- He refuses medications and any outpatient treatment.
- He is actively abusing substances and can no longer be monitored on an outpatient basis.

Hospitalizations need to be arranged by going to the emergency room of your local hospital. Your teen's doctor will probably help you arrange admission through the hospital at which the doctor has "admitting privileges." Not all doctors have an inpatient hospital practice, so your teen may or may not see his doctor while an inpatient, even if it is a hospital his doctor has recommended.

Understandably, many parents feel highly uncomfortable with hospitalizing their child, especially those who have never had to do so. Rest assured that "snake-pit" hospitals in which teens are locked up with dangerous, severely ill patients and given outdated treatments by uncaring doctors and nurses are a thing of the past (if not mainly of the movies). If your teen has been severely ill for years, a new hospitalization may not be as traumatic for you. But in either case, inpatient treatment can be the best thing you can do for your teen, especially if his doctor and therapist continue to provide consultation during the hospitalization period.

Be aware too that hospitalization is not the same as "institutionalization," which means committing a person for months and even years and taking away his basic freedoms due to mental illness. This rarely occurs nowadays, and when it does it usually involves lengthy court proceedings. In most cases, hospitalizations don't need to be longer than a week or two and are geared toward stabilization of the acute episode and preparation for a successful posthospital adjustment. Try to think of hospitalization as a period when your teen will get structured treatment, a reevaluation of medications, and advice on how to plan for a successful postdischarge period. It will also give your family a much-needed respite.

After a hospitalization, your teen may be discharged to a partial hospital program (that is, treatment during the day and going home at night) or an intensive outpatient program (for example, 2–3 hours of therapy each day). You will still need to deal with the complexity of the postmanic phase (see sections below), but you and your family will be able to regroup during the brief hospitalization and day hospitalization phases.

Enlisting the Help of Others in Your Support System

In Chapter 10, we talked about leaning on others to help you manage the stress of your teen's illness. This is especially important when your teen is fully manic because other family members can often accomplish what you can't at such times. Fifteen-year-old Carolyn impulsively ran away from home after a bad fight with her mother, Pam, during the height of a manic episode. Pam was understandably frightened when Carolyn called from her cell phone to say she had decided to live on her own because her home life was stifling her growth. Speaking rapidly, loaded with bluster and rage, and muttering about "going to live at the Krishna House," she admitted she had no money and nowhere to stay but argued she'd "figure it out." Pam notified the police, but what ultimately helped most was getting in touch with her ex-husband. Although Pam and Tom had a strained relationship, Carolyn was close to her father and agreed to stay at his apartment instead of on the street. The three then met with a family therapist, and Carolyn had an emergency session with her psychiatrist, who adjusted Carolyn's dosage of Zyprexa. Eventually, when the episode had stabilized, Carolyn returned to her mother's home.

Troubleshooting the Contract

If your teen has a manic recurrence despite the contract, arrange a session after the episode has resolved with the psychiatrist, therapist, and other relevant family members. You may be able to do this while the teen is in the hospital. Spend it reviewing, troubleshooting, and revising the plan: What went wrong? What strategies proved impossible to implement? Were there important prodromal symptoms that were not on the list? Laetitia's primary symptom during a recent episode was hiding food under her bed, but because this behavior didn't clearly relate to mania, it hadn't been listed on her contract. Her family's revision of the contract included adding this symptom.

If your teen's psychiatrist is often away, the doctor can write out emergency prescriptions in advance, with the understanding that you'll fill them the next time the teen's early warning signs appear and then arrange the emergency psychiatric session when the doctor returns. If potentially supportive family members did not return your phone calls when your teen's symptoms escalated, make clear to them the importance of quick responses, given the short window of opportunity of the prodromal phase. Was alcohol or marijuana available to your teen in your ex-spouse's neighborhood, where she lives on weekends? This requires more careful monitoring by your ex-spouse, who may be out of the loop. Finally, was your teen worried about her own feelings or behavior, but didn't feel comfortable calling her therapist or telling you? If not, who else could have been notified? Revising the plan to take into account these factors will make the contract far more successful the next time.

Of course, having a contract and implementing it are two very different things. Your teen may want no part of this kind of planning, or you may not feel that you can rely on others. Her doctor may be hard to reach in emergencies. Think of your contract as a work in progress. You can draw up these agreements and rehearse them when your teen is stable, but you may have to revise them further after an experience with a manic recurrence.

Picking Up the Pieces and Moving Forward

After Max's episode of mania had cleared, there were reparations that had to be made. Patrick and Wendy met with the school guidance counselor to discuss whether it made sense for him to continue in the same school or whether he would be ostracized by his peers and teachers. They agreed that he needed to have at least daily contact with the school psychologist for the month after his episode and that he should drop his math class for now. The guidance counselor also arranged to have his suspension lifted because his behavior was clearly a product of his disorder.

There were other reparations to make at home. He had been very cruel to his 12-year-old sister, Kara, calling her a "bitch, a whore, and a slut." Kara had been very upset by this, even though she knew he was ill. She deserved, and finally received, an apology. They also decided that Kara needed more individual time with both parents because Max's episode had left her feeling unimportant, unloved, and unprotected. They initiated family therapy with a clinician who understood bipolar disorder in teens. The relationship between Max and his sister, which was problematic even when Max was well, became the focus of these sessions.

After the "storm" of mania, your family will need some time to regroup and repair relationships damaged by hurtful words and actions—maybe between you and your teen or between you and your spouse or you and your ex. Your teen may have also mistreated his friends. Once your teen has been discharged from the hospital—or is clearly more stable following an episode treated on an outpatient basis—consider what needs to happen to bring his and your relationships back to the way they were. Sometimes, this will require family counseling; in other cases, supportive family discussions that don't involve an external person, using the communication techniques outlined in Chapter 9, will help you heal. Try to keep in mind that many of the things your teen said or did were the product of his biologically based illness, rather than an expression of his true feelings. Remind your other children and your spouse of this fact, although this explanation will not by itself be satisfactory to them. As one of our parents put it, "If you get run over by a bus, it may make you less angry to know that it was because the driver had a seizure. But you still got run over by a bus."

There may be practical consequences of the episode that need to be addressed. If your teen spent a lot of money, you'll have bills to pay, although some of the charges may be reversible (one parent was able to cancel her teen's order for plane tickets, for example). There may be legal issues to resolve that require an attorney. You may have to address your teen's impact on his schoolmates with the school officials. Please see Chapter 14 for some ideas on how to craft your teen's educational program to fit with the limitations imposed by his disorder.

Last, after an episode you may be left with an empty, hopeless feeling. You may wonder, Will my teen and family have to deal with this for the rest of our lives? Will my teen always be dependent on me? How can I encourage her to develop more independence? Will she always be in and out of hospitals? Will she ever be able to finish school, live independently, and have her own children?

We don't want to paint an unrealistic, rosy view of the future, but we also believe you have reason to be optimistic. People with bipolar disorder often have their worst episodes during the teen years; in late adolescence or early adulthood, they may realize that the key to their own independence is to stay on their medications, avoid drugs or alcohol, and maintain mood stability. Incorporating illness management strategies of the type described here will almost certainly make your teen's illness less recurrent. Likewise, getting your family on board with what to do in emergencies will eventually make those episodes that do occur seem less traumatic. Finally, new medications and psychotherapies are being developed all the time. It's likely that when she's an adult the treatments for bipolar disorder will be much more effective than they are now.

Having a mania prevention contract will make you feel more in control of your teen's and your family's future; it's an essential component of your teen's treatment plan. But the issues that arise during the development of depressive and/or suicidal episodes are different. Depressive episodes have a different set of prodromal symptoms from manic episodes (for example, depressive prodromal symptoms may show up as anxiety, pessimism, or the worsening of ongoing, milder forms of depression). While very disturbing to the teen and family, the onset of depressive episodes offer many opportunities for early intervention. There's a lot that family members can do for a teen who is spiraling downward or thinking about suicide, as you'll see in the next two chapters.

12

How to
Handle Depression

If you've been dealing with the chaotic, high-energy, risk-taking behavior of mania, depression may seem much easier to deal with—it might even feel like a welcome break. But it's important to take the "bi" part of bipolar seriously and exercise as much vigilance when your teen shows the signs of depression as when mania begins. Depression is a very real and frightening phase of bipolar disorder and is usually more distressing to your teen than to you. It can damage your teen's life. Your teen's depression and loss of interests can disrupt her education. Her withdrawal can damage her relationships with peers and relatives. Although it's a frightening prospect, the fact that untreated depression can progress into a full-blown episode and precipitate suicidal thinking or even a suicide attempt is a reality that must always be kept in mind.

You may also be subject to the common myth in our culture that those who are depressed can pull themselves out if it. Usually they can't, and that includes your teen. It can be incredibly frustrating for well-meaning parents to see a teen who once battled for her independence becoming increasingly dependent, unable to get herself ready for school, bathe, do her homework, or interact with the family. Depression can make life difficult for the whole family, but always remember that a depressed teen is in considerable pain.

Fortunately, there is reason for hope. With good psychiatric treatment and the practical tools offered here, the risks of the dire consequences of depression are vastly reduced. Depression is highly treatable, but, as with mania, you have to intervene early. It can be easy to miss the early warning signs, which are typically more subtle than for mania.

Therefore this chapter emphasizes the active role you must play in monitoring your teen for signs of depression. Then it gives a step-by-step plan for keeping prodromal depression from becoming a full-blown episode and tells you what action to take if it does.

The Many Faces of Depression in Bipolar Teens

Bipolar depression in teens consists of the same symptom constellations as for adults: depressed mood, loss of interest in activities, fatigue, slowing down, insomnia, poor concentration or indecisiveness, weight loss or weight gain, feelings of guilt or worthlessness, and, sometimes, suicidal thoughts or actions. The way these symptoms look is described in Chapter 2, but because many of them aren't highly visible, they can be hard to spot. Most teens don't admit to these symptoms except under careful evaluation by a professional. More often, they say they're angry, irritated, and bored. If you ask your teen how he feels while depressed, he may not be able to tell you or might give you clipped, irritated responses like "I don't know" or "Leave me alone."

Depression in bipolar disorder can be one of several types. In *dysthymia*, teens have a long-term (at least 1 year), stable, chronic depression that never gets extremely severe but is nonetheless debilitating. Teens with dysthymia complain of being bored and uninterested in the things they used to do (playing sports, playing the piano, listening to music) and are almost always irritable. They may become fixated on a particular activity (for example, video games) and will hole up in their room with the TV, computer, or a book for hours on end. Most teens get depressed from time to time, but dysthymia is chronic and impairing.

Bipolar teens often have *episodic depression.* This means that their mood has been stable (or even manic or hypomanic) and then sinks (sometimes rapidly) into a deep state of despair that, if untreated, can last for months. Episodic depression, like mania, has a prodromal phase in which the depression is worsening and during which early intervention can prevent a full episode. If teens do go on to develop a full major depressive episode, it's usually more severe than dysthymia. We don't know how long depressive episodes last in bipolar teens, but in adults they can go on for an average of 6–9 months if untreated.

Some teens have *double depression,* a persistent dysthymic mood with a more serious episode of depression on top of it. This kind of depression can be among the most difficult to treat, but again, like episodic depression, it usually has a recognizable prodromal phase. When teens who are dysthymic develop a depression, it usually shows up as a change in the degree to which they feel depressed, and as a result, the descent can be easy to miss. Nonetheless, you can detect these subtle changes in your teen's mood and help him implement the skills described in this chapter (for example, behavioral activation, cognitive restructuring).

Finally, depression in bipolar disorder often appears as *mixed episodes* (simultaneous mania and depression) or symptoms. It can be hard to recognize the sadness, low self-worth, and suicidal thinking beneath the anger, hostility, energy, and manic bravado, but it's still there, and still responsive to intervention. Mixed episodes can be the most distressing and uncomfortable for the teen, who may describe it as a "tired but wired" feeling.

One of the key differences between depression in teens and adults is that the onset in teens can be very rapid, whereas in adults it's usually gradual. Teens can experience a quick downward spiral in which one symptom begets another—negative mood reinforces negative thinking patterns, which causes physical and social withdrawal, which reinforces negative mood and thinking and causes more withdrawal. This spiral can be worsened by an environment full of stress and conflict. Thus it's best to (1) help your teen recognize depression at its first onset, (2) lower your expectations for academic performance and household responsibilities during this phase, (3) assist the teen in getting necessary outpatient mental health treatment, and (4) arrange hospitalization (also see Chapter 11) if the depression becomes debilitating enough that the teen can no longer function at home.

Step 1: Listing the Early Warning Signs of Depression

As in Chapter 11, start by listing the subtle changes in mood, activity, thinking, behavior, or sleep you notice when your teen is getting depressed (or, if your teen becomes seriously depressed very quickly, what symptoms signal to you a full episode of depression). Keep the list in a place where you and others can find it later. Try to base your observations on your teen's last episode of depression: What did you see, what did others see, and what did he report? It's important to identify early symptoms accurately—mild symptoms, if untreated, increase the risk of developing more serious depressions. You may want to rate the severity of the symptoms (where 1 = very mild and 10 = extremely severe). These ratings may

LISTING YOUR TEEN'S PRODROMAL SIGNS OF DEPRESSION

All of the following items refer to changes in your teen's usual mood, behavior, or sleep, rather than typical behavior. Consult with others who have observed your teen's mood during the depressive decline.

1. For any prior episode of depression, how long did it take (for example, a few hours, 1 day, 1 week) from the first observed symptom (for example, insomnia) to the point at which the depressive symptoms were severe? _____

2. List adjectives describing what your teen's mood is like when depressive episodes begin (examples: irritable, sad, fearful, anxious, angry, downhearted, grouchy, bummed, bored, blue, flat, numb).

_____

_____

_____

_____

_____

3. Describe changes in activity, energy, or physical behavior as the depression worsens (looks slowed down, won't talk to people, gets "clingy," talks slowly and doesn't say much, does less around the house, forgets to bathe, doesn't brush teeth, smells bad, clothes are dishevelled, smiles or laughs less, looks tired, loses appetite, loses interest in romantic partners).

_____

_____

_____

_____

_____

4. Describe changes in your teen's thinking and perception (thoughts seem to go slowly; seems uninterested in things; expresses many self-doubts, such as that she's worthless, unattractive, dumb, or uninteresting; feels guilty and regretful; expresses hopelessness or helplessness; can't concentrate or make simple decisions; thinks about hurting or killing himself; talks about death or other morbid topics; ruminates or worries excessively).

(cont.)

_____

_____

_____

_____

_____

5. Describe changes in sleep patterns (wants to sleep more or all the time, wakes up in middle of the night and can't fall back to sleep, wakes up an hour or two earlier than usual and is tired the next day, takes lots of naps).

_____

_____

_____

_____

_____

6. Describe anything else that seems _different_ about your teen.

_____

_____

_____

_____

7. Describe any circumstances that could have contributed to these symptoms (for example, stopped taking medications, drug or alcohol use, changes in home environment, loss of a romantic relationship, school failure, problems with a teacher or schoolmate, new use of a certain psychiatric drug, travel across time zones, more family conflicts).

_____

_____

_____

_____

_____

_____

help you distinguish your teen's prodromal phase from a more serious acute phase of depression.

Take special notice of how your teen's prodromal symptoms of depression differ from his prodromal symptoms of mania. Usually, the former involve being slowed down, subdued, and negative, whereas the latter involve being sped up, bouncy, expansive, and "over the top." But there are early symptoms that can signal the onset of either state: anxiety, irritability, and sleep disturbance occur in both states. Also, your teen may be developing a mixed episode, which can involve an unpredictable combination of symptoms from both poles.

Sometimes the best way to judge the polarity of the next episode is to examine your own reaction. If you're getting annoyed and impatient with your teen's lackluster behavior, she's probably getting depressed. If you're feeling bullied, pushed to your limits, and afraid of her, she's probably getting manic.

Once you've made your list of symptoms, note any special environmental circumstances that may be contributing, even if you're not sure of their causal role in your teen's mood. For Kari, the twists and turns of her relationships with boys were usually associated with her prodromal depressive symptoms, although when she was depressed she usually became more clingy, which drove boys away. Will's depressive prodrome was associated with an increase in his use of marijuana. For Jill, being rejected socially (not being selected for her chosen sorority in her first year of college) was the precipitant.

Step 2: Consulting Your Teen's Psychiatrist and Assuring Medication Consistency

As with mania, always consult with your teen's psychiatrist as soon as you have evidence that he's getting depressed. He may have information from recent evaluations of your teen that will help clarify what is causing the depression (for example, recent blood tests that suggest low lithium levels). His doctor may suggest an emergency session, which may consist of an evaluation, a blood workup, and, if indicated, a change in medications. The most likely approach will be to raise the level of the teen's mood stabilizer (for example, a higher dosage of lithium can be helpful in staving off depression), add an atypical antipsychotic with antidepressant properties (for example, Seroquel), or add the anticonvulsant Lamictal.

Your teen's doctor may or may not add an antidepressant. As we discussed in Chapter 6, antidepressants may precipitate mania or cause rapid cycling, although this is less likely if he is also taking a mood stabilizer. Some doctors are more likely to recommend antidepressants than others. If your teen's doctor does recommend an antidepressant, you'll need to monitor your teen very carefully in the days and weeks after he starts taking it for signs of agitation, hyperactivation, insomnia, aggression, or suicidal thoughts or actions. Nonetheless, some teens respond only to the addition of an antidepressant, so keep this option open.

This is also a good time to review the suggestions for assuring medication concordance in Chapter 8. Sometimes a teen who has secretly stopped taking his medications will have a "depressive rebound" (especially if he abruptly stops taking an antidepressant). Others who are getting depressed feel negative about everything, including their medications. They may mistakenly believe that the medications are the cause of their ill moods. Make good use of your teen's psychiatrist and therapist to help talk him into committing to the medication regimen—sometimes just hearing him out and correcting misinformation is all that is needed to get a teen back on board with treatment.

Step 3: Getting Your Teen Engaged and Active

Depression is not only about sadness; it's also about avoiding pain and anguish. The idea behind this third step, which psychologists call *behavioral activation*, is relatively straightforward: get your teen up and moving and increase her contact with her physical and social environment and she'll experience her emotional life differently. Specifically, behavioral activation is about helping your teen reengage and get active in the parts of her life she finds rewarding and solve the problems in her life that cause stress. But this is easier said than done: people who are depressed tend to withdraw from everyone and everything; withdrawing makes people more depressed, which makes them withdraw more in a vicious cycle. Getting your teen activated, engaged, and solving problems effectively is one of the best things you can do for her early in the depressive spiral and even later, if she becomes severely depressed.

It's understandable that when depressed your teen will not want to do the things that would make him feel better. Changes won't happen all at once—small steps build on one another. Your teen will need your support in reengaging with his environment, but once he's feeling better, the rewards of these activities will be incentive enough to keep it up. Until then, think of yourself as a coach and help him structure his daily routines so he remains active and engaged.

Educate Your Teen about Depression and Inactivity

To accept the behavioral activation approach, your teen needs to understand the importance of setting short-term goals and acting in accordance with those goals, rather than falling into the self-perpetuating, avoidant nature of depression. One way to frame this is to discourage her from "acting from the inside out" (letting her mood determine what she does and doesn't do) versus "acting from the outside in" (letting her behavior be driven by her environment and personal goals). Some teens and adults mistakenly believe depression needs to be combated with rest and "chilling out." "You need a good, restful vacation at home" is a common recommendation, but in fact these respites can make the depression worse.

Set Minimum Expectations

Although it's important to be empathetic about your teen's sadness and lethargy, it's also critical to hold him to a minimum set of expectations, even when severely depressed. These include getting out of bed by a certain hour every day (especially if he's going to school), including weekends; making his bed (which makes it less likely that he'll get back in it); taking a shower; and eating breakfast. You may want to limit the teen's access to the TV or computer to 1–2 hours per day. Weekends should not be spent "sleep bingeing," or catching up on sleep from the week.

As you learned in Chapter 10, daily routines and sleep–wake cycles can easily be disrupted by depressive or manic symptoms. Getting your teen back into a regular routine is critical to getting him to follow through on the behavioral activation exercises. So make a list of these minimum expectations and tack them up where they'll be easy to see. If your teen is clear about these expectations when well, he'll have an easier time adapting to them when getting depressed. They will be harder to fulfill when depression takes a more severe turn.

Be prepared for your teen to say that your attempts to activate her mean you don't understand the weight of her depression. Your teen may experience your efforts as nagging, controlling, or unsympathetic. Combine your efforts with statements of validation: "I understand how difficult this must be, I'm not saying it's easy, you are doing the best you can, but I think this will help." Help your teen realize that your goal is to make her feel better, not worse.

Develop a List of Pleasurable Activities

Sit down with your teen and look at the previous week. Are his days characterized by a lack of structure? Are there long periods when he seems to have nothing to do? Are there particular points in the day when he feels worst, when he's most likely to withdraw into his room? If he isn't in a regular 9:00 A.M.–4:00 P.M. school, are the mornings long expanses, with nothing to look forward to? Does he dread the weekends because he never has anything planned and therefore ends up sleeping? If he's active, are all of his activities "must do" activities, with nothing pleasurable?

Ask your teen to make a list of all of the things he used to enjoy, even if they seem unpleasant or impossible now. The List of Pleasurable Activities form includes a number of such activities—some of these have been reported by teens in our studies as things to do when they feel down. Ideally, these activities are rewarding or pleasurable, but be satisfied if your teen describes an activity as "That'd be okay, I don't know . . . whatever, I don't care." This may be the closest he can come to saying he wants to do something.

Next, help your teen complete the "Scheduling Pleasurable Activities" chart. Ask her to plan an activity that she can do each day, or even twice a day (morning and evening). This will require setting a target time for each activity. If you or she thinks twice a day or even once a day is too much, set a more modest goal, such as one pleasurable activity every 3 days, and then every 2 days, and then one. If she is beyond the early stages and has become more seriously depressed, pick the easiest tasks first (for example, listening to her iPod, putting on favorite pieces of clothing) and help her build up to more physically demanding or interactive activities (for example, exercise, going to a social event).

When you help her create her plan, try to be realistic about how these activities will fit into your family's routine. For example, your teen may think it will really help her mood if you could take her to Starbucks every morning, but that may disrupt your work routines and be too expensive. On the other hand, if going to Starbucks on her own in the morning (and paying for it herself) gets her up and out, it may be worth adding to the plan, at least during the prodromal phase. She may also

A LIST OF PLEASURABLE ACTIVITIES

List as many activities as you can imagine that your teen would find pleasurable, fun, rewarding, or at least a relief from boredom. Try to emphasize activities that will increase her engagement with other kids or her sense of competence or that will allow her to experience emotions other than depression (joy, excitement, pleasure). Distinguish between more demanding activities that the teen may still be able to do when in the earliest stages of a mood cycle (or when dysthymic) and less demanding activities for severe depression.

When less severely depressed:

_____   _____

_____   _____

_____   _____

_____   _____

(*Examples*: exercise, ride a bike or skateboard, play a musical instrument, play a sport, visit the Humane Society, practice a hobby, dance, cook something new, rearrange my room, change my hairstyle, help my sister with her homework, put on my favorite clothes, stretch my body or do yoga exercises, go to church or temple, go to a social event, go to the mall, play a game of cards, do something I've been meaning to do for someone else)

When more severely depressed:

_____   _____

_____   _____

_____   _____

_____   _____

(*Examples*: take photos; take a shower or soak in the bathtub; take a walk; scream into my pillow; paint, draw, or sketch; write letters; wash my face; listen to my iPod; instant-message or text-message a friend; go for a drive; call and talk to a friend; move my furniture around; read a comic book; read a novel; watch a comedy movie; play video games; sit outside in the garden; listen to a "soothing sounds" tape; meditate; burn incense; play with a pet; lie in the sun)

Sources: Lewinsohn, Munoz, Youngren, and Zeiss (1992); Miklowitz (2002).

suggest activities that require a lot of planning or funds (for example, going to a rock concert, going on a beach vacation). Praise her for coming up with good ideas, but steer her toward activities that can be done now, without a lot of planning or resources.

Once you and your teen have completed the first two columns of the plan, make sure you each have a copy. Then, once he completes each activity, ask him to record the day and time it was completed and his mood on a –5 (severely depressed) to +5 (severely manic) scale, before *and* after the activity. If these mood ratings mean little to the teen, simply ask him to describe his mood in words before (for example, "really angry") and after the activity ("less angry"). At the bottom of the chart, list any resources that will be needed to complete these activities. Will he need money? Does any of it require rides to town? Does it require that you or other family members reschedule any of your plans? For example, Tanika wanted to have pizza and watch a video with her family on Friday nights, but this plan excluded her younger brother, who had baseball games on Friday nights.

Why should your teen chart both high and low moods? Some pleasurable activities, like talking to friends on the phone, may overstimulate her (see Chapter 10) rather than reduce sadness or lethargy. Some people exercise right before they go to bed and then can't fall asleep, which can make them feel agitated or hypomanic the next day. Some of these side effects, of course, are unpredictable. A certain amount of trial and error will be needed to figure out what pulls your teen out of depression.

Troubleshooting the Plan

Once your teen has completed the first week of her behavioral activation plan, you'll have a general idea of whether the plan is improving her mood. Don't be surprised if you don't see results right away: it may take several weeks of effort, along with her usual medications and psychotherapy, before the depression starts to lift. The chart on page 272 will help you determine if the plan is working. Rate each day of the prior week as to your teen's mood on that day (or ask her to make the rating) and then make a check in the appropriate column if she generally followed her behavioral activation plan that day (did most, even if not all, agreed-upon activities). Use the rating that best characterizes the whole day, even if you think her mood bounced around. You may find it easier to rate whether it was a "good" or a "bad" day.

SCHEDULING PLEASURABLE ACTIVITIES

Day of the week and target time	Pleasurable activities	Actual time of day each activity was done	Mood before and after each activity (–5 to +5)
Monday _____ _____			
Tuesday _____ _____			
Wednesday _____ _____			
Thursday _____ _____			
Friday _____ _____			
Saturday _____ _____			
Sunday _____ _____			

List any resources (money, rides, appointments) that will be needed:

_____

_____

_____

Source: Adapted with permission from Miklowitz, D. J., *The Bipolar Disorder Survival Guide*. Copyright 2002 by The Guilford Press.

MONITORING THE SUCCESS OF YOUR TEEN'S BEHAVIOR ACTIVATION PLAN

Day of the week	Mood that day (–5 to +5)	Check (✓) if the activity plan was followed
Monday		
Tuesday		
Wednesday		
Thursday		
Friday		
Saturday		
Sunday		

Average mood rating for the days the plan was followed: _____

Average mood rating for the days the plan was not followed: _____

Source: Adapted with permission from Miklowitz, D. J., *The Bipolar Disorder Survival Guide.* Copyright 2002 by The Guilford Press.

If your teen's mood is better on the days that she followed the plan, you have evidence that her plan is working. If not, you may need to give it more time. If she's trying hard to follow through with the plan, give her plenty of praise. Remind her that the struggle against depression is tough, but that with continued effort she'll feel better in a few weeks.

Second, are the chosen activities too hard or unrealistic, or do they require resources or efforts from other family members? Sienna thought riding her bike to school would help her feel better in the morning. Unfortunately, her bike had a flat tire, which required her father to take her to the bike shop, which he had time to do only on weekends. The prior weekend, he had been out of town. Eventually, this plan was forgotten.

So, when choosing activities, make sure the resources that will be needed are easily accessible.

Third, is the plan posted in a place where your teen can find it and knows what events are coming up? Some parents complain that their teen loses the plan or forgets what's on it so that they always have to "remind her to have fun." One parent felt that implementing the plan had made her an ogre, because she frequently had to say "Remember? Today you were going to start practicing your violin again" or "Today you were going to call Debbie and ask her to go to the video arcade." The plan then began to seem like enforcing household chores. The ideas should come from your teen and reflect what she feels she can do at the present time, with support from you. Try to determine what kinds of reminders will and won't help in the "Resources needed" section of the plan.

Finally, when troubleshooting your plan, consider the balance between working with your teen to solve life problems and increasing pleasurable activities. Engage your teen in a discussion of whether her depression is more about the absence of positive reinforcers (too few pleasant activities) or the presence of too many negative reinforcers (many daunting problems that he avoids but that nonetheless make everything else seem less enjoyable). Brianna had been avoiding doing social studies homework all semester and was near failing. She listed riding her skateboard as an enjoyable activity, but in reality doing this had a very limited effect on her mood. Instead, her mother worked with her to take small steps toward solving her school problem: When could she read and summarize Chapter 5? When was a good time to start thinking about her end-of-semester project, and what resources would she need? Working on this school problem in small steps, while less pleasurable in the short term, had a more positive and longer-lasting impact on Brianna's depressive mood. You can use some of the problem-solving methods described in Chapter 9 to assist your teen in this process.

In contrast, Chris's plan contained too many "must do" activities and too few desirable activities. He thought it would make him feel better to schedule homework time because he knew he was falling behind and catching up would be a relief. Unfortunately, he scheduled homework on his plan up to six times a day, and when he couldn't follow through, he felt even worse. His father helped him develop a list of pleasurable activities and urged him to reward himself for completing homework with one of his chosen activities (in his case, playing the computer game "Zoo Tycoon" with his dad).

What If My Teen Won't Do It?

The biggest obstacle to implementing behavioral activation plans is an uncooperative teen. His lack of cooperation may be part of his depression, but it could also reflect a more generally uncooperative attitude toward treatment. So don't be surprised if, when you initially present this plan to your teen, he refuses or says it's stupid. Stay with it and try not to overreact. Say something like "Well, you may be right, it may turn out to be stupid. But we won't really know that until you try it. I can think of a number of reasons why it might be helpful to you, and I can also think of some why it wouldn't. Let's try to be open-minded."

Your teen's refusal may be rooted in fears that she won't be able to live up to your expectations. She may fear that she won't be able to do the things on the list, she won't feel any better, or you'll get annoyed and blame her if the plan isn't working. She may be afraid of disappointing herself. Depression can make the world seem like an endless stream of "try hard and fail" experiences. Although you won't be able to fully counter this view of her world, try to show an awareness of these fears and explain why you think they're unfounded.

Of course, negative thinking is part and parcel of what it means to be depressed and certainly part of what keeps your teen stuck in depression. Express your understanding of how hard it can be to figure out how to make things better. Reassure her that the two of you can collaborate on it: "Doing these things might help you feel better, and right now that's the only thing that matters to me. But if it were that simple, I know you would have already figured it out by yourself."

Consider offering the teen some rewards for carrying out the behavioral activation plan. Verbal praise is enough for some teens, but you can also reward him with access to valued privileges. For example, if your teen has been sleeping late so that he misses school, include "getting up in time for school" on the target list and make sure there's a reward at the end of the day (for example, you cook him a favorite meal, you allow him access to the TV) for following through. Remember, you can slowly withdraw these reinforcers as the teen's mood starts to stabilize and he can get up on his own.

Finally, troubleshoot the plan with your teen at the end of each week. What went well, what didn't, and how has her mood changed, if at all? What activities would she like to substitute if some didn't seem enjoyable or took too much effort? How can you be helpful if she forgets what's on the plan? Think about the plan as a work in progress. You may end up tweaking it or scrapping the whole thing and starting over, but at least you've developed a collaboration with your teen to confront his low mood and avoidance of the environment. As simple as behavioral activation sounds, it will do much to prevent your teen's depression from spiraling. As her mood improves, she'll gain a sense of mastery from having made her plan work. Hopefully, this feeling will be reinforcing enough that she'll continue to follow her agreed-on routines without your enforcement.

Step 4: Changing Negative Thoughts

A key symptom of depression in teens and adults is "automatic negative thoughts" or "negative self-statements." When depressed, people are prone to rapid, reflexive negative interpretations of events, usually involving considerable self-blame. These negative interpretations are usually a reflection of "core dysfunctional beliefs" such as "I'm unlovable," "My problems will always be with me," "I'll never be healthy," or "The world is a rejecting, unsafe place." Jessica, age 16, was pretty, popular, and very bright. When she got depressed, she would interpret minor events in highly personalized ways: a girl who chuckled when she walked by was laughing at her; her teacher's half-smile was hostile and meant to belittle her; her B grade in algebra was evidence that she was stupid.

In cognitive therapy, people learn to develop alternative ways of understanding the things that happen to them and to look at their situation from different vantage points. With a clinician's assistance, they learn to identify automatic thoughts and core beliefs and link them with negative mood states (anxiety, sadness, guilt). They evaluate the evidence for and against the veracity of these thoughts or beliefs and rehearse more adaptive and balanced interpretations of events. Then they rate the effects of these new thinking patterns on their mood states. Psychologists call this process *cognitive restructuring*. Jessica's first task in cognitive restructuring was to ask her classmates, in a benign way, what they were laughing about. When she discovered it had nothing to do with her, her therapist asked what other possibilities might explain why they were laughing at that particular moment. She developed and rehearsed the more balanced interpretation that "people are usually thinking about things that have nothing to do with me."

How can you tell if your teen would benefit from cognitive restructuring? First, this treatment is probably best when teens are becoming depressed or suffering from dysthymia rather than when they're in the depths of despair. When really down, your teen will have trouble identifying her negative thinking patterns and even more trouble believing in the more adaptive alternatives. Second, is she prone to negative thinking even when she's not depressed? Does she assume that other people dislike her because they've been recently unfriendly, discounting the possibility that they might have been having a bad day? Does she usually tend to see the "cloud in the silver lining"? It can be difficult to tell whether your teen's thinking patterns have changed as she became depressed, especially if she's been suffering from dysthymia. But in any of these cases she may benefit from cognitive therapy.

We're not encouraging you to adopt the role of cognitive therapist. This is a treatment that requires substantial clinical training and has many subtleties of technique. It's easy to do it badly. So if you're convinced your teen would benefit from cognitive therapy, we suggest you proceed as follows:

1. Locate a good individual cognitive therapist (or a cognitive therapy group). You can find a certified cognitive therapist in your area on the Academy of Cognitive Therapy website (*www.academyofct.org*; click on the "consumers" tab) or at the Association for Cognitive and Behavioral Therapies website (*www.aabt.org*; click on "find a therapist"), or through recommendations from your teen's doctor.

2. Read one or more self-help books on how to identify and challenge your own thinking patterns. These include *Mind over Mood* by Dennis Greenberger and Christine Padesky (1995) and *Feeling Good: The New Mood Therapy* by David Burns (1999). Your teen will probably need your help in completing exercises from these books (for example, the thought tracking record). If so, complete them with her, maybe using your own life experiences and thinking patterns as examples.

Step 5: Communicating Positively with Your Teen

> When my daughter gets depressed, I want to dive out of the window. I look at her haggard face and hear her whiny, monotone voice, and I just hate it and want to run away. Yet I know this is the time she needs me the most, whether she knows it or not. I say all the right things to her, listen like I should, but then she slams me by saying I don't care and that I'm not helpful. I have to put my own self aside and be like that cloth mother in those monkey experiments. She needs to cling to me like a little girl, and I need to be there to be clung to.
>
> —Mother of an 18-year-old with recurrent depressive episodes

Although family stress is at a maximum when your teen is getting depressed or manic, this is also the time when she most needs your compassion and support. Parent–child conflict is one of the most common precipitants for depression and suicidal behavior among teens. Family support is especially important when your teen is depressed, because she'll be isolated from peers and feel very alone.

There are some basic "do's and don'ts" of communication when your teen is depressed or getting depressed (and all of these also apply

TEENAGE DEPRESSION: DO'S AND DON'TS OF FAMILY COMMUNICATION

Do:

- Listen nonjudgmentally and express warmth, even when your teen is angry and rejecting.
- Validate the teen's feelings of despair, but express hope that she can overcome them.
- Encourage your teen to talk about his feelings, but gently back off if he doesn't want to.
- Highlight even small improvements or efforts (making her bed, combing her hair, returning phone calls).
- Put aside long-standing conflicts and call a truce.
- Express your expectations clearly and succinctly and in a calm tone of voice, even when you're saying something negative.
- Ask your teen if he wants to hear your advice before giving it.

Don't:

- Give commonsense advice of the form "pull yourself together" or "buck up and beat this thing"; these will be experienced as invalidating.
- Take your teen's anger and hostility personally—it's usually the illness talking.
- Express significant anxiety about the teen's mood state and where it will lead her; instead, discuss your worries with her doctor, your spouse, or a friend.
- Say things that your teen will experience as a guilt trip.
- Discuss your own or another family member's depression or suicidal feelings in front of your teen.
- Allow your teen to get embroiled in relationship conflicts between you and your spouse.

when she is expressing suicidal thoughts; see Chapter 13). Of course, depressed teens can challenge even the best, most compassionate of parents, so don't blame yourself if you slip into the "don't" category on occasion. If you apply these general guidelines, your teen is more likely to open up and view the family as supportive, even if at times she accuses you of being unsympathetic or unhelpful.

The "mantra" behind these tips is to give your teen plenty of support but also plenty of room. Balancing these two is hard but critical to helping alleviate her depression. Parents who have been able to sit with their teen, listen nonjudgmentally, back off when they've had enough, and keep their own boundaries usually report that their teens trust them more and more over time. We've been surprised at the number of bipolar teens who, when asked what helps them most when they're feeling down, say "talking to my mom or dad."

Sometimes the best tack to take is to admit your own limitations. For example, you can say "I can't deal with this right now; right now I'm too stressed/hungry/tired myself. I promise we'll talk later." This simple statement sets limits and draws boundaries. It will keep you from feeling that you're always "on call," allowing you to take care of yourself or your other kids while leaving open the option of talking later.

What Do I Do if My Teen Gets Depressed Anyway?

Despite your best efforts, your teen can slip into a severe depression in which she can't get out of bed; spends most of the day sleeping; develops a morose, mournful quality; can't go to school or misses significant portions of it; and expresses suicidal thoughts or intentions. There is no clear line between the prodromal phase and the acute phase of a bipolar depressive episode (and it can be even less clear in double depression, when there has been an ongoing period of dysthymia). The distinction is usually one of degree of symptom severity and functional impairment. For example, when transitioning from the prodromal phase to the severe phase, your teen may move from missing morning classes to missing school altogether. In the early stages, she may express unfocused thoughts about life not being worth living. When acutely depressed, she may express more frequent, intense suicidal thoughts and hopelessness or even make suicide attempts.

If your teen gets to this point, hospitalization is your best option (see also Chapter 11). Once again, you can arrange inpatient treatment with

THINGS THAT WORK AND DON'T WORK WHEN MY TEEN IS GETTING DEPRESSED

Below, check all the things you've tried and whether you think they clearly work, don't work, or if you're not sure. Keep this list so that the next time you see prodromal signs of depression in your teen, you can narrow the list to the most effective strategies.

Strategy	Tried?	Worked?	Didn't work?	Not sure?
Listing prodromal signs				
Behavioral activation planning				
Cognitive therapy				
Modifying medications				
Assuring medication adherence				
Providing support and reassurance				
Using good family communication skills				

From *The Bipolar Teen* by David J. Miklowitz and Elizabeth L. George. Copyright 2008 by The Guilford Press.

your teen's psychiatrist. The hospitalization will help assure her safety while depressed and also allow her psychiatrist to reevaluate her medications in a controlled environment. Psychiatric day hospitalization or intensive outpatient treatment may ease her transition back home after the hospitalization.

A Warning about Suicidality

When your teen is depressed, it is critical to be aware of any suicidal thoughts, to develop plans to keep your teen safe, and to be in reg-

ular contact with his treatment team. Suicidal thoughts are a common reality in adolescent bipolar disorder and must not be ignored. Fortunately, there's a lot you can do to alleviate your teen's feelings of despair and hopelessness, which is why we've devoted a whole chapter to the subject. *Whether or not you believe your teenager has had suicidal thoughts in the past, it's important for every parent of a bipolar teenager to read Chapter 13 so as to be prepared to prevent tragedy.*

If your teen is saying that life isn't worth living, becomes noticeably anxious, expresses feelings of hopelessness, or starts injuring himself (for example, self-cutting, burning himself with cigarettes), you must be alert to the possibility that he is contemplating a suicide attempt. If you see *any* such signs in your teen—even if you think they are manipulative or overdramatized—turn to the next chapter and be prepared to get professional help. Chapter 13 will help you recognize the early signs of suicidal thinking in your teen and intervene the minute they appear.

One of the hardest and most critical things that parents must learn is to speak openly with their bipolar teen about suicidal thoughts or intentions when the teen is getting depressed or is already there. Many parents are afraid that bringing up these issues will put ideas in their child's head. But knowing what your teen is thinking and feeling is important to preventing suicidal behavior, and it's up to you to bring the subject to the surface even though doing so can be very uncomfortable.

Teens hate the thought of going to the hospital and may avoid sharing suicidal thoughts with parents or providers for fear of getting locked up. So start by reassuring your teen that just because she is having suicidal thoughts doesn't necessarily mean she has to go to the hospital, although it will signal a need for more help and support. Then turn to the help provided in the next chapter.

13 Dealing with Suicidal Thinking and Behavior

Suicidal thinking and suicide attempts are unfortunate facts of bipolar disorder. We usually think of them as most likely to occur during depressive episodes, but actually suicidal thoughts and actions can occur almost anytime during the depressive descent, during mania, or even when your teen is doing well. Some teens have had suicidal thoughts all along, which get more intense as they get more depressed. *This is why it's important for every parent of a bipolar teen to read this chapter.* Understandably, you may not want to deal with this horrifying aspect of bipolar disorder if you see no signs of suicidality in your teenager, but be aware that suicide attempts are not always easy to foresee. They can take the form of sudden, impulsive self-destructive acts—some teens say they first thought about the act just minutes before doing it—or carefully planned, systematic efforts. *You should take every threat or self-injurious behavior seriously, even the seemingly most manipulative or staged.*

The purpose of this chapter is to help you protect your teenager in every way you possibly can. Being aware of the risk factors for suicide and the early warning signs that your teenager is thinking about it will help tremendously. So will getting your teenager to sign a safety plan, a written contract in which he agrees to take certain self-protective actions should thoughts of killing himself ever arise.

Why Do Teens Attempt Suicide?

Teens make attempts to take their own lives for any number of reasons: to gain attention from their parents or peers, to seek help, to express an-

DIRECT INDICATORS OF SUICIDAL INTENT

If you see any of these signs in your teenager, call her doctor **immediately.** If you have a safety plan such as the one described later in this chapter, now is the time to put it into action.

- Communication of a clear wish to die by a specific plan
- Persistent suicidal ideation and frequent preoccupation with death
- Expressed desire to escape a painful situation or emotion
- Evidence of planning: timing of the attempt to avoid getting caught, or confiding plans ahead of time
- Inability or refusal to promise to keep herself safe
- Preparatory behaviors (for example, giving away possessions)

ger or hostility, to escape an unbearable home or school situation, to relieve internal feelings of anguish, to induce guilt in others, or to seek revenge. For example, a teen can make a serious suicide attempt to punish a former boyfriend or girlfriend who now is with someone else. However, a reason that seems frivolous is no reason to take a teenager's suicidal intentions any less seriously. Regardless of their reasons for wanting to hurt themselves, and even if they don't really want to die, the outcome of a suicide attempt can be accidentally fatal.

We know it can be difficult to face the possibility that your teen is having self-destructive thoughts. Some people view thinking about suicide as a character weakness or moral failing. The truth is that suicidal thinking and attempts are symptoms of bipolar disorder. No teenager should have to feel alone or ashamed of these thoughts; many bipolar kids try very hard to control them but can't.

Maybe you feel that if your teenager is thinking about suicide, you're a failure as a parent. This is another misconception. We've seen suicidal thinking among teens whose parents were unfailingly conscientious in providing support for their teenagers and getting them into treatment.

There's no doubt that your task is tough and requires numerous balancing acts. You need to respond to any suicidal thoughts your teen has with compassion, but without rewarding suicidal behavior by being too attentive. Fortunately, as you'll learn in this chapter, you can help your teen through suicidal crises by selectively reinforcing adaptive, nonsuicidal behaviors—while at the same time taking care of yourself and other members of your family.

"Is My Teen at Risk?"

The risk of suicidal thoughts is high among adolescents in general: between 20 and 45% of all teens have them. But whereas 7–14% of all teens harm themselves at some point (including nonsuicidal acts such as scratching their wrists with a knife), the rate is closer to one in three among teens with bipolar disorder. In addition, suicidal thoughts in bipolar teens come frequently and intensely and are more likely to be acted on impulsively. The risk is highest when the teen is in the midst of a mixed or depressive episode.

If your teenager has a comorbid condition that tends to increase suicidal thoughts or actions, such as a substance misuse disorder, disruptive behavior disorder, or anxiety disorder, the risk goes up further. In addition, suicide attempts are intertwined with the genetics and biology of bipolar disorder. We know, for example, that the vulnerability to suicide can be inherited, and the functioning of the serotonin system is altered in the brains of people who attempt or complete suicide.

Factors that increase the risk of suicide attempts among teenagers can be biological, genetic, or clinical (that is, related to the teen's symptoms of bipolar disorder); they can also be environmental.

Clinical Features in Teens That Indicate a Greater Risk

- A prior suicide attempt or nonsuicidal self-injurious behavior
- Reacts to frustration with hostility and aggression (impulsive aggression)
- Pervasive hopelessness and pessimism
- Comorbid anxiety disorders, particularly panic attacks
- Substance or alcohol abuse
- Mixed episodes or psychosis
- A family history of suicide in a first-degree relative

Environmental Factors That Increase Risk for Suicide

- Unrelenting family discord
- A recent traumatic event involving loss or personal humiliation
- Legal, disciplinary, or school problems (for example, being bullied)
- Availability of firearms or pills
- Lack of availability of treatment
- Exposure to someone who has attempted or completed suicide
- Disconnection from major social support systems (family or school)

It's helpful to know about risk factors because some of them are amenable to intervention (for example, reducing access to guns, availability of treatment for substance abuse, medications for anxiety or psychosis). Use the preceding list to acquaint your teen's doctor—especially if she is new—with why you think your teen is at risk. Is your teen talking about suicide "passively" (for example, "I wonder what it would be like not to be here") or has she expressed more clearly articulated plans to you or to others (for example, says how she would do it and when)? Is he isolated from peers and doing poorly in school? Have there been recent instances of drug or alcohol abuse? Does she know someone who has attempted or completed suicide? *If one or more of the direct indicators or risk factors listed above is present, and especially if they co-occur with a depressive or mixed episode, treat it as an emergency and arrange immediate contact with the teen's treatment team (or call the hospital emergency service) to assess the need for hospitalization.*

Fortunately, the impact of some risk factors can be reduced. Other risk factors can be eliminated altogether. Chemical imbalances, for example, are treatable with medications: long-term lithium treatment significantly reduces the risk of suicide and suicide attempts, and other mood stabilizers or atypical antipsychotics can help control the anxiety, aggression, and agitation that sometimes translate suicidal thoughts into actions. Suicide attempts are also to some degree under environmental control. For example, suicide attempts can be reinforced inadvertently by well-meaning parents who ignore their teen's depressive ruminations but then become excessively concerned when she mentions suicide. Suicidal behaviors can be reinforcing to a teen if these behaviors eliminate internal feelings of distress. Some bipolar teens say they self-cut because it helps them feel better temporarily (which is possible because self-harm releases endogenous opiates in the brain). So even though the root cause of suicidal impulses is biology, its treatment should include modifications of the environment so that suicidal behavior is not reinforced (see examples given in the following sections).

One important environmental protection is a well-devised "safety plan," the main subject of this chapter. A successful safety plan can avert a suicidal episode, help your teen get the treatment she needs, and increase her belief that she can make it through seemingly unsolvable life problems. A safety plan involves (1) identifying when your teen is at risk, (2) decreasing her access to the means to commit suicide, and (3) increasing her access to *good coping strategies* (for example, distraction) and *social supports* (family, friends, and treatments) to help relieve her internal distress. With ongoing collaboration between your teen, family members, and her treatment team, a safety plan can be your teen's best protection against the suicidal impulses that bipolar disorder may impose.

Should your safety plan fail you, inpatient care is always an alternative that you must consider. If your teen has many of the risk factors listed so far and is thus at high risk for suicide or self-injurious behavior, hospitalization may be the only way to keep her safe and monitor her in a structured and protected environment. We'll discuss this option later in the chapter.

In the meantime, be aware of several *protective factors* that can work in your teen's favor:

- Positive parent–child connection (spending time together)
- Active parental supervision
- High parental expectations for conduct and academic achievement
- Positive connection between the school and the teen
- Religious or cultural beliefs against suicide

You can draw on these environmental supports when your teen is at risk for suicide. For example, teens are less likely to commit suicide when monitored closely by their parents, especially if the relationship was previously strained and the teen mistook his parents' lack of supervision for disinterest.

"How Do I Know That My Teen Is Thinking about Suicide?"

You can't always know with certainty that your teenager is thinking about ending her life. But you can learn to spot the early warning signs, and you can gain an understanding of four interrelated phenomena that we're talking about when we say "suicidality" or "suicidal behavior": *suicidal ideation* (thoughts about hurting or killing oneself), *suicide attempts* (a self-inflicted destructive act with the expressed or implicit purpose of killing oneself), *completed suicide* (actually taking one's life), and *nonsuicidal self-harm* (physical self-injury, usually in the form of self-cutting, which may or may not have a suicidal intent). Nonsuicidal self-harm, while unfortunately common among teens, is of particular concern in bipolar disorder because it can escalate into more serious suicide attempts.

Debbie, age 17, talked about ending her life and wondered aloud whether she would be better off dead, but never physically hurt herself (suicidal ideation). Dana, age 15, cut herself with glass after intense conflict with her teenage brother (who also had bipolar disorder) to "get her anger out," but never hurt herself badly enough to threaten her life (nonsuicidal self-harm). In contrast, Jake, age 17, actually made a suicide attempt by overdosing on Valium, although later he claimed he was "just really confused" at the time. After he'd taken the pills, he got scared when he realized he didn't really want to die.

Much of your prevention efforts for your teen will go into interrupting the transition from suicidal thoughts to suicide attempts or nonsuicidal acts of self-harm. Parents can sometimes spot the warning signs of an impending suicide attempt, especially if their teen has been very depressed, has had persistent ideas about suicide, or has made an attempt before. Look for sudden behavioral changes (for example, giving away possessions, jitteriness or agitation, increasing withdrawal from others), anxiety or panic symptoms, increased aggressiveness, or preoccupation with morbid topics. As we said above, these clinical features are considered to be risk factors that increase the probability of a suicide attempt.

Early warning signs may also include statements that life isn't worth living, that the teen wants to die, feelings of intense hopelessness and pessimism, self-injurious behavior (for example, self-cutting), and a worsening depressive mood. For many adolescents who attempt suicide, the motivations are not a wish to die as much as a desire to escape severe internal distress, anxiety, and intense loneliness. Usually, teens talk about a situation being unbearable or that their feelings are so intensely negative that they can only think of suicide as the way out. (To learn more about the thinking behind suicidal thoughts and actions, we recommend you read Kay Jamison's books *An Unquiet Mind* and *Night Falls Fast: Understanding Suicide.*)

Suicide attempts are not always linked to diagnosable episodes of depression or mania—teens can impulsively swallow an overdose of pills with little planning or foresight. This is most likely to happen if a stressful event has occurred (for example, a fight with a girlfriend/boyfriend), if they have "impulsive aggression" (the tendency to react to frustration with hostility), and if they have easy access to the means to hurt or kill themselves (for example, access to a gun or enough pills to cause poisoning). Some of these teens have had "hidden depressions" that no one, including their doctors, detected. *Your best strategy to reduce impulsive suicide attempts is to remove your teen's access to the means to kill himself, in addition to facilitating his ongoing psychotherapy and medication.*

Sixteen-year-old Neil had chronic thoughts about suicide but made only one attempt—slashing his wrists—in the midst of a bipolar, mixed episode. During this episode he became impulsive and aggressive: he broke objects in his room, smashed a window, cursed loudly at family members, and kicked the family dog. The second time he developed a mixed episode his parents had put a plan in place for preventing this progression, which included removing his access to sharp objects, getting his lithium dosage increased, and increasing his therapy sessions to give him an outlet for his anger. Although he did not make a suicide attempt during this second episode, he continued to have persistent suicidal thoughts that were a focus of his psychotherapy.

Preventing Suicide: Steps in Developing a Safety Plan

If you suspect your teen is at risk for making a suicide attempt, or even if you believe he is not suicidal but is seriously depressed, you should develop a signed safety plan in conjunction with your teen and his treatment team. Like the prevention contracts you developed for mania and depression, the safety plan includes a list of the teen's unique signs of suicidality (for example, morbid preoccupations, expressed feelings of hopelessness), a summary of environmental triggers (for example, conflicts with certain family members, events involving personal humiliation such as being bullied at school), and lists of what the teen, each family member, and the treatment team should do if the warning signs and/or triggers are present. The best safety plans prioritize the strategies to be used from most immediate (the teen agrees to tell at least one adult if he wants to kill himself, for example) to less immediate but possibly useful when other strategies don't work (for example, distracting her from her anxiety). The plan does not assume that your teen is developing a new manic or depressive recurrence—suicidal thinking is often on its own trajectory.

Step 1: Clear the House of All Potential Means of Self-Harm

There is a very clear association between the availability of firearms in the home and completed suicides among teens. One study found that overall rates of suicide were equal in the two geographically and socioeconomically similar cities of Seattle, Washington, and Vancouver, British Columbia. However, the suicide rate among 15- to 24-year-olds was

40% higher in Seattle than Vancouver, and the rate of youth firearm-related suicides was 10 times higher. This difference is probably due to the easier accessibility to guns among American teens. So the first step in any suicide prevention plan is to remove access to instruments of self-harm:

- *Remove guns from the house entirely or lock them up, unloaded, and store ammunition in a separate locked location, neither of which has keys your teen can locate.*
- *Make sure all pills, including Tylenol (acetaminophen or paracetamol), are inaccessible in large quantities.*
- *If you believe your teen has one or more direct indicators of suicide, dole out psychiatric medications in limited quantities,* especially those most likely to be used in suicide attempts (benzodiazepines like Valium or clonazepam). Keep only a limited number of the teen's pills around (maybe a few days' worth) and keep the rest in another location, such as at work or a relative's house.
- *Buy pills in "blister" or "bubble" packets, which make assembling large quantities much harder.* The introduction of blister packs in the United Kingdom was associated with a lower risk of suicide by overdose.

Step 2: Decrease Access to Alcohol or Drugs

The suicide rate among teens is clearly correlated with access to alcohol. Teens who make impulsive attempts often get drunk and swallow pills simultaneously. Make sure hard liquor is in a locked, inaccessible cabinet. If your teen has a comorbid substance abuse disorder as well as bipolar illness, make sure she's being treated for this disorder through drug or alcohol rehabilitation programs (see Resources). Your teen's psychiatrist should be monitoring his substance abuse through regular urine analyses (see Chapter 10).

Step 3: Talk Openly with Your Teen about Suicidal Feelings

The basis for determining whether your teen should be hospitalized is usually the potential lethality of his stated plans, intentions, and behaviors. Assessing lethality is best done by your teen's psychiatrist or psychologist, but sometimes teens refuse to go in. You can help by having an open conversation with your teen about his intentions. The best way to do this is to simply ask him, in a matter-of-fact but compassionate way, "Sometimes when kids start feeling depressed they think about hurting themselves or killing themselves. Have you ever had those thoughts?" It can be difficult to judge the appropriate timing of such an inquiry, although it's usually more effective when your teen is less rather than more emotionally aroused. He may shut down or refuse to talk, in which case you can assure him that "I'm ready to talk about this when you are."

It can be very painful for family members to openly discuss their teen's suicidal preoccupations. Nonetheless, these kinds of discussions are essential to your teen's safety. Some parents worry that having such discussions will make their teen become suicidal even if he's not, but there's no evidence that talking about suicide increases the chances that it will happen. In fact, it's *not* talking about it that creates the risk. Most people with bipolar disorder say it's a relief to openly discuss their suicidal thinking with family members, provided that these family members respond calmly and nonjudgmentally.

Encourage your teen to verbally express her suicidal despair, hopelessness, desire to escape, regrets, shame, or guilt. Try your best to respond calmly without becoming anxious, punitive, or resentful. A good strategy to follow is the "T-L-V-P" acronym: *T*alk openly, *L*isten, *V*alidate, and *P*roblem-solve about how to assure her safety. Try to get her to generate alternative solutions to suicide. *Help your teen realize that suicidal feelings will pass and that he is choosing a permanent solution to problems that are temporary.*

Step 4: Assess the Context

What is the event most closely associated in time with your teen's current suicidal thoughts or wishes? How similar is this event to past episodes in which she has had suicidal thoughts or harmed herself? Teens are highly reactive to family discord, "invalidating" communication from parents (interchanges in which their feelings are not acknowledged or legitimized), and perceptions that others don't care (which, of course, may be distortions). Loss experiences (for example, relationship breakups, death of a friend) and events involving personal humiliation—such as rape, sexual abuse by an adult, or a shaming experience in front of peers—can also be precipitants.

Teens may be unaware of the link between such events and suicidality. You may need to help your teen reconstruct the sequence of events and the thoughts and feelings that occurred at each step. Sarah got very upset after a friend humiliated her online, accusing her of sleeping with someone else's boyfriend and carrying a sexually transmitted disease. Not only was the event upsetting, but it occurred at a time when Sarah was questioning how she came across to boys—whether she was behaving in an overly sexualized manner, whether boys found her attractive, and whether she was attracted to girls as well as to boys. Her suicidal thinking began after the Internet experience but worsened when she went to school and was called a "slut" by a hostile cohort of her former friend. She swallowed pills and went to sleep for 12 hours, and only later realized she was trying to escape from this horrific experience of public humiliation.

The sequential chains of emotion, thinking, and behavior leading to a suicide attempt often reveal that the teen, at some point, felt she had no other alternative. When in the self-destructive, angry, anxious moods accompanying suicidal preoccupations, one's options seem increasingly narrow. Leslie, whose parents refused to let her go out one Saturday night, threatened to jump out of her third-floor bedroom window. Understandably, her parents found this threat unrealistic and manipulative, and did not take it seriously until she swallowed a handful of pills later the same night. After a trip to the emergency room, her father railed at her for "doing something so stupid." Leslie couldn't explain why she had swallowed the pills, which, after the fact, seemed stupid to her as well, but at the time "it was the only thing I could think to do." Moreover, she expressed shame and guilt at the pain she had caused her parents, which further fueled her suicidal thinking.

You may not feel comfortable trying to unearth the progression of these events, thoughts, and feelings with your teen. Of course, this is the job of her psychiatrist and therapist, but you may be the only person she's willing to talk to. Help her understand the chain of events such that, when they recur, you and she will be in a better position to alter the sequence and consider other behavioral options. For example, had Leslie been acquainted with "improving the moment" strategies (see page 212), and had her parents known of effective ways to distract her when she entered her most anguished states, her overdose might have been prevented.

Step 5: Construct a Safety Plan Contract

An important component of the safety plan is the safety contract (also called the "no suicide–no harm" contract), which is a signed agreement in which your teen agrees to take certain steps if the warning signs and triggers for suicidal behavior are present. As with most of the prevention contracts we've discussed, it's best to develop this contract when your teen is well, or right after a suicidal episode has been successfully resolved. Ideally, the contract incorporates the following elements:

1. *Your teen promises not to engage in further self-harm* and to notify her parents, psychiatrist/therapist, or another trusted adult if thoughts or impulses resurface.

2. *You and your teen develop a list of alternative strategies to combat suicidal thoughts when the precipitants occur.* What would she do if the initial precipitant (for Sarah, public humiliation by a friend) or something similar were to recur? How could she handle her distressing feelings other than by hurting herself? If her suicidal thoughts come frequently and persist, and she forgets what to do to combat them, encourage her to write a list of strategies on the back of a business card so she can easily access them.

Review the "stress thermometer" exercise in Chapter 10. This time, ask your teen at what point on the 1–100 scale she considers her "tipping point" (that is, the stress is severe enough to cause a suicidal thought or impulse). If her stress reaches that point (let's say 60), what can she do to relax and manage her emotions until she can get down to a 40? Common emotional self-regulation strategies include positive self-talk (see the *Mind over Mood* workbook of Greenberger and Padesky), mindfulness meditation (see the 3-minute breathing exercise in Chapter 9), and other "improving the moment" strategies like listening to relaxing music, walking, or, as one teen suggested, "crying into my pillow." Does your teen do well with distraction techniques (calling a friend, surfing the web, taking care of a pet, watching a movie, drawing, painting, or writing in a journal)? While only of short-term value, these distracting activities can derail the progression of thoughts and feelings into self-harm.

3. *Your teen lists her reasons for living.* People are most protected against suicide when they believe they'll be able to cope effectively with problems, that life has intrinsic value, or that others depend on their existence. The Reason for Living Inventory lists some common reasons to live identified by teens who had at one point considered suicide but then decided against it. Ask your teen to check the appropriate items when not actively suicidal. Then, when she admits to suicidal thoughts, remind her to review and think about her list.

Some teens supplement their Reasons for Living Inventory with visual reminders of the things that matter most to them. Lindsey, for example, kept her Inventory in a music box that played a tune she had enjoyed as a child, along with pictures of her cat, her younger sister, an award she won for her artwork, and a letter from her best friend.

4. *You and your teen discuss the necessity of emergency psychiatric treatment.* Your teen should be aware that you will call her doctor if she expresses a suicidal wish and that the doctor will probably want to see her and make changes to her medications. When suicidal, she will probably lack the insight necessary to make this call herself. However, reassure her that discussing her suicidal impulses with her doctor does not necessarily mean she will have to go to the hospital. In fact, tell her that if she's willing to get help on an outpatient basis and follow the other components of her safety plan, she's a lot less likely to need hospitalization.

Once you've constructed a safety contract, it should be signed by your teen, each family member, and, if possible, her doctor and therapist. Use the template on pages 294–296 below to construct your contract. It may go through several iterations if your teen becomes suicidal again and one or more elements of the contract prove unfeasible. Revising the contract in response to new events or suicidal episodes is not uncommon among families with bipolar teens and should not be viewed as a failure on your or your teen's part (see the example of Clare below).

Implementing a Safety Plan: Clare

Clare, a 17-year-old who lived with her parents and 15-year-old brother, suffered from bipolar I disorder. She admitted to thinking about suicide almost daily, even when she wasn't depressed. She had made two prior suicide attempts, both by overdosing on pain relievers she found in her parents' medicine cabinet. In both cases, she had managed to hide the attempts from her parents. She had vomited up the drugs and gone to sleep and managed to continue on as if nothing had happened. Her prior attempts were precipitated by loss experiences: in one case breaking up with a boyfriend and in another her parents' brief marital separation.

Her parents learned of Clare's prior suicide attempts during a session of family-focused treatment. They were upset, but neither seemed surprised by the news. Sessions were then devoted to problem solving to develop a safety plan: Was Clare willing to tell her parents when she became suicidal? Could Clare call her own doctor and therapist, or was it better to tell her mother and ask her to make the call? Was it safe for her

REASONS FOR LIVING INVENTORY FOR ADOLESCENTS

How important to you are each of the following reasons for NOT committing suicide? Check off each statement that is important to you.

_____ Whenever I have a problem, I can turn to my family for support and advice.

_____ It would be painful and frightening to take my own life.

_____ I accept myself for what I am.

_____ I have a lot to look forward to as I grow older.

_____ I feel loved and accepted by my close friends.

_____ I feel emotionally close to my family.

_____ I am afraid to die, so I would not consider killing myself.

_____ My friends care a lot about me.

_____ I would like to accomplish my plans or goals in the future.

_____ My family takes the time to listen to my experiences at school, work, or home.

_____ I expect many good things to happen to me in the future.

_____ I am hopeful about my plans or goals for the future.

_____ I believe my friends appreciate me when I am with them.

_____ I enjoy being with my family.

_____ I am afraid of using any method to kill myself.

_____ I can count on my friends to help if I have a problem.

_____ Most of the time, my family encourages and supports my plans or goals.

_____ My future looks quite hopeful and promising.

_____ My friends accept me for what I really am.

_____ My family cares a lot about what happens to me.

_____ I am happy with myself.

List other reasons for living:

_____

_____

_____

Source: Reprinted with permission of John Wiley & Sons, Inc. from Osman, A., Downs, W. R., Kopper, B. A., Barrios, F. X., Besett, T. M., Linehan, M. M., et al. (1998). The Reasons for Living Inventory for Adolescents (RFL-A): Development and psychometric properties. *Journal of Clinical Psychology, 54*, 1063–1078.

TEEN'S SAFETY PLAN

Teen's Agreement

If I, _____, am having suicidal thoughts or impulses, I promise to take some of the preventive actions listed below and to keep trying these actions until my suicidal thoughts subside. The following are signs that I may be at risk for a suicide attempt [list here typical early warning signs of a depressive episode or any statements or behaviors that in the past have signaled suicidal thinking or behaviors]:

_____

_____

_____

The following are *environmental triggers* that have upset me and made me think about suicide in the past (for example, family problems, relationship breakups):

_____

_____

If either I or my parents see any of the early warning signs of suicidality listed above, I agree to do the following:

1. Promise not to engage in any self-harm and to tell at least one parent, my psychiatrist, and/or my therapist if I have the impulse.
2. Stay away from alcohol or any illicit substances.

If the above is not enough, I will also try to reduce my suicidal thoughts in the following ways (circle all that apply):

3. Schedule pleasurable or distracting events (behavioral activation plans).
4. Use improving-the-moment strategies (for example, relaxation, meditation, dance, yoga, exercise).
5. Review my Reasons for Living Inventory.
6. Rely on input from trusted family members, friends, or spiritual sources (if relevant).

Other strategies I am willing to try:

_____

_____

Signature   **Date**

_____   _____
              (Teen)

Parents' Agreement

I, _____ (parents' names), agree to do the following if my teen has one or more signs of suicidal thinking or behavior (circle all that apply):

1. Get rid of all dangerous weapons in the house; leave them with friends or other family members who don't live with us.
2. Get rid of all pills that could be used to overdose, or replace them with a limited number of "blister packs."
3. If my teen is unable to do so, call the psychiatrist and therapist for emergency appointments.
4. Get rid of all alcohol or make it inaccessible.
5. Stay with my teen until he or she feels safe.

If the above are not enough, we can also help our teenager in the following ways (circle all that apply):

6. Talk openly about feelings: listen, validate, and discuss alternative strategies that don't involve self-harm.
7. Help my teen implement behavioral activation plans by scheduling low-key, rewarding, and/or distracting activities.
8. Try to avoid critical comments, judgments, or guilt-trips.
9. Reduce expectations for school performance or household responsibilities until the suicidal thoughts have cleared.
10. Make sure my teen is eating and sleeping regularly.

Other strategies we will try:

_____

_____

_____

Signature   **Date**

_____   _____
(Parent)

_____   _____
(Parent)

(cont.)

Doctor's/Therapist's Agreement

*I, Dr. _____, agree to do the following if _____
shows the above signs of suicide risk (circle all that apply):*

1. See the teen on an emergency basis and modify his or her medications (if appropriate).
2. Work with him or her on strategies to manage his or her emotions and interrupt the sequence from suicidal thoughts to actions.
3. Arrange a hospitalization (if necessary).
4. Other _____

Signatures   **Date**

_____   _____
                (Therapist)

_____   _____
                (Psychiatrist)

List members of your immediate family, neighbors, or close friends who could be contacted in an emergency:

Name   Phone numbers

_____   _____

                                                  _____

_____   _____

                                                  _____

List your doctors' names and phone numbers:

_____   _____

                                                  _____

_____   _____

                                                  _____

Number for local suicide hotline: _____

to be alone when she was thinking this way, and if not, what kinds of responses from her parents would she experience as supportive? Could her parents keep their pain relievers in a place where she couldn't find them?

Although considerable trial and error went into making the contract, Clare and her parents devised the plan in the sidebar. Clare agreed to contact her parents when her suicidal thoughts got very intrusive; in particular, she agreed to page her father, with whom she had a good relationship. All agreed that Clare would benefit from brief, supportive conversations with either parent and that her parents could be of help by recommending strategies to distract her from her suicidal ruminations. On a practical level, Clare agreed to stay out of her parents' bathroom when she had suicidal impulses.

Despite Clare and her parents' careful problem solving, Clare had another suicide attempt, this time precipitated by the move of her best friend (another loss experience). A bottle of Tylenol had been left on her mother's dresser, and she swallowed most of the tablets. She then became afraid and induced vomiting. This time, however, she contacted her father through his pager. This event was highly disturbing to her parents, who felt that she had let them down by not following their safety plan. Nonetheless, within a treatment session they were able to listen to Clare and validate her feelings of desperation. Likewise, Clare listened to her parents' frustration and practiced her own listening skills. She had an extra appointment with her psychiatrist, who checked her blood level, increased her lithium dosage, and then arranged a follow-up appointment the next week.

Clare remained mildly depressed throughout the rest of the family-focused treatment, but her parents' support made her feel more hopeful. She felt better that she had a list of alternative courses of action to follow when she felt most desperate. Her parents reported relief from knowing they had better access to her doctors than they thought they had.

Hospitalization for Suicidality

If your teen has been uncooperative with her safety plan, and you continue to have doubts about whether she'll be safe at home (see "Direct Indicators of Suicidal Intent," on page 282), we recommend that you arrange a hospitalization. Even if your teen has been cooperative, you may have to consider hospitalization if she is too emotionally distraught to know that her suicidal thoughts are putting her in real danger, in which case she may be unable to use the agreed-on strategies to combat them.

Suicide Prevention Plan for Clare, Age 17

Clare's list of her typical early warning signs of a suicidal episode:

I lose interest in watching my favorite TV shows.
I don't call my best friend back when she calls.
I don't want to come out of my room to eat dinner.
I start thinking about cutting myself.
I start daydreaming about how peaceful it might feel to be dead.
I imagine scenes of my funeral in detail: who is there, what everyone is saying.

Mom and Dad's list of Clare's early warning signs of a depressed episode:

She gets real withdrawn and won't talk to us or her friends.
She seems worried and anxious.
She lets her appearance go.

Clare's ideas about what she can do if one or more of the above early warning symptoms appear:

1. Agree not to hurt myself and to call my doctors if I have the impulse.
2. Page my father and, if I can't reach him, call my mother at work.
3. Stay out of my parents' bathroom (where medications are) when I'm home alone.

In addition to the above, Clare will try the following to help control her suicidal thoughts, in this order:

1. Do things that are distracting or make me feel better, like listen to music or read my poetry.
2. Read and think about my list of reasons for living.
3. Ask my best friend and parents to talk me through it.
4. Practice meditation and pray.
5. Do my yoga stretches.

Clare's ideas about things she'd like her parents to do:

1. Call my doctor to help me arrange an appointment.
2. Dad, carry your pager so that I can reach you easily.
3. If I need to call during the day, listen to me, don't get upset with me, and make suggestions for things I can do to distract myself.
4. Avoid being critical or blaming me for my bad feelings.

Mom and Dad's list of things they can do to help Clare if early warning signs appear:

1. Encourage her to call her therapist and psychiatrist; call them if she won't.
2. Check in with her by phone every few hours if she's home alone; listen to her and validate her feelings.
3. Show interest and appreciation when Clare shows adaptive coping strategies, such as positive self-talk, distraction, or pursuing new interests.
4. Avoid making her feel guilty or like she is a burden to the family.
5. Help Tom (younger brother) understand what she's going through.

Things Clare's doctor and therapist agree to do:

1. See her as soon as possible.
2. Change her medications if necessary.
3. Arrange a short time in the hospital if she can't promise not to hurt herself.
4. Help her understand where her suicidal thoughts are coming from.
5. Work with her on ways to stay safe.

Clare's ideas about things her friends can do:

1. Distract me by doing stuff with me we all like to do.
2. Stay with me until I feel like I'm not going to hurt myself.
3. Call my parents if I'm going to hurt myself and friends can't talk me out of it.

Source: Adapted with permission from Miklowitz, D. J., & Taylor, D. O. (2006). Family-focused treatment of the suicidal bipolar patient. *Bipolar Disorders, 8,* 640–651.

At minimum, the attending inpatient physician will put your teen on a 72-hour inpatient hold, which may be enough time to get the existing suicidal episode under control and plan for a more comprehensive outpatient program. It will also get your teen away from stimuli that provoke suicidal thoughts (calls from certain friends or romantic partners, access to instant messaging, conflicts with family members). Hospitalizations for suicide attempts can be short stays designed to reevaluate and restabilize medications or longer programs to identify triggers for suicidality, address the teen's feelings of hopelessness, and build better coping mechanisms. Unfortunately, the availability of longer programs is often determined by your insurance coverage, how cooperative your teenager is, and the availability of a hospital bed rather than his need for such a program.

If your teen is suicidal but refuses hospitalization, we recommend you institute procedures for involuntary hospitalization. After the 72-hour hold is over, a court proceeding will be necessary to guarantee a longer inpatient hold. You can consult with the teen's doctor or an attorney from the hospital if you feel this is necessary. Of course, your teen will resent an involuntary hospitalization, and you will probably be uncomfortable with it yourself, but the short-term costs of involuntary hospitalization are often outweighed by its long-term benefits (that is, a longer interval to achieve stabilization on a new medication regimen).

After the hospitalization, you may be able to arrange a transitional treatment program such as partial hospitalization (day treatment) or intensive outpatient treatment. After a brief hospitalization, Leslie, 18, entered a program consisting of 7 hours of treatment per week: 2-hour groups that met twice per week, two individual psychotherapy appointments, and a weekly psychiatry appointment to monitor her medications. This program lasted 10 weeks, and by its end she was considerably more stable and had a better grasp of why she had made a suicide attempt.

Coping during the Posthospital Period

Monitoring Your Teen

The risk for a reattempt of suicide is highest in the 3–6 months after the initial attempt. Even if your teen has not been in the hospital, the same triggers may reappear after the suicidal episode resolves (for example, seeing an ex-boyfriend with his new girlfriend) and can be even more potent if she is not clinically stable. So, if a transitional program is not available, make sure your teen has plenty of social supports, in the form of family members or close friends who can unobtrusively monitor her and make sure she is safe. After hospital discharge, she will still be depressed and anxious—and probably rejecting of help—but needs to know there are people to talk to if her feelings of despair return. She should not be left alone for long periods. She will probably resent your or others' intrusions into her world, but remind her that it is temporary, until she gains control over her self-destructive impulses.

Acts of kindness that show appreciation and love for your teen, and that show you value her companionship, can help significantly. Spend time with her in "nonclinical" activities that the two of you used to enjoy: playing cards, going out to get ice cream, or watching movies together. She may see through these acts of kindness, and may complain that you're being artificial, but this kind of positive reinforcement and social support will serve as a protective factor against impulsive attempts during the posthospital period. A study of teens and adults who had attempted suicide found that a simple intervention—postcards sent weekly to express encouragement—decreased repeat suicide attempts significantly in the year after the hospitalization.

If your teen is able to step outside of herself, she may benefit from activities that involve helping others or helping her community (for example, volunteering at a homeless shelter). Interestingly, after her third suicide attempt, Clare reported wanting to do more things to help her parents and younger brother, from whom she had felt isolated and disconnected. She wanted their relationships to become "more of a two-way street."

Personal and Family Coping

It's important to take good care of yourself—emotionally and physically—during the postepisode period. Family members often feel tremendous guilt, shame, and anger about the events that led up to their teen's suicide attempt. Your anger may be directed toward the teen, but it may also be directed toward your spouse or the treatment providers, especially if you feel they've been unhelpful when you most needed them. You may be constantly searching for an explanation for your teen's attempt and feel dissatisfied with the explanations given. Some parents feel an acute sense of stigma, as if they were being publicly humiliated for being ineffective or uncaring parents. You may feel tremendous anxiety that is not clearly linked to any one event.

If you or other members of your family are depressed, anxious, or suicidal, whether or not these symptoms relate directly to your teen's suicidality, make sure you're getting appropriate treatment and support from friends and family members. It's especially important that parents not express their own suicidal ideas within hearing range of the teen. Bipolar adolescents are more likely to think about or attempt suicide if they're exposed to a family member with similar symptoms, which is not uncommon in families in which more than one person has bipolar disorder. If you, your spouse, or one of your other children are feeling suicidal, some of the same safety plan strategies discussed in this chapter—such as removing weapons from the house—will apply.

Despite all the disruption your teen's suicidal episode has caused, try to return to normal family routines as soon as possible. Teens thrive on predictability, and it will be a comfort to your teen to know that, despite her recent suicide attempt, the family still eats dinner together, people still watch DVDs with her at night, and the dog still needs to be walked. Likewise, your other children and spouse will feel relieved by the return of predictable routines. Spend time away from the house doing things for yourself: going to the gym, walking in your favorite park, or spending recreational time with your spouse or your friends. Try to keep your own life positive to counter the negativity in the family environment brought on by your teen's suicide attempt. Recall one of the mantras in Chapter 9: don't allow your teen's mood to dictate the mood of everyone else in the family.

You will probably feel pulled in many different directions: How do I attend to my recently suicidal teen and make sure he's safe and at the same time pay more attention to his siblings, who felt neglected during the hospital period, and also take care of myself? And what about my spouse? Couple and family relationships often need repair during this period—in the form of talking privately, spending quality time together, and, if necessary, arranging to see a couple or family therapist. Where can I fit this in? There is no correct formula for obtaining this balance. *Rely on your teen's therapist and psychiatrist, and any extended family members who are available and willing, to help take some of the burden of your teen's care off your shoulders during the postepisode period.* Know when you've reached your own tipping point and ask others to step in.

Finally, be optimistic and don't give up! As your teen achieves stability and becomes more hopeful about the future, your lives will improve as well. Your considerable efforts will pay off over the long term, when your teen realizes that the structure and support you've provided have helped keep her alive.

14
Tackling the School Environment

Depending on a number of factors—such as how well controlled your teen's bipolar symptoms are and what kind of cognitive effects the disorder has had on him even when his symptoms aren't active—school may be either the biggest challenge you and your teen face or the least of your problems. Your teen may do well academically, at least outside of recurrences of mania and depression, or may be struggling to keep up. If your teen is one of the youth with bipolar disorder who at one point were designated "gifted," you may find it painful to see how bipolar disorder has hampered his performance. *Fortunately, there are many accommodations available that can help teens with bipolar disorder succeed academically.*

Most of the families we've worked with, even those who feel their teen's symptoms are controlled, report difficulties with the school setting. In this chapter we talk about the problems—with academics, the social arena, and homework—most commonly brought to our attention. Throughout the chapter you'll see highlighted quotes expressing concerns from parents that may be familiar to you; underneath them we offer strategies for intervening as well as sources of additional information on these complex topics.

A host of factors can affect your teen's academic achievement, including the influences of specific teachers and the school's expertise in special education and resources for managing disabilities, and the school's interest in being available to you and your teen. The strategies in this chapter should help your teen have a more successful school experience, but keep in mind that you'll have to adapt them to fit your teen's circumstances.

Finding the Right School and the Right Program

Teens with bipolar disorder vary widely in the amount of academic help they need and the type of environment in which they'll thrive emotionally and socially. If your teen is doing fine, you may need only to communicate with the teachers regularly to make sure things keep going smoothly. But if your teen is struggling, you'll have to request special accommodations or other services.

Many parents we've met aren't sure what they can expect from their teen's school. To start, teens diagnosed with bipolar disorder have a legal right to "a free appropriate public education . . . designed to meet their unique needs and prepare them for further education, employment and independent living," according to the Individuals with Disabilities Education Improvement Act of 2004 (IDEA 2004; see *http:// idea.ed.gov*). Figuring out how your teen's "unique needs" will be determined and the necessary services identified and delivered can, however, be a tricky navigational feat. A simple summary of the path to ensuring your teen gets the right services in the right school follows. But if a fairly straightforward approach doesn't lead your teen to an appropriate education, there are legal advocacy agencies that specialize in helping individuals with psychiatric or physical disabilities (see the Resources section).

Step 1: A Thorough Assessment

If you're going to ask for school accommodations, you'll need a thorough educational assessment of your teen. Help could vary from modifications in the classroom to "special education." Teens with bipolar disorder sometimes need help with behavior problems or a crisis management plan in addition to academic supports. The box on page 305 lists examples of the types of help for which your teen may be eligible.

Understanding and Educating Children and Adolescents with Bipolar Disorder: A Guide for Educators, published by the nonprofit Josselyn Center (2004; see the Resources), gives in-depth information about the role and process of the educational assessment. While the guide is intended for teachers, it will give you a good idea of what is available to your teen. In addition to reading this guide, talk to the person at school in charge of special education (usually a school psychologist or special education teacher) about the educational assessment process and how to request one.

Some parts of the evaluation can be done within the school system. However, you will want to ensure that they are not done in the service of excluding your teen from assistance because the school doesn't have the resources to provide it. If you're concerned about the school's ability to provide an appropriate assessment, you can hire a private psychologist to conduct the assessment to determine special education eligibility (see Chapter 7 on finding an appropriate therapist or assessor). If the school's assessment doesn't provide adequate information on your teen's problems or current performance, you have the right to ask the school district to reimburse you for assessments you seek privately, although there's no guarantee the school district will agree to do so.

A written report should be generated from the evaluation and should conclude with recommendations for school accommodations. Before you agree to any plan proposed, make sure you agree with (1) the problems identified in your teen, (2) the plan for addressing them, (3) how the plan's effectiveness will be assessed, and (4) how it will be revised if it's ineffective.

Step 2: A Section 504 Plan

We're calling this "step 2" because a Section 504 plan is the least intrusive level of help to which teens with a disability like bipolar disorder are legally entitled. It's a set of written agreements between parents and teachers about necessary school accommodations. To qualify, all you need to show is that your teen has a documented mental or physical impairment that limits a major life activity (for example, learning, recreation, socialization).

Generally, Section 504 plans are for teens who are having intermittent struggles in the classroom that interfere with but don't completely inhibit making strides at school. Often, parents have a Section 504 plan in place while determining whether the teen needs an individualized education plan (IEP) or are waiting for one to be implemented. The Section 504 plan can address issues such as how medication will be dispensed and taken at school, strategies for communication between the home and school, classroom accommodations (for example, timed test exemptions, behavior plans), and disciplinary actions if needed. Go to *www.wrightslaw.com/info/sec504.index.htm* to get more information about what a Section 504 plan is and how to initiate one.

Step 3: An IEP

An IEP offers a higher level of academic support than a Section 504 plan. The IEP typically has four components: (1) a summary of your teen's strengths and weaknesses (based on the school's evaluations and any you've obtained independently, no matter who pays for them), (2) goals for her academic success and development, (3) how these goals can be met given your teen's strengths or impairments, and (4) how progress will be assessed. Some potential accommodations for teens with an IEP are listed in the box below.

Though your teen may qualify for a Section 504 plan or an IEP without anyone knowing his diagnosis, he'll be eligible for more services if the diagnosis is divulged and made the basis of the plan. We discuss the pros and cons of disclosing your teen's diagnosis later in the chapter.

"My teen is bright but still makes only C's and D's even with all of the accommodations he's been given. We don't understand why this school can't help him succeed."

Despite receiving the types of accommodations listed below, your teen may still be failing, missing many days of school or not be able to make it to school at all (this is different from refusing to go to school, which will be discussed later), having significant peer conflicts, or having mood swings that are clearly connected to particular classes or

ELEMENTS OF AN IEP FOR BIPOLAR TEENS

- Having a designated place to use at any time of the day to calm down
- A signal your teen can use to leave the class for a time-out
- Reduced number of courses for graduation
- Adapted class schedules that may include a later start time to the day
- Testing accommodations (for example, untimed tests, oral exams, exemption from tests during symptomatic phases)
- Work/grade accommodations for when the teen has missed school due to symptoms or hospitalization
- Specific behavior plans for how the school should respond to more serious symptom-driven behaviors, to protect the teen from being suspended or expelled

teachers. Success may elude bipolar teens for many different reasons. You'll need to investigate the following areas before you can arrive at strategies that might help:

- If you feel that your teen's lack of success is related to the school, consider initiating special accommodations through a Section 504 plan or IEP as discussed above. If your teen has an IEP, the law requires that the plan be reviewed at least annually, at which point changes can be instituted.
- If your teen is continuing to have mood symptoms, her academic performance will almost certainly suffer. Using the mood chart (Chapter 10) and monitoring your teen over time will give you a sense of whether her symptoms are interfering with school productivity. In this case it may be necessary to meet with her psychiatrist and initiate changes to the medication regimen.
- When teens and their parents have a difficult time communicating effectively and resolving school-related problems, a teen's performance may falter. A therapist who is well versed in teaching communication and problem-solving skills (see Chapter 9) will be able to help your family identify the academic problems that need to be discussed and how to come up with more satisfactory solutions for them.
- Finally, you may need to take a realistic approach to your teen's performance and academic pathway. It may be helpful to recall how well she did in school before she began having symptoms. If she was a B student before, it may be unrealistic to expect her to reach beyond that level, although with proper treatment and continued mood stability she may be able to reclaim her former levels of achievement. If your teen previously made A's and is now making C's, you may need to assess over time if this is going to be her typical performance level now that she has bipolar disorder.

Factors that can contribute to your teen's getting poor grades despite high intelligence are complicated; naturally you have to take into account comorbid ADHD, pervasive developmental disorder, or dyslexia or other learning disabilities in addition to the possibilities already mentioned. If you've investigated all of these and haven't been able to identify obstacles that can be eliminated, you may need to accept that this is the best she can do for the time being. Alternatively, it may be time to look for a different academic program that will more effectively meet your teen's needs. Many teens in our treatment program have improved dramatically once they found the right school.

"Our daughter is adamant about not going to public school, but we're unsure of our other options."

We currently have no research data to tell us how well bipolar teens do in traditional school settings compared to nonbipolar teens. In our experience, though, teens who have *unremitting* symptoms of bipolar disorder and related cognitive and/or behavioral problems often do better in nontraditional settings because many public schools aren't equipped to provide the supports they need. Some teens do succeed in public school when their illness is finally stabilized. If the public school your teen is supposed to attend doesn't offer appropriate special accommodations, it will be up to the school to offer and cover the expenses of a viable alternative. But if the school district believes the services offered will meet your teen's needs and you disagree, you will probably have to find and pay for an alternative setting.

Finding such alternatives takes a bit of research, but you can start by investigating the other public schools in your area. Some areas offer open enrollment into other schools in the same district, and another school in your district may offer more expertise and resources for accommodating bipolar teens. Your teen may even be able to enroll in a school in another district, but this option is more costly.

Private schools are a second option for families that can afford the tuition. The typically smaller classes, more individualized attention, and more regimented behavior standards may be helpful to your teen, but be aware that private schools are not required by the state to provide special education services and you will have fewer legal rights in these settings. For a list of all of the public, private, and charter schools in your area, go to *www.nces.ed.gov/globallocator* but understand that you'll probably still have to rely on word of mouth and professional recommendations to find a school that fits your teen's specific needs.

Third, some schools contract with therapeutic day schools. If you and your school decide that this is the best placement for your teen, the school district will pay for these services, but it may spend a very long time unsuccessfully attempting to meet your teen's needs with less expensive alternatives (such as hiring a teacher's aide) before making this recommendation. Most of the teachers at these schools are well trained in mental health and behavioral issues. The schools typically offer psychiatric support, a secure environment, and intensive psychosocial intervention. These programs are good for a teen who is struggling in the academic environment due to symptoms or behavior problems but can still perform daily functions like self-care and minimal chores.

Fourth, consider homebound instruction or home schooling, especially if you live in an area with no other affordable options. Homebound instruction involves weekly meetings with a tutor to assign tasks to ensure your teen's progress. Parents often initiate this alternative, but the school may pay for the tutor and supplies (for example, textbooks).

With home schooling you're the tutor, which means a completely different education from the traditional route. If you and your teen work together well, you may find that the two of you can accomplish what needs to be covered with a couple of hours of focused work a day (teens say a lot of the traditional school day seems to be taken up with "dead air"). The educational requirements may be less for your teen if he goes the homebound route. However, teens may be less likely to follow through on assigned work when their parents are the only teachers. You should have in place a regular schedule for your teen, breaks within the day for each of you, and time when your teen is interacting with peers to enhance her social development.

Many families of a teen with bipolar disorder opt for a combination of settings. For example, your teen could start public school later in the morning, stay until after lunch, and then go to homebound instruction. Or he could be at a therapeutic day school in the morning and then bus over to his neighborhood school for the rest of the day. If you're curious about such options, talk with your school guidance counselors or district representatives.

Finally, some families of bipolar teens turn to residential treatment, especially if their teen is not progressing in school or there are serious concerns about his safety. A residential setting will keep your teen safe and offer psychiatric treatment and educational programming. Many teens who were running away, drinking, or injuring themselves and/or couldn't complete the simplest tasks at home or school (getting up on time, eating without prompting, and so on) have thrived in a residential environment. Residential treatment is usually time-limited (for example, 3–12 months); in other words, you are not consigning your child to a life away from family and friends, only a relatively short respite.

A good residential program will have a strong psychiatric staff, a high staff retention rate, good educational programming, and a focus on working with your family. However, you must thoroughly research a program before enrolling your teen because many programs turn out to be nontherapeutic "military schools in disguise." Though expensive, an educational consultant can help acquaint you with viable options and match your teen's needs to particular residential programs. The Resources section has a list of residential placements and educational consultants to help you find the best fit for your teen.

The downsides of residential programs are that they are very expensive (up to $120,000 a year, although there are options for financial assistance in most programs) and your teen may refuse to go. There are, however, services that will transport your teen to one of these placements if you are so inclined. This may seem like an extreme measure, but for those parents who are convinced that a residential placement is in their teen's best health and educational interests, it may be the only option.

"We've had such high hopes for our daughter—we're afraid her inability to complete a traditional education path will hinder her future."

Many parents say they've had to be flexible about the educational path their teens complete. This may be difficult due to your own dreams and expectations for your teen. You may never have thought about the possibility that your teen wouldn't finish high school and go to college, and you may have strong feelings about a change of educational plans. As mentioned in Chapter 4, many parents describe their bipolar teen as having been bright, curious, and enthusiastic as a child, as well as precocious and developmentally advanced in many ways. This perception can compound the disappointment many parents feel when their teen can't make it through the traditional academic system.

Some parents fear—often mistakenly—that a nontraditional educational route means that their teen's future will be unpromising. Getting a GED (a high school equivalency diploma) does not necessarily hinder teens from getting a job or attending college and can even prevent teens from feeling demoralized by trying to compete in a school setting that doesn't fit them. It may ease your disappointment and assuage your fears to know that you're not alone with this issue and that many bipolar teens succeed in a nontraditional academic environment.

Solving Day-to-Day School and Social Problems

Finding the best educational setting for your teenager is an important first step. But even in the best, most responsive setting, bipolar disorder typically generates problems that can disrupt your teen's functioning during the school day, either academically or socially. Your teen may not be dealing with all of the following difficulties now, but anticipating these common challenges can help you put solutions into action quickly in the future.

"We have an almost impossible time getting our son up and out of bed in the morning. Even once he's out of bed he seems so groggy that we're not sure it's even worth forcing him to go to school."

One of the most common complaints from parents is the lack of a morning routine. Parents consistently report difficulty awakening their teens, getting them going in the morning, and making sure they get to school on time. You may feel like you're taking a huge step backward in promoting your teen's independence when you have to help her get up each morning. Try the following strategies, but even if they work for you, you'll most likely need to lower your expectations for your teen's morning performance.

As discussed in Chapter 10, bipolar disorder makes it very difficult for teens to get up and ready for the challenges of the day, even on nonschool days. Marshall, for example, was so tired in the morning that he absorbed little from his classes. By the time he felt awake he was at lunch and had already missed half of the school day. One thing his parents found useful was to set an alarm that he couldn't turn off easily, placing it across the room from his bed. Some teens use a CD alarm clock that plays music they like to help them wake. You could also try rewarding your teen for getting up on time, such as giving him permission to hang out with a friend after school instead of coming straight home. Rewards are most effective when given within the same day as the behavior you want to reinforce.

If you and your teen have tried numerous strategies without success, you may need to talk with the school about a later start or a free first period. Also talk with your teen's psychiatrist about adjusting his nighttime medications if he experiences morning sedation.

"Our teen refuses to go to school, and we feel powerless to make him."

School refusal is, unfortunately, a common problem in bipolar disorder. Your teen may refuse to go to school because of ongoing mood symptoms, feeling hopeless and demoralized about the possibility of succeeding, boredom, social and/or academic performance anxiety, and/or peer problems. The reasons can be complex and intertwined.

If severe bipolar symptoms, anxiety, or psychosis (paranoia) are inhibiting your teen from wanting to go to school, make sure her psychiatrist is aware of the situation and has adjusted her medications accordingly. Even with a good IEP, dedicated teachers, and helpful parents, bipolar teens who are symptomatic will struggle in school and as a result try to avoid going.

In the case of adamant school refusal, you will probably want to meet with the school staff (for example, the special education teachers or school counselors) to get their input on how best to respond, or address the issue with your teen's individual or family therapist.

"The school refuses to understand that my son is having symptoms of a mood disorder—they think he just has a bad attitude and is lazy."

The neurobehavioral disorders, of which bipolar is one, are often referred to as "hidden disabilities" because you can't see the physical disability—only the resulting behavior. The concept of having a disability that isn't tangible is difficult to grasp, so you may understand why it's also difficult for those who aren't as closely connected to your experience, including teachers. Disclosing the teen's exact diagnosis can help teachers understand that there really is an illness behind the teen's inconsistent performance and defiance, but it's important to weigh the pros and cons of disclosure (see the box on page 312). Federal law entitles your teen to special services at school simply on the basis of having a diagnosis of bipolar disorder. But the reality is that Section 504 and IEP accommodations are often given on the basis of specific learning or behavioral problems (for example, dyslexia), and therefore the bipolar diagnosis doesn't need to be disclosed at all. Many teens and their parents decide to disclose the diagnosis only after it becomes clear that not revealing it is a disservice to the teen at school.

Maria didn't want her mother to disclose her diagnosis until her relationship with her teachers became strained. Her teachers interpreted

The *pros* of disclosing your teen's diagnosis:

- Documenting your teen's diagnosis means he will be protected under the Americans with Disabilities Act, and thus eligible for additional services and resources and protected from extreme disciplinary action (for example, expulsion) if any behavioral problems (for example, aggression) occur as a result of his illness.
- Knowing that your teen has a disorder may make school staff less likely to misinterpret her behavior as resulting from a bad attitude or laziness and more likely to put strategies in place for how to respond to her behavior.

The *cons* of disclosing your teen's diagnosis:

- Your teen may not want you to. He may be scared that his teachers will label him as a kid with a mental illness even when he is behaving like a typical teen.
- Your teen may also be concerned that her peers will find out and make fun of or harass her.

her inconsistent performance as the product of defiance and oppositionality. Maria's math teacher said, "I thought Maria and I had a close relationship, and some days things seem good, but on others she just seems irritated and resistant in class. Has something made her upset with me?"

Maria and her mother set up a meeting with this teacher, at which Maria's therapist explained the diagnosis and how her symptoms appeared at school. Maria's teacher was relieved that her relationship with Maria was not the cause, which opened the door to discussing how best to help her in math.

Make sure you and your teen talk about the benefits of divulging her diagnosis and the potential consequences before doing so. If you do plan to let her teachers know of the diagnosis, have a clear objective in mind. If you're just feeling frustrated and want support and validation for parenting a difficult teen, it would be better to get that support from a therapist, friends, or a support group of other parents of teens with mood disorders.

Before revealing information about your teen's diagnosis, ask yourself, "Can my teen manage with minor modifications that can be made without revealing his diagnosis?" If the answer is yes and your teen seems to function well at school with little impairment, there may never be a need to reveal his psychiatric diagnosis and put him at risk for the social stigma associated with psychiatric disorders.

"My teen is doing well with the two teachers who are compassionate, understanding, and well educated about his problems, but he's getting in deep trouble for ditching the classes of teachers who have a 'zero tolerance' or 'pull yourself up by the bootstraps' approach."

Despite an increasing willingness of most school systems to address mental health issues, your teen will nonetheless encounter teachers who do not have the education, experience, or desire to understand these issues in the classroom. Teachers may see your teen as spoiled and manipulative rather than ill. Even if you share your teen's diagnosis with his teachers, don't assume that the teachers will understand what it means. When Maria explained her diagnosis, one of the teachers said, "Well, I had dyslexia as a kid, and I got through school just fine." Not all teachers will see the diagnosis as a reason for them to be more helpful.

If you're going to reveal the diagnosis, it's important to provide education for the school staff. Maria's family used a list of bipolar symptoms to educate her teachers. You may use the handout from Chapter 9 (pages 205–206) that covers frequently asked questions about bipolar disorder.

No matter what level of help your teen needs, it's important to form an alliance with your teen's teachers. Many parents feel that the accommodations offered by their teen's school are less than ideal, which only emphasizes the importance of having a good relationship with the teachers. They are, after all, the individuals directly responsible for educating your teen and the sources of the greatest potential help. A good relationship will also make teachers feel more comfortable communicating their concerns to you and give you the opportunity to educate them about your teen's symptom-driven behaviors, like irritability and hostility, that they may have misread as intentional. Teachers who understand and express empathy for your teen's learning and behavior problems will make a tremendous difference in his day-to-day school performance.

It's important to try to work with your teen's teacher directly before going to the administration. Often, teachers will be much more amenable to helping if they sense you're giving them the benefit of the doubt. But if your teen's teacher is still neglecting to implement accommodations that are your teen's right by law, and you feel you've done what you can to work with the teacher, consult the administration about having your teen switched to a different class.

Consider this parent's interchange with her teen's teacher:

TEACHER: We had an incident after lunch with Harvey today.

PARENT: What happened?

TEACHER: Well, he was clearly upset when he came to my class and sat doodling. When I asked him to stop, he got very upset and threw his books on the floor. Then a classmate made a joke and Harvey yelled at him. He finally moved to the back of the room without asking permission and sat there sulking. When I asked him to join the class, he stormed out of the room and slammed the door. I'm going to move his desk away from the classmate who teased him. I know Harvey struggles, but when he's told to do something by a teacher he needs to follow directions. If he can't learn to control his behavior, he won't be allowed to return to my classroom.

PARENT: Thank you for telling me about this. I'm sorry about what happened yesterday and hope we can work together to make our strategies successful in your classroom. I think it makes sense to move Harvey away from the other student since he's so sensitive to being teased. But unfortunately, asking Harvey to control his behavior when he's in this mood state is like asking a student who uses a wheelchair to climb the stairs.

TEACHER: I'm not sure I follow.

PARENT: It's not that Harvey won't follow your directions. It's more that sometimes he *can't*. When you see him in the state he was in when he got to your classroom, he's in what we call "shutdown" mode. Basically, he's stuck and can't be reasonable. If he's pushed, the next stage is "meltdown." We've worked with him so he can recognize when he's in shut-down mode and can use strategies to keep it from going into a meltdown.

TEACHER: So what can I do?

PARENT: A couple of things that have worked have been for him to physically remove himself from an upsetting situation, or maybe change seats and draw by himself until he calms down. We understand that drawing or changing seats in the middle of class wouldn't be your choice, but when he's in this ready-to-blow space, leaving him alone to calm down is usually the best course of action.

"My teen's grades are all over the place, and we don't know whether he's just lazy on some days or it's bipolar symptoms."

Because a number of bipolar symptoms—difficulty concentrating, mental sluggishness, distractibility, racing thoughts—interfere with school performance, you're likely to see variation over time in your teen's schoolwork. Many families we know have developed a Plan A, Plan B, and Plan C system for matching their school performance expectations with their teen's symptoms. Plan A signifies that your teen's symptoms that day are not interfering with her ability to perform at school and that you can expect her to do better than when symptomatic. Plan B is used when your teen is having moderate symptoms that are interfering with her ability to attend and perform at school. She may still be able to go to school but may not do well on tests or be able to complete assignments. Plan C means your teen can't do any real work and may even need to take an extended break from school. Checking with your teen daily and using this common language will help you and your teen better gauge when you can expect her to achieve at her level of ability and when to lower your performance expectations.

"Our son continues to have outbursts in the classroom—they're a big concern to us and devastating to him."

Bipolar teens' externalizing behaviors (aggressive or hypersexual behavior, impulsivity, agitation, outbursts, or meltdowns) are usually the most demoralizing to teens and parents. If your teen is having frequent anger outbursts, let the school know about her diagnosis so that teachers can develop preventive strategies (see example of Harvey on the preceding page). Each school will have its own procedure for developing a behavioral plan, which is usually implemented as part of an IEP. Contact the school counselor or special education teacher to find out how your teen's school assesses and develops strategies for responding to classroom aggression. You may need to remind them that your teen has a legal right to the least restrictive academic setting.

You may still be able to positively influence the situation from the sidelines. Working with educators to prevent or at least minimize the negative consequences of aggressive outbursts will feel like a success in and of itself. First, you may be able to educate the teacher to the signs that your teen is getting agitated. Then share with the teacher the things that you've found helpful. For some teens, diversions in the classroom like drawing, working on the computer, listening to music with ear-phones, sitting in a softer chair, and distancing from other students may prevent a meltdown. In other situations your teen may need to leave the classroom altogether. Some schools set up support personnel or resource rooms for teens to access when they're having a hard time.

Teachers are often very open to being given solutions to these types of problems, especially because it's in their best interests not to have their classroom disrupted. Provide the school with a copy of the Josselyn Cen-ter's guide (see Resources) on educating bipolar teens as they develop pre-ventive measures for your teen.

Finally, as mentioned in Chapter 11, your teen may need to make reparations to his teachers or the students in his class (if they were specif-ically targeted) after an aggressive episode. It may be as simple as an apol-ogy to the teacher or classmate, but these gestures may go a long way in helping your teen minimize the social damage that accompanies manic outbursts.

"My daughter has such extreme anxiety at school that I'm constantly getting calls from her to come and get her in the middle of the school day."

Anxiety is a common symptom of bipolar disorder (see Chapter 3) and can make your teen unable to tolerate the demands of school. Being in-terrupted at work or at home by a teen at school isn't an uncommon oc-currence for parents, but it can be hard to know how to respond. Parents wonder if they should ignore the behavior, impose negative conse-quences for it, or simply be empathic and "rescue" the distressed teen from school.

First, do your best to manage your own anxiety about the situation. Staying calm and nonreactive, which is understandably difficult, may give you a better sense of how to respond in the moment. Second, you'll need to assess why your teen is calling you. If she's merely anxious, you may have one response (for example, reassurance). If she's becoming frankly psychotic (see Chapter 2, where the teen called his mother daily due to irrational fears), your interventions will usually involve the psy-chiatrist.

If your teen is anxious, you may walk her through some of the improving-the-moment strategies described in Chapter 13. For example, she may try to do relaxed breathing, confront her fearful thinking (see Chapters 7 and 12), or go through an informal problem solving (see

Chapter 9) to identify what she can do in the moment to cope with her anxiety (for example, go for a walk around the school, go to the bathroom and splash water on her face, have a snack, talk to a resource person).

"My teen struggles to make friends at school and feel accepted."

Although at some point most teenagers have trouble with peers and go through periods when they don't enjoy their friendships, teens with bipolar disorder have a particularly rough time. They are more socially impaired than nonbipolar teens and kids with ADHD. One study found that bipolar teenagers, even when not in the midst of an episode of illness, differed from their healthy peers in social functioning. They were more likely to be "inappropriately assertive" (they got into battles with teachers in which they challenged the teacher's right to set rules, for example) and had trouble empathizing with other kids. Interestingly, they did not differ from their peers in their knowledge of social rules, but because of their difficulty in regulating emotions, they often had trouble displaying this knowledge and doing the right thing in the right situation.

Some teens regain their social abilities when their moods stabilize, but this can take time and patience. They may complain in the interim that people avoid them or that friendships or romantic attachments are going sour. Other teens, particularly those who've had many episodes, have ongoing problems with their peers, including fights, on-again/off-again relationships, or overly sexualized relationships.

As a general strategy, we recommend providing as many opportunities as possible for your teen to have successful interactions with his peers. For example, if your teen has disobeyed household rules and you feel that a disciplinary consequence is required, we recommend withholding other privileges (maybe video gaming, allowance, or use of the computer) instead of withholding contact with friends. However, when his mood chart or list of stressors suggest that he's symptomatic and at risk for having his moods triggered by the social environment, suggest that he stay home rather than attend a social event and have a miserable experience. **Knowing when to be with peers and when he's not functioning well enough to socialize is a skill that will be important for your teen to have throughout life.**

Teens and parents often feel grief and loss related to peer problems. Many teens with bipolar disorder have never been invited to a birthday party, to a school dance, or to sit with other kids at lunch. This exclusion only robs them of more opportunities for social development—and may make their parents feel socially isolated too. Support that other parents take for granted—like having peers to share "war stories" with—may elude you.

Bipolar teens struggle in several areas of peer relations. Social awkwardness or immaturity may deny teens with bipolar disorder the chance to make friends. They may stand too close to other kids, talk too loud, or smell bad due to inconsistent hygiene. Teens with bipolar disorder say other teens call them mean, weird, or freaky. Whereas some bipolar teens are very sensitive to how others treat them, they can be interpersonally insensitive in their own behavior toward others. One 15-year-old girl we know asked a boy in her class if he had gotten his hair cut. When he said yes, she laughed at him and told him that it looked really stupid. When her mother, who overheard this comment, told her that she was being rude, she said that she was just being funny.

Due to bipolar teens' ever-changing moods, they often tire of or get irritated with friends. Many parents have described a "friend of the month" quality to their bipolar teen's social network: after a month the bipolar teen becomes bored or angry with a friend. Finally, when a teen is depressed, he may have a difficult time initiating and maintaining friendships due to lack of interest.

You may be able to help your teen in a number of ways. First, if your teen seems socially immature and does better with younger kids, try making connections with parents of these kids and arranging get-togethers either in the neighborhood or through other school and community activities. You can also investigate a social skills group or peer mentoring program within your teen's school or in the community. If your teen is the type who tires of friends, help her acknowledge this pattern and merely take a break from a friend rather than completely sever ties. After gaining some distance, your teen may realize that she didn't really want to lose another friend. If your teen was recently depressed, you may be able to help her by encouraging a gradual increase in social interactions until she is back up to her predepression levels (see the discussion of behavioral activation in Chapter 12).

"I'm not sure what to do—if anything—about the fact that my son is being bullied at school."

Bipolar teens are easy targets for class bullies. They may be teased for being less physically coordinated due to medication, being goofy or silly at times, missing class or school due to symptoms, being more emotional, receiving special services, being unkempt and/or unclean, being over-weight, or for a host of other things. A number of teens have told us that schoolmates provoke them into rages just to make fun of them. Teens with bipolar disorder are very reactive to the types of teasing that other students would be able to shrug off, making them an even easier target. It's no wonder that many teens with bipolar disorder give up and avoid peer interactions—or school—altogether.

As a parent it's hard to know how to respond to your teen's reports of being bullied. Will stepping in be helpful or make him a bigger target? It's probably best to talk to your teen about how he wants to handle challenging interactions with his peers. You and he can come up with strategies for ignoring, responding to, or getting help when faced with teasing or bullying. Most teens and parents report that trying not to engage the bully is usually the best strategy, keeping in mind that the bully may "up the ante" when ignored at first. However, if your teen struggles with being able to keep his cool, it may be best for him to leave a situation if he starts to feel upset.

On a larger scale, be sure you know your school's philosophy regarding bullying. Many schools have antibullying programs. When informed of the situation, the school will be in a better position to take preventive measures (for example, a teacher who knows the perpetrator well can intervene).

"Our daughter has been hypersexual when she's been manic. We're concerned that her symptoms create an impression among her classmates that doesn't fit who she is as a person."

Sexuality and dating are tough parent–teen topics even in the best of circumstances. In *Yes, Your Teen Is Crazy*, Michael Bradley offers some helpful strategies for talking to teens in general about dating, sexuality, pregnancy, and sexually transmitted diseases, issues that are particularly salient in bipolar disorder.

As mentioned in Chapter 2, many teens with bipolar disorder have been exposed to sex at an early age, sometimes because they've been victims of sexual abuse. Whether or not your teen has such a history, manic hypersexuality can put her at risk for sexual indiscretions or victimization. Many parents try to monitor their teen at all times and make sure she's safe, but there will be times when you have to trust others to monitor your teen, including school personnel.

The first thing that you can do to prevent a bad sexual experience related to poor judgment is to talk openly with your teen about sex in general and hypersexuality specifically. Normalize her curiosity (that is, most kids her age are interested in sex), but let her know that there's a difference between having intimate, romantic feelings for someone and the impulsivity and physical drive of hypersexuality.

It may be possible for the two of you to identify the difference between normal sexual feelings and hypersexuality. For example, typical teenage romance may include butterflies in the stomach, tentativeness, and a slow approach to experimentation, whereas hypersexuality may have an impulsive, fast-paced, "all or nothing" quality to it. If your teen understands what hypersexuality is, ask her to track it on her mood chart (see Chapter 10) and develop strategies for when she is having this symptom (for example, going out at night only with a trusted friend, educating a boyfriend about mania and bipolar disorder, checking in every hour with parents by phone).

If hypersexuality has led to rejection by peers, you may be able to respond as Hannah's mother Carol did. Before Hannah had severe symptoms of bipolar disorder, she had had a lot of friends in school who were on the honor roll and were leaders in the class. Carol said that the "weird sexual stuff" that Hannah began doing (doing strip teases at sleepovers and talking about sex with older men) alienated these girls and she had lost many of her friends.

Carol knew some of the mothers of these girls because they went to the same church. With Hannah's consent, she told the other mothers that Hannah's behavior was the result of her mood disorder and asked if the girls could still get together outside of school and at church. The mothers agreed, the girls were open to it, and over time with a medication change Hannah's inappropriate comments and behavior disappeared. Through these efforts she was able to keep her social circle despite her mood symptoms.

If your teen won't work on this issue with you, try dividing the problem into smaller units and apply the "basket strategy" suggested by Ross Greene in *The Explosive Child*. For example, you may treat "going out unattended" as a basket B item to be negotiated (i.e., your teen can go out without you only if she is in regular phone contact every hour), how she dresses as a basket C item that you could let go (unless it clearly puts her at risk), and safety issues as a basket A item on which you are unwilling to negotiate (i.e., staying out all night, allowing boys to stay over). In this way you may be able to pick your battles and make the ones affecting her safety the truly important ones.

Some parents are comfortable with their teen's sexuality, and others are not. Some make it clear to the teen that any premarital sexual activity is prohibited by their religious or cultural beliefs. Others tolerate their teen's forays into sexuality but make sure that their teen is on birth control and/or has a supply of condoms toward the goal of protection from sexually transmitted diseases. Planned Parenthood (*www.plannedparenthood.org*) is an excellent resource for counseling on sex-related issues, can provide education to your teen, and can help him or her attain birth control.

Your teen may prefer to discuss these problems with a counselor, but in most cases we've found that open communication between mothers and daughters or fathers and sons is more likely to prevent the negative effects of this unfortunate set of manic or hypomanic behaviors.

"My teen comes home from school in such a bad mood or so shut down that I can't get him to do anything related to school, including homework."

Bipolar teens often behave differently at home than at school. Many parents get good reports from the teachers at school about their teen's attitude and performance and are then shocked that the teen comes home from school and immediately flies into a rage or completely shuts down.

There are a number of reasons that teens may be in a bad mood by the end of a school day. Research by Mark Ellenbogen and colleagues at Concordia University found higher cortisol levels in teens at high risk for developing bipolar disorder (some of whom already had early symptoms) at 3:00 P.M. in the afternoon—just as school was letting out. Higher cortisol levels at this time of the day may explain parents' observations that these teens are wound up after school and have a hard time calming down and focusing.

There may be stressors at school that negatively affect your teen (for example, negative interchanges with a teacher, peer conflicts). One teen told his parents that when he was teased at school it instantly set the stage for him to be in a bad mood by the end of the day. On those days any additional stress at home, no matter how minor, made him "go ballistic."

As we discussed in Chapter 10, teens with bipolar disorder are prone to being hyperaroused or overstimulated. Unfortunately, the school environment may exacerbate your teen's already fluctuating states of arousal. For example, 16-year-old Cynthia found it very difficult to navigate the halls of the school between periods when hundreds of other teens were noisy, boisterous, and rushing to their next classes.

Finally, if your teen lacks initiative and motivation—due to various factors, such as depression, demoralization, or boredom with school—it may be very difficult to get him to complete work at home. This problem may go unnoticed by teachers, especially if your teen is quiet and withdrawn. One parent commented that her son's aloofness at school kept him "flying under the radar" of teachers, who assumed he was doing just fine.

Unfortunately, for many parents, homework becomes a struggle. You may not be able to get your teen to do his homework right after school at all. Instead, try planning physical activities (for example, swimming, playing a sport) to help your teen transition and burn off steam. Then allow him to complete homework when he has the most energy, which may be at night.

Many parents report that when their teen is already in a bad mood, she spends more time embroiled in arguments over homework than actually getting it done. In that case, consider hiring an evening tutor. Your teen may be more agreeable with someone outside the family, especially an older teen or young adult she can view as a mentor.

Some parents tell us that having their teen on a predictable schedule when she comes home from school is tremendously helpful. You may incorporate the family schedule from Chapter 10 to structure the interval between coming home from school, starting homework, and bedtime. Even older teens may be open to this level of assistance.

Finally, give your teen frequent breaks and rewards for homework completion. For example, a 5-minute break after every 30 minutes of homework may help with task completion. Some parents successfully tie their teen's allowance to the number of nights he completed homework without a fight.

Nonetheless, there will be times when medication changes, symptoms, or simple obstinacy will keep your teen from completing the required homework. Some parents leave work completion and consequences for incomplete work to the school and choose not to get embroiled in this issue with their teen. If your teen has a Section 504 plan or an IEP, you may be able to add modifications to the amount of work assigned or accommodations regarding when assignments must be handed in. A school counselor or special educator may be able to work with your teen on this issue.

What About the Future?

Aside from concerns about grades and school attendance or peer relations, most parents simply want their teen to develop skills for an independent life by challenging themselves and developing perseverance. When a teen falters in school, parents become understandably fearful about what this means for the future. Somehow, being able to face, withstand, and manage the challenges of school on a day-to-day basis feels like a preview for real life.

Success for bipolar teens appears to flow from a number of factors. In a letter about her experiences, a mother whose family took part in our treatment program credited her son's success in staying engaged and taking responsibility for his own behavior to "nurturing, responsible, competent, and attentive" teachers. She stated very clearly that part of her son's success was in managing his own expectations.

Needless to say, it was impossible for Leif, who was not medically stabilized, to meet anyone's expectations, even his own, under these conditions. Over time it was helpful that he discovered that it was acceptable not to be "even" all the time, and to have "off" days, and that on better days he could make amends, which he did very well.

Another ingredient in Leif's success was the ability to work toward self-management as a teen and young adult:

Another important improvement in Leif's life is his greater awareness of the benefits of exercising daily, of eating a healthy diet and of keeping his sleeping patterns as regular as possible, which is a challenge. But he tries a variety of holistic approaches that all help a little bit. He is physically active every day and walks our dog almost every evening, which helps him with insomnia. A positive aspect of Leif's life is the opportunity to volunteer twice a week. Mingling with the adults he works for, he engages in conversations, feels respected and appreciated, and his self-esteem is stronger.

This family was responsive to the communication and problem-solving skills taught in FFT and able to practice and put them into daily use. Leif's mother described how ongoing communication increased openness and trust between Leif and his family. For example, he became more willing to discuss difficult topics such as substance abuse with his parents:

We greet each day with optimism that it will be a good day, and when it's not, we reiterate our love and our commitment to Leif's well-being. We do not engage in destructive communication. Instead, we wait for the oasis in time where hearts and minds are ready for a meeting!

They also credited FFT with Leif having taken an active role in solving his own problems in and outside of the family:

During the course of our two years' participation in the family-focused treatment program, Leif developed his ability to speak for himself and to attempt taking responsibility for his needs. That helped him, and all of us, tremendously. One of the many benefits of our participation was the realization that our situation was not unique and that we were not alone in our struggle with schools, from individual teachers to special education resources, and with peers.

Finally, this family valued the commitment to ongoing treatment even with the strides they had made:

We have also been participating in weekly family therapy, including our other children, for over a year. I cannot overrate the benefits we all receive from each session. I am certain that without this guidance and experience we would have a very perturbed teenager and a broken down family. Learning together how to maintain positive family dynamics will be an asset for each member of our family forever.

We've been in contact with a number of other teens and parents who took part in our treatment program between 1999 and 2006. These teens are now young adults. Although we are only just beginning to collect systematic outcome data, we've been struck by the number who seem to be functioning very well in early adulthood. The worst symptoms seem to ease as teens approach their 20s. Most continue to have mood swings, but the demands of an independent adulthood, and often the requirements of a romantic partner or husband/wife, have made them behave more responsibly. Several are in college, the military, or working at steady jobs. Some have said that living through and learning to manage the illness has made them wiser and more compassionate and understanding toward others.

A few even have their own children. Interestingly, for these few, the presence of a child seems to have promoted stability rather than caused further dysregulation. Jessica, for example, had bitter conflicts with her mother when she was a teenager. As a teen she became pregnant and had an abortion, took numerous drugs, and was inconsistent with her medications. Now, at age 22, she has a 2-year-old daughter. Her boyfriend works steadily, and Jessica goes to community college part-time. She no longer abuses substances and is taking psychiatric medications because "I know I have to in order to save my relationship and make sure my daughter is getting what she needs." She gets her treatment through the mental health counseling services of the college.

What distinguishes the teens who do well from those who continue to be episodic or in and out of treatment programs? Certainly, taking regular medications is a big part of success, but it's not the only thing. Our impression has been that acknowledging the realities of the disorder and taking individual responsibility for it—in the form of tracking one's mood states, recognizing and getting help at the first signs of a relapse, staying away from alcohol or drugs, maintaining regular sleep–wake cycles, and avoiding social stressors that precipitate mood swings (for example, all-night parties)—make a tremendous difference in long-term functioning.

Importantly, continued contact and emotional support from parents and siblings can make the difference between a good and a poor long-term outcome. Most of the teens in our program have expressed appreciation for the parents who suffered along with them during their teen years. Several have wondered if they would be alive if it weren't for the commitment, love, and understanding they received from their parents. As Jessica put it, "If my daughter is unlucky enough to inherit this disorder, I hope I can be the mother to her that my mother was to me."

Resources

National Organizations

Depression and Bipolar Support Alliance (DBSA) (800-826-3632; *www. dbsalliance.org*) is devoted to educating consumers and their family members about mood disorders, decreasing the public stigma of these illnesses, fostering self-help, advocating for research funding, and improving access to care. DBSA has chapters in many cities that offer free, peer-led support groups.

National Alliance on Mental Illness (NAMI) (800-950-NAMI; *www.nami.org*) is a grassroots, self-help, support and advocacy organization for people with severe mental illnesses (including bipolar disorder, recurrent depression, and schizophrenia), their family members, and friends. NAMI offers parent support groups all over the United States and a structured educational program taught by parents of people with severe psychiatric disorders called "Family to Family."

Child and Adolescent Bipolar Foundation (CABF) (847-256-8525; *www.bpkids. org*), a parent-led organization, provides information and support to family members, health care professionals, and the public concerning bipolar disorders in the young. CABF advocates for health services and research on the nature, causes, and treatment of early-onset bipolar disorder. Note especially the material on navigating the public school system. The Learning Center contains examples of mood charts, articles on how to prepare for initial doctor visits, and information on research studies.

Juvenile Bipolar Research Foundation (JBRF) (866-333-JBRF; *www.jbrf.org*) is the first charitable organization dedicated to the support of research on early-onset bipolar disorder. Started by Demitri and Janice Papolos (authors of *The Bipolar Child*), JBRF raises and distributes funds for the most promising research into the causes, treatment, and prevention of bipolar disorder. The website contains substantial information on the diagnosis, causes, and treatment of the disorder, including articles on topics such as sleep inertia and setting up individualized educational plans for your teen. JBRF also allows you to join a listserv/chatroom for parents of bipolar kids.

Bipolar Significant Other Mailing List (*www.bpso.org*) is an e-mail exchange group in which members—relatives or friends of persons with bipolar disorder—share information about the illness, provide support to one another, and problem-solve about issues related to the impact of the illness on families and intimate relationships.

Massachusetts General Hospital Bipolar Clinic and Research Program (617-726-6188; *www.manicdepressive.org*) provides information, referrals for evaluation, treatment, research, and self-care tools to persons with bipolar disorder and their families. For a downloadable mood chart, click on "Resource Center," "Tools for All," and then "Blank Mood Chart."

National Institute of Mental Health Publications (866-615-6464; *www.nimh. nih.gov/publicat/index.cfm*) provides excellent up-to-date information on the symptoms, course, causes, and treatment of bipolar disorder. Separate sections are devoted to child and adolescent bipolar illness, suicide, medical treatments and their side effects, co-occurring illnesses, psychosocial treatments, sources of help for individuals and families, and clinical research studies.

American Academy of Child and Adolescent Psychiatry (202-966-7300; *www. aacap.org*) is the largest organization of child and adolescent psychiatrists. The site includes many educational materials and extensive lists of available child psychiatrists and how to contact them.

S.T.E.P. Up 4 Kids (866-992-KIDS; *www.stepup4bpkids.com*; e-mail: info@stepup4kids. com) is a nonprofit charitable foundation dedicated to supporting kids with bipolar disorder and their families. Resources include support groups, treatment seminars, and strategies for promoting public awareness. The site contains downloadable fact sheets and current research articles. The locations of summer camps and announcements of upcoming parent and mental health practitioner conferences are provided.

Websites Offering Information on Adolescent Bipolar Disorder for Teens and Parents

Child/Adolescent Bipolar Disorder website (*noetic.oathill.com/bipolar/chiladl.html*) gives information on diagnosis, treatment, and related issues for children and adolescents with bipolar disorder. It provides numerous links to Medscape (a comprehensive online summary of new research studies) and other relevant sites.

bpchildren.com is a great educational site for adults and teens, with an excellent list of resources for helping your teen manage at school.

bipolarchild.com, the Papoloses' website, offers information to families related to what they've learned in treating numerous children and teens with bipolar disorder.

pendulum.org has varied information on bipolar disorder and where to obtain additional books and articles concerning wellness techniques.

www.bpkids.org/site/DocServer/treatment_guidelines.pdf?docID=441 leads to an article presenting the expert consensus treatment guidelines for children and teens with bipolar disorder. The article was written for professionals, but it may be useful to share with your teen's treatment team or for you to use as a basis for evaluating a proposed treatment plan.

geocities.com/EnchantedForest/1068 contains selected articles for families of bipolar children and teens, book reviews, and practice guidelines; articles on how to work with the school system; and first-person accounts.

School Resources

www.schoolbehavior.com is a site developed to help educators understand the hidden disabilities (neurobehavioral disorders) that many students experience. Parents can send educators to this site to gain education and classroom strategies. Look for the article by Packer, L. E., "Classroom tips for children with bipolar disorder."

U.S. Department of Education (*www.ed.gov.com*; select "parents," select "my child's special needs," and then select "disabilities") gives detailed information about your teen's rights as a student with a disability. It also covers the individualized education plan (IEP) process.

Special Ed Advocate/Wrightslaw (*www.wrightslaw.com*) is the best place to find laws and other information related to special education.

Internet Special Education Resources (ISER) (*www.iser.com/index.shtml*) is primarily a site for learning disabilities, autism, and ADHD assessment and education. It contains a lot of helpful information for parents of teens with a disability.

Josselyn Center (847-441-5600; *www.josselyn.org/Store.htm*) has a guide for educators on understanding and educating children and adolescents with bipolar disorder. It contains many practical suggestions for teachers and parents on behavioral interventions and developing an IEP.

www.healthyplace.com has posted an article on the educational needs of children with bipolar disorder at *www.healthyplace.com/communities/bipolar/children_8.asp*.

The following are websites that can put you in contact with an educational consultant to help you find a school for your teen:

FamilyLight (800-PARENT-4; *www.familylight.com*). Thomas Croke is an expert consultant on finding schools for kids with bipolar disorder.

Independent Educational Consultants Association (IECA) (703-591-4850; *www. iecaonline.com*) provides a list of educational consultants in your area.

Legal Rights Pertaining to Psychiatric Disabilities

National Disability Rights Network (202-408-9514; *www.napas.org*) is a not-for-profit membership organization dedicated to protection, advocacy, and assistance for people with disabilities. The Protection and Advocacy (P&A) System and the Client Assistance Programs (CAP)—legally based disability rights agencies—are described in detail on the website, along with how the network remedies unfair or illegal treatment of the disabled.

Bazelon Center for Mental Health Law (202-467-5730; *www.bazelon.org/index. html*) is an organization whose purpose is to protect the rights of individuals with psychiatric disabilities. The site lists mental health advocacy resources in every state.

Therapeutic Boarding Schools

Each of the following has been recommended by at least one set of parents of bipolar teens.

King George School (2684 King George Farm Road, Sutton, VT 05867; 800-218-5122; *www.kinggeorgeschool.com*).

Grove School (175 Copse Road, Madison, CT 06443; 203-245-2778; *www. groveschool.org*).

Devereux Glenholme School (81 Sabbaday Lane, Washington, CT 06793; 860-868-7377; *www.theglenholmeschool.org*).

Aspen Achievement Academy (98 South Main Street [P.O. Box 509], Loa, UT 84747; 800-283-8334; *www.aspenacademy.com*).

SUWS Troubled Teens Wilderness Programs (911 Preacher Creek Road, Shoshone, ID 83352; 888-879-7897; *www.suws.com*).

The following are sites that offer a selection of treatment centers/therapeutic boarding schools:

National Association of Therapeutic Schools and Programs (NATSAP)—928-443-9505; *natsap.org*

Aspen Education Group—888-972-7736; *aspeneducation.com*

Summer Camps for Bipolar Kids

A complete list of summer camp opportunities for kids with mood disorders, learning disabilities, or disruptive behavior disorders was provided by the Child and Adolescent Bipolar Foundation (*www.bpkids.org/site/PageServer?pagename=res_index_23*; search by state) and the University of Wisconsin, Oshkosh (*www.uwosh.edu/phys_ed/programs/adaptedpe/campsforind.php*).

Camp New Hope (*www.campnewhope.net*) is the only camp devoted solely to bipolar kids. It is a weekend camp in Livermore, California, whose purpose is to help bipolar kids gain self-acceptance and knowledge of their disorder, as well as develop social networks in a supportive and fun environment. The camp medical directors are Drs. Kiki Chang and Shashank Joshi, both experts in the treatment of pediatric bipolar disorder. Contact *campnewhope_arroyo@yahoo.com* for more information.

Books for Teenagers

Anglada, T. (2006). *Intense minds: Through the eyes of young people with bipolar disorder*. Victoria, BC: Trafford.

Cobain, B. (1998). *When nothing matters anymore: A survival guide for depressed teens*. Minneapolis, MN: Free Spirit.

Copeland, M. E., & Copans, S. (2002). *Recovering from depression: A workbook for teens*. Baltimore: Brookes.

Irwin, C. (1999). *Conquering the beast within: How I fought depression and won . . . and how you can too*. New York: Random House.

Jamieson, P. E., & Rynn, M. A. (2006). *Mind race: A firsthand account of one teenager's experience with bipolar disorder*. New York: Oxford University Press.

Books for Parents

Amador, X., & Johanson, A. L. (2000). *I am not sick, I don't need help!* Peconic, NY: Vida Press.

Birmaher, B. (2004). *New hope for children and teens with bipolar disorder*. Roseville, CA: Prima Health.

Carlson, T. (2000). *The life of a bipolar child: What every parent and professional needs to know*. Duluth, MN: Benline Press.—A wonderful firsthand account of a parent's experience raising a bipolar child. Some parents have found the material a bit difficult as Carlson's son eventually commits suicide.

Findling, R. L., Kowatch, R. A., & Post, R. M. (2003). *Pediatric bipolar disorder: A handbook for clinicians*. London: Martin Dunitz.

Fristad, M. A., & Goldberg-Arnold, J. S. (2004). *Raising a moody child: How to cope with depression and bipolar disorder*. New York: Guilford Press.

Geller, B., & DelBello, M. P. (Eds.). (2003). *Bipolar disorder in childhood and early adolescence.* New York: Guilford Press.

Koplewicz, H. S. (2002). *More than moody: Recognizing and treating adolescent depression.* New York: Putnam Press.

Jamison, K. R. (1995). *An unquiet mind.* New York: Knopf.

Jamison, K. R. (1993). *Touched with fire: Manic–depressive illness and the artistic temperament.* New York: Maxwell Macmillan International.

Jamison, K. R. (2000). *Night falls fast: Understanding suicide.* New York: Vintage Books.

Lederman, J., & Fink, C. (2003). *The ups and downs of raising a bipolar child: A survival guide for parents.* New York: Simon & Schuster.

Lynn, G. T. (2000). *Survival strategies for parenting children with bipolar disorder.* London: Jessica Kingsley.

Miklowitz, D. J. (2002). *The bipolar disorder survival guide: What you and your family need to know.* New York: Guilford Press.—This is a book for late teens and adults with bipolar disorder and their relatives. It contains considerable information on the diagnosis, treatment, and self-management of the disorder, including how to function in the family and work settings.

Papalos, D., & Papalos, J. (2006). *The bipolar child: The definitive and reassuring guide to childhood's most misunderstood disorder* (3rd ed.). New York: Broadway Books.

Singer, C., & Gurrentz, S. (2004). *If your child is bipolar: The parent-to-parent guide to living with and loving a bipolar child.* Los Angeles: Perspective.

Steele, D. (2000) *His bright light: The story of Nick Traina.* Surrey, UK: Delta.

Summers, M. A. (2000). *Everything you need to know about bipolar disorder and manic-depressive illness.* New York: Rosen.

Waltz, M. (2000). *Bipolar disorders: A guide to helping children and adolescents.* Sebastopol, CA: O'Reilly & Associates.

Wright, P. W. D., & Wright, P. D. (2002). *From emotions to advocacy: The special education survival guide.* Hartfield, VA: Harbor House Law Press.

Relevant Books on Childhood Mental Health

Bradley, M. J. (2002). *Yes, your teen is crazy: Loving your kid without losing your mind.* Gig Harbor, WA: Harbor Press.

Faber, A., & Mazlish, E. (1999). *How to talk so kids will listen and listen so kids will talk.* New York: Collins.

Faber, A., Mazlish, E., & Koe, K. A. (1999). *Siblings without rivalry.* London: Piccadilly Press.

Faraone, S. V. (2003). *Straight talk about your child's mental health: What to do when something seems wrong.* New York: Guilford Press.

Greene, R. W. (1998). *The explosive child: A new approach for understanding and parenting easily frustrated, chronically inflexible children.* New York: Harper Collins.—This book, while not written specifically for bipolar disorder, contains practical strategies for avoiding "meltdowns" and using collaborative problem solving with your child or teen.

Kindlon, D., & Thompson, M. (2000). *Raising Cain: Protecting the emotional life of boys.* New York: Ballantine Books.

Pipher, M. (1994). *Reviving Ophelia: Saving the selves of adolescent girls.* New York: Ballantine Books.

Wilens, T. E. (2004). *Straight talk about psychiatric medications for kids* (rev. ed.). New York: Guilford Press.

Films for Adolescents, Siblings, and Parents

In our own words: Teens with bipolar disorder—A video documentary about teens and young adults sharing their stories of living with bipolar disorder (*www.josselyn.org/Store.htm*).

True life: I'm bipolar—MTV documentary inspired by Lizzie Simon's book *Detour* about the lives of teens and young adults living with bipolar disorder (*www.lizziesimon.com/consultant.htm*).

Changing minds: A multimedia CD-ROM about mental health (Royal College of Psychiatrists: tel. (country code 44) 020 7235 2351, ext. 259; *www.rcpsych.ac.uk/ campaigns/changingminds/materials/cdroms.aspx*) is part of an educational antistigma campaign intended for 13- to 17-year-olds. It covers addiction, stress, eating disorders, depression, schizophrenia, and self-harm.

Resources in Australia and New Zealand

Orygen youth health (*www.orygen.org.au*) is a service providing help to young people in the western area of Melbourne who have experienced mental health problems. Orygen Research Centre has a branch that focuses on first episode bipolar disorder.

Headspace (*www.headspace.org.au*) is Australia's new national youth mental health foundation and promotes early and effective treatment to young Australians affected by mental illness.

Richmond New Zealand (*www.richmondnz.org*)—if you click on the relevant links, you will get a host of mental health services for New Zealand and Australia, and one each for England and Scotland.

FYRENIYCE (*members.iinet.net.au/~fractal1*) is an Australian website that offers resources and links for people with bipolar disorder.

Resources in Canada

Canadian Mental Health Association (*www.cmha.ca*) is a nationwide charitable organization for gaining education and resources for mental health issues.

Mood Disorders Society of Canada (*www.mooddisorderscanada.ca*) gives links for the United States and Canada for anxiety and mood disorders including bipolar disorder.

Resources in England, Scotland, and Ireland

Glasgow Association for Mental Health (*www.gamh.org.uk*) is one of the principal providers of mental health support in greater Glasgow.

MDF the Bipolar Organisation (Castle Works, 21 St. George's Road, London SE1 6ES; 08456 340 540 [U.K. only]; 0044 207793 2600 [rest of world]; *www.mdf. org.uk*) is a user-led charitable organization that offers self-help groups, publications, and other practical information for living with bipolar disorder. There are separate sections for mental health professionals and for family members. The site appears to be geared to adults with the illness but contains information that may be useful for parents of bipolar teens.

SANE (0845 767 8000 [SANEline]; *www.sane.org.uk*) is a U.K. charitable organization with the goals of raising awareness and respect for those with mental health issues, undertaking research into the causes of these problems, and offering support to individuals and families.

YoungMinds (*www.youngminds.org.uk*) is a national charity that focuses on mental health in children and young people. If you search under "bipolar," you will find many references to resource fact sheets.

Royal College of Paediatrics and Child Health (50 Hallam Street, London W1W 6DE; 020 7307 5600; *www.rcpch.ac.uk*) can help you locate pediatricians and other child and youth health providers.

Royal College of Psychiatrists (*www.rcpsych.ac.uk/mentalhealthinformation.aspx*) is a site that offers fact sheets on many different topics (including bipolar disorder) including one for young people entitled *Mental Health and Growing Up* (Fact Sheet 33).

Rethink (5th floor, Royal London House, 22–25 Finsbury Square, London EC2A 1DX; 0845 456 0455; *www.rethink.org*) offers help to people with severe mental illness and their caregivers.

AWARE (helpline 1890 303 302; *www.aware.ie*) is a service to help people with depression. You can access information and locations of various branches in Ireland.

Mental Health Ireland (*www.mentalhealthireland.ie*) provides support to people with mental health problems and their caregivers.

Bibliography

Chapter 1

Egeland, J. A., Hostetter, A. M., Pauls, D. L., & Sussex, J. N. (2000). Prodromal symptoms before onset of manic–depressive disorder suggested by first hospital admission histories. *Journal of the American Academy of Child and Adolescent Psychiatry, 39,* 1245–1252.

Kessler, R. C., Chiu, W. T., Demler, O., & Walters, E. E. (2005). Prevalence, severity, and comorbidity of 12–month DSM-IV disorders in the National Comorbidity Survey Replication. *Archives of General Psychiatry, 62,* 617–627.

Lish, J. D., Dime-Meenan, S., Whybrow, P. C., Price, R. A., & Hirschfeld, R. M. (1994). The National Depressive and Manic–Depressive Association (DMDA) Survey of Bipolar Members. *Journal of Affective Disorders, 31,* 281–294.

Miklowitz, D. J., George, E. L., Axelson, D. A., Kim, E. Y., Birmaher, B., Schneck, C., et al. (2004). Family-focused treatment for adolescents with bipolar disorder. *Journal of Affective Disorders, 82*(Suppl. 1), 113–128.

Miklowitz, D. J., George, E. L., Richards, J. A., Simoneau, T. L., & Suddath, R. L. (2003). A randomized study of family-focused psychoeducation and pharmacotherapy in the outpatient management of bipolar disorder. *Archives of General Psychiatry, 60,* 904–912.

Miklowitz, D. J., & Goldstein, M. J. (1997). *Bipolar disorder: A family-focused treatment approach.* New York: Guilford Press.

Miklowitz, D. J., Goldstein, M. J., Nuechterlein, K. H., Snyder, K. S., & Mintz, J. (1988). Family factors and the course of bipolar affective disorder. *Archives of General Psychiatry, 45,* 225–231.

Rea, M. M., Tompson, M., Miklowitz, D. J., Goldstein, M. J., Hwang, S., & Mintz, J. (2003). Family focused treatment vs. individual treatment for bipolar disorder: Results of a randomized clinical trial. *Journal of Consulting and Clinical Psychology, 71,* 482–492.

Simoneau, T. L., Miklowitz, D. J., Richards, J. A., Saleem, R., & George, E. L. (1999). Bipolar disorder and family communication: Effects of a psychoeducational treatment program. *Journal of Abnormal Psychology, 108,* 588–597.

Chapter 2

Findling, R. L., Gracious, B. L., McNamara, N. K., Youngstrom, E. A., Demeter, C. A., Branicky, L. A., et al. (2001). Rapid, continuous cycling and psychiatric co-morbidity in pediatric bipolar I disorder. *Bipolar Disorders, 3,* 202–210.

Geller, B., Zimerman, B., Williams, M., Bolhofner, B., Craney, J. L., Frazier, J., et al. (2002). DSM-IV mania symptoms in a prepubertal and early adolescent bipolar disorder phenotype compared to attention-deficit hyperactive and normal controls. *Journal of Child and Adolescent Psychopharmacology, 12,* 11–25.

Lewinsohn, P. M., Seeley, J. R., & Klein, D. N. (2003). Bipolar disorders during adolescence. *Acta Psychiatrica Scandinavica, 108*(Suppl. 418), 47–50.

Pavuluri, M. N., Birmaher, B., & Naylor, M. W. (2005). Pediatric bipolar disorder: A review of the past 10 years. *Journal of the American Academy of Child and Adolescent Psychiatry, 44,* 846–871.

Wagner, K. D., Hirschfeld, R. M., Emslie, G. J., Findling, R. L., Gracious, B. L., & Reed, M. L. (2006). Validation of the Mood Disorder Questionnaire for bipolar disorders in adolescents. *Journal of Clinical Psychiatry, 67,* 827–830.

Wilens, T. E., Biederman, J., Kwon, A., Ditterline, J., Forkner, P., Moore, H., et al. (2004). Risk of substance use disorders in adolescents with bipolar disorder. *Journal of the American Academy of Child and Adolescent Psychiatry, 43,* 1380–1386.

Wozniak, J., Biederman, J., Mundy, E., Mennin, D., & Farone, S. V. (1995). A pilot family study of childhood-onset mania. *Journal of the American Academy of Child and Adolescent Psychiatry, 34,* 1577–1583.

Chapter 3

American Academy of Child and Adolescent Psychiatry. *www.aacap.org/publications/factsfam/72.htm.*

Biederman, J., Faraone, S. V., Chu, M. P., & Wozniak, J. (1999). Further evidence of a bidirectional overlap between juvenile mania and conduct disorder in children. *Journal of the American Academy of Child and Adolescent Psychiatry, 38,* 468–476.

Birmaher, B., Axelson, D., Strober, M., Gill, M. K., Valeri, S., Chiappetta, L., et al. (2006). Clinical course of children and adolescents with bipolar spectrum disorders. *Archives of General Psychiatry, 63*(2), 175–183.

Faraone, S. V. (2003). *Straight talk about your child's mental health: What to do when something seems wrong.* New York: Guilford Press.

Geller, B., Zimerman, B., Williams, M., Bolhofner, K., Craney, J. L., Frazier, J., et al. (2002). DSM-IV mania symptoms in a prepubertal and early adolescent bipolar disorder phenotype compared to attention deficit hyperactive and normal controls. *Journal of the American Academy of Child and Adolescent Psychopharmacology, 12,* 11–25.

Goldstein, T. R., Birmaher, B., Axelson, D., Ryan, N. D., Strober, M. A., Gill, M. K., et al. (2005). History of suicide attempts in pediatric bipolar disorder: Factors associated with increased risk. *Bipolar Disorders, 7*(6), 525–535.

Kovacs, M., & Pollock, M. (1995). Bipolar disorder and comorbid conduct disorder in childhood and adolescence. *Journal of the American Academy of Child and Adolescent Psychiatry, 34,* 715–723.

Kowatch, R. A., Fristad, M., Birmaher, B., Wagner, K. D., Findling, R. L., Hellander, M., et al. (2005). Treatment guidelines for children and adolescents with bipolar disorder. *Journal of the American Academy of Child and Adolescent Psychiatry, 44*(3), 213–235.

Kupfer, D. J., Frank, E., Grochocinski, V. J., Luther, J. F., Houck, P. R., Swartz, H. A., et al. (2000). Stabilization in the treatment of mania, depression, and mixed states. *Acta Neuropsychiatrica, 12,* 110–114.

Leverich, G. S., McElroy, S. L., Suppes, T., Keck, P. E. J., Denicoff, K. D., Nolen, W. A., et al. (2002). Early physical and sexual abuse associated with an adverse course of bipolar illness. *Biological Psychiatry, 51,* 288–297.

Lewinsohn, P. M., Klein, D. N., & Seeley, J. R. (2000). Bipolar disorder during adolescence and young adulthood in a community sample. *Bipolar Disorders, 2,* 281–293.

Post, R. M. (1992). Transduction of psychosocial stress into the neurobiology of recurrent affective disorder. *American Journal of Psychiatry, 149,* 999–1010.

Quinn, C. A., & Fristad, M. A. (2004). Defining and identifying early onset bipolar spectrum disorder. *Current Psychiatry Reports, 6*(2), 101–107.

Regier, D. A., Farmer, M. E., Rae, D. S., Locke, B. Z., Keith, S. J., Judd, L. L., et al. (1990). Comorbidity of mental disorders with alcohol and other drug abuse: Results from the Epidemiologic Catchment Area (ECA) Study. *Journal of the American Medical Association, 264,* 2511–2518.

Scheffer, R. E., Kowatch, R. A., Carmody, T., & Rush, A. J. (2005). Randomized, placebo-controlled trial of mixed amphetamine salts for symptoms of comorbid ADHD in pediatric bipolar disorder after mood stabilization with divalproex sodium. *American Journal of Psychiatry, 162*(1), 58–64.

Smoller, J. W., & Finn, C. T. (2003). Family, twin, and adoption studies of bipolar disorder. *American Journal of Medical Genetics, Part C: Seminars in Medical Genetics, 123*(1), 48–58.

Strakowski, S. M., DelBello, M. P., Fleck, D. E., & Arndt, S. (2000). The impact of substance abuse on the course of bipolar disorder. *Biological Psychiatry, 48,* 477–485.

Youngstrom, E. A., Findling, R. L., & Calabrese, J. R. (2004). Effects of adolescent manic symptoms on agreement between youth, parent, and teacher ratings of behavior problems. *Journal of Affective Disorders, 82*(Suppl. 1), S5–S16.

Youngstrom, E. A., Findling, R. L., Calabrese, J. R., Gracious, B. L., Demeter, C., DelPorto-Bedoya, D., et al. (2004). Comparing the diagnostic accuracy of six potential screening instruments for bipolar disorder in youths age 5 to 17 years. *Journal of the American Academy of Child and Adolescent Psychiatry, 43*, 847–858.

Chapter 4

Akiskal, H. S. (1996). The prevalent clinical spectrum of bipolar disorders: Beyond DSM-IV. *Journal of Clinical Psychopharmacology, 16* (Suppl. 1), 4–14.

Alda, M. (1997). Bipolar disorder: From families to genes. *Canadian Journal of Psychiatry, 42*, 378–387.

Butzlaff, R. L., & Hooley, J. M. (1998). Expressed emotion and psychiatric relapse: A meta-analysis. *Archives of General Psychiatry, 55*, 547–552.

Cicchetti, D., & Rogosch, F. A. (2002). A developmental psychopathology perspective on adolescence. *Journal of Consulting and Clinical Psychology, 70*(1), 6–20.

Greenberg, J. S., Kim, H. W., & Greenley, J. R. (1997). Factors associated with subjective burden in siblings of adults with severe mental illness. *American Journal of Orthopsychiatry, 67*(2), 231–241.

Greene, R. W. (1998). *The explosive child: A new approach for understanding and parenting easily frustrated, chronically inflexible children.* New York: HarperCollins.

Harris, G. (2006, November 23). Proof is scant on psychiatric drug mix for young. *New York Times*, p. A1. Retrieved from *www.nytimes.com/2006/11/23/health/23kids.html?ex=1321938000&en=fl766195258101f2&ei=5088partner=rssnyt&emc=rss*.

Miklowitz, D. J. (2002). *The bipolar disorder survival guide.* New York: Guilford Press.

Miklowitz, D. J., Goldstein, M. J., Nuechterlein, K. H., Snyder, K. S., & Mintz, J. (1988). Family factors and the course of bipolar affective disorder. *Archives of General Psychiatry, 45*, 225–231.

Perlick, D. A., Hohenstein, J. M., Clarkin, J. F., Kaczynski, R., & Rosenheck, R. A. (2005). Use of mental health and primary care services by caregivers of patients with bipolar disorder: A preliminary study. *Bipolar Disorders, 7*(2), 126–135.

Robertson, H. A., Kutcher, S. P., Bird, D., & Grasswick, L. (2001). Impact of early onset bipolar disorder on family functioning: Adolescents' perceptions of family dynamics, communication, and problems. *Journal of Affective Disorders, 66*, 25–37.

Simeonova, D. I., Chang, K. D., Strong, C., & Ketter, T. A. (2005). Creativity in familial bipolar disorder. *Journal of Psychiatric Research, 39*(6), 623–631.

Simoneau, T. L., Miklowitz, D. J., & Saleem, R. (1998). Expressed emotion and interactional patterns in the families of bipolar patients. *Journal of Abnormal Psychology, 107*, 497–507.

Chapter 5

Alda, M. (1997). Bipolar disorder: From families to genes. *Canadian Journal of Psychiatry, 42*, 378–387.

Chang, K., Adleman, N. E., Dienes, K., Simeonova, D. J., Menon, V., & Reiss, A. (2004). Anomalous prefrontal–subcortical activation in familial pediatric bipolar disorder: A functional magnetic resonance imaging investigation. *Archives of General Psychiatry, 61*, 781–792.

Chang, K., Steiner, H., & Ketter, T. (2003). Studies of offspring of parents with bipolar disorder. *American Journal of Medical Genetics C: Seminars in Medical Genetics, 123*, 26–35.

DelBello, M. P., Adler, C. M., & Strakowski, S. M. (2006). The neurophysiology of child and adolescent bipolar disorder. *CNS Spectrums, 11*, 298–311.

Hammen, C., & Gitlin, M. J. (1997). Stress reactivity in bipolar patients and its relation to prior history of the disorder. *American Journal of Psychiatry, 154*, 856–857.

Kim, E. Y., Miklowitz, D. J., Biuckians, A., & Mullen, K. (2007). Life stress and the course of early-onset bipolar disorder. *Journal of Affective Disorders, 99*(1–3), 37–49.

LaPalme, M., Hodgins, S., & LaRoche, C. (1997). Children of parents with bipolar disorder: A meta-analysis of risk for mental disorders. *Canadian Journal of Psychiatry, 42*, 623–631.

Malkoff-Schwartz, S., Frank, E., Anderson, B., Sherrill, J. T., Siegel, L., Patterson, D., et al. (1998). Stressful life events and social rhythm disruption in the onset of manic and depressive bipolar episodes: A preliminary investigation. *Archives of General Psychiatry, 55*, 702–707.

Manji, H. K., Quiroz, J. A., Payne, J. L., Singh, J., Lopes, B. P., Viegas, J. S., et al. (2003). The underlying neurobiology of bipolar disorder. *World Psychiatry, 2*(3), 136–146.

Miklowitz, D. J., Biuckians, A., & Richards, J. A. (2006). Early-onset bipolar disorder: A family treatment perspective. *Development and Psychopathology, 18*, 1247–1265.

Pavuluri, M. N., Henry, D. B., Nadimpalli, S. S., O'Connor, M. M., & Sweeney, J. A. (2006). Biological risk factors in pediatric bipolar disorder. *Biological Psychiatry, 60*(9), 936–941.

Post, R. M., & Weiss, S. R. (1996). A speculative model of affective illness cyclicity based on patterns of drug tolerance observed in amygdala-kindled seizures. *Molecular Neurobiology, 13*, 33–60.

Rich, B. A., Vinton, D. T., Roberson-Nay, R., Hommer, R. E., Berghorst, L. H., McClure, E. B., et al. (2006). Limbic hyperactivation during processing of neutral facial expressions in children with bipolar disorder. *Proceedings of the National Academy of Sciences, 103*(23), 8900–8905.

Smoller, J. W., & Finn, C. T. (2003). Family, twin, and adoption studies of bipolar disorder. *American Journal of Medical Genetics, Part C: Seminars in Medical Genetics, 123*(1), 48–58.

Chapter 6

Biederman, J., Mick, E., Faraone, S. V., Wozniak, J., Spencer, T., & Pandina, G. (2006). Risperidone for the treatment of affective symptoms in children with disruptive behavior disorder: A post hoc analysis of data from a 6-week, multicenter, randomized, double-blind, parallel-arm study. *Clinical Therapeutics, 28*(5), 794–800.

Bowden, C. L., Brugger, A. M., Swann, A. C., Calabrese, J. R., Janicak, P. G., Petty, F., et al. (1994). Efficacy of divalproex vs. lithium and placebo in the treatment of mania: The Depakote Mania Study Group. *Journal of the American Medical Association, 271*, 918–924.

Bowden, C. L., Calabrese, J. R., Ketter, T. A., Sachs, G. S., White, R. L., & Thompson, T. R. (2006). Impact of lamotrigine and lithium on weight in obese and nonobese patients with bipolar I disorder. *American Journal of Psychiatry, 163*(7), 1199–1201.

Bowden, C. L., Calabrese, J. R., Sachs, G., Yatham, L. N., Asghar, S. A., Hompland, M., et al. (2003). A placebo-controlled 18–month trial of lamotrigine and lithium maintenance treatment in recently manic or hypomanic patients with bipolar I disorder. *Archives of General Psychiatry, 60*, 392–400.

Brown, E. B., McElroy, S. L., Keck, P. E. J., Deldar, A., Adams, D. H., Tohen, M., et al. (2006). A 7–week, randomized, double-blind trial of olanzapine/fluoxetine combination versus lamotrigine in the treatment of bipolar I depression. *Journal of Clinical Psychiatry, 67*(7), 1025–1033.

Calabrese, J. R., Sullivan, J. R., Bowden, C. L., Suppes, T., Goldberg, J. F., Sachs, G. S., et al. (2002). Rash in multicenter trials of lamotrigine in mood disorders: Clinical relevance and management. *Journal of Clinical Psychiatry, 63*, 1012–1019.

Chang, K., Saxena, K., & Howe, M. (2006). An open-label study of lamotrigine adjunct or monotherapy for the treatment of adolescents with bipolar depression. *Journal of the American Academy of Child and Adolescent Psychiatry, 45*, 298–304.

Chang, K. D., Keck, P. E. J., Stanton, S. P., McElroy, S. L., Strakowski, S. M., & Geracioti, T. D. J. (1998). Differences in thyroid function between bipolar manic and mixed states. *Biological Psychiatry, 43*(10), 730–733.

DelBello, M. P., Findling, R. L., Kushner, S., Wang, D., Olson, W. H., Capece, J. A., et al. (2005). A pilot controlled trial of topiramate for mania in children and adolescents with bipolar disorder. *Journal of the American Academy of Child and Adolescent Psychiatry, 44*(6), 539–547.

DelBello, M. P., & Kowatch, R. (2006). Pharmacological interventions for bipolar youth: Developmental considerations. *Development and Psychopathology, 18*, 1231–1246.

DelBello, M. P., Kowatch, R. A., Adler, C. M., Stanford, K. E., Welge, J. A., Barzman, D. H., et al. (2006). A double-blind randomized pilot study comparing quetiapine and divalproex for adolescent mania. *Journal of the American Academy of Child and Adolescent Psychiatry, 45*(3), 305–313.

DelBello, M. P., Schwiers, M. L., Rosenberg, H. L., & Strakowski, S. M. (2002). A double-blind, randomized, placebo-controlled study of quetiapine as adjunctive treatment for adolescent mania. *Journal of the American Academy of Child and Adolescent Psychiatry, 41*, 1216–1223.

Faraone, S. V. (2003). *Straight talk about your child's mental health: What to do when something seems wrong.* New York: Guilford Press.

Findling, R. L., McNamara, N. K., Youngstrom, E. A., Stansbrey, R. J., Gracious, B. L., Reed, M. D., et al. (2005). Double-blind 18–month trial of lithium versus divalproex maintenance treatment in pediatric bipolar disorder. *Journal of the American Academy of Child and Adolescent Psychiatry, 44*(5), 409–417.

Goldberg, J. F. (2000). Treatment of bipolar disorders. *Psychiatric Clinics of North America, 7*, 115–149.

Goodwin, G. M., Bowden, C. L., Calabrese, J. R., Grunze, H., Kasper, S., White, R., et al. (2004). A pooled analysis of 2 placebo-controlled 18-month trials of lamotrigine and lithium maintenance in bipolar I disorder. *Journal of Clinical Psychiatry, 65*, 432–441.

Hunkeler, E. M., Fireman, B., Lee, J., Diamond, R., Hamilton, J., He, C. X., et al. (2005). Trends in use of antidepressants, lithium, and anticonvulsants in Kaiser Permanente-insured youths, 1994–2003. *Journal of Child and Adolescent Psychopharmacology, 15*, 26–37.

Joffe, H., Cohen, L. S., Suppes, T., McLaughlin, W. L., Lavori, P., Adams, J. M., et al. (2006). Valproate is associated with new-onset oligoamenorrhea with hyperandrogenism in women with bipolar disorder. *Biological Psychiatry, 59*(11), 1078–1086.

Kafantaris, V., Coletti, D. J., Dicker, R., Padula, G., Pleak, R. R., & Alvir, J. M. (2004). Lithium treatment of acute mania in adolescents: A placebo-controlled discontinuation study. *Journal of the American Academy of Child and Adolescent Psychiatry, 43*(8), 984–993.

Kowatch, R., & DelBello, M. P. (2003). The use of mood stabilizers and atypical antipsychotics in children and adolescents with bipolar disorders. *CNS Spectrums, 8*, 273–280.

Kowatch, R. A., Fristad, M., Birmaher, B., Wagner, K. D., Findling, R. L., Hellander,

M., et al. (2005). Treatment guidelines for children and adolescents with bipolar disorder. *Journal of the American Academy of Child and Adolescent Psychiatry, 44*(3), 213–235.

Kowatch, R. A., Suppes, T., Carmody, T. J., Bucci, J. P., Hume, J. H., Kromelis, M., et al. (2000). Effect size of lithium, divalproex sodium, and carbamazepine in children and adolescents with bipolar disorder. *Journal of the American Academy of Child and Adolescent Psychiatry, 39*, 713–720.

Melkersson, K., & Dahl, M. L. (2004). Adverse metabolic effects associated with atypical antipsychotics: Literature review and clinical implications. *Drugs, 64*, 701–723.

Patel, N. C., DelBello, M. P., Bryan, H. S., Adler, C. M., Kowatch, R. A., Stanford, K., et al. (2006). Open-label lithium for the treatment of adolescents with bipolar depression. *Journal of the American Academy of Child and Adolescent Psychiatry, 45*(3), 289–297.

Post, R. M., Uhde, T. W., Roy-Byrne, P. P., & Joffe, R. T. (1986). Antidepressant effects of carbamazepine. *American Journal of Psychiatry, 143*, 29–34.

Scheffer, R. E., Kowatch, R. A., Carmody, T., & Rush, A. J. (2005). Randomized, placebo-controlled trial of mixed amphetamine salts for symptoms of comorbid ADHD in pediatric bipolar disorder after mood stabilization with divalproex sodium. *American Journal of Psychiatry, 162*(1), 58–64.

Strober, M., Schmidt-Lackner, S., Freeman, R., Bower, S., Lampert, C., & DeAntonio, M. (1995). Recovery and relapse in adolescents with bipolar affective illness: A five-year naturalistic, prospective follow-up. *Journal of the American Academy of Child and Adolescent Psychiatry, 34*, 714–731.

Suppes, T., Baldessarini, R. J., Faedda, G. L., Tondo, L., & Tohen, M. (1993). Discontinuation of maintenance treatment in bipolar disorder: Risks and implications. *Harvard Review of Psychiatry, 1*, 131–144.

Thase, M. E. (2006). Bipolar depression: Diagnostic and treatment challenges. *Development and Psychopathology, 18*, 1213–1230.

Tohen, M., Kryzhanovskaya, L., Carlson, G., DelBello, M. P., Wozniak, J., Kowatch, R., et al. (2005). Olanzapine in the treatment of acute mania in adolescents with bipolar I disorder: A 3-week randomized double-blind placebo-controlled study. *Neuropsychopharmacology, 30*(Suppl. 1), 176.

Tohen, M., Vieta, E., Calabrese, J., Ketter, T. A., Sachs, G., Bowden, C., et al. (2003). Efficacy of olanzapine and olanzapine-fluoxetine combination in the treatment of bipolar I depression. *Archives of General Psychiatry, 60*, 1079–1088.

Tondo, L., & Baldessarini, R. J. (2000). Reducing suicide risk during lithium maintenance treatment. *Journal of Clinical Psychiatry, 61*(Suppl. 9), 97–104.

Vitiello, B., & Swedo, S. (2004). Antidepressant medications in children. *New England Journal of Medicine, 350*, 1489–1491.

Wagner, K. D., Kowatch, R. A., Emslie, G. J., Findling, R. L., Wilens, T. E., McCague, K., et al. (2006). A double-blind, randomized, placebo-controlled trial of oxcarbazepine in the treatment of bipolar disorder in children and adolescents. *American Journal of Psychiatry, 163*(7), 1179–1186.

Chapter 7

Feeny, N. C., Danielson, C. K., Schwartz, L., Youngstrom, E. A., & Findling, R. L. (2006). CBT for bipolar disorders in adolescence: A pilot study. *Bipolar Disorders, 8*(5, Pt. 1), 508–515.

Frank, E., Kupfer, D. J., Thase, M. E., Mallinger, A. G., Swartz, H. A., Faglioni, A. M., et al. (2005). Two-year outcomes for interpersonal and social rhythm therapy in individuals with bipolar I disorder. *Archives of General Psychiatry, 62*, 996–1004.

Geller, B., Tillman, R., Craney, J. L., & Bolhofner, K. (2004). Four-year prospective outcome and natural history of mania in children with a prepubertal and early adolescent bipolar disorder phenotpye. *Archives of General Psychiatry, 61*, 459–467.

Goldstein, T. R., Axelson, D. A., Birmaher, B., & Brent, D. A. (2007). Dialectical behavior therapy for adolescents with bipolar disorder: A 1-year open trial. *Journal of the American Academy of Child and Adolescent Psychiatry, 46*, 820–830.

Hlastala, S. A. (2003). Stress, social rhythms, and behavioral activation: Psychosocial factors and the bipolar illness course. *Current Psychiatry Reports, 5*, 477–483.

Johnson, S. L. (2005). Life events in bipolar disorder: Towards more specific models. *Clinical Psychology Review, 25*, 1008–1027.

Lam, D. H., Watkins, E. R., Hayward, P., Bright, J., Wright, K., Kerr, N., et al. (2002). A randomized controlled study of cognitive therapy for relapse prevention for bipolar affective disorder: Outcome of the first year. *Archives of General Psychiatry, 60*(2), 145–152.

Linehan, M. M. (1993). *Cognitive-behavioral treatment of borderline personality disorder.* New York: Guilford Press.

Miklowitz, D. J., George, E. L., Richards, J. A., Simoneau, T. L., & Suddath, R. L. (2003). A randomized study of family-focused psychoeducation and pharmacotherapy in the outpatient management of bipolar disorder. *Archives of General Psychiatry, 60*, 904–912.

Miklowitz, D. J., Otto, M. W., Frank, E., Reilly-Harrington, N. A., Wisniewski, S. R., Kogan, J. N., et al. (2007). Psychosocial treatments for bipolar depression: A 1-year randomized trial from the Systematic Treatment Enhancement Program. *Archives of General Psychiatry, 64*, 419–427.

Pavuluri, M. N., Graczyk, P. A., Henry, D. B., Carbray, J. A., Heidenreich, J., & Miklowitz, D. J. (2004). Child and family-focused cognitive behavioral therapy for pediatric bipolar disorder: development and preliminary results. *Journal of the American Academy of Child and Adolescent Psychiatry, 43*, 528–537.

Bibliography

Rea, M. M., Tompson, M., Miklowitz, D. J., Goldstein, M. J., Hwang, S., & Mintz, J. (2003). Family focused treatment vs. individual treatment for bipolar disorder: Results of a randomized clinical trial. *Journal of Consulting and Clinical Psychology, 71,* 482–492.

Scott, J., Paykel, E., Morriss, R., Bentall, R., Kinderman, P., Johnson, T., et al. (2006). Cognitive behaviour therapy for severe and recurrent bipolar disorders: A randomised controlled trial. *British Journal of Psychiatry, 188,* 313–320.

Chapter 8

Coletti, D. J., Leigh, E., Gallelli, K. A., & Kafantaris, V. (2005). Patterns of adherence to treatment in adolescents with bipolar disorder. *Journal of Child and Adolescent Psychopharmacology, 15*(6), 913–917.

Cromer, B. A., & Tarnowski, K. J. (1989). Noncompliance in adolescence: A review. *Developmental and Behavioral Pediatrics, 10*(4), 207–215.

DelBello, M. P., Hanseman, D., Adler, C. M., Fleck, D. E., & Strakowski, S. M. (2007). Twelve-month outcome of adolescents with bipolar disorder following first-hospitalization for a manic or mixed episode. *American Journal of Psychiatry, 164*(4), 582–590.

Frank, E. (2005). *Treating bipolar disorder: A clinician's guide to interpersonal and social rhythm therapy.* New York: Guilford Press.

Hack, S., & Chow, B. (2001). Pediatric psychotropic medication compliance: A literature review and research-based suggestions for improving treatment compliance. *Journal of Child and Adolescent Psychopharmacology, 11*(1), 59–67.

Jamison, K. R. (1993). *Touched with fire: Manic–depressive illness and the artistic temperament.* New York: Maxwell Macmillan International.

Jamison, K. R. (1995). *An unquiet mind.* New York: Knopf.

Jamison, K. R., Gerner, R. H., & Goodwin, F. K. (1979). Patient and physician attitudes toward lithium: Relationship to compliance. *Archives of General Psychiatry, 36,* 866–869.

Kowatch, R. A., Fristad, M., Birmaher, B., Wagner, K. D., Findling, R. L., Hellander, M., et al. (2005). Treatment guidelines for children and adolescents with bipolar disorder. *Journal of the American Academy of Child and Adolescent Psychiatry, 44*(3), 213–235.

Liptak, G. S. (1996). Enhancing patient compliance in pediatrics. *Pediatric Review, 17,* 128–134.

Miller, W. R., & Rollnick, S. (2002). *Motivational interviewing (2nd ed.): Preparing people for change.* New York: Guilford Press.

Millett, K. (1990). *The loony-bin trip.* New York: Simon & Schuster.

Reilly-Harrington, N. S., & Sachs, G. S. (2006). Psychosocial strategies to improve concordance and adherence in bipolar disorder. *Journal of Clinical Psychia-*

try, 67(7), e04. Retrieved from *www.medfair.com/content/cme/classes/pubweb/ bipolarreports7/harrington.htm.*

Schou, M. (1979). Artistic productivity and lithium prophylaxis in manic–depressive illness. *British Journal of Psychiatry, 135,* 97–103.

Simeonova, D. I., Chang, K. D., Strong, C., & Ketter, T. A. (2005). Creativity in familial bipolar disorder. *Journal of Psychiatric Research, 39*(6), 623–631.

Strakowski, S. M., Keck, P. E., McElroy, S. L., West, S. A., Sax, K. W., Hawkins, J. M., et al. (1998). Twelve-month outcome after a first hospitalization for affective psychosis. *Archives of General Psychiatry, 55,* 49–55.

Strober, M., Schmidt-Lackner, S., Freeman, R., Bower, S., Lampert, C., & DeAntonio, M. (1995). Recovery and relapse in adolescents with bipolar affective illness: A five-year naturalistic, prospective follow-up. *Journal of the American Academy of Child and Adolescent Psychiatry, 34,* 714–731.

Tondo, L., & Baldessarini, R. J. (2000). Reducing suicide risk during lithium maintenance treatment. *Journal of Clinical Psychiatry, 61*(Suppl. 9), 97–104.

Wilens, T. E. (2004). *Straight talk about psychiatric medications for kids* (rev. ed.). New York: Guilford Press.

Chapter 9

Karp, D. A. (2002). *The burden of sympathy: How families cope with mental illness.* New York: Oxford University Press.

Miklowitz, D. J., & Goldstein, M. J. (1997). *Bipolar disorder: A family-focused treatment approach.* New York: Guilford Press.

Simoneau, T. L., Miklowitz, D. J., & Saleem, R. (1998). Expressed emotion and interactional patterns in the families of bipolar patients. *Journal of Abnormal Psychology, 107,* 497–507.

Chapter 10

Bricker, J. B., Russo, J., Stein, M. B., Sherbourne, C., Craske, M., Schraufnagel, T. J., et al. (2006). Does occasional cannabis use impact anxiety and depression treatment outcomes?: Results from a randomized effectiveness trial. *Depression and Anxiety, 0,* 1–7. Retrieved from *www3.interscience.wiley.com/cgi-bin/abstract/113456498/ABSTRACT.*

Deas, D., & Brown, E. S. (2006). Adolescent substance abuse and psychiatric comorbidities. *Journal of Clinical Psychiatry, 67*(7), e02.

Geller, B., Cooper, T. B., Sun, K., Zimerman, B., Frazier, J., Williams, M., et al. (1998). Double-blind and placebo-controlled study of lithium for adolescent bipolar disorders with secondary substance dependency. *Journal of the American Academy of Child and Adolescent Psychiatry, 37,* 171–178.

Jamison, K. R. (2000). Suicide and bipolar disorder. *Journal of Clinical Psychiatry*, *61*(Suppl. 9), 47–56.

Post, R. M., & Leverich, G. S. (2006). The role of psychosocial stress in the onset and progression of bipolar disorder and its comorbidities: The need for earlier and alternative modes of therapeutic intervention. *Development and Psychopathology*, *18*, 1181–1211.

Sonne, S. C., & Brady, K. T. (1999). Substance abuse and bipolar comorbidity. *Psychiatric Clinics of North America*, *22*, 609–627.

Strakowski, S. M., DelBello, M. P., Fleck, D. E., & Arndt, S. (2000). The impact of substance abuse on the course of bipolar disorder. *Biological Psychiatry*, *48*, 477–485.

Strakowski, S. M., Keck, P. E., McElroy, S. L., West, S. A., Sax, K. W., Hawkins, J. M., et al. (1998). Twelve-month outcome after a first hospitalization for affective psychosis. *Archives of General Psychiatry*, *55*, 49–55.

Wilens, T. E. (2004). *Straight talk about psychiatric medications for kids* (rev. ed.). New York: Guilford Press.

Wilens, T. E., Biederman, J., Kwon, A., Ditterline, J., Forkner, P., Moore, H., et al. (2004). Risk of substance use disorders in adolescents with bipolar disorder. *Journal of the American Academy of Child and Adolescent Psychiatry*, *43*, 1380–1386.

Chapter 11

Birmaher, B., Axelson, D., Strober, M., Gill, M. K., Valeri, S., Chiappetta, L., et al. (2006). Clinical course of children and adolescents with bipolar spectrum disorders. *Archives of General Psychiatry*, *63*(2), 175–183.

Kowatch, R. A., Fristad, M., Birmaher, B., Wagner, K. D., Findling, R. L., Hellander, M., et al. (2005). Treatment guidelines for children and adolescents with bipolar disorder. *Journal of the American Academy of Child and Adolescent Psychiatry*, *44*(3), 213–235.

Newman, C., Leahy, R. L., Beck, A. T., Reilly-Harrington, N., & Gyulai, L. (2001). *Bipolar disorder: A cognitive therapy approach*. Washington, DC: American Psychological Association Press.

Chapter 12

Beck, A. T., Rush, A. J., Shaw, B. F., & Emery, G. (1979). *Cognitive therapy of depression*. New York: Guilford Press.

Brent, D. A., & Poling, K. (1997). *Cognitive therapy treatment manual for depressed and suicidal youth*. Pittsburgh, PA: University of Pittsburgh STAR Center Publications.

Burns, D. D. (1999). *Feeling good: The new mood therapy* (rev. ed.) New York: Avon Books.

Greenberger, D., & Padesky, C. A. (1995). *Mind over mood*. New York: Guilford Press.

Jacobson, N. S., Martell, C. R., & Dimidjian, S. (2001). Behavioral activation treatment for depression: Returning to contextual roots. *Clinical Psychology: Science and Practice, 8,* 255–270.

Lewinsohn, P. M., Munoz, R. F., Youngren, M. A., & Zeiss, A. M. (1992). *Control your depression*. New York: Fireside/Simon & Schuster.

Perlis, R. H., Ostacher, M. J., Patel, J., Marangell, L. B., Zhang, H., Wisniewski, S. R., et al. (2006). Predictors of recurrence in bipolar disorder: Primary outcomes from the Systematic Treatment Enhancement Program for Bipolar Disorder (STEP-BD). *American Journal of Psychiatry, 163*(2), 217–224.

Poling, K. (1997). *Living with depression: A survival manual for families* (3rd ed.). Pittsburgh, PA: University of Pittsburgh Star Center Publications.

Chapter 13

Baldessarini, R. J., Tondo, L., Davis, P., Pompili, M., Goodwin, F. K., & Hennen, J. (2006). Decreased risk of suicides and attempts during long-term lithium treatment: A meta-analytic review. *Bipolar Disorders, 8*(5, Part 2), 625–639.

Brent, D. A., Perper, J. A., Goldstein, C. E., Kolko, D. J., Allan, M. J., Allman, C. J., et al. (1988). Risk factors for adolescent suicide: A comparison of adolescent suicide victims with suicidal inpatients. *Archives of General Psychiatry, 45,* 581–588.

Bridge, J. A., Goldstein, T. R., & Brent, D. A. (2006). Adolescent suicide and suicidal behavior. *Journal of Child Psychology and Psychiatry, 47*(3–4), 372–394.

Carter, G. L., Clover, K., Whyte, I. M., Dawson, A. H., & D'Este, C. (2005). Postcards from the Edge Project: Randomised controlled trial of an intervention using postcards to reduce repetition of hospital treated deliberate self-poisoning. *British Medical Journal, 331,* 805.

Fawcett, J., Golden, B., & Rosenfeld, N. (2000). *New hope for people with bipolar disorder*. Roseville, CA: Prima Health.

Goldstein, T. R., Birmaher, B., Axelson, D., Ryan, N. D., Strober, M. A., Gill, M. K., et al. (2005). History of suicide attempts in pediatric bipolar disorder: Factors associated with increased risk. *Bipolar Disorders, 7*(6), 525–535.

Goldston, D. B., Daniel, S. S., Reboussin, D. M., Reboussin, B. A., Frazier, P. H., & Kelley, A. E. (1999). Suicide attempts among formerly hospitalized adolescents: A prospective naturalistic study. *Journal of the American Academy of Child and Adolescent Psychiatry, 38,* 660–671.

Greenberger, D., & Padesky, C. A. (1995). *Mind over mood*. New York: Guilford Press.

Hawton, K., Sutton, L., Haw, C., Sinclair, J., & Harriss, L. (2005). Suicide and attempted suicide in bipolar disorder: A systematic review of risk factors. *Journal of Clinical Psychiatry, 66*(6), 693–704.

Linehan, M. M. (1993). *Cognitive-behavioral treatment of borderline personality disorder.* New York: Guilford Press.

Mann, J. J., Oquendo, M., Underwood, M. D., & Arango, V. (1999). The neurobiology of suicide risk: A review for the clinician. *Journal of Clinical Psychiatry, 60*(Suppl. 2), 7–11.

Miklowitz, D. J., & Taylor, D. O. (2006). Family-focused treatment of the suicidal bipolar patient. *Bipolar Disorders, 8,* 640—651.

O'Carroll, P. W., Berman, A. L., Maris, R. W., Moscicki, E. K., Tanney, B. L., & Silverman, M. M. (1996). Beyond the Tower of Babel: A nomenclature for suicidology. *Suicide and Life-Threatening Behavior, 26,* 237–252.

Sloan, J. H., Rivara, F. P., Reay, D. T., Ferris, J. A., & Kellerman, A. L. (1990). Firearm regulations and rates of suicide: A comparison of two metropolitan areas. *New England Journal of Medicine, 322,* 369–373.

Turvill, J. L., Burroughs, A. K., & Moore, K. P. (2000). Change in occurrence of paracetamol overdose in UK after introduction of blister packs. *Lancet, 355,* 2048–2049.

Chapter 14

Bradley, M. J., & Giedd, J. N. (2003). *Yes, your teen is crazy!: Loving your kid without losing your mind.* Gig Harbor, WA: Harbor Press.

Ellenbogen, M. A., Hodgins, S., & Walker, C. D. (2004). High levels of cortisol among adolescent offspring of parents with bipolar disorder: A pilot study. *Psychoneuroendocrinology, 29,* 99–106 .

Geller, B., Bolhofner, K., Craney, J. L., Williams, M., Delbello, M. P., & Gunderson, K. (2000). Psychosocial functioning in a prepubertal and early adolescent bipolar disorder phenotype. *Journal of the American Academy of Child and Adolescent Psychiatry, 39,* 1543–1548.

Goldstein, T. R., Miklowitz, D. J., & Mullen, K. (2006). Social skills knowledge and performance among adolescents with bipolar disorder. *Bipolar Disorders, 8*(4), 350–361.

Greene, R. W. (1998). *The explosive child: A new approach for understanding and parenting easily frustrated, chronically inflexible children.* New York: HarperCollins.

Josselyn Center. (2004). *Understanding and educating children and adolescents with bipolar disorder: A guide for educators.* Chicago: Josselyn Center for Mental Health.

Leverich, G. S., McElroy, S. L., Suppes, T., Keck, P. E. J., Denicoff, K. D., Nolen, W. A., et al. (2002). Early physical and sexual abuse associated with an adverse course of bipolar illness. *Biological Psychiatry, 51,* 288–297.

Index

Index

Index

Index

About the Authors

David J. Miklowitz, PhD, is Professor of Psychology and Psychiatry at the University of Colorado, Boulder. His award-winning research on family-focused treatments for bipolar disorder has been funded by the National Institute of Mental Health, the MacArthur Foundation, the National Alliance for Research on Schizophrenia and Depression, and the Robert Sutherland Foundation. Dr. Miklowitz is the author of the bestselling *Bipolar Disorder Survival Guide* and of *Bipolar Disorder: A Family-Focused Treatment Approach.*

Elizabeth L. George, PhD, is coinvestigator with Dr. Miklowitz on the Colorado Family Project and a psychologist with a private practice based in Boulder, Colorado.